PERSPECTIVES ON THE HISTORY
OF ECONOMIC THOUGHT
VOLUME X

METHOD, COMPETITION, CONFLICT
AND MEASUREMENT IN THE
TWENTIETH CENTURY

Perspectives on the History of Economic Thought Volume X

Method, Competition, Conflict and Measurement in the Twentieth Century

Selected Papers from the
History of Economics Society Conference
1992

Edited by
Karen I. Vaughn

Published for the History of Economics Society
by Edward Elgar

Published by
Edward Elgar Publishing Limited
Gower House
Croft Road
Aldershot
Hants GU11 3HR
England

Edward Elgar Publishing Company
Old Post Road
Brookfield
Vermont 05036
USA

British Library Cataloguing in Publication Data
Method, Competition, Conflict and
Measurement in the Twentieth Century:
Selected Papers from the History
of Economics Society Conference, 1992. –
(Perspectives on the History of Economic
Thought; Vol. 10)
  I. Vaughn, Karen Iversen   II. Series
  330.1

ISBN 1 85278 807 0
Printed on FSC approved paper
Printed and bound in Great Britain by Marston Book Services Ltd, Oxfordshire

Contents

PART IV   JOHN MAYNARD KEYNES

PART V   PROBLEMS OF MEASUREMENT

Contributors

Henry T. Burley, Department of Econometrics, La Trobe University, Bundoora, Victoria, Australia. At present Assistant Professor in Stategic Management and Business Environment, Erasmus University, Rotterdam, The Netherlands.

Anna Carabelli, Dipartimento di Scienze Economiche, Università di Padova, Italy.

John B. Davis, Department of Economics, Marquette University, Milwaukee, Wisconsin, USA.

Mary Ann Dimand, Department of Economics, Yale University, New Haven, Connecticut, USA.

Robert W. Dimand, Yale University, New Haven, Connecticut, USA.

John E. Elliot, Political Economy and Public Policy Program, University of Southern California, Los Angeles, California, USA.

Frank Kalshoven, Faculty of Economics and Econometrics, University of Amsterdam, Amsterdam, The Netherlands.

Maria Cristina Marcuzzo, Dipartimento di Economia Politica, Università di Modena, Italy.

Ellen O'Brien, Department of Economics, University of Notre Dame, Notre Dame, Indiana, USA.

Andrea Salanti, Dipartimento di Scienze Economiche, Università di Bergamo, Bergamo, Italy.

Bo Sandelin, Department of Economics, University of Gothenburg, Gothenburg, Sweden

Mark K. Tomass, Department of Economics, Babson College, Babson Park, Massachusetts, USA.

Alex Viskovatoff, Department of Economics, Harvard University, Cambridge, Massachusetts, USA.

Emiel F. M. Wubben, Department of Strategic Management and Business Environment, Erasmus University, Rotterdam, The Netherlands.

Acknowledgement

We wish to thank The Macmillan Press, Ltd for granting Anna Carabelli permission to quote from J.M. Keynes, *A Treatise on Probability* in *The Collected Writings of John Maynard Keynes* (London: The Macmillan Press, Ltd. 1989).

Ideas and themes in twentieth-century economic thought

Karen I. Vaughn

This collection of essays was chosen from among those presented at the nineteenth annual meeting of the History of Economics Society held at George Mason University in Fairfax, Virginia in May, 1992. While the subjects discussed at that meeting ranged over a wide spectrum of topics from the ancient world to the modern, this collection is limited to themes in twentieth-century economic thought. Issues in modern economic thought dominated the meeting, making the choice of a theme for this volume a simple one. Despite the apparent limitations of a single century – not yet completed – however, these papers cover a wide variety of interesting and important issues in economic thought.

Part I of the book is devoted to problems of methodology, a recurring concern at meetings of the History of Economic Society. The three papers published here all deal in various ways with the disarray of modern economic methodology caused by the abandonment of positivism.

Alex Viskovatoff begins the volume with his provocative chapter, 'Unity of theory: the role for theoretical maps'. Viskovatoff begins by calling attention to the common agreement among methodologists that positivism is defunct as a philosophy of science, and goes on to present an alternative to positivism that answers both its critics and defenders: unity theory. Unity theory, based on the work of philosopher Philip Kitchner, combines elements of Kantian apriorism with the empirical testing of positivism. The apriorism applies to the overall picture of the world the theorist brings to his confrontation with reality – his theoretical map – while the role of empirical testing is to describe and define the relationships among entities in the map. The fundamental contribution of unity theory is to draw the distinction between global and local confirmation of theory. Global confirmation applies to the theoretical map as a whole with its ability to generate knowledge and to orient the practitioner in the use of data. Local confirmation refers to the more conventional empirical tests that help to link various parts of the map together. The theoretical map serves to limit the possible interpretations of empirical tests, and empirical testing need not be exhaustive to provide local confirmation as long as it is intelligible within the context of the map.

The demise of positivism is also the inspiration for Andrea Salanti in Chapter 2, 'Popper, Lakatos and economics: are we begging the questions?' Salanti, however, not only criticizes positivism; she also points to the methodological difficulties inherent in some of the alternatives proposed to fill the void left by positivism. She offers a critique of the latest arguments by Hutchison and Blaug in support of positivism as well as the proposed alternatives of critical rationalism and evolutionary epistemology, both of which she accuses of circular reasoning. Her final plea is to recognize the value of methodological pluralism as the only alternative left.

The advantages of methodological pluralism are demonstrated in a concrete fashion in Chapter 3. Mark Tomass proposes to evaluate two rival theories that have otherwise been considered incommensurable: Marshall and Marx on money. In a sense, Tomass is attempting to compare the implications of two 'theoretical maps' by translating the claims of one into the language of the other. He demonstrates both that Marx's theory of money can be expressed in Marshallian language and that Marshall's theory of money can be shown to be a truncated form of Marx's theory. He concludes that Marx's theory is superior to Marshall's in its ability to explain monetary phenomena. In effect, Tomass presents an exercise in translating from one language of discourse to another to compare the merits of the two, an exercise he claims as evidence of the benefits of pluralism.

Part II is comprised of chapters on three aspects of economic processes: competition, conflict and capital. Maria Marcusso's contribution (Chapter 4) is to set the historical record straight regarding the origin of the theory of imperfect competition. Although both R.F. Kahn and Joan Robinson claim Pierro Sraffa as the inspiration for their theories of imperfect competition, Marcusso argues that Kahn and Robinson each had very different projects in mind in following up on Sraffa's lead. Neither, moreover, was entirely faithful to the source of their inspiration. Specifically, when Sraffa called attention to the inconsistencies in perfect competition, his desire was to break away completely from the Marshallian apparatus, as he did later with *The Production of Commodities by Means of Commodities*. Kahn and Robinson, on the other hand, both stayed strictly within the Marshallian framework, Kahn by examining the characteristics of the short period based on actual, empirical cost data, and Robinson by generalizing the partial equilibrium approach, and making monopoly theory the norm and perfect competition a special case of market theory. While Robinson's view dominated Kahn's in the profession, Marcusso points to the irony that in her later years, Robinson regretted her contribution, accepting instead the route Kahn took to a theory of effective demand.

While Marcusso examines the origin of a theory of market competition, in Chapter 5 Robert and Mary Ann Dimand explore some early theories of conflict. They call our attention to two contributions to game theory developed within the context of theories of war strategies: the mathematical approach of Fredrick Lanchester to battle strategies, and the approach of Lewis Richardson to the study of arms race strategies. While neither man's model was sophisticated by modern standards, Lanchester's model formed the basis for later military operations research. Richardson, on the other hand, whose models have not found much confirmation in applied work, was nevertheless both a precursor of conflict resolution theory and an early user of chaos theory whose models were developed to try to avoid war.

In Chapter 6, Bo Sandelin treats us to a close look at the intellectual development of one of the giants of economic theory: Knut Wicksell. Wicksell is widely known for his penetrating development of the theory of capital. This chapter is an interesting exploration of the way in which Wicksell's capital theory evolved over the course of his lifetime. Further, it is an excellent example of why an historian should be wary of finding complete consistency in the entire *oeuvre* of any brilliant intellect. Wicksell's ideas changed as he learned, a phenomenon that is surely widespread among intelligent people. In particular, Sandelin shows how Wicksell moved from the influence of the wages fund shown in his description of capital as a subsistence fund, to capital as invested capital at different distances from the beginning of the production process, to a notion of capital as saved-up labour and land in which intermediate goods were important, to a concern with capitalist processes rather than capital *per se*, to distinguishing between real and money capital, and finally to giving up 'stored-up labour' as an unwieldy and unmeasurable concept. Throughout, Sandelin tells us, Wicksell continued to improve and modernize his theory of capital, although the underlying core concept remained much the same.

The period between the two world wars was a fruitful one for the development of modern economic analysis, as we see in Parts III and IV of this book. Part III examines two issues that came to the fore during the 1920s and 1930s: the development of Marxist themes in neoclassical language, and the examination of the implications of uncertainty for economic theory.

In Chapter 7, 'From Marxism towards neoclassicism: on the decline of Dutch Marxist political economy in the inter-war period', Frank Kalshoven chronicles the decline of Marxism as it was reinterpreted into neoclassical mathematical economics. Two Dutch Marxists, J. van der Wijk and S. de Wolff were economists who wished to gain more respect for Marxist ideas from the academic community. Their approach was to make Marxist economics more scientific by using mathematical analysis to defend Marxist claims. The result was that they evolved into neoclassical economists themselves, and ended by showing that Marxism was a special case of neoclassical assumptions. Here, the attempt to translate a set of ideas from one language of discourse to another ended not with an increasing respect for Marx as Chapter 3 suggests, but in the abandonment of Marxism altogether.

Emile Wubben's ambitious contribution, 'Mainstream economics and uncertainty in the inter-war period', (Chapter 8) examines another challenge to neoclassical economics during this turbulent time; that is, the introduction of the notion of uncertainty into economic theory. Frank Knight's distinction between risk and uncertainty is well known to economists. Wubben argues that the important challenge that Knight's theory presented to the competitive theory of markets was never explored by the economics profession. After Knight, economists either translated his concept of uncertainty into risk in order to make it more tractable, or ignored it completely. Despite their apparent engagement with Knight's theory of uncertainty, Hicks down played its importance, Robbins used static theory because it was more manageable, and Hart defined it away by transmuting it into risk. One could add that uncertainty is still troubling to economists and unincorporated in economic theory more than 70 years after Knight wrote.

Challenges to contemporary economics are also discussed in all three chapters in Part IV, which is devoted to the work of John Maynard Keynes. The rich and varied work of Keynes is of perennial interest to historians of economics partly because of the enigmatic nature of *The General Theory*, and partly because of the enormous impact his ideas had on economic theory and policy in the post-war years. All three chapters address the meaning of Keynes's writing itself and particularly the questions of subjectivity in Keynesian thought.

In Chapter 9, 'The locus of Keynes's philosophical thinking in *The General Theory*: the concept of convention', John Davis traces the development of Keynes's early philosophical views on intuition in the context of his economics, and especially in the role that convention plays in his theory of market behaviour. Davis argues that questions of intuition and judgement manifest themselves in Keynes's economics in the functioning of convention. To the extent that economic activity requires making judgements in a world of limited knowledge, people rely on established conventions to simplify their task. Specifically in Keynes's theory, interest rates, attitudes toward liquidity and investment and employment are matters of convention to which market forces must adjust. Davis suggests that Keynes's theories were differentiated from his more market-oriented opponents by his introduction of a set of constraints (conventions) that were not included in rival theories.

John Elliott, in Chapter 10, 'Two perspectives on Keynes in *The General Theory* and after', attempts to sort out the rival claims about the 'real' Keynes: Keynes of the neoclassical synthesis, versus the radical Keynes who saw capitalism as inherently cyclical and unstable. Elliott concludes on the basis of textual and contextual evidence that although both kinds of arguments (equilibrium and disequilibrium) are present in Keynes's writing – partly to make a point – the real Keynes is the radical one. Hicks may have effectively aborted the Keynesian revolution by finding an equilibrium statement of the relationships presented in *The General Theory*, but Shackle's interpretation of Keynes is more cohesive: as the author of a theory of disorder rather than of order.

Part IV concludes with Anna Carabelli's very close reading of Keynesian texts, including some that have never been published, in order to explain, 'Keynes on mensuration and comparison' (Chapter 11). Carabelli argues that throughout his life, Keynes was preoccupied with questions of measurement and units of comparison. The *Treatise on Probability* is particularly instructive in demonstrating Keynes's early awareness of the problems of intuition and judgement (aspects of Keynes's thought taken up by Davis) in assessing probabilities of impending situations. Carabelli argues persuasively that Keynes was from the beginning interested in questions about the quality of our knowledge. He emphasized particularly that rationality does not necessarily mean calculation, but involves subjective judgements to reach decisions. Carabelli draws attention to similar attitudes Keynes had toward the economic entities of his general theory such as index numbers, income, aggregate capital, utility and general price levels, all of which defied accurate calculation and measurement. Carabelli's reading of Keynes lends support to Elliott's claim that Hick's neoclassical synthesis was a misinterpretation of *The General Theory*.

Keynes hovers in the background of Chapter 12, in Part V of this book. Ellen O'Brien's fascinating paper, 'How the 'G' got into the GNP', tells the story of the debates and interests that led to government expenditure being included in the national income accounts. Contrary to general belief, O'Brien shows that Keynesian theory had very little to do with the final construction of the accounts. In fact, no theory seems to have played much of a role in setting them up. The accounting practices actually used emerged out of a struggle, largely between Simon Kuznets who wanted to limit the special government section to a portion of war expenditures, and government bureaucrats who were primarily interested in emphasizing the role of government in the economy. The bureaucrats won, and the accounts, the product of historical contingencies and the powers of the disputants, have become entrenched in economic theory and practice.

Finally, Chapter 13 is a tribute to a generally overlooked economist, M. J. Farrell, whose empirical work shows the important relationship between theory development and empirical practice. In 'Farrell, data envelopment analysis and Leibenstein on efficiency measurement', Henry Burley argues that Farrell's techniques of measuring efficiency by creating an envelope curve of actual firm performance to identify the most efficient firms, is consistent with Leibenstein's theory of *X* efficiency. Leibenstein shows why Farrell found so much variation in firm performance, and Farrell's technique provides a way of measuring efficiency in light of Leibenstein's theory.

Clearly, this collection of independent but thematically related chapters is testimony to the vibrancy of research in the history of economic thought. Some have referred to the history of economic thought as the study of the dead ideas of dead economists. This volume, on the contrary, puts the lie to that definition. It explores the vibrant and exciting ideas of economists who remain very much in intellectual community with the present, enlivening debate and inspiring the rethinking of old ideas and the creation of new ones.

PART I

ECONOMIC METHOD

1 Unity of theory: the role for theoretical maps

Alex Viskovatoff[1]

If one looks at recent methodology literature, one routinely encounters three claims. First, the ascendancy of positivism is over, so an important question on the methodologist's agenda is: what lies beyond positivism (Caldwell, 1989, p. 14). Second, the 'Duhemian Problem' is particularly difficult in economics; the complexity of economic phenomena and questions about the empirical basis of the discipline make empirical testing an extremely complex affair (Hands, 1990, p. 73; see also Boland, 1989). Third, instead of declaring what constitutes good scientific practice and laying out the 'correct' criteria for theory choice as these have been developed by philosophers in their armchair reflections on what physicists do, methodologists should study the practice of economists more closely, 'to help us to understand better what the practice of economics is all about' (Caldwell, 1989 p. 15; see also Hausman, 1988).

In this chapter we address all three claims. Specifically, we try to show how a recent successor to positivism in the philosophy of science that has not yet been introduced into the methodological literature can offer an account of what constitutes the empirical basis of economics for which the difficulty of testing is not a problem, and how it can provide a rational reconstruction (to use a positivist term well worth preserving) of economists' practice in terms of their own understanding of that practice.

The philosophical account of science we have in mind is a Kantian variety of holism which stresses the importance of explanatory unification in science; it has been developed most extensively by Philip Kitcher (1981, 1986, 1989). As we have noted, the methodology literature stresses the decline of positivism, but aside from noting the importance of Kuhn, and picking up one strand of contemporary philosophy of science–realism (Mäki, 1989), methodologists have tended not to look too closely at how philosophers themselves have responded to this situation. If one does pick up recent volumes of philosophy of science (such as Boyd, Gasper and Trout, 1991 or Kitcher and Salmon, 1989), one finds that explanatory unification is one of the most interesting ideas floating around in the discipline at the moment. Furthermore, Kitcher initiated his research programme as a response to the fact that a science can be obviously successful like biology but make few predictions – although prediction is central to science according to the positivist view. Economics also is not noted for its success at making predictions. So, it is worth seeing how his ideas can be applied to economics.

This chapter is divided into three sections. The first sketches Kitcher's account of science, contrasting a Kantian view of science with an empiricist one. It stresses the difference between local and global confirmation – the criterion of explanatory unification operates primarily on the latter level – and introduces the idea of a theoretical map. The second shows how two descriptions by economists, from very different vantage points (one given by a graduate macroeconomics textbook, the other made in the course of some reflections by a game theorist) of what the validity of economic knowledge derives from fit in nicely with the account of science just presented. Finally, some implications of the idea of explanatory unification for economic methodology are considered.

Kant's philosophy of science

As we have noted, methodologists have emphasized that the testing of hypotheses is especially difficult in economics. There have been two main responses to this problem: either it is argued that economists should face the problem head-on and be more zealous in their testing (Hutchinson, 1977; Blaug, 1980), or that they should be more aware of and sensitive to means that are used to appraise theories other than testing (Caldwell, 1988; McCloskey, 1985). In our view these responses, despite their recognition that one should move beyond positivism, are still too close to it. At the core of positivism is the idea, inherited from the British empiricists, that knowledge is constituted in a bottom-up fashion, from experience. (That is why testing is paramount: when one does a test, one checks whether one's theory is confirmed by experience.) This view has not been directly challenged by methodologists, and this may be the reason why the question of what one is to make of economic theory is still unresolved. Kant did challenge this view, and argued that knowledge is constituted in a top-down fashion, by the theoretical activity of the scientist: the basis of scientific empirical knowledge is the slicing up of the world by means of the right theoretical categories.[2]

According to empiricism, theories are nothing more than efficient generalizations of observations, since all the reason one has for believing in the truth of a given theory comes from one's belief in the veracity of the observations confirming it. Theories have an epiphenomenal role in science: there is nothing in the structure of a theory itself, apart from its empirical implications, that can have any bearing on its truth or validity. (Of course, some theories with the same empirical implications might be more useful than others with identical implications, but that is just because of the limited cognitive abilities of scientists.) This notion of theoretical truth was formalized by the logical positivists with the 'hypothetico-deductive account of justification': one takes a theory and applies it to a given situation, adding the appropriate initial conditions to obtain a prediction; if the prediction is confirmed, one is justified in holding the theory to be true. The logical positivists' account of course abstracted entirely from a very interesting aspect of science: it said nothing about where the theories that were held up for testing came from; nor could it really make sense of why theories play such a central role in science. These problems were brushed aside however with the distinction between context of discovery and context of justification: the source of a hypothesis is irrelevant to its justification, which should be the sole concern of the philosophy of science.

A much more serious flaw of logical positivism concerned its central empiricist assumption – that of the self-justificatory nature of 'direct' empirical experience. It turns out that many observations made by contemporary science depend upon theoretical assumptions to such an extent that there is no way one can sensibly hold that the observations are epistemically prior to the theory, or indeed that one has more confidence in the observations than in the theory. A related problem is the Duhem–Quine thesis. When the test of a theoretical hypothesis is performed, one cannot in general deduce in a straightforward manner that the hypothesis is false if the results of the test turn out to be negative: hypotheses are not tested alone, but together with different auxiliary hypotheses, and it may be the falsity of one of these that produces the negative results. These and other problems led to the gradual realization that the logical positivist approach is not workable.[3]

For Kant, in contrast to the logical positivists, the way in which hypotheses are constructed plays a central role in science. This is because nature does not present us with a ready-made structure from which its basic principles and laws are manifestly apparent. One cannot simply observe if these laws are empirically validated. The kinds of inquiry and tests that one can do are infinite in number; if one does not do the right ones, however, one will make little progress. As scientists started employing the experimental method, they

learned that reason has insight only into that *which it produces after a plan of its own*, and that it must not allow itself to be kept, as it were, in nature's leading strings, but must itself show the way with principles of judgment based upon fixed laws, constraining nature to give answer to questions of reason's own determining. Accidental observations, made in obedience to no previously thought-out plan, can never be made to yield a necessary law, which alone reason is concerned to discover (Kant, 1950, B xiii; emphasis added).

The natural question to ask at this point is what particular principles science uses for the formulation of hypotheses. The answer that Kant proposed is that science proceeds under the supposition that underlying nature there is a systematic unity and order. Before detailed empirical investigations are undertaken, science projects an order of nature which, if correct, gives one reason to think that when investigations are conducted, the right questions will be asked. A projected order of nature is broader than a specific scientific theory consisting of specific propositions: several such theories may fall under the same projected order (the notion thus has affinities to Kuhn's notion of the paradigm, or Lakatos's notion of the research programme). Rather than specifying precise laws, a projected order of nature delineates the various entities that constitute nature, the significant properties of these entities, and how they are interrelated. It thus maps out nature, and we can accordingly use the non-Kantian term 'theoretical map' to denote the same thing. Implicit in an order of nature or map is a specification of how the truth of empirical statements is to be determined: for example, if one decides that what is important about the motion of physical objects is their velocity, and that this velocity is to be thought about quantitatively, then a sensible way to go about studying motion is to measure the velocities of objects under various circumstances. (In other domains where precise measurement is not possible, measurement may not play a central role in truth fixation.) Since the basic regulative principle for the formulation of hypotheses which science operates under is that of unity, it follows that both at the level of theoretical maps and at the level of specific theories, the more connections that can be made between different theories and the greater the generality of theories, the better.

According to Kant, the principle that nature exhibits a systematic order is a priori: it does not follow directly from empirical evidence. Kant provides a transcendental argument justifying the adoption of the principle. Not to suppose that nature is ordered in a systematic way would undermine the very idea of scientific inquiry and, more generally, would undermine reason itself. Therefore, if the idea of scientific inquiry is to make any sense, it must incorporate the idea that nature is systematically ordered. This is quite apart from the question of whether in fact nature is so ordered.[4]

We now turn to the account of theory confirmation that follows from the above account, as it has been sketched out by Kitcher (1986). In contrast to the empiricist justificatory account, a Kantian confirmation theory comes in two parts. The global part deals with major reorientations in the theoretical map used by a science. Such reorientations will occur when the community of practitioners of the science comes to believe that the order projected by the existing framework cannot adequately account for the body of empirical knowledge accepted by the community. A reorientation will consist in a change in the projected order, which amounts to a change in the constituent entities and qualities that are projected, along with a change in the basic patterns of argument that are used for the construction of explanations and in the language in which these explanations are expressed. A central principle used for the evaluation of rival projected orders or theoretical maps is the principle of explanatory unification: if the explanations used within one map are able to account for the accepted body of knowledge in a more unified manner than are the explanations used within another map, then the first map will be preferred. Local confirmation works within the theoretical map that has been selected by the process of global confirmation, and consists of a process of testing basically like the one described by logical positivism. The selection of a map 'constructs for us a space within which the hypotheses we devise to tackle outstanding research problems must fit. That space may be partitioned into a finite number of alternatives – possibly a small number – and we may proceed to eliminate those that are incompatible with the observations' (Kitcher, 1986, p. 230).

This two-part confirmation theory is able to deal with an aspect of scientific practice for which the empiricist account runs into difficulties and which is of particular relevance to economics. A given set of observations can be accounted for by an infinite number of alternative theories. Scientists nevertheless tend to describe a theory as true if it has passed different tests successfully, without worrying about all the other possible alternative theories that no one has ever thought of. This means that the possibility always exists that even if a theory is 'confirmed', there is another theory that could account for the same observations better. But this would undermine the sense in which the first theory is confirmed: if there exists a theory that is better, how could the first theory be true? Nevertheless, social as well as natural scientists routinely disregard this problem, searching for an explanation from a small set of candidate theories, and settling upon the theory that performs best by a process of elimination. While this cannot really be justified from an empiricist perspective,

> the Kantian emphasis on our need for a projected order of nature (the source for the causal claims that we must make if we are to have experience) makes way for the possibility of confirmation by contextual elimination of rivals. Provided that there is an answer to the question of the rational acceptability of scientific practices (which are associated with a projected order), Kant may contend that elimination of rivals relative to an accepted practice solves the problem of local confirmation (Kitcher, 1986, p. 230).

The basic idea is that if one has a particular theoretical map and that map generates a number of alternative hypotheses which one can take to span the space of possible explanations within the map, then if one of these hypotheses is confirmed, that hypothesis provides the true explanation, since all other hypotheses are either within the map and perform worse, or outside it and are invalid by definition.

We conclude this section with some implications of the Kantian account concerning models and explanation of particular importance to economics. The first is that there is a clear distinction to be made between maps and models and in the way that they are appraised. Often when one refers to a scientific theory, one is thinking more about a map than a model. Models facilitate the explanation of specific phenomena by describing them in a way such that the available theoretical apparatus can be applied to them. Since models are often constructed with specific applications in mind, they often can be (provisionally) evaluated by means of a few tests, without taking related but not directly raised issues into account. This is the process of local confirmation. A map on the other hand is not constructed with a specific application in mind: it projects an order of nature which is supposed to be universally valid for the entities it defines, and it forms the context in which models are developed, applied and interpreted. Since it performs an essential integrative function, and since its purpose is to define the kinds of entities and properties that constitute its domain, rather than to provide detailed explanations of specific phenomena, it is not evaluated by testing. Rather, it is evaluated holistically, by its ability to facilitate the generation of new knowledge. This is global confirmation.

Another implication of the account is that the view that explanations are discrete entities, typically showing how some law-like statement of greater or lesser generality implies the phenomenon to be explained, needs to be abandoned. This view seems to originate from a superficial examination of the practice of physics, where the period of a pendulum, say, is derived from Newton's laws and the gravitational constant. If one actually looks at Newton's *Principia* on the other hand, one finds that the complexity of some phenomena required him to make simplifying assumptions in order to make a mathematical derivation; he then compared the model defined by the assumptions with the known, real world, sometimes repeating the process several times. The explanation then consisted in linking up the subsidiary explanations based on the models, and making it clear that the whole procedure was consistent with the map (Cohen, 1985, pp. 165–70).

The last point suggests something that is desirable in models: they must on the one hand allow us to use whatever modelling tools we have at our disposal, while on the other hand – since in general each model will not be able to give a complete explanation of a phenomenon of interest, but only of one aspect of it – it should be possible to link the explanations that they provide into longer, more complete explanations. Here another function of the map becomes apparent: since all model-based explanations are expressed in terms that it defines, it ensures that explanations can be linked. We will return to these points in the final section.

Justification of economic theory by economists

The tendency of economists as well as other social scientists to take a positivist view of scientific practice has often been noted. To see that the tendency is real, one merely has to look at Milton Friedman's essay 'The Methodology of

Positive Economics' (1953), with all its emphasis upon the testing of predictions, and consider the fact that it is the best-known methodological piece in the profession. Nevertheless we shall try, by looking at two examples taken from opposite ends of the 'empirical–theoretical spectrum', to show that there also exists among the practitioners of theory what might be called a Kantian strain in thinking about justification of theory.

The first example is Olivier Blanchard and Stanley Fischer's graduate textbook, *Lectures in Macroeconomics* (1989). In contrast to what is often the case with microeconomics textbooks, Blanchard and Fischer set out to explicitly show in what way economics functions as an empirical science. Their demonstration can be divided into two parts: a justification of the basic framework, and a demonstration of how theory evolves within this framework, largely as a response to empirical information. They justify the framework in the following way:

> One of our main choices has been to start from a neoclassical benchmark, with optimizing individuals and competitive markets. As our guided tour indicates, this is not because we believe that such a benchmark describes reality or can account for fluctuations. We are sure that incomplete markets and imperfect competition are needed to account for the main characteristics of actual fluctuations. We also believe that such nonneoclassical constructs as bounded rationality ... or interdependent utility functions ... may be needed to understand important aspects of financial and labor markets. We believe, however, that looking at their effects as arising from deviations from a well-understood benchmark is the best research strategy. Alternative strategies that have started squarely from a different benchmark have for the most part proved unsuccessful (Blanchard and Fischer, 1989, p. 27).

The authors carry out the second part of their demonstration by illustrating how macroeconomic theory changes, by means of a brief chronology of developments in the field since its inception (Blanchard and Fischer, 1989, pp. 275–8). As a result of its responses to various macroeconomic phenomena, such as the Great Depression and the stagflation of the 1970s, there are today in macroeconomics two main research programmes, real business cycle theory and (a revamped) Keynesianism. The authors state that they go on in the rest of the book to explore various models developed by both camps, and to 'examine whether we can in such models generate the fluctuations in output and its components, as well as the fluctuations in employment, that are observed in reality' (Blanchard and Fischer, 1989, p. 278).

Two points about macroeconomic method that emerge from Blanchard and Fischer's description are of interest in the present context. The first point is that macroeconomics operates with an articulated criterion of empirical adequacy; the existence of this criterion shows how macroeconomics is an empirical science. The criterion takes account of the fact that in economics, precise predictions of observed phenomena are not possible. Accordingly, the method of confirming theories by assembling assumptions and then subjecting them to a test is modified in two ways. First, rather than trying to predict the precise sequence of values that are contained in the time series of a given economic aggregate, macroeconomists try to construct a model that can generate the temporal pattern that this sequence displays. And second, rather than considering one test by itself to confirm or disconfirm a theory, macroeconomists look at many data sets of the same kind together, and see whether a model can generate the basic pattern that seems to be common to them.

The second point of interest in the macroeconomic method as described by Blanchard and Fischer is that it matches the Kantian picture of scientific method much better than it does the empiricist one. One indication of this is the empirical criterion that has just been noted: it requires a much more complicated process of reasoning and judgement than is implied in the logical positivist account.[5] Another indication is the broader context in which the criterion is applied. The authors 'start from a neoclassical benchmark, with optimizing individuals and competitive markets' (Blanchard and Fischer, 1989), and then proceed to see how models (either using the benchmark without modification or making certain modifications to it) perform empirically. As we have seen, this kind of practice, where one starts off from a limited set of tentative models and then tries to eliminate them as likely candidates, does not make very much sense from an empiricist point of view.[6] From the Kantian point of view however, what is being followed here is simply normal scientific procedure.

Still, one part of Blanchard and Fischer's approach to the justification of economic theory is not as strong as one would like. This is their assertion that the use of the benchmark of optimizing behaviour and competitive markets is advisable because these are 'well understood'. They are well understood because they have been studied the most; that they have been so is however a contingent, historically determined fact with no implications one way or the other about the correctness of the approach. Specific reasons for thinking that there is something about the benchmark that does lead to the right questions being asked are desirable. (The need for them would not be so great once the important questions have been answered, but as Blanchard and Fischer note, that is not yet the case.) To find such reasons, we can turn to Robert Aumann's paper 'What Is Game Theory Trying to Accomplish?' (1985).

Aumann takes the position that 'on the most basic level, what we are trying to do in science is to understand the world' (Aumann, 1985, p. 29). Understanding is quite different from prediction, and has three components: 'fitting things together, relating them to each other' so that frequently occurring patterns are isolated; unification, in which 'many different phenomena are pulled together' by means of a theory; and simplicity, according to which 'as few as possible exogenous parameters should be used to account for any particular phenomenon'. Because game theory and economic theory in general exhibit these traits, their statements, 'while perhaps not falsifiable, do have some universality, do express some insight of a general nature' (Aumann, 1985, pp. 29–31, 42).

The criteria of theoretical adequacy that Aumann proposes are of course the Kantian criterion of explanatory unification. In one respect however, his account is very non-Kantian: he makes a very strong distinction between theoretical and empirical statements. 'The concept of truth applies to *observations*; one can say that such and such were truly the observations. It also applies to all kinds of everyday events, like whether or not one had hamburger for dinner yesterday. It does not, however, apply to *theories* (Aumann, 1985, p. 34). Aumann is led to this position because of his strong distinction between understanding and prediction, and his interpretation of economic theory as not making predictions, but as a means for understanding. His position is unsatisfactory for us because since he does not require theory to be empirically confirmed, his grounding of economic theory is too subjective. (Aumann in fact advocates viewing game theory and mathematical economics as art forms, and seeing their validity in the same way one sees the validity of good art.) It is probably fair to say however that his account does a good job of expressing the appeal that economic theory has for many theorists, so that his account serves to show that acceptance of that theory is based largely upon holistic considerations of unifying power.

What these two accounts suggest is that the confirmation of economic theory can be seen as proceeding along the lines of the Kantian two-part account of confirmation. Particular hypotheses that are selected as candidates for the explanation of a given phenomenon are suggested by the theoretical map accepted by the community of economists; since this map by definition is supposed to be correct, it is taken to demarcate the relevant plausible hypotheses exhaustively, so that the hypothesis from the candidate set which performs best can be taken to offer the correct explanation for the phenomenon in question. In addition to this process of local confirmation, there is also a process of global confirmation. The latter consists in making the observation that models that directly follow from the map have been the most extensively studied, so that further study should proceed by making straightforward modifications of these models (Blanchard and Fischer), or in observing that the map must be valid in some way, since it gives one a subjective feeling of understanding (Aumann). In both variants, unification plays a major role.

While the local part appears to be unproblematic, unfortunately the same cannot be said for the global part. This is because the first variant is essentially an appeal to tradition, and hence should have little normative force in a scientific context,[7] while the second is able to make the case that the map is unified and leads to understanding only by avoiding the problem of empirical confirmation. But this may reflect shortcomings of economic theory, rather than indicate an inadequacy of the Kantian account of confirmation. The important point is that one can find among different aspects of economic practice as articulated by economists different pieces of what a justification of economic theory along Kantian lines would look like, and that the Kantian view provides a philosophical explication of aspects of economic practice that are not brought into a clear focus by other approaches.

Theoretical unity as connectability of explanations
If one compares current trends in methodological thinking with the general views of economists as represented by Blanchard and Fischer and by Aumann, one finds both agreement and disagreement. Methodologists and practising economists both hold that the testing of theories is especially difficult in economics. They tend to disagree however on how one should respond to this problem, with its implication that the truth or empirical validity of economic theory is not clear cut; they tend to disagree also on the more pointed problem that despite the difficulty of testing, there are bodies of evidence that indicate that fundamental assumptions of economic theory are violated under a broad range of empirical conditions. Economists usually hold that one should adhere to the generally accepted neoclassical theory because it is the only one that is able to explain a wide range of economic phenomena in a unified manner; methodologists on the other hand tend to argue for a more pluralistic approach, recommending that economics should part with its 'grand vision that a single theory could provide one with a basic grasp of the subject matter' (Hausman, 1992, p. 225). In this remaining section we draw implications for these issues of the philosophical framework outlined in the first section. While testing is certainly problematic, from the present perspective this does not have fundamental implications one way or the other as to the empirical validity of economic theory, taken as a basic framework; that is because testing is not the fundamental way in which theory is justified. Furthermore, the economist is not faced with a trade-off between theoretical unity on the one hand and the ability to account in a detailed manner for wide ranges of phenomena on the other (which because of this alleged trade-off are hence often taken to be outside the purview of the theory): unity is present at the level of theory taken as a map, not at the level of theories that take the form of models; the role of the latter is to allow one to take account of the specific characteristics of phenomena.

The belief that testing is the basis of empirical confirmation, and the failure to distinguish between theory in its role as a map and models (which leads to the belief that there is a necessary trade-off between theoretical unity and empirical generality) derive in our opinion from an over-simplified view of scientific explanation which reached its peak in logical positivism. The kind of explanation which the positivists took as paradigmatic was the derivation of the value of a particular physical parameter for a given situation from known initial conditions and one or more general laws. This is certainly one type of scientific explanation. But there are also other types, and as the phenomena one tries to understand become more complicated, so do the forms of the explanations one constructs to do so. This and the implications it has for the empirical confirmation of theories can be seen by considering once more how Newton proceeded. When Newton explained the motion of the planets, he did not derive their trajectories in a single explanatory step from a long series of equations. Instead he introduced a sequence of models making various simplifying assumptions, and showed how as models were refined to take into account more features of the physical system he was concerned with, his predictions matched the measured values more and more closely. This was partly a matter of pragmatics – one starts with the simple cases first, and since one's time and techniques are limited, one only models in as much detail as is required for the task at hand – but it was not only that. Until he wrote the *Principia*, he was not always able to get his predictions to match measured values within known experimental errors. So his confidence in his theory did not come from the theory being able to pass all the tests to which it was subjected. Rather, it came from the facts that when faced with a discrepancy between prediction and measurement he could repeatedly refine his model to eliminate the discrepancy (so that he had reason to think that even a particularly stubborn discrepancy could be eliminated in the future), and that he was able by means of the same explanatory strategy to account for phenomena that were previously thought to be unconnected, such as the motion of falling bodies near the earth's surface, the paths of the planets, and the tides (Hall, 1983). What made him think that his theory was true was thus that he was able, by always considering the same properties of objects and using the same explanatory strategies, to account increasingly well for all phenomena related to motion. A specification of such properties and strategies is what we have called a theoretical map; since the models, no matter how refined, always used the same principles, and since the specification was universally applicable, the map was highly unified.

Certainly, Newton's theory was unified in another way also: it explained everything in terms of a small set of universal laws. But there is reason to think that the unity of these laws is derivative of the unity of the theoretical map. First, the laws have no meaning without the map, since it is the map that specifies what the laws refer to and how to go about verifying them. Second, the grounds for believing the laws to be true are precisely that the map is unified as just described, and that, in conjunction with the laws, it leads to successful predictions. (If the map were not unified, one would not have a great deal of confidence in the truth of the laws, since the confirming evidence – the verifications – would be hard to evaluate.) This order of dependence is indeed fortunate, for it leads one to believe that whether a given object domain is characterized by laws or not has no bearing on whether it can be the subject matter for a science: even if it exhibits no laws, it may still be amenable to treatment by a unified map, specifying a unified set of theoretical categories and explanatory strategies, and it is this unity that appears to be constitutive of science.

This brings us back to economics. Economists have adopted a mode of explanation which in effect assumes that economic phenomena are characterized by laws (whether they believe that these phenomena actually are so characterized is beside the point). Thus, to take the most important example, economists take the common sense, folk-psychological idea that people generally speaking are rational – their behaviour can be explained in terms of their beliefs and desires – and formalize this explanatory strategy by constructing utility theory, which supposes that individual agents have determinate expectations and preferences, and that these, when combined with the constraints agents face, lead to a specific choice in a lawful manner, in accordance with axioms precisely defining rationality. Thus, in the same way that Newton, before specifying any quantitative laws of motion, first mapped out the mechanical view of the world, according to which the motion of objects is understood in terms of their masses and the forces acting upon them, and not in terms of their qualities, economists start off from the map concept of rationality – which states merely that to understand people's actions, you must look at their beliefs and desires – without specifying a precise relationship between the three. And in the same way that Newton went on to formalize the map notion of motion and to specify specific quantitative relationships between the variables it laid out, economists formalized the notion of rationality.[8] According to the mode of explanation they adopted, the unity of the discipline of economics taken as a science must lie in this formalization of rationality,[9] in the same way that the unity of physics on the positivist view lies in the universality of its laws. As we have just argued however, while physics does seem to have this unity, it is not the fundamental one; it is not what makes physics a science. (It is probably better looked on as a property of the object domain: physical objects just happen to obey quantitative laws.) In any case, this unity at the level of law-like descriptions and formal models used in one-step explanations does not appear to be attainable for economics. A good case can be made that the unity of economic theory lies in its purely formal aspects, and not in an ability to unify diverse empirical phenomena.[10] It appears that rationality can only be a fully coherent concept at the map level.

Even if unity in terms of lawful empirical regularities were attainable for economics, this is not where economists should first of all seek theoretical unity, if the account of science we have presented in this chapter is more or less correct. Scientists are seldom able to give a complete explanation of all aspects of a given phenomenon by means of a single model or theory. Instead, they use different models to explain different regularities. Therefore, they of course put effort into developing abstract models and theories that are not quite true, but that can be useful for solving certain scientific problems. But they also put considerable effort into showing how these different theories relate to each other and can be linked to each other, because it is in this linkability that the unity of science (as opposed to that of the physical world) lies.[11] We would venture to suggest that economists should follow this practice.

The account of science we have adopted thus turns out to bolster the methodologists' case for trying out different theoretical approaches and undermines the economists' claims that this would sacrifice unity. The unity that is fundamentally constitutive of science is unity of explanatory patterns; any unity of generalizations taking the form of laws or lawlike statements, of which the proposition that agents optimize is an instance, is derivative. If using a wider range of types of models allows economists to explain more regularities that occur in the economy, this would not reduce the unity of the discipline, but increase it.[12] This is precisely what methodologists advocate. However, while authors such as Caldwell (1988) and Hausman (1992) recommend that economists should be more willing to try different theoretical approaches, we would add that a simultaneous effort should be made to relate these approaches to each other, and to tie them together if possible.

This is of course one function of the theoretical map. The mathematical physicist David Ruelle has remarked that once the physical framework defining a certain class of phenomena has been specified, 'you still have to choose a mathematical theory and establish a correspondence between the objects of this mathematical theory and the physical concepts. It is this correspondence that constitutes a *physical theory*' (Ruelle, 1991, p. 11; emphasis in original). It is precisely this correspondence which is not at all clear in much of economic theory, and it is safe to say that this problem is a major reason why there exists a separate field of methodology in economics – something not to be found in such a developed form in other disciplines outside of the humanities. One reason why one needs maps is that sometimes it is necessary to venture away from home, so that one can find one's way in unfamiliar territory. But another reason is simply to have a complete and objective understanding of where one's home town is: unless you can pick up a globe and point to a spot, you can't really say where 'here' is – even if the other people in the room with you think they know what you mean when you say it (Tugendhat, 1982). It is not enough for economists to know how a model relates to a given set of data: they also have to know how their theory relates to a coherent and reasonably complete picture of the world. Economics cannot be a separate science because, as the arguments of this chapter suggest, there is no such thing.[13]

Notes

1. I would like to thank Don Lavoie, Bruce Caldwell, William Parker, Philippe Fontaine, Elias Khalil, Donald McCloskey and Simon Saunders for helpful comments on earlier versions of this paper.
2. Of course, Donald McCloskey and other writers who discuss the rhetoric of economics. influenced by the philosopher Richard Rorty and the literary theorist Stanley Fish, also emphasize the constructed nature of scientific knowledge. But Kant, unlike those authors, gives arguments for the objective validity of scientific theories and hence can maintain the difference between science and literature.
3. Quine's solution to both problems was to adopt a position of (confirmation) holism similar to Kant's: 'our statements about the external world face the tribunal of sense experience not individually but only as a corporate body, (Quine, 1953, p. 41).
4. Kant held this question to make no sense. Scientific realists answer it in the affirmative. For a critique of scientific realism, see Putnam (1987).
5. Indeed, it requires holistic rather than discrete evaluation of results at the local, and not just the global, level.
6. One can of course follow Friedman and take an instrumentalist position, which amounts to saying that if a theory is 'confirmed', that is all that is required – whether it is true or refers to anything real is beside the point – but Blanchard and Fischer do not seem to want to do this.
7. To see the problem with Blanchard and Fischer's argument, it is necessary to take the idea of a projected order of nature seriously. They argue that one must carry on one's research in terms of the models they advocate because these models are the best understood. But if it is the case that the projected order of nature that leads to a satisfactory understanding of the macroeconomy is significantly different from the one they project, then no matter how well understood those models are, or how much one studies their extensions, one will not come one step closer to understanding the macroeconomy, since one has not isolated the right natural kinds, that is, the features of the macroeconomy that govern its behaviour. It is this possibility that makes the kind of arguments made by Aumann necessary, and which prompted Kant to say that there is an ineluctable a priori aspect to natural science. Of course, one might hold that after physical theory became highly confirmed, the a priori justification of its categories provided by Kant became more or less a luxury. (Kant would disagree, holding that such a justification will always be required, in order to have something more than mere 'empirical' validation of theory.) Even under this view however, one can still argue that before that confirmation was arrived at, a priori justification was required to let scientists know that they were on the right track.
8. While economists followed the practice of physics of formalizing and making more specific a map notion, they did not adopt the general mode of explanation in physics, but a simplified variant of it. One does of course find exceptions – Koopmans (1957) for instance speaks of sequences of increasingly more realistic models – but these have not generally been very influential.
9. Together with the other centrepieces of neoclassical analysis, the concepts of equilibrium and markets, which we are not considering here.
10. Restricting ourselves to utility theory, there are three reasons for thinking so. First, explaining decisions in terms of utility theory involves inferring preferences, expecta-

tions, and the decision taken from each other in a holistic process of interpretation, rather than measuring the three independently from each other as would be required for a strict causal explanation, so that explanations using utility theory seem to be interpretations rather than a description of an objective causal process (Rosenberg, 1988; Shafer, 1986). Second, there are wide ranges of situations under which phenomena occur – such as those that the psychologists Tversky and Kahnemann (1986) have described as framing effects – which cannot be explained by utility theory for fundamental reasons. It therefore turns out not to be a general theory of decision-making, as it was originally believed to be. Third, utility theory, if taken as a complete theory of decision-making referring to empirically occurring processes, rather than as simply an uninterpreted formalism, leads to infinite regresses, and is hence logically problematic, quite apart from its failure to explain specific empirical phenomena (Conlisk, 1988).

11. Newton has described this by saying that science uses both the methods of analysis and of synthesis (1952, pp. 404-5). Not all natural scientists place a pre-eminent value on theoretical unity: Ruelle (1991), for instance, thinks that physics should aspire to unity but can do without it – the unity of nature is enough.

12. Thus utility maximization models of decision-making could be complemented by cognitive science models, when the former fail.

13. Hausman (1992) argues that economists want economics to be a separate science, and that they are wrong to do so. For arguments that not even physics is a separate science, see Dreyfus (1991).

References

Aumann, R.J. (1985), 'What is Game Theory Trying to Accomplish?', in Arrow, K.J. and Honkapohja, S. (eds.), *Frontiers of Economics*, Oxford: Basil Blackwell.

Blanchard, O.J. and Fischer, S. (1989), *Lectures on Macroeconomics*, Cambridge, Mass.: MIT Press.

Blaug, M. (1980), *The Methodology of Economics*, Cambridge: Cambridge University Press.

Boland, L. (1989), *The Methodology of Economic Model Building: Methodology after Samuelson*, London: Routledge.

Boyd, R., Gasper, P. and Trout, J.D. (eds) (1991), *The Philosophy of Science*, Cambridge, Mass.: MIT Press.

Caldwell, B.J. (1988), 'The Case for Pluralism', in de Marchi, N. (ed.), *The Popperian Legacy in Economics*, Cambridge: Cambridge University Press.

Caldwell, B.J. (1989), 'The Trend of Methodological Thinking', *Ricerche Economiche*, **43**, pp. 8–20.

Cohen, I.B. (1985), *Revolution in Science*, Cambridge, Mass.: Harvard University Press.

Conlisk, J. (1988), 'Optimization Cost', *Journal of Economic Behaviour and Organization*, **9**, pp. 213–28.

Dreyfus, H.L. (1991), *Being-in-the-world: A Commentary on Heidegger's Being and Time, Division I*, Cambridge, Mass.: MIT Press.

Friedman, M. (1953), 'The Methodology of Positive Economics', in *Essays in Positive Economics*, Chicago: University of Chicago Press.

Hall, A.R. (1983), *The Revolution in Science 1500–1750*, London: Longman.

Hands, D.W. (1990), 'Thirteen Theses on Progress in Economic Methodology', *Finnish Economic Papers*, **3**, pp. 72–6.

Hausman, D.M. (1988), 'Economic Methodology and Philosophy of Science', in Winston, G.C. and Teichgraeber, R.F. III (eds), *The Boundaries of Economics*, Cambridge: Cambridge University Press, pp. 88–116.

Hausman, D.M. (1992), *The Inexact and Separate Science of Economics*, Cambridge: Cambridge University Press.

Hutchinson, T.W. (1977), *Knowledge and Ignorance in Economics*, Chicago: University of Chicago Press.

Kant, I. (1950), *Critique of Pure Reason*, trans. N.K. Smith, London: Macmillan.

Kitcher, P. (1981), 'Explanatory Unification', *Philosophy of Science*, **48**, pp. 507–31.

Kitcher, P. (1986), 'Projecting the Order of Nature', in Butts, R.E. (ed.), *Kant's Philosophy of Physical Science*: Metaphysische Anfangsgründe der Naturwissenschaft *1786–1986*, Dordrecht, Holland: D. Reidel.

Kitcher, P. (1989), 'Explanatory Unification and the Causal Structure of the World', in Kitcher and Salmon.

Kitcher, P. and Salmon, W.C. (eds) (1989), *Scientific Explanation (Minnesota Studies in the Philosophy of Science*, vol. 13), Minneapolis: University of Minnesota Press.

Koopmans, T.C. (1957), *Three Essays on the State of Economic Science*, New York: McGraw-Hill.

Mäki, U. (1989) 'On the Problem of Realism in Economics', *Ricerche Economiche*, **43**, pp. 176–98.

McCloskey, D.N. (1985), *The Rhetoric of Economics*, Madison, Wisconsin: University of Wisconsin Press.

Newton, I. (1952), *Opticks*, New York: Dover.

Putnam, H. (1987), *The Many Faces of Realism*, La Salle, Ill.: Open Court.

Quine, W.V.O. (1953), 'Two Dogmas of Empiricism', in *From a Logical Point of View*, Cambridge, Mass.: Harvard University Press.

Rosenberg, A. (1988), *Philosophy of Social Science*, Boulder, Colorado: Westview Press.

Ruelle, D. (1991), *Chance and Chaos*, Princeton: Princeton University Press.

Shafer, L. (1986), 'Savage Revisited', *Statistical Science*, **1**, pp. 463–501 (with commentaries).

Tugendhat, E. (1982), *Traditional and Analytical Philosophy: Lectures on the Philosophy of Language*, Cambridge: Cambridge University Press. (Translation of *Vorlesungen zur Einführung in die sprachanalytische Philosophie*, Frankfurt am Main: Suhrkamp, 1976.)

Tversky, A. and Kahneman, D. (1986) 'Rational Choice and the Framing of Decisions', *Journal of Business*, **59**, pp. S251–78.

2 Popper, Lakatos and economics: are we begging the questions?

Andrea Salanti[1]

Until very recently, the two aspects of science, the activity itself and the resulting knowledge, have been studied separately. ... An analysis of science which unites these two aspects will be able to resolve the apparent paradoxes in its nature: that out of a personal endeavour which is fallible, subjective, and strictly limited by its context, there emerges knowledge which is certain, objective, and universal. (Ravetz, 1971, p. 71)

[P]rogress in science can be assessed rationally. This possibility explains why, in science, only progressive theories are regarded as interesting; and it thereby explains why, as a matter of historical fact, the history of science is, by and large, a history of progress. (Science seems to be the only field of human endeavour of which this can be said. ... It should be obvious that the objectivity and the rationality of progress in science is not due to the personal objectivity and rationality of the scientist. (Popper, 1981, pp. 94–5)

Introduction

Over the last decade or so, a substantial portion of the literature on economic methodology has been concerned with the adequacy of Popper's falsification-ism with respect to a number of issues: the proper framework for the appraisal of economic theories, the supposed virtues of his epistemological perspective, the feasibility of a Lakatosian reconstruction of the history of economics, and/or the possibility of identifying progressive research programmes within contemporary economics.[2]

Whether these were the right and/or the only issues worthy to be addressed may be doubted.[3] What cannot be disputed, however, is that the ensuing debate has centered on such themes, raising many highly controversial and still unsolved questions. Nevertheless most participants – whose number has grown no less quickly than their propensity to apply for admission to the invisible college of methodologists – seem to agree on the following minimal points:

1. Falsificationism, the methodology of bold conjecture and severe test, is often preached in economics but it is almost never practised;
2. [What hinders from practicing falsificationism in economics is, among other things, that] the 'Duhemian Problem' is particularly difficult in economics; the complexity of economic phenomena and questions about the empirical basis of the discipline make empirical testing an extremely complex affair;

19

3. Though 'hard cores' and 'positive heuristics' abound, 'novel facts' as defined by the Lakatosian school have been few and far between in the history of economic thought.

(Hands, 1990a, p. 73)

Such a thin area of consensus has been paralleled by a wide disagreement on virtually everything else regarding Popper, Lakatos and economics,[4] that establishing the existence of a truly Popperian and/or Lakatosian approach in economic methodology remains a daunting task. In spite of such an awkward situation, however, a number of economic methodologists continue to regard their own work as belonging to the realm of the Popperian and possibly Lakatosian tradition.[5] Among them we may find those who openly advocate falsificationism and those who, rejecting Popper's methodology but retaining some aspects of his epistemology, advocate some elements of Popper's fallibilism and/or critical rationalism. At the same time all methodologists (and historians) seem to agree with Caldwell (1989, p. 15) that 'the purpose of the new methodology is to help us to understand better what the practice of economics is all about.'[6]

Given such premises, the emergence of some difficulties should have been expected. Indeed, Popper's methodology (and epistemology, for that matter) has a pervasive prescriptive character that may not be easily isolated from the descriptive *obiter dicta* it undoubtedly contains.[7] Thus we have the problem of reconciling what is actually practised with what should be epistemologically trustworthy and, vice versa, of resisting the temptation to infer how science ought to be practised by mere reconstructions of what is actually done (because of Hume's guillotine).

The purpose of this chapter is to argue that some recent assessments in economic methodology involving Popperian issues have been caught precisely in this trap, particularly as far as the task of providing an account of the progressiveness of economics is concerned. How can it be possible, indeed, to discover how progress *should* be attained in economics simply by observing what economists actually do? What should we conclude in the light of the fact that seemingly sound prescriptions are widely disregarded?[8] It will be concluded that both 'falsificationists' and 'critical rationalists', although animated by respectable concerns, are doomed to leave unanswered the important question of how progress in economics is actually achieved. To some extent their assessments seem to be concerned with the task of providing a more or less direct answer to the growing stream of criticisms coming from the anti-modernist crusade (that is, in economics, mainly from advocates of hermeneutics and rhetoric). However welcome such efforts may be (compare Salanti, 1990), they do not appear to lead to entirely satisfactory conclusions. Indeed, the paradoxical outcome of this state of affairs is that 'Popperians' encounter just the same kind of difficulty as those alternative approaches they are trying to resist.

The quest for falsificationism in economics

As is commonly acknowledged, the two most coherent and tenacious spokesmen for falsificationism in economics are Terence Hutchison and Mark Blaug. What has characterized for decades Hutchison's quest for falsificationism has always been his strong and explicit agreement with Popper's ethical and political concerns. He openly states that

> Any significant case for adopting, or 'striving after', a methodological principle must rely ultimately on some ethical, moral, or political argument (as Popper emphasized in the debate with Habermas and elsewhere). Insofar as methodological principles are critical principles, then, the criticism they contain, or imply, must rest on some kinds of normative standards or presuppositions. (Hutchison, 1988, p. 169)[9]

Quite coherently, as far back as 1938, he made explicit his worry that:

> The most sinister phenomenon of recent decades for the true scientist, and indeed to Western civilization as a whole, may be said to be the growth of Pseudo-Sciences no longer confined to hole-in-corner cranks. [. . . Testability is] the only principle or distinction practically adoptable which will keep science separate from pseudoscience. (Hutchison, 1938, pp. 10–11)[10]

and exactly fifty years later he is still warning that:

> [A] kind of superhuman utopianism seems to prevail, even regarding economists themselves, who are urged to disregard all rules except 'honesty, clarity and tolerance' (McCloskey, 1983, p. 482). Of course, if we were all intellectually superhuman, [...] there might well be no role for critical codes of discipline, demarcation, and adequacy. For we would be living in an intellectual utopia. But for those of us concerned with the discussion of economic processes and policies in the real world, within a reasonably free democratic framework, a vital role may always remain for critical principles and criteria of adequacy, such as the falsifiability principle. (Hutchison, 1988, pp. 180–1)

The problem with such a plea for falsificationism in economics is that it is far from clear who is more utopian, whether McCloskey, who takes somewhat for granted scientists' 'honesty, clarity and tolerance', or Popper, who invites us to adopt critical rationalism as a safeguard against violence (see note 9). Anyway, apart from the thesis that in the field of social studies, because of the greater risk of ideological contaminations, outright methodological permissiveness would be even more harmful than in the natural sciences, and the consequent argument that the important policy implications of economics makes desirable the grounding of economists' authority and expertise on objective criteria,[11] Hutchison does not provide more arguments than those due to Popper. His passionate advocacy of falsification and falsifiability is thus open to all the well-known criticisms raised against Popper.[12]

A possible line of defence against such critiques is to observe that falsificationism is a *prescriptive* methodology that, as such, escapes those critiques concerning either what is actually practised, or prospective obstacles to actually practising it. As Hutchison puts it quite roughly:

> In reviewing objections to the falsification and falsifiability principle the observation need not long detain us that, in fact, in economics not much attention is paid to it (though a good deal of lip service is paid). But insofar as lip service is not translated into action, so much the worse for economics. Anyhow, we are concerned here with norms and standards and not with actual behavior. (Hutchison, 1988, p. 177)

One who makes much use of this type of argument, restated in more elegant terms, is Mark Blaug. In many respects his methodological vision is more sophisticated than Hutchison's (naïve) falsificationism, because of his endorsement of both Popper's falsificationism and Lakatos's methodology of scientific research programmes (MSRP).[13] As I have pointed out elsewhere (Salanti, 1992 and 1994), however, his methodological position is not beyond question. His repeated justification of Popperian falsificationism is based on the observation that falsificationism is a normative proposal which, as such, cannot be faulted for failing to describe scientific practice; no wonder, therefore, if economists preach it but nevertheless rarely practise it. But then, how is it possible – as Blaug must perforce claim when he reconstructs pieces of the history of economics along Lakatosian lines – to have *progress* in economics? For the sake of consistency Blaug ought to admit that falsificationism is simply useless and/or unnecessary as a simple prescription for doing good science, if 'good science' is to be taken as 'working out *progressive* research programmes'.[14] Otherwise one would not understand how it is possible to do good science without taking falsificationism seriously. How may it be possible to be 'critical of what economists actually do as distinct from what they say to do' (Blaug, 1984, p. 33) and at the same time maintain that (important pieces of) what economists actually do can be shown to be progressive according to Lakatosian criteria? Alternatively, Blaug might maintain his advocacy of falsificationism, but then he ought to show that Lakatosian progressive chapters of the history of economics (for example, the Keynesian revolution) were marked by an effective practice of falsificationism: a claim, in its turn, that may be subject to criticism[15] (and that Lakatos himself, to be sure, would have dismissed on the basis on his criticisms of falsificationism).

Almost surely Blaug would reject these critical remarks by denying both that economists never practice falsificationism and that he ever argued in that way. This is precisely what he has maintained, commenting upon a previous draft of Salanti (1994), in private correspondence. One point (what Blaug has really said) does not need further discussion: his writings are housed in libraries for all to see. My excuse for insisting on the other point is that I, along with Caldwell (1991a) and Hands (1992), continue to doubt that we may convincingly argue for many examples of progressive research programmes within economics and to believe that Lakatos's (1971) praise of historiographical criticism should hold for MSRP itself. Indeed, even if we concede to Blaug the former point, it remains to be clarifiedwhy he is obliged to resort to the same kind of argument (that normative proposals cannot be faulted for failing to describe actual scientific practice) in order to rescue Lakatos from his critics (see Blaug, 1991b). Note that Popper's advocacy of falsificationism exhibits a manifest normative component directed at the single scientist, while Lakatos's MSRP deals with the outcome of the activity of a whole community of specialists. If single scientists practised falsificationism and we could easily detect progressive research programmes there would not be any problem about Blaug's methodological approach, but what use is MSRP to us if scientists usually do not follow the falsificationist prescriptions (as Blaug himself admits of economists)? If nevertheless we encountered 'progressive' research programmes, we should have to explain these unintended consequences of scientists' behaviour. Otherwise, if their activity could not be 'rationally' reconstructed along Lakatosian lines, we should have to justify somehow the progressiveness of an apparently irrational scientific activity.

A third possibility, of course, might be to doubt that economics is a science. But this option, as Caldwell points out, 'is not open to a Lakatosian economist [. . .] who is forced to judge the MSRP as deficient if it cannot rationalize the history of the discipline' (Caldwell, 1991a, p. 107). It is just this conclusion that Blaug refuses to draw, as is apparent in his most recent pronouncement on this matter, where we are told that:

There is a subtle distinction in Lakatos between MSRP, the methodology of scientific research programs, and MHRP, the methodology of historiographical research programs, that is, between the notion of an SRP, made up of a hard core and a protective belt, plus the proposition that the evolution of an SRP *should* be appraised in terms of excess empirical content, and the quite distinct historical thesis that scientists in fact adopt and reject SRPs in accordance with that appraisal criterion. [...] In other words, it is one thing to define an SRP as 'progressive' because it accurately predicts novel facts and quite another to assert that scientists actually subscribe to the progressive SRPs that can be found in the history of a science. [...] Thus, in my Methodology of Economics (1980), I argued that modern economists preach the methodology of falsificationism but rarely practise it: they are 'innocuous falsificationists'. This thesis may be expressed by saying that in economics MHRP is largely false; however that in no way denies the force of MSRP: the normative case for falsificationism might stand up even if the positive one fell to the ground. (Blaug, 1991b, pp. 502–3)

In economics, according to Blaug, we would have progressive SRPs in spite of the actual practices of economists who adhere to them for many reasons besides their progressiveness. While it might be understandable that Popper (a philosopher) can find 'obvious that the objectivity and the rationality of progress in science is not due to the personal objectivity and rationality of the scientist' (Popper, 1981, p. 95), one would have thought that Blaug (an economist) would oppose such a view. How can it be that 'the normative case for falsificationism might stand up even if the positive one fell to the ground'? Is this not equivalent to arguing that the scientist is led by an invisible hand to promote an end which is no part of his intention? Yet would we be likely to believe that the normative case for the benevolence of the butcher, the brewer or the baker might stand up, even if the positive case made by Adam Smith was empirically irrelevant? Similarly, would we be content to make the normative case of perfect competition without worrying about actual markets and second best complications? Were this the case, we should all look for other jobs.

The quest for critical rationalism in economic methodology

One may well reject falsificationism and/or MSRP and at the same time be unwilling to join the anti-modernist camp because unwilling to remain completely without criteria of appraisal. What Popper offers us is his epistemology of critical rationalism that one may subscribe to even if he rejects his falsificationism (after all, people reject falsificationism not because they doubt *modus tollens*, but for its inadequacy on either descriptive or prescriptive grounds when advocated as the *deus ex machina* of scientific enterprise), while Lakatos may be taken as a source of inspiration for 'creative' use of his insights on history and methodology.[16]

Among those who have recently explored such possibilities,[17] Wade Hands's (1993) attempt stands out because of its clarity in identifying the very issues at stake. Hands has been for a decade one of the most prolific critics of falsificationism and MSRP (Hands, 1984, 1985a, 1985b, 1990b, 1991 and 1992), but this does not prevent him from concluding that the Popperian tradition, despite its various *methodological* vices, can be appreciated because of its *epistemological* virtue(s). Hands's argument is that the virtues of the Popperian philosophical framework emerge when compared with its potential rivals, and especially with the different instances of the anti-modernist movement. Critical rationalism, according to him, 'is capable of addressing many of the issues raised by recent antimodernist discourse' (Hands, 1993, p. 171).

Such a response, however, is based on a particular version of critical rationalism that has his own problems, as Hands himself is ready to recognize (Hands, 1993, p. 193, n. 31). Indeed, critical rationalism, deprived of strict methodological rules (such as falsification and falsifiability), becomes a non-justificationist philosophy whose descriptive and/or normative adequacy requires some additional support. In this respect the best support presently available seems to be the 'evolutionary epistemology' interpretation of the Popperian perspective provided by, among others, Bartley, Campbell and Popper himself (compare Radnitzky and Bartley, 1987). According to such an interpretation, as Caldwell points out:

> Evolutionary epistemology provides the epistemological foundations for critical rationalism. This doctrine emphasizes the similarities between the growth of animal (including human) knowledge and the evolution of species. Bold conjectures are analogous to blind variations (mutations) in nature; the process of criticism is analogous to the process of natural selection. Evolutionary epistemology provides an empirical basis for epistemology (in processes found in nature) as well as an argument for realism (the survival of both ideas and organisms depends on their fit within their environment, and the assumption of an existing environment is consistent with realism). (Caldwell, 1991b, pp. 23–4)

Note, however, that human beings, somewhat differently from other living creatures, are capable of self-representation and purposeful action (among other things), so that the evolution of scientific knowledge is more likely to be of the Lamarckian (rather than Darwinian) type. But a Lamarckian approach would require the identification of the inner force(s) supposed to be responsible for the evolutionary process (undoubtedly no easy task).

Indeed, the discussion of the context of discovery has always been a source of much confusion and the hope of finding a satisfactory assessment was abandoned long ago. It is difficult to see why evolutionary epistemology should be able to escape the well-known pitfalls of that discussion. What is likely to happen, in my opinion, is that advocates of evolutionary interpretations of critical rationalism will have to resort, in the end, to the usual all-powerful metaphor of the invisible hand. The point has not gone unnoticed by Hands who observes:

> For Bartley the Chicago view of rationality, incentives, and markets is clearly integrated into his view of the growth of knowledge and the institutional structure of science. 'The central concern of that branch of philosophy known as epistemology or the theory of knowledge should be the growth of knowledge. This means that the theory of knowledge is a branch of economics' (Bartley, 1990, p. 89). For Bartley epistemology is basically a branch of economics, although only of a certain type of economics: the economics of Smith's *Wealth of Nations* and the modern economics of the Chicago, public choice, and transactions cost schools. (Hands, 1993, p. 167)

Hands seems to be willing to suspend his judgement. He comments that 'evolutionary epistemology is a possible solution to Popper's problem; time will tell if it can be worked into a full adequate solution' (Hands, 1993, p. 193, n. 31). While appreciating his fair-minded abstention from killing off infant lines of research in economic methodology,[18] we cannot keep quiet about the fact that Bartley's conjecture is likely to prove to be a dead-end track. This is because the view that the problem of the growth of knowledge and its inner rationality should be approached with the typical tools of economics, fascinating as it may be, is open to the objection of circular reasoning.

It would be quite surprising, indeed, if a discipline whose main methodological puzzle is the methodological status of the rationality hypothesis[19] could rescue epistemology from the difficulties encountered in dealing with the rationality of scientists and/or of science itself. The metaphor of the invisible hand is surely appealing (especially to economic methodologists, of course), but it is doomed to remain what it is, just a simple metaphor.

In order to convert it into a convincing explanation we ought to grasp both the difference between practical and scientific rationality and the economics of the institutional setting in which science is currently practised, two issues that do not make economists comfortable. As far as the difference between practical and scientific rationality is concerned, we need only remember that one of the most frequent criticisms of the standard notion of rationality in economics is simply that it is descriptively false,[20] especially when strictly individualistic preferences cannot be reasonably assumed (as at first sight seems to be the case in scientific practice). How can it be possible, then, to avoid the same objection as far as the actual practice of science is concerned?

The second issue seems even more daunting. The Smithian metaphor of the invisible hand may well suggest the relevant questions of normative economics, but it is at best descriptively inadequate, and at worst plainly false, if taken as a piece of positive economics. As Frank Hahn puts it:

> When the claim is made – and the claim is as old as Adam Smith – that a myriad of self-seeking agents left to themselves will lead to a coherent and efficient disposition of economic resources, Arrow and Debreu show what the world would look like if the claim is to be true. In doing this, they provide the most potent avenue of falsification of the claims. (Hahn, 1973, p. 324)

Given such premises, what can we expect from applying the same argument to the growth of knowledge? Even if we concede the possibility of adequately representing the problem of scientists' choice, at best we might hope to find a set of very idealized (and descriptively false) circumstances under which the growth of knowledge would be 'optimally' pursued (note, by the way, that the definition of optimality in this context is far from obvious). Furthermore, as is also well known, a market economy needs some institutional framework (at least a minimum of legal rules) in order to work properly. So we meet again the same kind of question: what corresponds to such rules in the growth of knowledge business?

At present we do not hold firm answers to such questions. Whether some answer will be found in the future we cannot tell (but I doubt it). What I can say now is that we have already had to relinquish hope of finding a set of all-purpose methodological rules, but this is not a good reason for replacing a much needed epistemological explanation of scientific progress with an over-simple and incomplete metaphor.

A final remark

Behind the efforts of all economic methodologists who advocate some facet of the Popperian tradition (falsificationism, MSRP, critical rationalism) there is the respectable desire to provide an account of what constitutes 'progress' in economics, without endorsing either anarchist/nihilist postmodernism, or merely sociological explanations typical of other current perspectives. With all my sympathy for their attempts and their concerns,[21] I cannot abstain from noticing that really convincing answers still remain to be found.

We know that scientific rationality (like economic rationality, for that matter) is likely to be bounded and procedural rather than perfect and substantive. The problem is that we know very little of what use we may make of such a notion as 'imperfect' rationality. To be sure, while there is life, there is hope too. In the meantime, however, the best thing to do is to make our best efforts to take pluralism seriously. As recently stressed by Warren Samuels:

> Pluralism means tolerance of epistemological criteria and discursive understanding that are different from those that we prefer, and a studied resistance to establish those that we prefer as the privileged ones. (Samuels, 1991, p. 522)

Notes

1. Without implying their responsibility in any way, I wish to thank Bruce Caldwell and Wade Hands for their comments. Financial support from MURST (the Italian Ministry for the University and Scientific Research) is also gratefully acknowledged.
2. The relevant literature is too extensive to permit detailed references. For a (partial) bibliography, see Redman, 1989, pp. 210–13 and 232–6.
3. See, for instance, Mäki (1990) and Weintraub (1989). Even more forceful strictures in this respect come from Lawrence Boland; for two fresh restatements of his criticism, see Boland (1992a and 1992b).
4. Compare, for instance, the different views expressed by contributors to de Marchi (1988) and de Marchi and Blaug (1991).
5. Here I am taking for granted that works along Lakatosian lines are altogether in the Popperian tradition. Lakatos's methodology of scientific research programmes (MSRP) may well be seen as an attempt to apply Popper's falsificationist methodology (originally conceived as a prescriptive response to the classical questions of demarcation and appraisal of scientific *theories*) to the mainly descriptive question (originally raised, among

others, by Kuhn) of scientific *progress* and its determinants. Note that if the problem of the progressiveness of a scientific enterprise is a serious one within a Popperian perspective, it becomes really crucial for MSRP. While for Popper, after all, the *potential* falsifiability of a theory is enough to guarantee its scientific status, MSRP can ascertain the scientific status of a research programme (and the 'rationality' of scientists committed to it) *only* through its compliance with Lakatos's criteria of theoretical and empirical progress. This because, if loosely interpreted (cf. Caldwell, 1991a), most Lakatosian categories turn out to fit almost any discipline, whether 'truly scientific' or not.

6.   For other quotations in the same vein and an account of the state of economic methodology, see Salanti (1989).

7.   As I argue below, the same cannot (or should not) be said of Lakatos's MSRP.

8.   Of course, I take for granted that progress in economics does exist. By this I do not mean, however, that economics is *always* progressive in the short run: sometimes it may well happen that a theory or even a whole paradigm is superseded by one that is no better, or that is conflicting, and controversies between opposite approaches last for a long time. But I think, nevertheless, that there would be general agreement that our understanding of economic problems has notably progressed if compared, for instance, with that of a hundred years ago.

9.   The indirect reference is to Popper (1976), who went so far as to claim that, differently from other species: 'Man has achieved the possibility of being *critical of his own tentative trials, of his own theories*. These theories [...] can be critically discussed, and shown to be erroneous, without killing any authors or burning any books [...]. If the method of rational critical discussion should establish itself, then this should make the use of violence obsolete: *critical reason is the only alternative to violence so far discovered*. It seems to me clear that it is the obvious duty of all intellectuals to work for *this* revolution – for the replacement of the eliminative function of rational criticism.' (Popper, 1976, p. 292, italics in the original). Popper repeatedly expressed similar concerns in many of his writings. The most explicit discussions may be found in Popper (1950 and 1957).

10.   Quoted – of course as an example of a mistaken belief – in McCloskey (1989, p. 233).

11.   See, for instance, Hutchison (1976, 1981 and 1988).

12.   For surveys and discussions of such critiques by economic methodologists, see Caldwell (1982, ch. 12; 1984 and 1991b), Hands (1984 and 1985a) and Hausman (1985 and 1988).

13.   See Blaug (1976, 1980, 1984, 1990, 1991a and 1991b).

14.   The reader should note that I am not maintaining that progress can never be gained through falsifications. After all, the 'growth of knowledge' story may well be told according to a strictly Popperian perspective (see Popper, 1963, ch. 10). What I want to say is rather that it would be very surprising if in economics it proved to be possible to be more falsificationist than Lakatos believed to be the case in the natural sciences.

15.   For instance, the possibility of applying successfully Lakatosian standards of progress to Keynes's *General Theory* is the object of a controversy between Blaug and Hands. See Blaug (1990, 1991a and 1991b) and Hands (1985b and 1990b).

16.   For a provocative discussion of the necessity of a more 'creative' exploitation of Lakatos's methodological insights both in economic methodology and in the history of economics, see de Marchi (1991). He blames methodologists for having focused their attention on too narrow a set of questions (unduly neglecting topics such as the evolution of heuristics, its 'local' as opposed to 'programme-wide' aspects, the role of empirical work, the possible epistemic value of the discovery context, and so on), and historians for having embraced, among other things, too static and mechanical a notion of research programmes.

17.   See, for instance, Roger Backhouse's (1992) attempt to retain Lakatos's appraisal criterion by replacing the concept of a scientific research programme with 'something much broader' together with his (1991 and 1993) critical assessments of post-modernist challenges to economic methodology, and Bruce Caldwell's (1991a and 1991b) explicit advocacy of critical rationalism as the inspiring source of his (1982 and 1988) proposals of methodological pluralism.

18.   Indeed, as we can see in Hands (1993), he is perfectly aware of the very tentative character of Bartley's economic metaphor.

19. For a discussion of how such difficulties emerge within Popperian approaches to economic methodology, see Hands (1985a). Another author who places his trust in critical rationalism is Caldwell. He argues that 'Popper's writings on critical rationalism provide a way out of the dilemma posed by the conflict between falsificationism and situational logic' (Caldwell, 1991b, p. 25). If this simply means that some problems can be solved by discarding naïve falsificationism, it is difficult to disagree. On the other hand, if the claim is that we might usefully apply situational logic to scientists' behaviour, it is difficult to abstain from asking 'how' and 'why'.
20. For a more detailed discussion of the consequences of such a distinction for Popperian approaches to economic methodology, let me refer to Salanti (1987).
21. For an open acknowledgement of the uneasiness due to the abandonment of 'modernist' certitudes, see Beed (1991).

References

Backhouse, Roger E. (1991), 'The constructivist critique of economic methodology', *Methodus*, 4 (1), pp. 65–82.

Backhouse, Roger E. (1992), 'Lakatos and Economics', in Lowry, S. Todd (ed.), *Perspectives on the History of Economic Thought, Vol. 8*, Aldershot: Edward Elgar, pp. 19–34.

Backhouse, Roger E. (1993), 'Rhetoric and Methodology', in Hébert, R.F. (ed.), *Perspectives on the History of Economic Thought, Vol. 9*, Aldershot: Edward Elgar, pp. 3–17.

Bartley, W.W. III (1990), *Unfathomed Knowledge. Unmeasured Wealth*, La Salle, Ill.: Open Court.

Beed, Clive (1991), 'Philosophy of science and contemporary economics: An overview', *Journal of Post Keynesian Economics*, 13 (4), pp. 459–94.

Blaug, Mark (1976), 'Kuhn versus Lakatos or Paradigms versus Research Programmes in the History of Economics', in Latsis, Spiro J. (ed.), *Method and Appraisal in Economics*, Cambridge: Cambridge University Press, pp. 149–80.

Blaug, Mark (1980), *The Methodology of Economics: Or How Economists Explain*, Cambridge: Cambridge University Press.

Blaug, Mark (1984), 'Comment 2', in Wiles, P. and Routh, G. (eds), *Economics in Disarray*, Oxford: Basil Blackwell, pp. 30–6.

Blaug, Mark (1990), 'Reply to D. Wade Hands' "Second Thoughts on Second Thoughts": Reconsidering the Lakatosian progress of The General Theory', *Review of Political Economy*, 2 (1), 102–4.

Blaug, Mark (1991a), 'Second thoughts on the Keynesian revolution', *History of Political Economy*, 23 (2), pp. 171–92.

Blaug, Mark (1991b), 'Afterword', in de Marchi, Neil and Blaug, Mark (eds), *Appraising Economic Theories. Studies in the Methodology of Research Programs*, Aldershot: Edward Elgar, pp. 499–512.

Boland, Lawrence A. (1992a), 'Understanding the Popperian legacy in economics', *Research in the History of Economic Thought and Methodology*, Vol. 9, pp. 265–76.

Boland, Lawrence A. (1992b), 'Methodology in the 1980s: Fads and false hopes', Simon Frazer University, mimeo.

Caldwell, Bruce J. (1982), *Beyond Positivism. Economic Methodology in the Twentieth Century*, London: Allen & Unwin.

Caldwell, Bruce J. (1984), 'Some problems with falsificationism in economics', *Philosophy of the Social Sciences*, 14 (4), pp. 489–95.

Caldwell, Bruce J. (1988), 'The Case for Pluralism', in de Marchi, Neil (ed.), *The Popperian Legacy in Economics*, Cambridge: Cambridge University Press, pp. 231–44.

Caldwell, Bruce J. (1989), 'The trend of methodological thinking', *Ricerche Economiche*, 43 (1–2), pp. 8–20.

Caldwell, Bruce J. (1991a), 'The Methodology of Scientific Research Programmes in Economics: Criticisms and Conjectures', in Shaw, G.K. (ed.), *Economics, Culture and Education. Essays in Honour of Mark Blaug*, Aldershot: Edward Elgar, pp. 95–107.

Caldwell, Bruce J. (1991b), 'Clarifying Popper', *Journal of Economic Literature*, **29** (1), pp. 1–33.

Hahn, Frank H. (1973), 'The winter of our discontent', *Economica*, **40** (159), pp. 322–330.

Hands, D. Wade (1984), 'Blaug's economic methodology', *Philosophy of the Social Sciences*, **14** (1), pp. 115–25.

Hands, D. Wade (1985a), 'Karl Popper and economic methodology. A new look', *Economics and Philosophy*, **1** (1), pp. 83–99.

Hands, D. Wade (1985b), 'Second thoughts on Lakatos', *History of Political Economy*, **17** (1), pp. 1–16.

Hands, D. Wade (1990a), 'Thirteen theses on progress in economic methodology', *Finnish Economic Papers*, **3** (1), pp. 72–6.

Hands, D. Wade (1990b), 'Second thoughts on "second thoughts": Reconsidering the Lakatosian progress of the General Theory', *Review of Political Economy*, **2** (1), pp. 69–81.

Hands, D. Wade (1991), 'The Problem of Excess Content: Economics, Novelty and a Long Popperian Tale', in de Marchi, Neil and Blaug, Mark (eds), *Appraising Economic Theories; Studies in the Methodology of Research Programs*, Aldershot: Edward Elgar, pp. 58–75.

Hands, D. Wade (1992), 'Falsification, Situational Analysis and Scientific Research Programs: The Popperian Tradition in Economic Methodology', in de Marchi, Neil (ed.), *PostPopperian Methodology of Economics*, Boston: Kluwer, pp. 19–53.

Hands, D. Wade (1993), 'The Popperian Tradition in Economic Methodology: Should It Be Saved', in *Testing, Rationality and Progress: Essays on the Popperian Tradition in Economic Methodology*, New York: Roman and Littlefield, pp. 149–201.

Hausman, Daniel H. (1985), 'Is falsificationism unpractised or unpractisable?', *Philosophy of the Social Sciences*, **15** (3), pp. 313–19.

Hausman, Daniel H. (1988), 'An Appraisal of Popperian Methodology', in de Marchi, Neil (ed.), *The Popperian Legacy in Economics*, Cambridge: Cambridge University Press, pp. 65–85.

Hutchison, Terence (1938), *The Significance and Basic Postulates of Economic Theory*, London: Macmillan.

Hutchison, Terence (1976), 'On the History and Philosophy of Science and Economics', in Latsis, Spiro J. (ed.), *Method and Appraisal in Economics*, Cambridge: Cambridge University Press, pp. 181–205.

Hutchison, Terence (1981), 'On the Aims and Methods of Economic Theorizing', in *The Politics and Philosophy of Economics*, Oxford: Basil Blackwell, pp. 266–307.

Hutchison, Terence (1988), 'The Case for Falsification', in de Marchi, Neil (ed.), *The Popperian Legacy in Economics*, Cambridge: Cambridge University Press, pp. 169–81.

Lakatos, Imre (1971), 'History of Science and Its Rational Reconstruction', in Buck, Roger C. and Cohen, Robert S. (eds), *PSA 1970. Boston Studies in the Philosophy of Science*, vol. 8, Dordrecht: Reidel, pp. 91–136.

Mäki, Uskali (1990), 'Methodology of economics: complaints and guidelines', *Finnish Economic Papers*, **3** (1), pp. 77–84.

de Marchi, Neil (ed.) (1988), *The Popperian Legacy in Economics*, Cambridge: Cambridge University Press

de Marchi, Neil (1991), 'Introduction: Rethinking Lakatos', in de Marchi, Neil and Blaug, Mark (eds), *Appraising Economic Theories. Studies in the Methodology of Research Programs*, Aldershot: Edward Elgar, pp. 1–30.

de Marchi, Neil and Blaug, Mark (eds) (1991), *Appraising Economic Theories. Studies in the Methodology of Research Programs*, Aldershot: Edward Elgar.

McCloskey, Donald M. (1983), 'The rhetoric of economics', *Journal of Economic Literature*, **21** (2), pp. 481–517.

McCloskey, Donald M. (1989), 'Why I am no longer a positivist', *Review of Social Economy*, **47** (3), pp. 225–38.

Popper, Karl (1950), *The Open Society and Its Enemies*, London: Routledge & Kegan Paul.

Popper, Karl (1957), *The Poverty of Historicism*, London: Routledge & Kegan Paul.

Popper, Karl (1963), *Conjectures and Refutations*, London: Routledge & Kegan Paul.

Popper, Karl (1976), 'Reason or Revolution?', in Theodor W. Adorno *et al.*, *The Positivist Dispute in German Sociology*, London: Heinemann, pp. 288–300.

Popper, Karl (1981), 'The Rationality of Scientific Revolutions', in Hacking, Ian (ed.), *Scientific Revolutions*, Oxford: Oxford University Press, pp. 80–106, (first printed in Harré, Rom (ed.), *Problems of Scientific Revolutions*, Oxford: Oxford University Press, 1975).

Radnitzky, Gerard and Bartley, W.W. III. (eds) (1987), *Evolutionary Epistemology, Rationality, and the Sociology of Knowledge*, La Salle, Ill.: Open Court.

Ravetz, Jerome R. (1971), *Scientific Knowledge and Its Social Problems*, Oxford: Oxford University Press.

Redman, Deborah A. (1989), *Economic Methodology. A Bibliography with Reference to Works in the Philosophy of Science, 1860–1988*, New York: Greenwood Press.

Salanti, Andrea (1987), 'Falsificationism and fallibilism as epistemic foundations of economics: A critical view', *Kyklos*, **40** (3), pp. 368–92.

Salanti, Andrea (1989), 'Recent work in economic methodology: Much ado about what?'. *Ricerche Economiche*, **43** (1–2), pp. 21–39.

Salanti, Andrea (1990), 'Review of Arjo Klamer, Donald N. McCloskey and Robert M. Solow (eds), *The Consequences of Economic Rhetoric*, Cambridge: Cambridge University Press, 1989', *Kyklos*, **43** (3), pp. 518–20.

Salanti, Andrea (1992), 'Review of Neil de Marchi and Mark Blaug (eds), *Appraising Economic Theories. Studies in the Methodology of Research Programs*, Aldershot: Edward Elgar, 1991', *Economic Journal*, **102** (415), pp. 1534–6.

Salanti, Andrea (1994), 'On the Lakatosian apple of discord between historians and methodologists', *Finnish Economic Papers*, **7** (1), pp. 30–41.

Samuels, Warren J. (1991), '"Truth" and "discourse" in the social construction of economic reality: An essay on the relation of knowledge to socioeconomic policy', *Journal of Post Keynesian Economics*, **13** (4), pp. 511–24.

Weintraub, Roy E. (1989), 'Methodology doesn't matter, but the history of thought might', *Scandinavian Journal of Economics*, **91** (4), pp. 477–93.

3. An exercise in theory evaluation: should rival theories of money and credit continue to survive?

Mark K. Tomass[1]

Prelude

Prominent economic theorists, the founders of modern economics, disagreed about the general propositions of what determines the welfare of individuals and nations and they specifically disagreed about what determines the levels of output, employment and prices. Those theorists typically cited facts to serve the purpose of an empirical verification of their interpretations. Contemporary economists continue to disagree about the same issues. They, in turn, present their verified interpretations through the use of econometrics as a presumably more sophisticated method of empirical testing (Mirowsky, 1989). Despite econometric testing of theories against the facts, however, disagreements continue to persist and rival economic theories survive next to each other without any sign of diminished disputes or a triumph of one theory over the other. Each theory is often described by its rival as 'irrelevant', 'useless', 'ideologically biased', 'unscientific', or all of the above.

One can argue that disagreements persist because the proponents of rival theories are dogmatic or have vested interests. However, if we take the propositions of rival economic theories at their face value, then what are the criteria to be met for a proponent of a rival theory to be characterized as dogmatic? Are these criteria philosophical, ideological, or psychological? It may be said that being dogmatic means not being 'scientific', since scientific thinking implies the undertaking of a process of self-criticism in the search for the ultimate causes of natural and social phenomena. But, does science possess uniform criteria according to which rival theories can be judged? Despite their claim to be basing their interpretations of phenomena upon observed facts, rival theories may still either establish different criteria for what makes them scientific or focus on different facts altogether, thus rendering empirical testing unable to solve the dispute. Does this mean that each theory is equally true according to its own criteria and that rival theories cannot be evaluated against each other because each operates within its own 'paradigm' (Kuhn, 1970)?

More than two decades after Kuhn's *Structure of Scientific Revolutions*, some methodologists are taking relativist positions on the question of the validity and truth of rival economic theories in a new wave of 'postmodernist discourse analysis' (Samuels, 1990). Others, influenced by modern French philosophy (Lyotard, 1984 and Foucault, 1972; 1973), are even arguing that rival economic theories are incommensurable. They imply that economic theories are equally valid within their own conceptual frameworks, for there are no commonly accepted standards according to which the propositions of rival theories can be evaluated against each other (Amariglio, 1988; 1990; Amariglio, Resnick and Wolff, 1990). Although there is no consensus on whether such standards are subjective or objective, they seem to apply to the methodologies as well as to the contents of rival theories. A theory cannot be characterized as superior or more comprehensive than another. It can only have different consequences or implications for social practice. While the latter assertion is widely accepted, the former is controversial. If we accept the proposition that no theory is superior to any other, neither methodologically nor substantively, then theory choice becomes a matter of aesthetic preference that is either arbitrary or caters to psychological needs. In this, we do not deny or underestimate any link between aesthetic preference and theory choice, but rather question the assertion that aesthetic preferences regarding economic theories are not based on a conception of truth (Dyer, 1986; 1988). Since it is implied that rival philosophical criteria are themselves incommensurable, then the acceptance of such a relativist position on the truth and validity of rival theories implies the rejection of any notion of a 'correspondence' between theory and a *social* reality.[2] Indeed, the denial of commonly accepted philosophical foundations to evaluate the propositions of rival theories against each other renders the philosophy of science an irrelevant enterprise to the social sciences in general.[3] Philosophical criteria are then replaced by 'rhetoric' (McCloskey, 1985).

This chapter evaluates the incommensurability thesis by choosing to examine the extent to which rival conceptions of the nature of money and its role in production are bounded by their philosophical foundations. We focus on rival theories of money rather than 'grand theories' claiming to explain all social phenomena for two reasons: first, in order to have a disciplined dialogue and avoid falling into slippery discussions concerning the validity of all the propositions of a 'grand theory' versus the other, and second, because the role of money in production has been controversial since the inception of economic thought. We will consider Alfred Marshall's and Karl Marx's rival theories of money.[4] We choose to discuss Marshall versus Marx not only because of their different positions on the relationship between money and the production process (Dillard, 1987; 1988), but also because they have both given thought and credence to the philosophical foundations that generated their economics.

This chapter is divided into five sections. In the first two sections, the metaphysical, epistemological and methodological foundations of Marshall's and Marx's theories of money are briefly established. In the third and the fourth sections, an attempt is made to translate Marshall's and Marx's theories of money by using the rival philosophical foundations. In light of this, we conclude that the two rival theories of money are commensurable and that the implications that Marx draws from his treatment of money as capital are superior to Marshall's.

Marshall's philosophical foundations and his theory of money

In defining the conditions for establishing the validity and truth of knowledge, Marshall positions himself within the bounds of empiricism when he states that 'the function of the science is to collect, arrange and analyse economic facts and to apply the knowledge, gained by observation and experience, in determining what are likely to be the immediate and ultimate effects of various groups of causes' (Marshall, 1920, p. v). Sensory observations therefore play the role of the ultimate kind of data upon which knowledge is based. This epistemological position also informs us about the metaphysical foundation of knowledge, for if sensations are the only data for knowledge, then sensations are also the underlying nature of the universe and the categories which we use to describe it (Mill, 1979, pp. 180–2).

The view that knowledge is gained by observation and experience and that the latter informs us of the effects of causes is built on Hume's and J.S. Mill's empiricism. Hume, for example, argues that 'all reasoning concerning matters of fact seem to be founded on the relation of *Cause and Effect*. The knowledge of this relation ... arises entirely from experience' (Hume, 1975, p. 26). We investigate past observations in order to find those which 'are constantly conjoined with each other' (Hume, 1975, p. 27). The question however is, what kind of past observations should one focus on? Marshall found the answer in Mill who believes that the truths known to us by immediate consciousness are 'our own bodily sensations and mental feelings' (Mill, 1974, p. 7). Such knowledge does not imply necessary truths but empirical truths as they are observed in nature. Those empirical truths are derived in his inductive–deductive–inductive methodology which can be summarized in two processes; one analytic, the other synthetic (Tomass, 1991, pp. 58–83).

In the analytic process, the observer must analyse the existing state of society into its elements and collect 'all those facts and reasoning which are similar to one another in nature' (Marshall, 1920, p. 39). However, since the study of political economy focuses exclusively on the actions of people in their pursuit of wealth, the relevant elements of the existing state of society become the observer's feelings, desires, or motives that induce him to act. Therefore, after classifying as motives the feelings that induce the individual to act, the inductive process proceeds by focusing on the observations 'in which the action of motive is so regular that it can be predicted and the estimate of the motor-force can be verified by results' (Marshall, 1920, p. 26). Marshall's purpose in focusing on motives that cause people to act in a regular pattern is to identify regularities of sequence which, in turn, serve to identify causes and effects. But can these motives be measured? Marshall builds on J.S. Mill's belief in our ability to quantify motives and desires, since the 'desires of man and the nature of the conduct to which they prompt him, are within the reach of our observation' (Mill, 1948, p. 149). Thus, 'an opening is made for the methods and tests of science as soon as the force of the person's motives – not the motives themselves – can be approximately measured by the sum of money which he will just give up in order to secure a desired satisfaction: or again by the sum which is just required to induce him to undergo a certain fatigue' (Marshall, 1920, p. 15). Money therefore measures the ratio of the exchange between pleasure and pain.

By focusing on the strength of motives rather than the motives themselves, Marshall attempts to free economics from heavy dependence on inaccessible psychological states. As a result, money enters the sphere of economic analysis as a fundamental methodological instrument that links Marshall's epistemology with his methodology, rather than as a fundamental social and economic institution. Indeed, Marshall insists that money 'is the centre around which economic science clusters' not because money 'is regarded as the main aim of human effort', but because 'it is the one convenient medium of measuring human motive on a large scale' (Marshall, 1920, p. 22). These measurements provide the epistemological bases for any explanatory statement, since those measured strengths of psychological states are the only data on which knowledge of human action can be based. The fact that the strength of psychological states represents the values that people cast on objects makes money a measure of value. This shows that the functions of money as a measure of value and as a medium of exchange are interdependent.

Through induction, Marshall generates alternative ratios of exchange between pleasure and pain regarding consumers and producers. This involves abstracting observations regarding the sum of money that measures the strength of motives, from any other observation which might influence it, by the addition of *ceteris paribus* clauses. Marshall abstracts the sum of money which a consumer is willing to give up in order to acquire an amount of pleasure, from any other circumstance that may affect the ratio of the exchange. The induction of alternative ratios of the consumer's exchange of pleasure and pain, determines the law of demand. The latter is a locus of correlations between prices and quantities demanded. Given the empiricist criterion for establishing causation, these correlations are regular sequences of observations that establish causation between prices and quantities demanded subject to *ceteris paribus* clauses. Marshall also abstracts the sum of money which the producer requires in order to undergo the pain of producing the commodity, from any other circumstance that may affect the ratio of the exchange. In the same manner, the induction of alternative ratios of the consumer's exchange of pleasure and pain, determines the law of supply. Now causation is established between prices and quantities supplied and demanded.

Marshall's synthetic process starts when he forms a synthesis of outcomes to deduce the effects of all the causes acting simultaneously. Thus, 'induction, aided by analysis and deduction, brings together appropriate classes of facts, arranges them, analyses them and infers from them general statements or laws' (Marshall, 1920, p. 781). For instance, a decline in the consumers' strength of motive for the pleasure embodied in a commodity implies that people are willing to exchange less money (fatigue, pain, or energy) for it. This leads to a surplus of the commodity at the initial ratio of exchange, thus causing its price to decline. The decline in the price becomes in turn, a cause, the effect of which is less production of the commodity. Since producers (labour and capital) are offered a smaller sum of money to induce them to undergo the same fatigue, they respond by reducing their supply of work effort and capital. Conversely, when consumers desire more of a commodity, the increase in its price causes a higher level of production. As a result, Marshall establishes regularities of sequence between the sum of money that measures the strength of motives, prices, quantities desired and quantities produced (Whitaker, 1975, p. 165). Finally, the magnitude and ratio of exchanges of pain and pleasure across individuals determines the kind and level of output to be produced in a society. The levels of output and employment therefore are determined by the strength of people's motives for action. Marshall then claims that as we keep focusing on the regularities of sequence 'we get gradually nearer to those fundamental unities which are called nature's laws: we trace their action first singly and then in combination' (Marshall, 1920, p. 40).

The analytic process therefore provides the synthetic process with the laws of human nature which could be also referred to as empirical generalizations.

> Then for a while deduction plays the chief role: it brings some of these generalizations into association with one another, works from them tentatively to new and broader generalizations or laws and then calls on induction again to do the main share of the work in collecting, sifting and arranging these facts so as to test and 'verify' the new law. (Marshall, 1920, p. 781)

With the latter inductive–deductive–inductive methodology, Marshall constructs in his *Principles* an edifice of 'verified', yet abstract laws. These laws have been extracted from the concrete nexus of experience by conscious and selective induction of constantly conjoined facts. Within this edifice however, the purchasing power of money is assumed to be 'fixed' (Marshall, 1920, pp. 593–4).[5] Furthermore, its social role in production is neutral. One may argue that Marshall's characterization of money in the *Principles* is not intended to be a complete theory of money but an abstract framework of analysis within which resources are shown to be optimally allocated for the purpose of production, distribution and consumption. What concerns us however, is whether abstracting from money's function as an institutional process by which a system of production based on private property realizes the value of output, has a serious consequence for the conclusions drawn from such a framework (Dillard, 1987, p. 1624).

In order for us to be fair in evaluating the consequences of abstracting from the institution of money, we must investigate Marshall's treatment of money in his later works and particularly, his last work on *Money, Credit and Commerce*.[6] There, he allows the value of money to vary, depending on its quantity in circulation. By maintaining his initial thesis of money as a measure of the strength of motives, he formulates his 'Quantity Doctrine' in which he concludes that 'the value of a unit of a currency varies, other things being equal, inversely with the number of the units and their average rapidity of circulation' (Marshall, 1965, p. 48). In other words, 'there is a direct relation between the volume of currency and the level of prices, that, if one is increased by ten percent, the other also will be increased by ten percent' (Marshall, 1965, p. 45). This also affirms a similar conclusion in *Memorials of Alfred Marshall*, where he asserts that changes in the money supply affect long-term prices (Pigou, 1956, p. 192). Marshall however expresses a dissatisfaction in the quantity theory for not accounting for the velocity of money. Changes in the velocity of money, he asserts, will alter the proportional relationship between money and the price level (Marshall, 1965, pp. 43–5). But no short-run analysis is provided regarding the relationship between the quantity of the circulating money and the rate of production. In his *Official Papers*, Marshall states that the influx of gold from the mines of the New World for a period of thirty years 'has not in the long-run any great effect; that has caused the movements [of prices and quantities produced] to be spasmodic; but that the increased production would have been very much the same without the new gold' (Marshall, 1926, pp. 168–9). The existence of more or less money in circulation therefore does not disturb the level and the kind of production because the latter is determined by the strength of the motives of producers and consumers to exchange their pain for pleasure, given their preferences and resource endowments.

Marshall distinguishes between the transactions and precautionary demand for money (Marshall, 1965, p. 44) and hints at the opportunity cost of holding idle money (Marshall, 1965, p. 39 and Whitaker, 1975, pp. 167, 174). However, he does not proceed to investigate the implications of an asset demand for money with regard to the level of production. In *Economics of Industry* however he establishes a link between credit crises and economic crises (Marshall, 1879, pp. 151–2). Later, in *Money, Credit and Commerce*, Marshall devotes an entire chapter to this link. An unreasonable expansion of credit following a series of good harvests results in short-term economic crises (Marshall, 1965, pp. 246–51). An increase in the volume of credit leads to high prices, wages and profits as well as to a sharp rise in speculative activity. The latter prompts sceptical creditors to reduce lending and call back selective loans, causing a series of bank failures and a fall in prices. The fall in prices increases the value of money. As a result, entrepreneurs prefer to hold money due to the rise in its value (hoarding!),[7] thus leading to a faster decline in prices and to a rise in unemployment, for entrepreneurs resist a reduction in profits by laying off labour (Marshall, 1920, pp. 594–5). Unemployment however will soon decline as entrepreneurs expect a rebound in prices. They will increase the quantity of goods supplied in order to profit by it (Marshall, 1879, pp. 155, 162). Excessive credit expansion and contractions are therefore not neutral. They generate short-term business cycles through their impact on short-term price level changes, independent of changes in the monetary base (Gaynor, 1991, pp. 47–51 and Tomass, 1991, pp. 96–101).

Marshall suggests a neutral money cycle but a non-neutral credit cycle! In his exposition of the credit cycle, Marshall came close to a monetary theory of production. Why then did he fail to treat the mere existence of money as a disturbing element in production in the short-run or in the long-run, with or without the presence of a credit crisis? The answer lies in his insistence that 'Money is, firstly, a medium of exchange' and secondly, 'a standard of value … to indicate the amount of general purchasing power' (Marshall, 1965, p. 16). Money is 'command over capital' but, in itself, is not given the significance that capital has for production (Marshall, 1965, p. 256). In this however Marshall is being inconsistent with his belief in Spencer's and Hegel's representation of 'Principle of Continuity', for, the spirit of continuity prompts him to state that 'there is not in real life a clear line of division between things that are and are not Capital' (Marshall, 1920, p. ix). In fact, he applies the term interest and profit to what is regarded 'free', 'fluid', or 'floating' capital which does not seem to be anything other than money advanced for the purchase of equipment (Marshall, 1920, pp. viii, 411–12). If his philosophical foundations do not obstruct his conception of money as capital, then would they obstruct an effort to map out its implication for monetary crises occurring independent of a credit crisis? The third section will provide an answer to this question.

Marx's philosophical foundations and his theory of money
Regarding the metaphysical foundations of Marx's economics, he argues in favour of a 'naturalism' that shifts the polemic between idealism and materialism towards a realism (Marx, 1975, p. 336). For Marx, the thinking process forms categories of thought when it receives 'an impulse from outside' (Marx, 1986b, p. 38). Such impulses are in the form of perception and conception of the social and living conditions of people. His statement that 'the real subject [society] remains outside the mind and independent of it' makes him metaphysically a realist (Marx, 1986b, p. 38). His realism is also manifested in his distinction between the 'real-concrete' and the 'mental-concrete'. The real-concrete is the world of circumstances as it presents itself to the mind from concrete conditions existing outside it. The mental-concrete however is 'a product of thinking, of comprehension;' it is the mind's comprehension of an independent real-concrete (Marx, 1986b, p. 38). Knowledge is a product of a thinking process that assimilates and transforms the perceptions and images of the real-concrete into the concepts and categories of the mental-concrete.

Since the practical activity of people and their social relations change, implying a change in the real-concrete, then our conception of them in the mental-concrete changes as well. Each one of the concretes shapes the other. The relationship between the two concretes therefore is bidirectional. In this sense, it is a dynamic relationship. It implies that objects of thought are not independent of human contemplation. When the object of thought is the society in which the subject finds himself, then 'society must always be envisaged as the premise of conception even when the theoretical method is employed' (Marx, 1986b, p. 39). But the minds of people, the subject, while conceptualizing and interpreting these circumstances, also change them in the process of entering into social relationships with one another. The subject lives within the object and is changed by it, since not only people change circumstances but circumstances change people also. Marx, accordingly, charges that 'the materialist doctrine concerning the changing of circumstances and upbringing forgets that circumstances are changed by men and that the educator must himself be educated' (Marx, 1976, p. 4). Hence, Marx criticizes traditional metaphysics for not capturing the metaphysical significance of human activity as objective social activity that changes people's perception and conception of circumstances. He writes: 'The chief defect of all previous materialism (that of Feurebach included) is that things, reality, sensuousness are conceived only in the form of the *object, or of contemplation*, but not as *sensuous human activity, practice*, not subjectively' (Marx, 1976, p. 3). Marx therefore finds an escape to the endless metaphysical polemics between idealism and materialism in human activity.

Regarding his epistemological foundations, the criterion with which Marx validates his economic categories is people's consciousness of their social practice. Consciousness is a question of interpretation, of a comprehension of a human predicament. The investigation of the processes that underlie such comprehension does not seem to be of relevance to Marx's intellectual project. His concern is not the search for empiricist or rationalist criteria for the validity of knowledge. The practical problems facing people are the categories that must be based on empirically verifiable premises. Both empiricists and rationalists can observe and verify such premises. The meaning of these premises for people however, is contingent on their practices in the given historical conditions. Thus:

> the premises from which we begin are not arbitrary ones, not dogmas, but real premises from which abstraction can only be made in the imagination. They are the real individuals, their activity and the material conditions of their life, both those which they find already existing and those produced by their activity. These premises can thus be verified in a purely empirical way. (Marx and Engels, 1976, p. 31)

The general foundations of the kind of knowledge that Marx is concerned with therefore are people's consciousness of their practical activity. This conception of the nature of categories of the mental-concrete introduces an interpretive element into the formation of economic theory and practice. The consciousness of people of their practice implies that they collectively cast different meanings on the categories of the real-concrete depending on the various elements shaping their social practice. Practice, as a criterion for the meaning of a category does not cast a static meaning on it, but rather a dynamic one. By dynamic, we imply that the meaning of a category may change depending on the relationship between the real and the mental concretes. Anthropological studies, for example, show that money meant different things to different communities. Money was not uniformly treated as a multi-function institution as we treat it now (Neale, 1976). The truth of each function of money is established by the communities' practices as they treat money according to what it means to them.

The task of methodology is to construct a logical process in order to explain a historical process. But from what type of data may one initiate a logical process? Marx's naturalism informs him that such a process must start from 'the activity and the material conditions' of people's lives. While being aware that any starting point is an abstraction from a historical process, Marx adopts Hegel's analytic method (Hegel, 1975, p. 285) in order to abstract from the population of society and 'move to more and more tenuous abstractions until one arrived at the simplest determinations' (Marx, 1986b, p. 37). Such determinations define the function of the concept at any moment of time. Money, for example, is a store of value when it is hoarded, but it is capital when advanced for production. Marx then uses Hegel's synthetic method (Hegel, 1975, p. 286) in order to take these simplest determinations for 'a return journey until one finally arrived once more at population, which this time would not be a chaotic conception of a whole, but a rich totality of many determinations and relations' (Marx, 1986b, p. 37). The mental-concrete which he arrives at 'is a synthesis of many determinations, thus a unity of the diverse. In thinking, it therefore appears as a process of summing-up, as a result, not as the starting point, although it is the real starting point' (Marx, 1986b, p. 38).

A determination is a one-sided abstraction that has a special function depending on the form of production, distribution and circulation of the societies they exist in. Exchange in communal societies, for example, was not an integral part of them but took place in trade with other communities. Money played a role in exchange only among communities whose primary activity was trading between the surrounding communities. In ancient Rome and Greece, Marx argues, payments were made in kind rather than in money. Money did exist in ancient societies for different and mutually independent purposes before wage labour and capital existed. It has become a many-sided concrete economic category only in capitalist societies. As an abstract simple economic category, money:

> can express relations predominating in a less developed whole or subordinate relations in a more developed whole, relations which already existed historically before the whole had developed the aspect expressed in a more concrete category. To that extent, the course of abstract thinking which advances from the elementary to the combined corresponds to the actual historical process. (Marx, 1986b, p. 39)

In order for the logical process to be conceptualized in a unity with the historical process, the abstract concepts should always be referred to the specific institutions of society in which they are practised. Only then does their concrete nature acquire a historical character and meaning. In the course of the evolution of societies, the abstract concepts take on more relations and meanings and reach a level where they have a multiple significance in the most diversified form of society.

Being 'a crystallization of exchange value of commodities', money is conceptualized as a *relation* of production. People put their trust more in money than in one another precisely because money 'is the objectified relationship of persons to each other; as objectified exchange value and exchange value is nothing but a mutual relation of the productive activities of persons;' (Marx, 1986c, p. 97) it is a relation among the labour of individuals (Marx, 1987, p. 289). Unlike the quantity theory, Marx conceptualizes money as a relation rather than an object. Furthermore, the classical quantity theorists 'fall into the error of confusing *money* as distinct from *currency* with *capital* or even with commodities' (Marx, 1987, p. 416). Currency is a physical form of money, it is money as a medium of circulation, it is the one-sided form of money. Marx charges that the quantity theorists have, in general, failed to

> examine money in its abstract form in which it develops within the framework of simple commodity circulation and grows out of the relations of commodities in circulation. As a consequence they continually vacillate between the abstract forms which money assumes, as opposed to commodities and those forms of money which conceal concrete factors, such as capital, *REVENUE* and so forth. (Marx, 1987, p. 417)

Because his predecessors failed to examine money in its abstract form as a general equivalent of commodities, they failed to trace its development dynamically, that is, as its relations with other abstractions develop. As a result, they could not conceptualize the one-sided abstraction of money as a medium of circulation as it becomes a unity of meanings in a multi-sided mental-concrete and acquires multiple functions. Instead, they refer to one-sided abstract forms of money and often confuse the different forms with one another. Marx's charge is a methodological one. It is the methodology of Marx's predecessors that lacks the means to investigate money's origin and essence and thus fails to distinguish its abstract forms from its multi-sided concrete forms.

If money only circulates commodities, as the quantity theorists assumed in an equilibrium approach, then the entire stock of money available could be in circulation. It follows that commodities enter circulation without a price and money without value and that the prices of commodities spontaneously adjust in response to the quantity of money in the market (Marx, 1987, pp. 123–4). For Marx however money 'circulates commodities which have prices, that is commodities which have already been equated nominally with definite quantities of gold' (Marx, 1987, pp. 338–9). This implies that the determined prices of commodities presuppose that the exchange value of the quantity of gold is given by the labour time embodied in its production. Therefore, the quantity of money required for circulation is determined by 'the sum of the commodity prices to be realized' (Marx, 1987, p. 339). The latter, in turn, is determined by 'the price level, the relative magnitude of the exchange values of commodities in terms of gold' and by 'the quantity of commodities circulating at definite prices' (Marx, 1987, p. 339). The quantity of money in circulation 'must be determined by the aggregate of the prices it circulates divided by its velocity' (Marx, 1987, p. 193). A change in the value of money maintains the proposition that prices determine the quantity of money in circulation. An increase in the value of gold in terms of the labour time necessary for the production of one unit of it, for example, will reduce the prices of the commodities because a change has taken place in their standard of value.[8] Consequently, the quantity of gold in circulation will decrease as a result of a decrease in the sum of prices (Marx, 1987, p. 391).

But where would the additional quantity of money spring from or flow off when prices rise or fall? Marx responds that the mass of money must 'be capable of expansion and contraction. At one time money must be attracted in order to act as circulating coin, at another, circulating coin must be repelled in order to act again as stagnant money. This condition is fulfilled by money taking the form of hoards' (Marx, 1967, p. 134). Thus, the incorporation of a two-sided form of money (a medium of circulation and a store of value) into the mental-concrete allows Marx to reverse the order of causality of the quantity theory.

When the store of value function is emphasized, the sale of one commodity does not mean the immediate purchase of another commodity. Money could be held for a prolonged period of time or exported, thus interrupting the domestic flow of circulation. A monetary crisis occurs not because of a 'scarcity of currency' but a disproportion between the disposable capital and the vastness of the industrial, commercial and speculative enterprises then in hand' (Marx, 1986a, p. 117). Since commodities under capitalism are produced directly for the purpose of trade and indirectly for the purpose of consumption, production 'must get caught up in this incongruity between trade and exchange for consumption just as much as, for its own part, it must produce it' (Marx, 1986c, pp. 86–7). Say's Law – supply creates its own demand – is also reversed, because more supply does not mean more consumption demand, but vice versa. Moreover, when money is transformed into capital as people cast an additional meaning to it, its relation to production acquires a new function. Its two-sided relation as a medium of exchange and a store of value, now becomes three-sided. Hoards can now be transformed into money-capital depending on the value of the productive capital to be renewed (Marx, 1967b, pp. 83, 451), or can remain out of circulation in order to accumulate capital for production on an extended scale (Marx, 1967b, pp. 120, 321, 472, 489–95). Any net hoarding or net dishoarding produces an inequality between the level of demand and the exchange value of the produced commodities to be realized. Net hoarding will make the market price lower than the exchange value.[9] This reduces the rate of profit, thus leading to more hoarding and economic crises while net dishoarding will be associated with economic expansion. It is not the shortage of money that causes a crisis, but the net hoarding of money. Net hoarding implies a deliberate reduction in the level of total expenditures. It is evident that once money is conceived as capital, the reason for hoarding becomes embedded within the conditions of production. As Marx ascends with the logical one-sided abstract function of money to the historical multi-sided concrete, the neutrality of money in capitalist production can no more be argued for (Hilferding, 1981, part IV).

When bank credit replaces the circulation of commodities by means of money, money becomes loan capital. Money acquires a new use value. 'Its use-value then consists precisely in the profit it produces when converted into capital. In this capacity of potential capital, as a means of producing profit, it becomes a commodity' (Marx, 1967c, pp. 338–9). The formula for the money capital that is handed over to the functioning capitalist for a period of time as loan capital is expressed as M–M', where M' is the initial loan plus interest. This however doesn't mean that money itself possesses the property of bearing profit. Marx demystifies what is commonly perceived as the object of money as self-expanding by bringing out its essence as a relation between people. The essence of interest, he argues, is in its being part of the profit that the functioning capitalist acquires when he converts loan capital into money capital and advances it as productive capital in order to absorb the surplus value created by wage workers in the process of production. It is therefore 'not until capital is money-capital that it becomes a commodity, whose capacity for self-expansion has a definite price quoted every time in every prevailing rate of interest' (Marx, 1967c, p. 393).

The development of the function of money as a means of payment in addition to its use-value as loan-capital however, reflects a further aggravation of the contradictions of commodity production, adding the antagonism of creditors and debtors to the previously existing one between buyers and sellers. By increasing the mutual dependence of commodity producers on each other, money used as a means of payment separates the circulation of commodities from the payments for them and creates new possibilities for crises to develop, in addition to intensifying crises which arose independent of credit (Marx, 1967c, pp. 488–91). The default of a few debtors may result in a series of failures and bankruptcies of commodity owners interconnected by debt obligations. The sign for a credit crisis is felt by banks 'as soon as their clients deposit more bills of exchange [IOUs] than money' (Marx, 1967c, pp. 447). The banks, as a result, decrease credit in an attempt to raise their stocks of hoards.

Any disturbance of the credit payment mechanism, 'no matter what its cause, suddenly and immediately transforms money from its merely ideal shape as a money of account into hard cash. Profane commodities can no longer replace it' (Marx, 1967c, p. 447). It is the function of money as a store of value therefore that exacerbates a payment crisis. The contradiction between the use-value of commodities and their independent money-form sharpens and the latter prevails as the absolute form of wealth. A credit crisis becomes a monetary crisis and undermines the function of money as a medium of circulation in order to bestow on it the feature of an ultimate object of satisfaction in the form of hoards. As a result of the relative scarcity of money in circulation as money-capital, and the rise in the interest rate (Marx, 1967c, pp. 570–2), '"the poor stand still, because the rich have no money to employ them, though they have the same land and hands to provide victuals and clothes, as ever they had; ... which is the true Riches of a Nation and not the money"' (Marx, 1967a, p. 138).[9]

The construction of a Marxian theory of money with Marshall's philosophical foundations

The apparent differences in the philosophical foundations of Marshall and Marx are a matter of scope rather than substance (see Table 3.1).[11] Regarding metaphysics, neither defends the material or the ideal origin of being. While Marx does not investigate the metaphysical nature of the categories of thought, he acknowledges their realism, a classification which Marshall would have accepted if confronted with it (Marshall, 1920, p. 53), for he believes that 'every change in social conditions is likely to require a new development of economic doctrines' (Marshall, 1920, p. 37). This seems to suggest a distinction similar to the one made by Marx regarding the 'real' and the 'mental' concretes. Unlike Marshall however, Marx shows with what he refers to as 'the fetishism of commodities' that the meanings of the categories of thought are socially produced and are not characteristics springing from the objects of thought themselves (Marx, 1967c, pp. 71–83). Then, regarding epistemology, would Marshall's empiricism reject Marx's commodity fetishism? Or, is Marx's commodity fetishism epistemologically incommensurable with the empiricism of Marshall? Despite the fact that Marx does not explicitly endorse either empiricism or rationalism as the sole premise for his conception of commodity fetishism, he does state that people's social activities are the empirical premises from which his categories are conceived.

Commodity fetishism, we believe, is not in conflict with empiricism, it rather demands more introspection and understanding of the process that generates meanings which Marshall would not have rejected, had he been more patient while reading Marx. Wouldn't an empiricist observe that capital equipment are products of past labour and do not produce value by themselves but in conjunction with living labour? Marshall's argument that capital is not a free good and deserves a reward in the form of profit is a moral statement that justifies but does not explain the source of profit. It is designed to refute Marx's notion of exploitation.

Furthermore, would empiricists not relate at all to the idea that 'utilities' or 'values' are socially constructed and are not characteristics of the things-in-themselves? (Amariglio and Callari, 1989). It is true that empiricists are inclined to separate the observed object from the observing subject (Tomass, 1990, pp. 19–56). This however is a shortcoming of empiricists. Empiricism is not procedurally destined to reject processes of introspection and self-understanding that lead to conceptions like commodity fetishism. To observe one's own psychic phenomena is not alien to Mill nor to Marshall. The

Table 3.1 Comparison of ideas in Marshall and Marx

	Marshall	Marx
Metaphysics	Sensations are the underlying nature of the universe. They stimulate thought and cause human action. No scholastic defence is provided on the source of sensations being material or ideal.	No evidence of a consistent scholastic defence of either materialism or idealism. Suggests a realism under the label of 'naturalism or humanism'. Social practice (the real-concrete) generates interpretations of social relations among people (the mental-concrete), which, in turn, cause human action. Through these social relations, people cast meanings onto objects, then assume that these meanings are not socially produced and historically contingent but are characteristics springing from the objects themselves (Commodity Fetishism).
Epistemology	We know the world through sensations. Sensations of pain and pleasure are the only data for knowing human action and for explaining it.	People's social and productive activities are the empirical premises from which they produce conceptions and ideas. No elaboration is provided about the role of sensations versus reason in the way in which people know such empirical premises.
Methodology	**Three Processes:** 1. *Analysis by induction*: Money measures the strength of the individual's motive to exchange pain and pleasure. A constant conjunction of two measured quantities is sufficient to establish causation between them. Thus, forming a singular and abstract law subject to *ceteris paribus*. 2. *Syntheses by deduction*: The combined effect of all causes acting simultaneously is deduced in order to synthesize broader generalizations or new laws.	**Three** Processes to combine the logical (space) and historical (time): 1. *Analysis by abstraction*: Abstract from society to arrive at the simplest determination which define the function of a concept at any moment of time. 2. *Syntheses by deduction*: Take the simplest determinations into a reverse process to arrive once again at society but with a synthesis of many simple determinations and relations. The historical element in the synthetic process is manifested in the change of the meaning of the functional concepts through time and in the increasing complexity of the determinations within the mental-concrete. While deducing new circumstances from earlier premises, one should be aware of the change in meaning

3. *Verification by induction*: To test and verify the new laws.	associated with the use of concepts. Functional concepts are dynamic, that is, they take additional functions when related to new abstractions in the process of the ascent from the abstract to the concrete. 3. *Realisticness of premises and verification*: The reality of concepts must be proven in practice. The truth of the deduced circumstances are empirically verifiable.	
Economic laws	Since different causes may act in opposing directions, economic laws are statements of tendencies. Furthermore, different social conditions give rise to different economic doctrines, but no elaboration is given on how the above methodology can narrate an evolutionary economic theory.	Countervailing forces prevent the accurate prediction of future circumstances, thus rendering economic laws as statements of tendencies. Furthermore, economic laws are historically contingent depending on the institutions which people create. They are not universally true.
The economy	An abstraction of capitalist relations of production that is based on the interaction of the strength of the motives of the individuals involved in the exchange of pleasure and pain.	A multi-sided instituted process embedded within property relations of production. No explicit discussion of the role of sensations of pleasure and pain in the determination of the level and kind of output. Such role for sensations, however, is implied in the capitalist's profit motive, in the worker's instinct of survival, and in the concept of use-value.
The concept of money	A generally accepted medium of exchange.	A social relation in symbolic material form.
Explicit functions of money	1. Medium of exchange. 2. Standard of value, or standard for deferred payments. 3. Store of value.	1. Medium of exchange. 2. Standard of value, or standard for deferred payments. 3. Store of value. 4. Capital (an institution that makes the employment of resources possible).

Table 3.1 continued

	Marshall	Marx
Implicit functions of money	1. Measure of value (of sensations). 2. 'Free', 'floating', or 'fluid' capital.	1. Measure of value (through the cost of labour).
The definition of money	(Gold = monetary base) + bank notes.	Gold + bank notes.
Changes in the money supply	Changes in the supply of gold leads to long-term, sustainable price changes and is neutral with regard to the level of output or relative prices. Short-run impact of fluctuations in gold supply is not discussed. Causality runs from M to P.	The stock of money is divided into circulating money and hoards. An *increase* in the money supply can, in the short-run end up in hoards or in circulation depending on the conditions for production and accumulation. The long-run impact is a higher rate of production and accumulation. The impact of a *decrease* in the money supply depends in the short-run on the availability of hoards. In the long-run, as hoards are depleted, a realization crisis occurs. Causality runs from P to M and vice versa.
Monetary crises	Exogenous shocks associated with unreasonable expansion of credit leads to short-term high prices, wages, profits, and higher speculative activity. Banks reduce lending, leading to a credit crisis, a fall in prices, lower output, and unemployment. A rebound in prices eliminates the crisis.	The use of money as a medium of exchange creates an abstract possibility of a monetary crisis, for the circular flow is interrupted whenever money is held for itself as an asset. When the demand for money is incorporated within the conditions of production and accumulation, monetary crises occur in the form of a 'realization crisis', that is, the circulating quantity of money is insufficient to realize the exchange values, thus leading to a fall in prices, lower profit rates, lower output, higher unemployment. Credit crises intensify existing monetary crises.

problem lies first in empiricism's lack of a methodological mechanism that synthesizes additional concepts and axioms attained by introspection. Such a synthetic process allows for changes in the meaning of the categories used to explain phenomena by incorporating 'non-economic' forces that shape preferences which Marshall considers to be exogenous. Marx's methodology, for instance, informed him to synthesize more abstractions and concepts than Marshall's. This adds a dynamic element to Marx's methodology in accounting for the change in the meaning of the economic categories used in interpreting a phenomenon as more abstractions are linked together. Relations of ideas that are otherwise unavailable for immediate observation become incorporated in an explanation of a phenomenon. Marx's theory of money therefore becomes less abstract and more concrete than Marshall's for first using fewer auxiliary clauses and second, for permitting a change in the meaning and significance of the categories used through time.

By keeping these philosophical criteria in mind, this section aims to construct a Marxian theory of money as an active element in capitalist production with the realist (as distinct from idealist or materialist) metaphysics, the empiricist epistemology and the inductive–deductive–inductive methodology of Marshall. In other words, we will attempt to partially reduce Marx to Marshall. Partially, because we are focusing only on Marx's theory of monetary crises and we do *not* intend to reproduce Marx's analysis of the historical development of capitalism nor his labour theory of value.

We divide this section into two subsections. The first attempts to construct a theory of monetary production; the second focuses exclusively on the reason for the difference between Marshall's and Marx's view on the order of causality between money and the price level, and also examines the possibility of attaining a Marxian order of causality without violating the logic of Marshall's philosophical foundations. The purpose of this examination is to conclude whether any particular conception of the order of causality from money to prices or vice versa is influenced by the meaning and theoretical significance which is cast on money.

The construction of Marx's monetary theory of production with Marshall's philosophical foundations
In the section on Marshall, we saw how he assigns an epistemological role to the sensations which an individual experiences, observes and subsequently measures within himself. These sensations of pleasure and pain not only explain human action but also provide the individual with the only data from which he can derive knowledge of human action. Basing knowledge on sensations of pleasure and pain, we observe that individuals act to satisfy their desires. They use objects of nature to fulfil their needs in a rational and efficient manner that maximizes their utility. They also, for the same purpose,

act on objects in different ways to create new objects in form and content. We refer to this type of action as labour or production. Individual labourers sooner or later observe that by specializing in a particular skill they can produce a quantity of a good that exceeds their need for it. Thereby, they can exchange that surplus for a variety of other goods to satisfy their other needs. The result of this specialization will culminate in a greater total utility derived after exchange than if they had produced each object individually. Through sense experience, they also soon discover that barter exchange is time consuming and difficult to attain in ideal proportions. An individual and, consequently, individuals conclude that utility will be maximized if one good can be considered as money and conveniently exchanged for all other goods. Gold possesses the proper characteristics of money and is thereof treated as a medium of exchange.

The use of money as a medium of exchange however splits the act of exchange into two separate acts: buying and selling. In order for an individual to buy what he desires, he has to sell the commodity that he produces first. The individual observes that it is more difficult to sell a good than to by it because money is now conceived as a special asset of universal demand. This implies that the marginal utility of money does not decrease as fast as the marginal utility of other goods. The use of money as a medium of exchange, however, has given its store of value function a special significance in the form of postponed utility. This raises the possibility and desirability to acquire and keep money for an indefinite period of time. Money has become a powerful instrument by which an individual can acquire pleasure at any time and in any form. Money, in other words, acquires an independent existence. It is demanded for itself. Marshall therefore should not deny that money's dominant role in economics should stem out of being 'an aim of endeavour' (Marshall, 1920, p. 782).

When money acquires an existence independent of the goods it exchanges for, an individual is able to purchase goods for the purpose of exchanging them for a larger sum of money with which he can acquire a greater satisfaction (M–C–M′).[12] The exchange here takes the form of M–C ... C′–M′, where M–C and C′–M′ are exchanges of equals. Between C and C′ lies the additional value of the sacrifice or 'waiting' involved in advancing money-capital (Marshall, 1920, p. 587). Alternatively, an individual can purchase goods for his consumption with the additional amount of money he acquired, then advance the original amount once again in the same fashion to acquire a larger sum of money. This type of activity makes the individual who is carrying it out a trader whose prime concern is to amass more money, the object of universal utility. A number of individuals practising this type of trade form a distinguished class in society whose success in amassing money allows them to expand their trading activity by commissioning individuals to produce commodities, while providing them with the raw material and equipment. The class of traders soon realize the efficiency involved in having the individual producers perform their work in one or few factories, where the traders can maximize productivity by reducing transportation costs. The introduction of cost-saving technologies enables traders to increase production at lower per-unit cost, thus leading to the bankruptcy of individual producers who cannot sell their products at prices as low as those of the traders. Given the new conditions, the individual producers realize that they can maximize utility by selling their labour to the trader for a money-wage.

Individuals are now divided, according to their source of income, into two major classes: capitalists and workers. The income of the traders who now have become capitalists depends upon profits generated from the sale of commodities. They attempt to maximize the rewards for their 'waiting' by attaining a greater sum of money in which a greater promised pleasure is embodied. They therefore advance their money as capital into the most profitable activities. The workers attempt to maximize the pleasure embodied in money-wages by exchanging their labour for the highest alternative money-wage offered by the competing capitalists. This new social order will be stable as long as the capitalists can smoothly convert the produced commodities into money in a period of time sufficient to insure stable wages and a rate of profit that equals or exceeds the sacrifice endured by capitalists in 'waiting' and supervisory effort. Basing economic action on individual motives however, separates the motives of consumers from those of producers. The periodic change in the degree of difficulty and time involved in converting commodities into money causes a divergence of market prices from the supply price. This divergence alters the rate of profit because changes in demand levels exceed or fall short of supply prices. The degree to which the profit rate is altered will affect future decisions of the rational and profit maximizing capitalists concerning whether or not they should advance money as capital to enter another cycle of production, or at least alter the magnitude of capital advanced for production. The change in the magnitude of production, in turn, gives rise to unemployment and/or overproduction. Once money, the medium of circulation, becomes the aim of circulation as well, the possibility of economic crisis cannot be ruled out. As long as the marginal utility of holding money exceeds the marginal utility of 'waiting', a crisis will continue to worsen, since capitalists advance less money as capital, thus leading to a lower level of output and employment.[13]

The attainment of Marx's order of causality between money and the price level with Marshall's philosophical foundations
Marshall has generally conceived of causality as a one-directional relationship among isolated phenomena. The notion of mutual determination how-

ever was not alien to him. He criticizes Ricardo for not perceiving that 'in the problem of normal value, the various elements govern one another *mutually* and not successively in a long chain of causation' (Marshall, 1920, p. 816). By 'normal value', Marshall implies the long run price; and by 'the various elements', he implies the supply price (the initial price demanded by the producer), the demand price and the amount produced. These elements, for Marshall, mutually determine one another to culminate in a long-run equilibrium price. If Marshall's methodology does not have a conceptual difficulty with the notion of mutual determination, why did he not argue that causality between money and the price level runs in both directions? The answer to this lies in the theoretical insignificance which Marshall attaches to the demand for money as an asset in the absence of a credit crisis. When no theoretical implications are construed from money being a store of value and possible capital, its remaining and *de facto* active function is the medium of exchange that is contrasted in its entirety with the volume of the circulating commodity. Such treatment of money facilitated the methodological dichotomization of classical economic theory into a monetary theory and a value theory. Consequently, the production of commodities is abstracted from the production of money (Mason manuscript, ch. IV). This is why a change in its quantity is translated into a change in its value and in a change in the price level. If however money is held for itself, then not all of its quantity will circulate against a definitive quantity of commodities. Its circulating quantity will vary, depending on the requirements for hoarding and the volume of transactions taking place at any period of time (see the section on Marx above). A change in the quantity of money therefore may be counterbalanced by net hoarding or net dishoarding depending on the extent of capital accumulation and on the state of the convertibility of commodities into money in the market.

Despite the fact that Marshall defines economics to be the study of people in their pursuit of wealth, he does not incorporate the consequences of pursuing wealth into his system of exchange between pain and pleasure. A statement implying that people are utility maximizers does not have the same implication as a statement implying that people are money maximizers, for the demand for money as an asset has a disturbing impact on the circular flow. The conversion of commodities into money is not seen to be problematic because producers and consumers are perceived to be exchanging pain and pleasure and not pain and money. Pleasure is seen in the utility embodied in commodities and not in money. There is no reason for an individual to hold money for a prolonged period of time if it is only a means and not an end. There is no reason therefore for Marshall to think about an abstract direction of causality from the price level to the quantity of money in circulation, because the realization of the sum of prices by the quantity of money is not seen as a problem. The relationship between money and prices is seen as a 'microeconomic' endeavour, dichotomized from the 'macroeconomic' one in which the problem of the realization of the sum of prices (effective demand) arises. Marx's ascent from the abstract to the concrete avoids the micro/ macro dichotomy. The realization of the sum of prices by the quantity of money in circulation, for him, determines market prices and, consequently, contributes to the instability of the business cycle.

Suppose however that we had asked Marshall to generate a direction of causality from the sum of prices to the quantity of money in circulation and vice versa. Let us consider whether he could have done that without violating the internal consistency of his philosophical foundations. In order to do this, we have to look for a price in Marshall's analysis that will perform the theoretical function of Marx's 'ideal price'.[14] Marshall's supply price can serve the function of Marx's ideal price. In order for supply prices to be realized by the quantity of money in circulation at a given point in time, the commodities produced must be sold at their supply prices. Below, we shall consider two cases: first, when money is conceived only as a medium of circulation, and second, when the accumulation of money is conceived as an end.

To take the first case, we have established in the section on Marshall that the supply price reflects the ratio of the desired exchange between the pain that the capitalist has to undergo for postponing consumption, and the utility accruing to him from consuming the amount of commodities represented in the value of his monetary profits.[15] If all capitalists wish to fulfil a higher level of desired utility at a given period of time, then given that the entire quantity of money is in circulation, the velocity of money in circulation may increase to realize the supply prices. There is no reason therefore for Marshall to think that a net increase in prices, and therefore in the price level, can or does cause variations in the quantity of money. The quantity theory of money will also hold in this context. With money functioning only as a means of exchange, had any quantity of it been, for any reason, withdrawn from circulation, the result would have been a reduction of the price level to maintain the previous level of production or transactions. This is consistent with Marshall's central argument that production is determined by the pain/ pleasure trade-off independent of the monetary sphere, thus, maintaining the micro/macro dichotomy.

In the second case however, when money is considered to be the aim of circulation as well as its medium, there must be some quantity of it that is hoarded. Net hoarding may vary to realize the sum of the supply prices. But what is the motive of the hoarder to change the magnitude of his net hoarding of money in response to changes in supply prices? Basing motives on individual psychologies, one may argue that an individual will decrease his net hoarding if the marginal utility embodied in a commodity exceeds the marginal utility of the unit of money which he will forego in dishoarding it.[16] Now, if we conceive of commodities and money as entering the exchange process without predetermined values, actual prices must be determined instantaneously at the time of their interaction. This means that at any given moment of time and a given volume of transactions, a quantity of money associated with a certain value must have accommodated market prices. The materialization of a volume of transactions indicate that hoarding could have varied already. The desire to buy may be translated into the ability to buy through net dishoarding. Since equilibrium prices reflect actual transactions, the formation of equilibrium market prices implies that the quantity of money in circulation varies with the variation of demand to generate actual market prices. This allows us to conclude that if we consider the accumulation of money to be the aim of production, then causality can run from prices to the quantity of money in circulation with the use of Marshall's philosophical foundations.

The abstraction of Marshall's 'quantity doctrine' with Marx's philosophical foundations

In this section, we will argue that Marshall's theory of money is a one-sided abstract determination that fits within Marx's multi-sided analysis of money. In the section on Marx, we saw how he starts his economic analysis with a socially determined individual. The social relations, which the individual is part of, are constituted by the synthesis of many one-sided abstractions. Each specific configuration of abstractions casts a particular meaning upon sense observations. This enhances the observer's awareness that the object of thought takes on a multitude of relations to other abstractions.

An example of a one-sided abstraction is Marx's apparent adoption of a logic similar to Marshall's 'Quantity Doctrine' when he abstracts one function of money from its other functions. He wrote that:

> if the paper money exceed its proper limit, which is the amount of gold coins of the like denomination that can actually be current, it would, apart from falling into general disrepute, represent only that quantity of gold, which *in accordance with the laws of the circulation of commodities*, is required and is alone capable of being represented by paper. If the quantity of paper money issued be double what it ought to be, then, as a matter of fact, £1 would be the money-name not of $1/4$ of an ounce, but of $1/8$ of an ounce of gold. The effect would be the same as if an alteration had taken place in the function of gold as a standard of prices. Those values that were previously expressed by the price of £1 would now be expressed by the price of £2 (Marx, 1967a, p. 128, italics added).

It is clear that in the above passage, Marx is abstracting one function of money from its other functions. The Quantity Theory's order of causality that runs from money to the price level therefore is possible within Marx's methodology, given that he is considering the question 'in accordance with the laws of the circulation of commodities' and in isolation from other laws which he has not yet developed. We would be misinterpreting Marx's theory of money if we consider this abstract law of circulation to be true as a phenomenon in the concrete. We would be violating his method of the ascent from the abstract to the concrete. For Marx to be faithful to his methodology, he must reject that mechanical conception of causality of the quantity theory. For, an increase in the supply of paper money never occurs in the abstract, or at least not in the more advanced sections of *Capital*, when money, the medium of circulation, becomes capital and where its other functions, especially as a store of value, come into play. The increase in the supply of paper money must take place at some point in the general formula of capital with respect to individual capitalists and at some stage of the business cycle. Any analysis of the consequences of an increase in the money supply therefore should take place within the context of the mutual determination of all the abstract concepts contained in the mental-concrete.

Conclusion
In the preceding two sections, we examined the hypothesis that a dialogue among economists of different philosophical foundations is futile. We challenged the ability of the proponents of the two rival theories of money to continue to shield themselves with their own philosophical foundations against unfriendly attacks and consequently, to continue to defend their theory versus the theory of their rival on philosophical grounds.[17] The construction of Marx's theory of money with Marshall's philosophical foundations showed that Marx's theory of money could have been arrived at and potentially evaluated by Marshall's philosophical foundations. However, the fact that Marshall's philosophical foundations would not have obstructed an attempt to arrive at Marx's formulation of a monetary crisis without violating its logical consistency, means that the validity of Marshall's theory of money cannot be defended in terms of his empiricist epistemology and inductive–deductive–inductive methodology, as the correct theory of money's role in capitalist production. In addition, we have seen that Marshall's theory of money can be explained within Marx's philosophical foundations, though such a theory is only an abstract (or truncated) one according to Marxian methodological standards. Despite their different ideological and normative components, the two rival theories of money and credit and their philosophical foundations are therefore commensurable.

Dialogue among economists regarding monetary theory therefore is not futile. If incommensurability applies neither to monetary theory nor to the philosophical foundations of theories, then this opens the way for further case studies in economic theory and the social sciences where rival 'grand theories' can be focused on their sub-theories that attempt to explain concrete variables such as profit, wages, etc. Their comparative validity can thus be determined in relation to the concrete variables that they are attempting to explain. Such variables are socially constructed institutions that people have devised and acknowledged regardless of their intellectual tradition or ideological sympathies. By this, we do not ignore or underestimate the significance of the bidirectional relations between a 'grand theory' and its sub-theories, but rather emphasize that the sub-theories are the statements to be evaluated against other statements made by the sub-theories of a rival 'grand theory'.

Beside its functions in capitalist economies as a measure of value, a medium of exchange, a standard of value and a store of value, money is treated by all the participants in our contemporary civilization as an institution that realizes the value of output and as one that permits or inhibits growth. Money, with all its functions, is a social reality that we have created. Any 'grand theory' therefore must account for that social reality, for the meaning of fundamental variables is collectively generated. A theory that does not account for the peculiarities of money as a fundamental institution of modern civilization is inferior to one that does. The relativity of their metaphysical or epistemological status therefore does not apply in their case. A partial (or abstract) representation of the role of money in production becomes inferior to a more comprehensive (or less abstract) representation of it. It may be however, that the incommensurability thesis does not apply to interpretations of institutions in space, but applies to interpretations of institutions in time. That is to say, we cannot equate institutions throughout history that emerged in different time periods and two different social realities, for they may have different meanings to each community. The choice between rival economic theories therefore becomes relative to the importance of the variable that each is attempting to explain given the institutions of the time.

By rejecting the isolationist attitude of postmodernism towards the social sciences as manifested in the incommensurability thesis, we endeavour to emphasize postmodernism's better side, the one that tolerates a pluralistic attitude towards methodologies. Our case study shows that conceptual frameworks should not imprison the social scientist. The social scientist should be able to surmount a theory's conceptual boundaries by adding concepts that enable it to explain phenomena with broader perspectives, even if this requires variables that may be unavailable for immediate observation. On the other hand, the social scientist should also be able to dismiss concepts that were once central to a theory, if such concepts become obsolete in describing social and economic institutions and cripples the theory from having the intended influence in social practice. This however requires him to abandon stalwart sectarianism and prejudices. Regarding our case study, such sectarianism applies to Marshall, to Marx and to many of their contemporary followers. It is not only unreasonable, but also unscholarly for orthodox economists to dismiss the entire corpus of Marx's analysis of capitalist production as useless and unscientific, for we have shown above that Marx's criteria for scientific thought are not only commensurable with Marshall's but also include broader categories. They both conclude that economic laws are statements of tendencies. On the other hand, Marx's and Marxists' intolerance to criticism regarding the adequacy of some of his concepts for social practice cannot be consistently defended either, for it has inhibited serious development in Marxian thought and relegated Marxists to a well-intentioned but fundamentalist fringe group that is having a marginal impact on the shaping of modern civilization.

Notes

1. I am indebted to Alan Dyer and Steven Nathanson for the time and effort they expended to clarify my thoughts on this subject. I am grateful to Will Mason and Paul Wendt for helpful suggestions, and to Jack Amariglio and George Caffentzis for inspiring conversations. I also thank Oscar Brookings, John Parsons, and especially Charles Peake for their comments.
2. We refer to 'reality' as a 'social reality' in order to stress its relation to the role of our social beliefs and practices in the shaping of such reality by casting meanings on it.
3. By philosophical foundations, we imply the metaphysical, the epistemological, and the methodological foundations of rival theories. By metaphysics (or ontology), we refer to the process that casts meanings onto the category under study and investigates its material versus its ideal origin. By epistemology, we first refer to the way in which knowledge of such categories is acquired; second to the relationship of this knowledge to the world in itself. Finally, by methodology, we refer to the process that organizes a logical and explanatory structure with the acquired data. Methodology therefore is concerned with the *means* of cognition rather than with its substantive foundations. Such means of cognition form a process of transition that follows certain unifying principles.
4. In *Memorial of Alfred Marshall* (Pigou, 1956, pp. 27–33) Keynes considers Marshall to be the originator of the Cambridge Theory of Money.
5. Marshall defines money to include precious metals as the monetary base, legal tender notes issued by the government, and privately issued bank notes or 'bills of exchange' which could be considered as bank credit (Marshall, 1965, pp. 12–15).
6. For a review of Marshall's position on monetary issues and for an evaluation of his influence on his contemporaries and pupils see Eshag, 1965 and Gaynor, 1991.
7. We use the term 'hoarding' in this context in order to be consistent with Marx's use of the term in the following section to refer to the demand for money as asset.
8. Notice here that both relative prices and the price level are determined by value relations. Marx therefore does not treat 'the sum of prices' and 'the price level' as two independent variables. The price level, for him, is also formed by value relations. A change in the price level, Marx argues, may take place either from a change in exchange values of commodities given the value of money, or from a change in the value of money given the value of commodities (Marx, 1967a, p. 99).
9. Marx distinguishes between the market price, the ideal price, and the exchange value of a commodity. While market prices are determined by short term supply and demand forces, ideal prices are attained by dividing the exchange value of the commodity by the exchange value of the money-commodity. Exchange values, in turn, are determined by the

socially necessary labour time embodied in commodities (Marx, 1986c, pp. 74–6 and Marx, 1987, p. 308).

10. Marx quotes a footnote from John Bellers (1696), 'Proposals for Raising a College of Industry', London, p. 3.

11. Some philosophers may object to this schematization of philosophical categories. We would like to comfort them by pointing out that we chose to schematize them for pedagogical reasons. In this schematization we do not intend to draw lines of demarcation between metaphysics, epistemology, and methodology but rather outline their different emphases.

12. Notice that this equation is a pure equation of exchange that does not incorporate Marx's theory of the extraction of surplus value which is part of his philosophical foundations, thus is intentionally excluded from the forthcoming scenario.

13. At this point the reader should note that it would be hard to distinguish Marshall from Keynes with regard to the relationship between money, aggregate demand, and crises. Thus, combining Marshall's empiricist epistemology and methodology with Marxian analysis of money gives rise to Keynes's monetary theory of production.

14. Marx's 'ideal price' is the price at which the capitalist hopes to sell his product in order to realize a profit.

15. The magnitude of this temporary abstinence from consumption is determined by the sum of the cost of raw materials and the pain/pleasure trade-off represented by wages.

16. We are aware of the charge that this could be considered by orthodox economics a misapplication of 'micro' reasoning to a 'macro' problem. Given our interpretation of Marshall's philosophical foundations however, it is evident that any statement regarding an economic phenomenon must be based on individual psychology. Therefore, one aim of our reconstruction of Marshall's reasoning is to overcome the micro/macro dichotomy.

17. The mainstream trend of twentieth-century economic doctrines adheres to an essentially empiricist epistemology and to a variation on the inductive–deductive–inductive methodology (with the exception of Friedman's instrumentalism). The current schools of philosophy which had an influence on economics, such as Logical Positivism (Ayer, 1952) or the Falsificationism of Karl Popper (Popper, 1968) hold primarily empiricist epistemological positions. Their differences however are methodological rather than epistemological. The basic themes of their methodologies are also influenced by John Stuart Mill's methodology of cognition.

References

Amariglio, Jack (1988), 'The body, economic discourse, and power: an economist's introduction to Foucault', *History of Political Economy*, **20** (4).

Amariglio, Jack (1990), 'Economics as a Postmodern Discourse', in Samuels, Warren (ed.), *Economics as Discourse*, Boston: Kluwer Academic Publishers.

Amariglio, Jack and Callari, Antonio (1989), 'Marxian Value Theory and the Problem of the Subject: The Role of Commodity Fetishism', *Rethinking Marxism*, **2** (3), Fall.

Amariglio, Jack, Resnick, Steven and Wolff, Richard (1990), 'Division and Difference in the "Discipline" of Economics', *Critical Inquiry*, **17** (3), Autumn.

Ayer, Alfred Jules (1952), *Language, Truth and Logic*, New York: Dover Publications.

Dillard, Dudley (1987), 'Money as an Institution of Capitalism', *Journal of Economic Issues*, **21** (4), December.

Dillard, Dudley (1988), 'The Barter Illusion in Classical and Neoclassical Economics', *Eastern Economic Journal*, **14** (4), October–December.

Dyer, Alan W. (1986), 'Veblen on Scientific Creativity: The Influence of Charles S. Peirce, *Journal of Economic Issues*, **20** (1), March.

Dyer, Alan W. (1988), 'Economic Theory as an Art Form', *Journal of Economic Issues*, **22** (1), March.

Eshag, Eprime (1965), *From Marshall to Keynes: An Essay on the Monetary Theory of the Cambridge School*, Fairfield, NJ: Augustus M. Kelley.

Foucault, Michel (1972), *The Archaeology of Knowledge*, trans. A.M. Sheridan Smith, New York: Harper.

Foucault, Michel (1973), *The Order of Things*, New York: Vintage.

Gaynor, W.B. (1991), 'Price Trends and Economic Crisis in Marshall's Monetary Theory, *Journal of the History of Economic Thought*, (13), Spring.

Hegel, Georg W.F. (1975), *Logic*, trans. William Wallace, Oxford: Oxford University Press.

Hilferding, Rudolf (1981), *Finance Capital*, trans. Morris Watnick and Sam Gordon, London: Routledge & Kegan Paul.

Hume, David (1975), *An Inquiry Concerning Human Understanding*, Oxford: Clarendon Press.

Kuhn, Thomas (1970), *The Structure of Scientific Revolutions*, Chicago: University of Chicago Press.

Lyotard, Jean François (1984), *The Postmodern Condition: A Report on Knowledge*, trans. G. Bennington and B. Massumi, Minneapolis: University of Minnesota Press.

Marshall, Alfred and Marshall, Mary (1879), *The Economics of Industry*, London: Macmillan.

Marshall, Alfred (1920), *Principles of Economics*, vol. I, London: Macmillan.

Marshall, Alfred (1926), *Official Papers*, London: Macmillan.

Marshall, Alfred (1965), *Money, Credit and Commerce*, Fairfield, N.J.: Augustus M. Kelley.

Marx, Karl (1967a), *Capital*, trans. Samuel Moore and Edward Aveling, vol. 1, New York: International Publishers.

Marx, Karl (1967b), *Capital*, trans. Samuel Moore and Edward Aveling, vol. 2, New York: International Publishers.

Marx, Karl (1967c), *Capital*, trans. Samuel Moore and Edward Aveling, vol. 3, New York: International Publishers.

Marx, Karl (1975), 'Critique of The Hegelian Dialectic and Philosophy as a Whole', *Karl Marx Friedrich Engels: Collected Works*, vol. 3, Moscow: Progress Publishers.

Marx, Karl (1976), 'Theses on Feurebach', *Karl Marx Friedrich Engels: Collected Works*, vol. 5, Moscow: Progress Publishers.

Marx, Karl and Engels, Friedrich (1976), 'The German Ideology', *Karl Marx Friedrich Engels: Collected Works*, vol. 5, Moscow: Progress Publishers.

Marx, Karl (1986a), 'The Causes of the Monetary Crisis in Europe', *Karl Marx Friedrich Engels: Collected Works*, vol. 15, Moscow: Progress Publishers.

Marx, Karl (1986b), 'Introduction', *Karl Marx Friedrich Engels: Collected Works*, vol. 28, Moscow: Progress Publishers.

Marx, Karl (1986c), 'Outlines of the Critique of Political Economy' (rough draft of 1857–8), *Karl Marx Friedrich Engels: Collected Works*, vol. 28, Moscow: Progress Publishers.

Marx, Karl (1987), 'A Contribution to the Critique of Political Economy', *Karl Marx Friedrich Engels: Collected Works*, vol. 29, Moscow: Progress Publishers.

Marx, Karl (1988), 'A letter from "Marx to Kugelmann"', 11 July 1868, in *Karl Marx Friedrich Engels Collected Works*, vol. 43, Moscow: Progress Publishers.

Mason, Will E. (manuscript), *Classical Versus Neoclassical Monetary Theories: The Roots, Ruts, and Resilience of Monetarism – and Keynesianism.*

McCloskey, Donald (1985), *The Rhetoric of Economics*, Madison: University of Wisconsin Press.

Mill, John Stuart (1948), 'On the Definition of Political Economy and the Method of Investigation Proper to It', *Essays on Some Unsettled Questions of Political Economy*, London: University of London.

Mill, John Stuart (1974), *A System of Logic*, London: University of Toronto Press.

Mill, John Stuart (1979), *An Examination of Sir William Hamilton's Philosophy*, London: University of Toronto Press.

Mirowsky, Philip (1989), ''Tis a Pity Econometrics Isn't an Empirical Endeavor: Mandelbrot, Chaos, and the Noah and Joseph Effects', *Ricerche Economiche*, **43** (1–2).

Neale, Walter C. (1976), *Monies in Societies*, San Francisco: Chandler & Sharp Publishers, Inc.

Pigou, A.C. (ed.) (1956), *Memorials of Alfred Marshall*, New York: Kelley & Millman, Inc.

Popper, Karl (1965), *Conjectures and Refutations: The Growth of Scientific Knowledge*, New York: Harper Torchbooks.

Samuels, Warren (ed.) (1990), *Economics as Discourse*, Boston: Kluwer Academic Publishers.

Tomass, Mark Kharpoutly (1991), *Rival Theories of Money and Credit: The Epistemologies and Methodologies of Marshall and Marx*, Ann Arbor, MI: University Microfilms International.
Whitaker, J.K. (ed.) (1975), *The Early Economic Writings of Alfred Marshall, 1867–1890*, vol. I, New York: The Free Press.

PART II

COMPETITION, CONFLICT AND CAPITAL

4. At the origin of imperfect competition: different views?

Maria Cristina Marcuzzo[1]

I

Sraffa's article in the December issue of the *Economic Journal* of 1926 (Sraffa, 1926) paved the way for development of the theory of imperfect competition in Cambridge, England, in the 1930s. Although Sraffa's article was referred to as the source and the inspiration of both Kahn's *The Economics of the Short Period* and Robinson's *The Economics of Imperfect Competition*, the ideas presented in these works can hardly be regarded as genuine developments of Sraffa's arguments.

In this chapter I will argue that the contributions by R.F. Kahn and J. Robinson differ from Sraffa's in the reasons given for abandoning perfect competition and, consequently, in the role assigned to imperfect competition. After summarizing Sraffa's argument (section 2) I shall discuss Kahn's peculiar measure of the imperfection of the market (section 3) and Robinson's approach to cost curves (section 4). My conclusion is that in its early stage, the theory of imperfect competition reflected different views on what should be accepted or discarded in the received doctrine. While Sraffa was inclined to dispose of the entire Marshallian apparatus, Kahn and Robinson came to rescue it (section 5).

Kahn introduced market imperfection to account for an observed fact, that firms worked below capacity. His approach consisted in investigating the shape of the actual cost curves faced by the firms in the short period. According to Kahn, the usefulness of the device of the short period is based 'on the fact that the life of fixed capital is considerably greater than the period of production. ... It cannot be too strongly emphasized that this is a *fact*, which could not be deduced by a priori reasoning'. (Kahn, 1989, p. xiii).

Joan Robinson introduced market imperfections to prove the generality and validity of the partial equilibrium approach based on the theory of monopoly which had been adapted to this purpose by employing the marginal technique. In so doing she discarded the analysis based on the actual costs incurred by an observed firm in favour of the analysis of possible configurations of supply and demand curves.

It was her view – derived from 'a purely *a priori* set of assumptions' (Robinson, 1979, p. 114) – which proved successful and became the 'accepted' view.

II

The reasons Sraffa gave for abandoning the hypothesis of perfect competition were twofold. First, he held that the *theory* in which that hypothesis was embedded was logically inconsistent; second, that the behavioural descriptions implied in the hypothesis of perfect competition were at variance with the known facts.

The particular theory under attack was of course the Marshallian–Pigouvian representation of the working of individual markets. Drawing on his previous article, published in Italian,[2] Sraffa showed that many of the assumptions upon which the theory rested were ill founded. (Sraffa, 1925).

The assumption that long period costs for the firm are increasing when conditions of perfect competition hold was the result of attributing to a single firm what was attributable, under particular circumstances, only to an industry. Since each firm is too small to have an appreciable influence on the price of its factors, the result of an increasing marginal cost for the firm can be obtained only by assuming that the number of firms is fixed within each industry and that each firm, as it expands production, experiences a decrease in productivity by the factor which is constant for the industry (Sraffa, 1925, p. 301). But this can be justified only for an industry that happens to be the only employer of a factor that cannot be augmented. Furthermore, the assumption that the number of firms within a given industry is fixed violates one of the postulates of perfect competition, that is, open entry and exit of firms from any industry.[3]

The assumption of decreasing average costs is also shown to be inconsistent with the theory of perfect competition. If it is admitted that there is a firm whose costs per unit of output decrease when production increases, what prevents that firm from expanding production indefinitely and becoming a monopolistic producer in that market?

The assumption that firms operate with constant costs creates a further difficulty for the theory of perfect competition in the Marshall–Pigou tradition, which assumes that the firm faces a perfectly horizontal demand curve. Thus, given constant costs, either the equilibrium is undetermined or, if it is postulated that firms always produce as much as possible, the possibility of one single firm monopolizing the market cannot be ruled out.

The lack of realism in the assumption of perfect competition is revealed by the common knowledge that producers are not usually constrained by costs – which are normally diminishing for the producers of manufactured consumer's goods – but by demand. However, the theory of perfect competition assumes that while firms can sell any quantity whatsoever at the given market price, they are unable to lower prices or to increase marketing expense in order to increase their market share. Unfortunately, quite the opposite behaviour is observed in most markets.

In Sraffa, abandonment of the hypothesis of perfect competition means abandoning a *particular* theory, i.e. a theory that sees competition as a situation where the expansion of firms is halted by rising costs. While the producer cannot have any influence on price, the consumer is indifferent among the products of any given industry. The assumption of a perfectly elastic demand curve encapsulates the idea that products are homogeneous and therefore that there is perfect substitution or indifference in consumption.

Assumption of variable costs is necessary to the theory of perfect competition in the Marshall–Pigou tradition for reasons imposed by the particular price theory adopted, but it is not required by the theory of competition in the classical tradition.

In the Marshall–Pigou apparatus costs are made dependent on the quantity produced in order to exhibit the fundamental symmetry of demand and supply curves in the determination of relative prices. The theory based on the symmetry between the forces of supply and demand holds on the condition that the law of variations in costs, as output varies, has the same degree of generality as the law of variation of demand price, in relation to the quantity demanded (Sraffa, 1925, p. 317). If costs were not made dependent on the quantity produced, there could be no symmetry and commodity price would be dependent on the expenses incurred in production while demand would influence only the quantity produced, as the classical economists had it.

Sraffa's point was that the assumption of constant costs was the correct hypothesis to derive a *general* theory of competition, that is, a first approximation to reality, which needed to be supplemented with the analysis of the actual mechanism of price formation by firms.[4] This explains why Sraffa favoured the approach based on constant costs, since:

> it does not lead us astray when we desire to study in greater detail the conditions under which the exchange takes place in particular cases, for it does not conceal from us the fact that we cannot find the elements required for this purpose within the limits of its assumptions. (Sraffa, 1926, p. 541)

For Sraffa the adoption of the hypothesis of imperfect competition is only one of the 'three potential alternative routes for the elaboration of the theory of prices', the other two being 'first, to attribute general importance to the case of constant returns; second, the recognition of the general interrelations among the costs of production of various industries and the analysis of these interrelations by means of a system of general equilibrium' (Roncaglia, 1978, p. 12).

On one hand, adopting the hypothesis that competition is imperfect seems to serve the purpose of illustrating a paradox. Far from being restricted to very special circumstances, the hypothesis that – within the Marshall–Pigou apparatus – firms can be regarded as single monopolies, functioned better than perfect competition, in accounting for the evidence, that is, that the expansion of firms is halted not by rising costs but by the limitation of the market. On the other hand, the idea of competition, conceived in the context of a *different* theory, could still be retained as a 'first approximation'. This point became clear only much later, in the writing of *Production of Commodities by Means of Commodities*. (See Panico, 1991). Only then did Sraffa succeed in providing a satisfactory analysis of simultaneous determination of all prices, showing that the assumption of constant returns could be dispensed with in a different theory of competition.[5]

III[6]

In the first major contribution to the theory of imperfect competition in the Cambridge tradition,[7] *The Economics of the Short Period* by R.F. Kahn, the reason given for abandoning perfect competition is that the Marshallian–Pigouvian apparatus could not account for an observed fact: that firms could earn a positive profit while working below capacity. In competitive conditions, when price is greater than average cost firms are supposed to produce up to capacity output; if price falls below average cost, they should close down. However, the observed behaviour of firms during the Depression was that, when demand fell, firms stayed in business by working below capacity.

The short period is a situation in which plants and machinery are assumed to remain unchanged. It is characterized by two types of costs: quasi-fixed costs, which remain unchanged irrespective of the level of output, and prime costs, which respond to changes in output.

Kahn's approach is to investigate the shape of the firm's prime cost curves by looking into the technical method with which output can, in practice, be varied in the short period. In the face of a fall in demand, and on the assumption that the effective length of the working day is given, the firm has to decide 'whether to work part of the machinery every day or all of the machinery some days' (Kahn, 1989, p. 46).

The answer is given by the shape of the average cost curve under the two methods. The crucial factors are the quasi-fixed element of costs: the expenditure on fuel, lighting, repairs and salaries of foremen and key-men, and the degree of uniformity of machinery. Clearly the quasi-fixed costs are greater when production is carried on every day – which we shall call Method 1 – than when the number of days in which work is done is reduced, which we shall call Method 2. However, when production is reduced by reducing the number of machines employed, as in Method 1, the degree of uniformity of machinery plays a major role. If the machinery is equally efficient, the average prime cost decreases continuously until it reaches a minimum at the point of full capacity output. If the machinery is not uniform, and more inefficient machinery is used to increase output, then minimum cost is reached at a lower level of output. The cost curve takes the characteristic U-shaped form, until full capacity output is reached.

With Method 2, the number of *days* of production is reduced and the fixed costs involved in the periods of idleness are assumed to be constant, whatever the length of the period of stoppage. Since the difference between the total cost of a full working day and the fixed cost per day – which is called the prime cost per day – is independent of the length of the period over which production is daily carried on, it follows that, for any given level of daily output, the average prime cost (the ratio of the prime cost per day and the daily output) is independent of output. Therefore, under the assumption that the machinery is equally efficient, marginal prime cost is equal to constant average cost until full capacity is reached. In Figure 4.1 the two methods are compared.

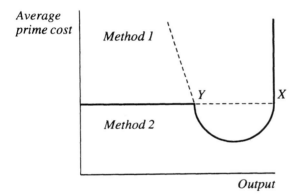

Figure 4.1   Comparison of two methods of varying output

At *X*, the point of full capacity output, all machines are used each working day. Up to *Y*, where the two curves cross, costs are lower with Method 2 than with Method 1, because working fewer days entails lower quasi-fixed costs.

In the range from *Y* to *X*, working every day with a reduced number of machines is more economical than reducing the days in which production is carried on, assuming that the machinery is not uniform. The greater the importance of quasi-fixed cost and the more uniform the machinery, the higher will be the level of output at which the two curves cross and, consequently, the wider the range for which Method 2 is more economical.

Indeed, Kahn produced evidence which showed that the most common method of reducing output in the cotton industry and in coal mining was 'to close down the whole plant on some days and to work the whole plant a full shift on other days.' (Kahn, 1989, p. 57).

The shape of the marginal cost curve – a reversed L – and the evidence of short time working in the cotton and coal industries during the Depression, are a serious challenge to the theory of perfect competition. When faced by a perfectly elastic demand curve, a constant marginal cost curve loses its significance as the determinant of output. Whenever the price exceeds the average cost curve, firms are supposed to be producing at the full capacity level of output. But if this were so, the only firms that worked below capacity would be the inefficient ones whose prime cost exceeded price, and this goes against the evidence. Therefore the conclusion is that 'the existence of short-time must often be incompatible with a state of perfect competition' (Kahn, 1989, p. 83).

The obvious step is then to introduce the assumption of an imperfect market. The main difference with a perfect market is that output is no longer determined by the equality of price and marginal cost. As in monopoly, 'the product of output and the difference between price and average prime cost [is] a maximum' (Kahn, 1989, p. 86). Kahn applies here the standard definition of 'maximum monopoly net revenue' provided by Marshall (1961, p. 397),[8] but he also offers an ingenious method for measuring market imperfection.

Assuming a linear demand curve and a perfectly horizontal prime cost curve until full capacity output is reached, Kahn starts his analysis by proving the following equation

$$(p - r)/x = \tan \theta$$

where r is the average prime cost, x the maximizing profit level of output, p the corresponding price and $\tan \theta$ the slope of the individual demand curve. At the equilibrium level of output $\tan \theta$ is then equal to the excess of unit price over unit prime cost. This can be expressed as:

$$p - r = fq \qquad f \leq 1$$

where $f (= \frac{x}{x*})$ is the ratio if x, to the capacity output, $x*$, and

$$q = x* \tan \theta$$

In Figure 4.2 we have drawn two demand curves with identical slope and an average cost curve shaped as a reversed L. As the demand curve and the cost curve are both straight lines, the maximum net revenue is given at a level of output equal to half of the horizontal cathetus and at a level of price corresponding to a point equal to half the vertical cathetus of the triangle formed by each demand curve with the horizontal segment of the average

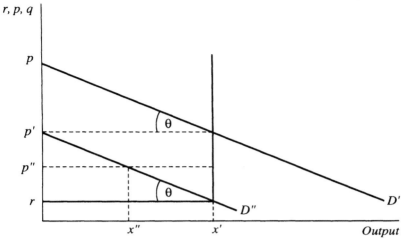

Figure 4.2   Different levels of demand

cost curve. The tangent to the angle formed by the demand curve with the average cost, q, when x^* is set equal to 1, is termed by Kahn the 'annihilation coefficient'. In his own words, 'the function q, which would be equal to the gradient of the individual demand curve if the capacity output were the unit of output, is a measure of the imperfection of the market' (Kahn, 1989, p. 121). The reason for this name is that, for a linear demand curve, q is the increase in price necessary to reduce output by an amount equal to capacity output. In fact, a useful graphic interpretation of q is that it is equal to the 'vertical distance between the points at which the individual demand curve cuts the y axis and the ordinate at the position of capacity output (Kahn, 1989, p. 121n).

When demand is equal to D', $p - p' = q$ and $f = f' = 1$, that is, the equilibrium level of output is full capacity. In this case the difference between the profit maximizing level of price, p', and the average cost, r, is equal to q, given that $p - p' = p - r$. When demand drops to D'', $p' - r = q$, the maximizing net revenue level of output falls to x'', i.e. to f'' (<1) of capacity output and p falls of $(1 - f'')q$. In this case the difference between the profit maximizing level of price, p'', and the average cost, r, is less than $p' - r = q$. A proportionality is therefore maintained between f, the degree of utilization of the plant, and the difference between price and cost, which is given by q: 'Imperfection of the market is now playing the role for which it was cast. It provides an explanation of the apparent paradox that firms work short time although they are making a prime profit.' (Kahn, 1989, pp. 122–3).

For a linear demand curve, when x^* is set equal to 1, q is equal to its slope. So the flatter the demand curve is, *ceteris paribus*, the lower the degree of market imperfection will be. When the demand curve is perfectly horizontal, $q = 0$ and the market is said to be perfect.

It must be noted that Kahn reached his results along a route that did not take in the tool of marginal revenue – a concept that had yet to see the light of day when he was engaged on his fellowship dissertation. Formally the results are equivalent,[9] but above and beyond the interest of historical accuracy, the importance of stressing this element lies in the fact that Kahn's analysis requires special assumptions, that is to say, linear demand curves and linear average cost curves. Moreover Kahn's analysis was meant to be applicable to particular circumstances, an exceptionally low level of demand, which would induce firms to reduce the level of plant utilization, thus finding themselves on the horizontal segment of their marginal costs curve.

However, the 'view' expressed in the dissertation was not successful. Keynes followed an alternative route to explain the persistence of underutilization of resources in the short period that did not require imperfect competition, and remained unconvinced of its importance;[10] while Joan Robinson although she wrote the *Economics of Imperfect Competition* under the close scrutiny of Kahn – adopted a completely different 'view'.

IV

Joan Robinson did not invent the marginal revenue[11] curve nor christen it,[12] but she was responsible for its extensive use. The novelty[13] of the approach taken by Joan Robinson in *The Economics of Imperfect Competition* was the extension of the rule of marginal revenue = marginal cost to all market forms.

The purpose of the analysis contained in *The Economics of Imperfect Competition* is to apply the technique based on individual decisions as they are incorporated in the supply and demand curves of commodities and factors of production. The starting point is Sraffa's proposal 'to rewrite the theory of value, starting from the conception of the firm as a monopolist' (Robinson, 1969, p. 6), but with the aim of extending the marginal technique to market forms other than perfect competition. By doing so it is possible to unify the analysis of monopoly and perfect competition according to a single principle.[14]

The supply side of value theory became firmly based on the profit-maximizing equilibrium of the individual producer.[15] The demand side of value theory allowed for substitution and preferences on the part of consumers. Perfect competition becomes a special case in a general theory of competition allowing for different values of the elasticity of demand. As she remarked in the final chapter of her book:

> It is customary, in setting out the principles of economic theory, to open with the analysis of a perfectly competitive world, and to treat monopoly as a special case.

It has been the purpose of the foregoing argument to show that this process can with advantage be reversed and that it is more proper to set out the analysis of monopoly, treating competition as a special case. (Robinson, 1969, p. 307)

Joan Robinson's book, *The Economics of Imperfect Competition* is built upon a general relation between average value, marginal value and elasticity of the average value. If *e* is the elasticity of the average value, *A* the average value, *M* the marginal value, then:

$$e = \frac{A}{A-M}; \; M = A\frac{(e-1)}{e}; \; A = M\frac{e}{(e-1)}$$

The above set of relationships (See Robinson, 1969, p. 36)[16] can be applied both to the average and marginal revenue curve and to the average and marginal cost curve. For the revenue curve, there are two points to note. First, it is only with a down-sloping demand curve that the marginal revenue becomes a distinct curve.[17] Second, with a down-sloping demand curve *any* assumption about the shape of the marginal cost curve provides for the determinacy of equilibrium.

For the purpose of the condition of maximum profit, i.e. MR = MC equality, it makes no difference whether marginal costs are constant, rising or falling, provided that the MR revenue curve is downward sloping. The generality of the statement that, both in competition and monopoly, production will be carried up to the point where marginal cost is equal to marginal revenue lies in the fact that it can equally accommodate constant, decreasing, and increasing costs.

There are three logical situations to consider the determination of equilibrium: (*i*) the short period, when the productive equipment of the firm is fixed, and some costs do not vary with output; (*ii*) the quasi-long period, when the productive equipment is adapted to changes in output, 'and all costs except the minimum reward of the entrepreneur may vary with output' (Robinson, 1969, p. 47); (*iii*) the long period, when the number of firms vary. However, from the point of view of the existing firms within a given industry, the quasi-long period and the long period are equivalent. In the short period, the marginal cost is constant, because prime costs do not vary with output; the average cost curve is decreasing, because of the fixed element of cost, and lies above the marginal cost curve.

The characteristic of the long period is that profits are normal, that is, there are no incentives for the number of firms to change. Since each firm is earning normal profits when price equals average cost, and the condition of maximum profit is given by marginal revenue = marginal cost, full equilibrium requires the demand curve to be tangential to the average costs (Robinson, 1969, p. 94).

Under perfect competition, full equilibrium can only be obtained when marginal cost is equal to average cost. Since marginal revenue is equal to price, the 'double condition' for equilibrium becomes $MC = P$ and $AC = P$, i.e. $MC = AC$. Marginal and average cost are equal at the minimum point on the average cost curve; therefore only in perfect competition is each firm at the optimum size. The following passage summarizes the argument:

> Now if average costs are continually falling, as the firm expands, and never reach a minimum point, marginal cost will always lie below average cost. Marginal costs may be rising (over a certain range of outputs) or may be falling. If marginal costs are rising it will be possible for the firm to reach equilibrium, where price is equal to marginal cost. But price will be less than average cost, profits will be less than normal, and the industry will not be in equilibrium. And if marginal costs are falling the firm will continue to expand. The expansion of one firm (or the growth of the firm by amalgamation with others) will reduce the number of firms until competition ceases to be perfect. Thus, under perfect competition, marginal and average cost must be equal in equilibrium, and average cost must be at a minimum, simply because, if this condition is not fulfilled, competition is not perfect. (Robinson, 1969, p. 96)

Under monopoly, since average cost is falling and the demand curve is downward sloping, the tangency solution implies that the equilibrium level of output is to the left of the point of minimum average cost and therefore less than full capacity.

Joan Robinson's discussion of equilibrium conditions shows a change of perspective in the notion of costs. Far from representing the actual costs incurred by an observed firm, the cost curves necessary to the construction of the supply curve of a commodity or of a factor of production, reflect the assumptions of the particular theory embraced.

The shape of the supply curve of a factor of production is said to reflect the degree of homogeneity and heterogeneity of a factor. Land, labour, capital and entrepreneurship can be heterogeneous from the point of view of the industry for which the supply curve is drawn and homogeneous from the point of view of other industries. Heterogeneity of the factor from the point of view of the industry is not a *sufficient* condition for the supply curve of a factor to be rising, since if the factor is homogeneous from the point of view of other industries – if it has the same efficiency[18] in other industries – it will have an elastic supply.

However, homogeneity of the factor from the point of view of the industry, but heterogeneity from the point of view of other industries, implies a rising supply curve. Furthermore, if a factor is heterogeneous both from the point of view of the industry for which we are drawing the supply curve and from the point of view of other industries, the supply curve of the factor will be rising.

So when a factor is in imperfectly elastic supply to an industry, it means that it is 'scarce' from the point of view of that industry. A scarce factor is a factor which earns rent, and rent is the difference between the earnings actually received by a certain factor and its transfer price to other industries. (Robinson, 1969, p. 110).

It follows that if a factor is in perfectly elastic supply, it means that is homogeneous and that it will not earn rent. If a factor is not homogeneous, it means that it is scarce, therefore there is rent and its supply curve will be rising.

Besides the heterogeneity of a factor, from the point of view of either one industry or the other industries or both, the shape of the supply curve of a factor of production also depends on the elasticity of substitution among various factors, i.e. on the technical possibility of substituting factors for each other, which expresses the possibility of economizing in the use of the scarce factor as its cost rises (Robinson, 1969, p. 123):

> When the scarce factors are not homogeneous, so that there is rent, their cost will rise, as more is employed, both because the efficiency of a marginal unit, relatively to its price, is reduced as more of the factor is employed, and because the transfer cost of intramarginal units is raised. (Robinson, 1969, pp. 142–3)[19]

Thus the shape of the supply curve of a factor, and therefore the supply curve for a commodity, depends both on the degree of heterogeneity and indivisibility of the 'factors' of production and on the degree of their substitutability in the production process. The theoretical framework can accommodate any possible world and by enlarging its scope it gains generality.

V

Kahn took seriously Sraffa's charge that the theory of perfect competition lacked realism. He showed that demand sets limits to the expansion of the firms, since, in the short period and for low levels of demand, the relevant range of the marginal cost curve is horizontal. However, it was the theory of effective demand – which Kahn contributed to with his analysis of the short period and of the multiplier – which gave truly general validity to this proposition. Joan Robinson tried to by-pass the inconsistencies of perfect competition, by extending the condition of MC = MR to all market conditions, i.e. perfect and imperfect competition. In so doing, however, she blurred the distinction between two different approaches to the theory of competition which was implied or, rather, adumbrated in Sraffa's articles.[20] Furthermore, while Kahn was concerned with the short period, Robinson followed Sraffa through the intricacies of the long period and looked into the theoretical – as opposed to actually observed – cost curves of the firms and the supply curves of commodities and factors of production. So one is tempted to agree with Loasby that 'Joan Robinson's first book gave a powerful impulse towards the development of formalism which has been so characteristic of the last fifty years, and which she came to regard with such dismay' (Loasby, 1991, p. 41).[21]

The point is that with Joan Robinson imperfect competition lost its paradoxical nature, i.e. that of showing the 'impossibility' of perfect competition in the conditions postulated by the Marshall–Pigou apparatus. Rather than changing the apparatus or looking for the actual conditions in which firms operate, she successfully sought out the new conditions in which the Marshallian theory of value could be made consistent. A central piece of this strategy was acceptance of the technique of marginal analysis and its underlying assumption:

> It is the assumption that any individual, in his economic life, will never undertake an action that adds more to his losses than to his gains, and will always undertake an action which adds more to his gains than to his losses, which makes the analysis of value possible. And it is this assumption that underlies the device of drawing marginal curves. (Robinson, 1969, p. 6)[22]

The Economics of Imperfect Competition was a response to Sraffa's challenge, although – as Kaldor noted – the book gave the impression that the points raised were not addressed.[23] The challenge was to construct tools that did not break down when confronted with facts.

In the meanwhile, the theory of effective demand provided the alternative explanation – more promising and exciting than imperfect competition – of the malfunctioning displayed by free competition. Her collaboration with Kahn, which had started with work on her book, was cemented with their common involvement in the Keynesian revolution. She came to consider her first book 'a blind alley' (Robinson, 1979, p. x) and rehabilitation of imperfect competition was confined to its connection with the theory of effective demand. In fact, it was Kalecki's 'view' – once again centered on observed rather than imagined costs curves – that she ended up by praising.

Notes

1. I wish to thank the participants to the History of Economics Society Annual Meeting, George Mason University, to the Seminar of the National Research Council Group on 'Economic theory and Realism of Hypotheses', Università di Venezia and to William Darity Jr., Gary Mongiovi and Fernando Vianello for helpful comments. I am grateful to Annalisa Rosselli for her help in improving the paper in many respects.
2. The English translation of the 1925 article has not yet been published. For a summary and a comparison with the 1926 article, see Maneschi, 1986.
3. Whitaker (1989, p. 169) pointed out that while, according to Marshall, 'competition is defined broadly, resting fundamentally on the openness of markets', for Pigou it was identified with atomistic price-taking behaviour.

4. Sraffa's point was *not* that in real life constant costs prevail. This is also confirmed by the following passage contained in the letter sent by Sraffa to Keynes on June 6, 1926, a few months before the publication of the 1926 article: 'although I believe that Ricardo's assumption is the best available for a simple theory of competition (*viz.* a first approximation), of course in reality the connection between cost and quantity produced is obvious. It simply cannot be considered by means of the system of particular equilibria for single commodities in regime of competition devised by Marshall' (Roncaglia, 1978, p. 12).

5. In the Preface to his book, Sraffa wrote, 'Anyone accustomed to think in terms of the equilibrium of demand and supply may be inclined, on reading these pages, to suppose that the argument rests on a tacit assumption of constant returns in all industries. If such a supposition is found helpful, there is no harm in the reader's adopting it as a temporary working hypothesis. In fact, however, no such assumption is made. ... The temptation to presuppose constant returns is not entirely fanciful. It was experienced by the author himself when he started on these studies many years ago – and led him in 1925 into an attempt to argue that only the case of constant returns was generally consistent with the premises of economic theory' (Sraffa, 1960, pp. v–vi).

6. This section is mainly derived from Marcuzzo, 1994.

7. The 'Cambridge tradition' is taken here as the development of ideas stemming from the works of Marshall and Pigou. No attempt is made to compare it with the theory of imperfect competition in the Young–Chamberlin tradition. The reader is referred to O'Brien, 1983.

8. Cost conditions under a monopoly are represented by Marshall with a downward-sloping supply curve. With a downward-sloping demand curve, the maximum revenue corresponds to the point at which the difference between the two curves times output is a maximum.

9. 'If the demand curve is assumed to be linear, this equation [i.e. $p - r = fq$] can be rewritten $p - fq = p - xq/u = p - \tan \theta = r$; [where u stands for capacity output] which can be readily recognized as equating marginal revenue to marginal cost ...' (Maneschi, 1988, p. 162). See also Newman, 1986, p. 116, who also points out that Kahn did not use marginal revenue.

10. In 1941, in defence of Kalecki, Joan Robinson wrote to Keynes: 'I must protest at your calling Imperfect Competition an esoteric doctrine. It may be awful rot – as you have always suspected – but for better or worse it is in all the textbooks now.' (See Keynes, 1973, pp. 830–2).

11. Harrod is probably right when he claims he was the first to present the concept of MR, in print, albeit under a different name, in his article *Notes on supply* (Harrod, 1930, p. 239). As he explained in a letter to Joan Robinson on 1 July 1933:

> As a matter of history it may interest you to know that I devised and wrote an article about the M.R. curve which I sent to the Journal in the Summer of 1928. Unfortunately the article contained some other matter with which Maynard didn't agree and he handed it over to Ramsey to refute. I became ill about that time and didn't bother about it for a year or so. When I took it up again, I wrote to Ramsey replying to his refutation, and he replied in a letter which I have got, entirely surrendering and indeed provides a rather elaborate mathematical demonstration of my points – these were points other than those connected with the M.R. curve. Meanwhile I became dissatisfied with the article on other grounds and did not press for its publication. I scrapped it; and in 1930 wrote quite a different article but embroidered in it my original construction of the M.R. curve. (JVR Papers, Correspondence, King's College Archives)

Permission from Dominick Harrod to quote from this unpublished letter is gratefully acknowledged.

12. Apparently the name was given by Austin Robinson. According to his recollections, he was supervising a young undergraduate mathematician who had turned to economics, Charles Gifford, who had produced early in 1930, what 'we subsequently called a marginal revenue curve on a day that Richard Kahn was lunching with us' (Robinson, 1977a,

p. 27). In Austin Robinson's opinion, imperfect competition 'started as a joint game between Joan and Richard Kahn' (Robinson, 1977b, p. 80).

13. Shove's priority in developing the analysis of 'conditional monopoly', i.e. the intermediate cases between competition and monopoly, is more difficult to assess. We can rely mainly on the lecture notes taken by John Saltmarch for the 1928–29 academic year of his Economic Theory course. (See in particular, Part II, lectures 5–10; King's College Archives.) Here, without explicitly using the concept of marginal revenue, Shove defines equilibrium as equality between marginal cost and the algebraic sum of the two component parts of the variation in revenue. He states the equilibrium condition as $\Delta c = p\Delta x - x\Delta p$, where x = quantity produced; p = price; c = cost. The issue of 'priority' between Joan Robinson and G. Shove is documented by the extant letters by Shove in Joan Violet Robinson Papers, Correspondence, King's College Archives. (Excerpts are published in Turner, 1989, pp. 27–8). On this point see Marcuzzo, 1991.

14. Joan Robinson considered this an advance on Marshall's approach:

'It is clear that the marginal method of analysis will produce exactly the same results as the method, used by Marshall, of finding the price at which the area representing 'monopoly net revenue' is at a maximum, since net revenue is at a maximum when marginal revenue and marginal cost are equal. Both methods can be applied to problems of competition and monopoly. Marshall introduced in his system of analysis an artificial cleavage between monopoly and competition, by treating competitive problems only by the 'marginal' method, and monopoly problems only by the 'areas' method'. (Robinson, 1969, p. 54n).

15. According to Shackle (1967, p. 11), Joan Robinson 'abandoned value theory itself in favour of her new invention, the theory of the firm'. Also according to Whitaker (1969, p. 187) Robinson provided 'a full and unified treatment of profit-maximizing equilibrium for a firm facing a fixed market environment'.

16. The algebraic demonstration of the relation between the curves of average and marginal values is given by Harrod (1931, pp. 566–76).

17. As it has been noted 'nobody had previously wanted the *general* concept of marginal revenue since they conceived of marginal revenue in the special form of *price*' (Shackle, 1967, p. 42).

18. 'Two portions of a certain factor ... will be counted as consisting of an equal number of efficiency units if they can be substituted for one another without altering physical productivity' (Robinson, 1969, p. 109).

19. The transfer cost is the price that has to be paid to keep a factor in a particular employment; it resembles the modern concept of opportunity cost (see Robinson, 1969, pp. 105–7).

20. Although she did not read the original Italian article, she must have been familiar with its contents, since she attended Sraffa's lectures. Whitaker is not right in saying that 'Sraffa had ceased to lecture by the time the Robinsons returned from India.' (op. cit. p. 191n.). Joan Robinson came back from India in the summer of 1928 – five months earlier than her husband – together with the Committee of British people who had been in charge of solving a dispute between the State of Gwalior and the Central Government of India over a matter of taxation and with whom Joan had worked to win the case for the State (see her curriculum, January 1935, in John Maynard Keynes's papers, King's College Archives, file UA/9. 1). Sraffa gave his course 'Advanced Theory of Value' in the Michaelmas and Lent Terms of the 1928–9 and 1929–30 academic years and in the Lent Term of 1931 (see Cambridge University *Reporter*).

21. Also in Loasby, 1989, p. 79.

22. In the 'Introduction' she noticed that 'When Mr. Sraffa declared that the time had come to re-write the theory of value, starting from the conception of the firm as a monopolist, he suggested that the familiar tool, "maximum monopoly net revenue", was ready to hand and that the job could begin at once. But that tool is at best a clumsy one and it is inappropriate to many of the operations which are required of it. In its place the "mar-

ginal" technique must be borrowed from the competitive chapters of the old textbooks, and adapted to new purposes' (Robinson, 1969, p. 6). The wording of the last sentence was suggested by J.M. Keynes. (See Draft of Book I in JVR papers, King's College Archives.) Moreover, the first draft of the Introduction presented many similarities with the opening passage of Robinson, 1932 in which she defended the methodology of considering economics as a 'box of tools'.

23. 'One almost has the feeling that Mrs. Robinson could have written much the same book if Mr. Sraffa's path breaking article (to which she acknowledges so much debt) had never been written' (Kaldor, 1980, p. 55).

References

Clifton, James A. (1977), 'Competition and the evolution of the capitalist mode of production', *Cambridge Journal of Economics*, **1** (1), March.

Harrod, Roy F. (1930), 'Notes on Supply', *Economic Journal*, 40 (158), June.

Harrod, Roy F. (1931), 'The Law of Decreasing Costs', *Economic Journal*, **41** (164), December.

Kahn, Richard F. (1989), *The Economics of the Short Period*, London: Macmillan.

Kaldor, Nicholas (1980), 'Mrs. Robinson's "Economics of Imperfect Competition"', in *Essays on Value and Distribution*, 2nd edn, London: Duckworth.

Keynes, John Maynard (1973), 'Economic Articles and Correspondence: Investment and Editorial', in Moggridge, D. (ed.), *The Collected Writings of John Maynard Keynes*, vol. XII, London: Macmillan.

Loasby, Brian J. (1989), *The Mind and Method of the Economist*, Aldershot: Edward Elgar.

Loasby, Brian J. (1991), 'Joan Robinson's "Wrong Turning"', in Rima, Ingrid (ed.), *The Joan Robinson Legacy*, Armonk: M.E. Sharpe.

Maneschi, Andrea (1986), 'A comparative evaluation of Sraffa's "The Laws of returns under competitive conditions" and its Italian precursor', *Cambridge Journal of Economics*, **10**, (1), March.

Maneschi, Andrea (1988), 'The place of Lord Kahn's "The economics of the short period" in the theory of imperfect competition', *History of Political Economy*, **20**, (2).

Marcuzzo, Maria Cristina (1991), 'Joan Robinson e la formazione della Scuola di Cambridge', in Joan Robinson, *Occupazione, distribuzione e crescita*, Bologna: Il Mulino.

Marcuzzo, Maria Cristina (1994), 'R.F. Kahn and Imperfect Competition', *Cambridge Journal of Economics*, **18**, (1), March.

Marshall, Alfred (1961), *Principles of Economics*, London: Macmillan.

Newman, Peter (1986), 'Review of R.F. Kahn, "The Economics of the Short Period"', *Contributions to Political Economy*, **5**.

O'Brien, Dennis P. (1983), 'Research Programmes in Competitive Structure', *Journal of Economic Studies*, **10** (4).

Panico, Carlo (1991), 'Some Notes on Marshallian Supply Functions', *Economic Journal*, **101** (406), May.

Robinson, Austin (1977a), 'Keynes and his Cambridge Colleagues', in Patinkin D. and Leith J.C. (eds), *Keynes, Cambridge and the General Theory*, London: Macmillan.

Robinson, Austin (1977b), 'Discussion' in Patinkin, D. and Leith, J.C. (eds), *Keynes, Cambridge and the General Theory*, London: Macmillan.

Robinson, Joan V. (1932), *Economics is Serious Subject. The Apologia of an Economist to the Mathematician, the Scientists and the Plain Man*, Cambridge: Heffer.

Robinson, Joan V. (1969), *The Economics of Imperfect Competition*, 2nd edn, London: Macmillan.

Robinson, Joan V. (1978), *Contributions to Modern Economics*, Oxford: Blackwell.

Robinson, Joan V. (1979), *Collected Economic Papers*, vol. V, Oxford: Blackwell.

Roncaglia, Alessandro (1978), *Sraffa and the Theory of Prices*, New York: Wiley.

Shackle, G.L.S. (1967), *The Years of High Theory. Invention and Tradition in Economic Thought 1926–1939*, Cambridge: Cambridge University Press.

Sraffa, Piero (1925), 'Sulle relazioni tra costo e quantità prodotta', *Annali di Economia*, **2** (1).

Sraffa, Piero (1926), 'The Laws of Returns under Competitive Conditions', *Economic Journal*, **36** (144), December.

Sraffa, Piero (1960), *Production of Commodities by Means of Commodities. Prelude to a Critique of Economic Theory*, Cambridge: Cambridge University Press.

Stigler, George J. (1957), 'Perfect Competition, Historically Contemplated', *Journal of Political Economy*, **65** (1), February.

Stiglitz, Joseph E. (1992), 'The Meanings of Competition in Economic Analysis', paper presented at the International Conference on 'The Value of Competition', Milan, mimeo.

Turner, Marjorie S. (1989), *Joan Robinson and the Americans*, Armonk: Sharpe.

Whitaker, John K. (1989), 'The Cambridge Background to Imperfect Competition', in Feiwel, George F. (ed.), *The Economics of Imperfect Competition and Employment. Joan Robinson and Beyond*, London: Macmillan.

5 Early mathematical theories of conflict: the contributions of Lanchester and Richardson

Robert W. Dimand and Mary Ann Dimand

Game theory deals with the mathematical modelling of conflict and co-operation. Formal mathematical analysis of conflict emerged from the First World War in the writings of Frederick William Lanchester (1868–1946) and Lewis Fry Richardson (1881–1953). Their concerns were sharply distinct. Lanchester's *Aircraft in Warfare* (1916) examined how to win battles by choosing an appropriate strategy such as concentrating forces. Richardson was a pacifist Quaker who, from his *Mathematical Psychology of War* (1919) onward, attempted to understand the dynamics of arms races and the statistics of outbreaks of war as aids to preventing war.

Lanchester, an English engineer, built an experimental automobile engine as early as 1895 and began producing the Lanchester automobile in 1900. The Physical Society of London declined in 1897 to print a Lanchester paper on the inherent stability of model aeroplanes, for which thirty years later the Royal Aeronautical Society awarded Lanchester a gold medal (Newman, 1956, 2136n.). His interest in aircraft extended beyond their physical properties to their effect on military strategy which he expounded in 1914 in a series of articles in *Engineering*, which were the basis for his book two years later.

In the course of examining the role of aircraft in warfare, Lanchester essayed a mathematical analysis of the relationship between opposing forces in battle, to determine the conditions under which a smaller force could defeat a larger force. Neither Lanchester or Richardson used an explicit payoff function. Implicitly, the payoffs in Lanchester's analysis were victory or failure to achieve victory without consideration of the cost of winning a battle in one way rather than another. Lanchester's payoffs would thus be of the form $(-1, 1)$, so that he was analysing a two-person, zero sum game. Considering two armies, with b the numerical strength of the Blue army and r the numerical strength of the Red army, Lanchester represented the time derivatives of the size of the two forces as

$$db/dt = -N\,r \times \text{constant} \tag{5.1}$$
$$dr/dt = -M\,b \times \text{constant} \tag{5.2}$$

where N and M are positive and represent the fighting value of the individual units on each side. The fighting values would reflect differences in armament. The attrition of each force's numbers thus depended on the number of opponents shooting at it. This formulation led directly to Lanchester's recommendation of concentration rather than division of forces, so that a larger force would be shooting at a given enemy force.

If the Blue and Red forces were equal in fighting strength, then

$$\frac{db}{b\,dt} = \frac{dr}{r\,dt} \tag{5.3}$$

which, together with (5.1) and (5.2), implied

$$-Nr/b = -Mb/r \tag{5.4}$$

and $$Nr^2 = Mb^2: \tag{5.5}$$

'In other words, the fighting strengths of the two forces are equal when the *square of the numerical strength multiplied by the fighting value of the individual units are equal*' (Lanchester, 1956, 2145). From this result, which depended for its validity on the assumed equality of fighting strength of the two sides, Lanchester concluded too hastily that the fighting strength of a force would depend on the square of its numerical strength, according to his '*n*-square law'. He gave several illustrations, with application for example to Nelson's strategy before and at Trafalgar, but took the foundations of his law as established.

Lanchester allocated a role for strategy both in concentration of forces (maximizing the initial value of b or r) and in increasing M or N through improved training or armament. He also considered the possibility that long range weapons might nullify the advantages of superior number, and indicated that closing the distance between two numerically disparate forces to reduce the value of the smaller's long-range weapons could benefit the larger force:

let us imagine a 'Blue' force of 100 men armed with the machine gun opposed by a 'Red' 1,200 men armed with the ordinary service rifle. Our first assumption will be that both forces are spread over a front of given length and at long range. Then the 'Red' force will lose 16 men to the 'Blue' force loss of one, and, if the combat is continued under these conditions, the 'Reds' must lose. If, however, the 'Reds' advance, and get with short range, where each man and gunner is an individual mark, the tables are turned ..., and, even if 'Reds' lose half their effective [*sic*] in gaining the new position, with 600 men remaining they are masters of the situation; their strength is $600^2 \times 1$ against the 'Blue' $100^2 \times 16$. (Lanchester, 1956, 2148)

Lanchester's suggestion was that with long range weapons, a force's power might no longer be proportional to the square of its number. The Reds could return the 'rules of the game' to their former state by changing tactics. In Lanchester's illustration, the fighting power coefficients of the forces did not change, but the larger force could square its effectiveness by approaching the enemy.

The precise way in which effectiveness depended on weaponry, proximity, and other factors was not modelled. Lanchester considered formally only the strategies of division versus concentration of forces. Such strategies as 'run away' or 'burn a village' were not on his palette. He did not formally consider the choice of an optimal strategy from among a set of possible strategies (other than the choice of concentration over division of forces) to maximize the probability of victory (equivalent to maximizing expected pay-off in Lanchester's framework). His mathematical analysis of two-person, zero sum conflict with regard to strategic choice, though limited, is a clear precursor of the mathematical theory of strategic games although, like Lanchester's work on aerodynamics, it had little immediate impact.

Lanchester's contribution has been recognized by the establishment of the Frederick W. Lanchester Prize of the Operations Research Society of America. The Lanchester equations are the basis for much later work in military operations research (see Shubik, 1982, 404, for references on Lanchester games, and Taylor, 1979 for a survey). The then-novel military use of aircraft which inspired Lanchester's analysis was also the occasion for the first operational research group, the Anti-Aircraft Experimental Section of the British Ministry of Munitions led by A.V. Hill, brother-in-law of J.M. Keynes and later Nobel laureate in physiology (Hill, 1960, 265–6, 307–8). Another novel feature of the First World War, submarine warfare, led Thomas Edison in 1915 to devise a war game to simulate 'zigzagging' as a way for merchant ships to evade submarines (see Whitmore, 1953) and William (later Lord) Beveridge, then Assistant General Secretary of the British Ministry of Munitions, to develop 'Swish', a submarine war game, in 1916.

While Lanchester hoped to win battles by concentration of air power, and Hill to shoot down the aircraft, Richardson wished to prevent wars by learning how arms races provoked them. Richardson took first-class honours in Part I of the Natural Sciences Tripos at Cambridge in 1903, but his first degree was the DSc. in physics awarded him by the University of London for his published work on meteorology in 1926, the same year that he was elected a Fellow of the Royal Society. He also took second-class honours in the London special BSc. examination in psychology as an external student in 1929. His meteorological research, which led to his work on approximation methods for differential equations, provided the background to his use of differential equations to represent arms races. According to Richardson's son, 'calculations took longer to complete than did the predicted weather to arrive. Richardson undertook one of these enormous computations and included the results in *Weather Prediction by Numerical Process*, even though they did not agree with the facts' (S. Richardson, 1957, 300). This policy also provides some background to his work on arms races.

As a conscientious objector in the First World War, Richardson served with the Friends' Ambulance Unit in France, and after the war he resigned from the meteorological office when it was transferred to the Air Ministry. 'Despite his achievements in meteorology and their recognition in the 1920's, he was not offered any positions in British universities, largely because of his stand as a conscientious objector, which disqualified him according to the then prevalent ideas' (S.A. Richardson, 1957, 300–302). He was finally offered a professorship in 1940, but chose instead to retire after eleven years as principal of Paisley Technical College in Scotland at the early age of fifty-nine, to devote himself to studying the causes of war.

Richardson wrote his first study on the *Mathematical Psychology of War* while serving with the Friends Ambulance Unit in France. 'There was no learned society to which I dared to offer so unconventional a work. Therefore I had 300 copies made by multigraph, at a cost of about 35 pounds, and gave them nearly all away. It was little noticed. Some of my friends thought it funny. But for me it was quite serious, and was the beginning of the investigations on the causes of war which now occupy me in my retirement' (Richardson, 1960b, xxix). Sixteen years later, Richardson (1935a, 830n.) announced that the last few copies were still available from the Geneva Research Centre in Switzerland. This monograph is now scarce, available in British copyright libraries (Richardson, 1957, 305), but the core of the work is available in extracts that Richardson published in 1935 in *Nature*, the prestigious weekly British scientific journal.

The approach of another World War provided Richardson with the scientific audience he had lacked: in 1938 he presented a paper on 'Generalized Foreign Politics', summarizing his three *Nature* contributions (1935a, 1935b, 1938), in Cambridge to Section J of the British Association for the Advancement of Science, and in June 1939 the *British Journal of Psychology* published a monograph supplement by Richardson with the same title as his British Association paper (eventually revised and enlarged as Richardson, 1960a). *Nature* remained the main forum for Richardson's research on the causes and frequency of wars, printing contributions by him on those topics in 1941, 1944, 1945, 1946 and 1951. After the war, his studies on war and peace appeared in a great variety of scholarly periodicals: *British Journal of Medical Psychology*, *British Journal of Sociology*, *British Journal of Statistical Psychology*, *Eugenics Review* (on the pacifying effect of intermarriage), *Journal of the American Statistical Association*, *Journal of the Royal Statisti-*

cal Society, Psychometrika, and *Sankhya, the Indian Statistical Journal* (see L. Richardson, 1957, 306–7 for references).

Not all journal editors, however, accepted Richardson's opinion of the importance of his work. 'In 1939, when the clouds of the Second World War were ominously gathering over Europe, an American journal received for publication a paper from Lewis F. Richardson. The paper contained the essentials of chapters ii and iii of the present book, as well as fractions of other chapters. In his letter of transmittal Richardson urged that the paper be published immediately because its publication might avert an impending war. The editors of the journal not only did not rush the paper but rejected it (Rashevsky and Trucco, preface to Richardson, 1960a, ix: a 'story, for the authenticity of which the editor cannot vouch but which he heard from a responsible source and has every reason to believe to be true').

Richardson's model was based on a system of differential equations strikingly similar to those of Lanchester. Richardson viewed arms races as the interaction of fear and threat. 'It was asserted in the years 1912–14 that their [Germany and Austria–Hungary] motives were fixed and independent of our behaviour, whereas our motives were a response to their behaviour and varied accordingly. In 1914 Bertrand Russell put forward the contrary view that the motives of the two sides were essentially the same, for each was afraid of the other; and it was this fear which caused each side to increase its armaments as a defence against the other' (Richardson, 1950a, 1244). Taking x and y as the preparedness for war of two groups of nations, Richardson (1935b) stated the equations

$$dx/dt = ky - ax + g \qquad (5.6)$$

$$dy/dt = lx - by + h \qquad (5.7)$$

where a and b are positive constants representing resistance to armament costs, k and l are positive 'defence coefficients' and g and h are positive or negative constant grievances, modified by friendly feelings or treaties. He took annual defence budgets as representing x and y. In this formulation, even complete disarmament, setting $x = y = 0$, could not prevent the restarting of an arms race if the grievance variables g and h were positive. Since defence budgets could not be negative, no equilibrium level of defence spending would exist as long as g and h were positive.

Richardson (1938) amended this model by redefining x and y as 'threats minus co-operation', $x = U - U_0$, $y = V - V_0$, where threats U and V were measured by annual defence budgets and co-operation U_0 and V_0 in the form of trade, travel and correspondence was taken to have been constant through the 1909–13 arms race of France and Russia against Germany and Austria–

Hungary. Here *g* and *h* represented gross rather than net grievances. Setting *k* = *1* and *a* = *b* on the grounds that 'These two pairs of nations were very roughly equal', Richardson derived the equations

$$d(x + y)/dt = (k - a)(x + y) + g + h \tag{5.8}$$

and $$d(U + V)/dt = (k - a)(U + V) + \{g + h - (k - a)(U_0 + V_0)\} \tag{5.9}$$

The rate of change of defence spending, $d(U + V)/dt$, would be a linear function of the level of defence spending, $U + V$, with a slope of $k = a$. Using annual data for the years 1909–10 to 1912–13, so that he had only four data points, Richardson confirmed that the relationship between $U + V$ and the rate of change of $U + V$ appeared to be linear, with a slope of 0.73/year. He found that the line cut the axis at 194, so that $d(U + V)/dt = 0$ when $U + V =$ 194 million pounds sterling per year (Richardson, 1919, analysis without diagram; with diagram, 1938, 793; 1950a, 1246; 1960a, 33). 'This 194 million sterling is the amount of defence expenditure, by the four nations concerned, that would just have been mutually forgiven in view of the amount of goodwill then existing. It is, to say the least, a remarkable coincidence that the trade between these opposing pairs of nations was on the average 206 millions sterling, close to 194' (Richardson, 1938, 793). Any level of defence spending less than 194 would lead to a stable equilibrium defence spending of 0 in this model. Defence spending of 194 is an unstable equilibrium, but any deviation of $U + V$ above 194 would start a spiralling arms race.

As Ian Bellany (1975, 119) noted, Richardson used the flow of defence spending rather than the stock of armaments to represent military preparedness, and sometimes wrote as if the two formulations were equivalent. In later work (1950a, 1951, 1960a) he represented war-like preparations by 'warfinpersal' (war-finance per salary or 'warlike worktime'), annual defence expenditure divided by the annual earnings of a semi-skilled engineer, which he related to Keynes's wage-unit (Richardson, 1960a, 132–3, where he also cites Hawtrey). The alternative stock formulation has been the basis for at least one successful forecast. Lorie Tarshis (personal communication) recalls that at the American Economic Association annual meetings in December 1936, Wassily Leontief predicted that the risk of a European war would be greatest in August or September 1939, when the German lead over Britain and France in stock of armaments would be at its peak. In general, in line with the theory developed in capital accumulation games, we would expect that only investments in war-use *stocks* would have deterrence value, although some of these stocks might be composed of human capital.

'There have been only three great arms-races. The first two of them ended in wars in 1914 and 1939; the third is still going on' wrote Richardson (1951,

567). Could the third great arms race end without fighting? Incorporating measures of 'submissiveness' and of objection to the cost of rearmament into his equations, Richardson concluded that the arms race could end without war.

One aspect of Richardson's later work that was ahead of his time was the application of chaos theory, which he had elsewhere applied to the probability of encounters between gas molecules, to the number of nations on each side of a war, which he modelled as a chaos, restricted by geography, and modified by the infectiousness of fighting (Richardson, 1946; 1960b, pp. 247–87).

Richardson was aware of the limitations of his specific models: 'It is instructive to regard large groups as deterministic, and to represent their behaviour by differential equations, provided that we remember that such a treatment is a caricature' (Richardson, 1951, 567). Even those writers who have most praised Richardson for applying mathematics to the analysis of conflict have expressed reservations about the details of formulations, such as using the flow of defence spending rather than the stock of armaments. Kenneth Boulding demurred at Richardson's use of the volume of trade as a measure of co-operation, suggesting instead the difference between actual trade and what trade would be if there no were no restrictive tariffs or quotas as the appropriate variable (quoted by Rashevsky and Trucco in preface to Richardson, 1960a, vii–viii).

Although the motivation for Richardson's studies was the prevention of war, he provided no explicit discussion of what nations should do to halt an arms race. He stated that his 'equations are merely a description of what people would do if they did not stop to think. ... It is what *would occur if instinct and tradition were allowed to act uncontrolled*' (Richardson, 1960a, 12). Implicitly, intervention to halt the process by actors who understood the model would mean changing the game, a parallel with Lanchester. Unlike Lanchester's, however, Richardson's formulation included a simple mechanism for such change: the co-operation, or net grievance, parameters. He did not discuss alternative strategies using trade, treaties, or intermarriages when using the 1919 arms escalation model, but later articles make it clear that he envisioned such policies as military deterrents. In his *n* nation model, Richardson explicitly supposed that 'When an alliance is formed, the defence coefficients between allies sink to zero' (Richardson, 1960a, 170).

Richardson's model differed sharply from later game theory by not starting from the optimizing actions of rational agents. Indeed, he did not give an explicit payoff function. The context in which Richardson worked, and what he said about his system, indicates that he felt that the lower the probability of war was or the smaller the stock of armaments, the higher the joint payoff. For Richardson, however, 'peace or war' was not a binary zero-sum payoff

alternative. In his statistical studies of conflicts (1950b, 1960b), his concern
with the number of people killed is evident. He may also have been concerned that arms competed with civilian expenditures in government budgets,
but this is much less clear. (By contrast, Lanchester's concern with the mere
winning of a conflict as opposed to losing it is transparent.) It is as though
Richardson bypassed discussion of the game being played and considered
only the Cournot-type reaction functions of the player-nations to some unstated
game (see Boulding, 1962 for interpretation of the Richardson equations as
reaction functions). Richardson (1960a) gave what are basically phase dia-
grams to show the areas of stability and instability of his system depending
on the values of the coefficients of defence and net grievance. Presumably
the wise government would alter its coefficients and initial position accordingly.

As considering Richardson's equations as reaction functions makes evident, a Richardson equilibrium is a Nash equilibrium: neither player can
better its status by its individual actions. Just as in the case of rival oligopolistic
firms, however, the players in this model would seem to forgo potential gains
from collusion. If they could agree not to attack each other, they would have
both security and no need for stockpiling arms.

Richardson (1960a) also considered extending the number of players beyond two, and analysing his approach at this point becomes much more
difficult. Richardson assumed that the behavioural function of the ith of n
players was $dx_i/dt = g_i + \sum_{ij}x_j$ $(i, j \neq i)$ Richardson, 1960a, 146), where g_i was
the ith country's net grievance. If the behavioural equations are to be viewed
as reaction functions, this means that all players play Nash strategies regardless of the number of their potential allies. Richardson's analysis went on to
consider the stability of a three-player system, and concluded that even if all
pairs of nations would be stable in two-player versions of the game, the
triplet may not have a stable equilibrium (Richardson, 1960a, 154–6). It is
surprising that Richardson's representation of a three-player arms race with
Nash players bears this striking resemblance to the three-player transferable
utility log-rolling game. When he considered alliances between countries
explicitly in the theory of n nations, Richardson assumed that alliances changed
the defence coefficients between the two allies, rather than changing the
behavioural equations in any more fundamental way. While he considered
the effect of differing degrees of information on other nations's stocks of
arms, Richardson modelled perfect information by a nation's concern with
the difference between its own stocks and those of each other nation, rather
than by any bargaining process connected with alliance formation (Richardson,
1960a, 160–2, 170–6).

Although Richardson did not model agent choice explicitly, Brito (1972)
and Simaan and Cruz (1975a, 1975b) have shown that the Richardson model

and more general Richardson-type models can be derived from goal-oriented rational calculations. Simaan and Cruz (1975a) also demonstrated that Richardson's model can be reformulated in the language of the modern theory of differential games.

Richardson's influence on the area of game theory known as conflict resolution (Kenneth Boulding's term) or peace science (Walter Isard's term) can be seen most clearly in *Fights, Games and Debates* by Anatol Rapoport, who acknowledges 'the methods exemplified in the work of Rashevsky and specifically of Richardson, which dominate Part I of this book' (Rapoport, 1960, xi), and in the discussion of Richardson-process models by Boulding (1962, 25–40). Quincy Wright (1942) gave an early discussion of Richardson's work, and he and the pioneering mathematical social scientist Nicholas Rashevsky edited Richardson's manuscripts (1960a, b) for posthumous publication. Richardson's analysis is the starting point for modelling of arms races in the *Journal of Conflict Resolution*, of which Rapoport is gaming editor and whose editorial board includes the noted game theorists John Harsanyi, Reinhard Selten and Martin Shubik.

Empirical application of the Richardson model has been disappointing. Stephen Majeski and David Jones (1981) suggest that this is because the form in which the model has usually been applied, converted to difference equations because budget data is discrete, is overly restrictive, relating arms spending in one country only to last year's arm spending in another country, rather than to a distributed lag of past expenditure. Even using the more general distributed lag model, Granger causality testing by Majeski and Jones found independence (no arms race) for seven of twelve pairs of arms expenditures commonly proposed as arms races. While this is plausible for the five (out of six) South American pairs, where animosity was unaccompanied by recent or prospective military conflict, it is surprising for USA–USSR (1949–75) and India–Pakistan (1948–75). The only instance of two-way causality as predicted by Richardson was between Israel and the Arabs (Egypt, Syria and Jordan). Contrary to the Richardson model, in this case it was instantaneous causality, with only current spending mattering, not even last year's spending by the other side. Iraqi spending affected Iranian spending, and Peruvian spending affected Brazilian spending, but there was no influence in the opposite direction, either instantaneous or lagged. Greek and Warsaw Pact spending depended on current and lagged Turkish and NATO spending, respectively, but Turkey and NATO responded only to current, not lagged, Greek and Warsaw Pact spending. Majeski and Jones (1981, 281) concluded that 'we have found no evidence to support the classic Richardson discrete arms race model'.

Great activity in building upon Richardson's foundations does not necessarily imply satisfaction with the results. Charles Anderton observes that

We have over one hundred Richardson-process (differential equations-type) arms race models in the literature. We have considered dozens of variables in these models under deterministic and stochastic conditions. One could argue that this reflects the popularity and success of Richardson-type models. I believe, however, that the search for bigger and better differential equations is a reflection of frustration over the limited applicability of Richardson-type models. This is a sign, not of a successful research program, but of a degenerating one. ... I am *not* arguing that Richardson's *work* on arms races is theoretically weak. Richardson offers an extensive and plausible verbal justification in *Arms and Insecurity* and *Mathematical Psychology of War* that provides a theory, understanding, and explanation of the arms race process. What I am arguing is that the Richardson *model* and Richardson-process models in general do *not* add much to the understanding already given in the verbal justification. Modeling efforts that take account of gross behaviour and strategy from the start are attempts to push the arms race modeling enterprise to a deeper level than Richardson and other Richardson-process modelers have pushed it. ... This is a noble effort and Richardson was the first to attempt the application of mathematics in the analysis of arms races. This was his genius, not the models that he developed. (Anderton, 1989, 349, 356–7)

It may be taken as a testimonial to the vitality of Richardson's work that seventy years after his first, barely-noticed monograph, and after the publication of over a hundred Richardson-type models, a researcher finds it necessary to argue the case for going beyond the specifics of Richardson's mathematics while highly praising his contribution.

Lanchester and Richardson built models of conflict whose basic differential equations startlingly resembled each other in assuming linear feedback between two players. Their approaches, however, were diametrically opposed: Lanchester's concern was that battles be won, with no apparent concern for human cost, while Richardson's work was motivated by pacifism. Curiously enough, a nation exercising Lanchester-type behaviour would wish to build up its forces in order that it could produce good concentrations at a number of locations, thus producing a Richardson arms-race. While each author's analysis concerned the competitive behaviour of two players, neither modelled available strategies explicitly or was fully conscious of any payoff function involved. Nonetheless the work of each has had a lasting influence on writers in the now more mature fields of game theory and operations research.

References

Anderton, C.H. (1989), 'Arms Race Modeling: Problems and Prospects', *Journal of Conflict Resolution* **33** (2), pp. 346–67.

Bellany, I. (1975), 'The Richardson Theory of "Arms Races": Themes and Variations', *British Journal of International Studies*, **1** (2), pp. 119–30.

Boulding, K.E. (1962), *Conflict and Defense: a General Theory*, New York: Harper & Brothers for the Center for Research in Conflict Resolution, University of Michigan.

Brito, D.L. (1972), 'A Dynamic Model of an Armaments Race', *International Economic Review* 13, pp. 359–75.

Hill, A.V. (1960), *The Ethical Dilemma of Science and Other Writings*, New York: Rockefeller Institute Press, and Oxford: Oxford University Press.

Lanchester, F.W. (1916), *Aircraft in Warfare*, London: Constable.

Lanchester, F.W. (1956), Except from Lanchester (1916) in Newman (1956), pp. 2138–57.

Majeski, S.J. and D.L. Jones (1981), 'Arms Race Modeling: Causality Analysis and Model Specification', *Journal of Conflict Resolution* 25 (2), pp. 259–88.

Newman, J.R. (1956), *The World of Mathematics*, 4 vols., New York: Simon and Schuster.

Rapoport, A. (1957), 'Lewis F. Richardson's Mathematical Theory of War', *Journal of Conflict Resolution* 1 (3), pp. 249–99.

Rapoport, A. (1960), *Fights, Games and Debates*, Ann Arbor, University of Michigan Press.

Rapoport, A. (1974), *Conflict in Man-Made Environment*, Harmondsworth: Penguin.

Rashevsky, N. (1948), *Mathematical Theory of Human Relations*, Bloomington, Indiana: The Principia Press.

Richardson, L.F. (1919), *Mathematical Psychology of War*, Oxford: William Hunt.

Richardson, L.F. (1935a), 'Mathematical Psychology of War', *Nature* 135, pp. 830–1.

Richardson, L.F. (1935b), 'Mathematical Psychology of War', *Nature* 136, p. 1025.

Richardson, L.F. (1938), 'The Arms Race of 1909–13', *Nature* 142, pp. 792–3.

Richardson, L.F. (1939), *Generalized Foreign Politics*. Cambridge: Cambridge University Press; *British Journal of Psychology*, Monograph Supplement No. 23.

Richardson, L.F. (1946), 'Chaos, International and Intermolecular', *Nature* 158, p. 135.

Richardson, L.F. (1950a), 'Mathematics of War and Foreign Politics', in T.H. Pear, ed., *Psychological Factors of Peace and War*, London: Hutchinson, as reprinted in Newman (1956), pp. 1240–53.

Richardson, L.F. (1950b), 'Statistics of Deadly Quarrels', in T.H. Pear, ed., *Psychological Factors of Peace and War*, London: Hutchinson, as reprinted in Newman (1956), pp. 1254–63.

Richardson, L.F. (1951), 'Could an Arms Race End without Fighting?', *Nature* 168, pp. 567–8, 920.

Richardson, L.F. (1957), 'A Bibliography of Lewis Fry Richardson's Studies of the Causation of Wars with a View to their Avoidance', *Journal of Conflict Resolution*, 1 (3), pp. 305–7.

Richardson, L.F. (1960a), *Arms and Insecurity*, N. Rashevsky and E. Trucco (eds), Pittsburgh: The Boxwood Press, and Chicago: Quadrangle Books.

Richardson, L.F. (1960b), *Statistics of Deadly Quarrels*, Q. Wright and C.C. Lienau (eds), Pittsburgh, The Boxwood Press, and Chicago: Quadrangle Books.

Richardson, S.A. (1957), 'Lewis Fry Richardson (1881–1953): A Personal Biography', *Journal of Conflict Resolution* 1 (3), pp. 300–4.

Russell, B.A.W. (1914), *War, the Offspring of Fear*, London: Union for Democratic Control.

Shubik, M. (1982), *Game Theory in the Social Sciences*, Cambridge, MA: MIT Press.

Simaan, M., and J.B. Cruz, Jr. (1975a), 'Formulation of Richardson's Model of the Arms Race from a Differential Game Viewpoint', *Review of Economic Studies*, 42, pp. 67–77.

Simaan, M. (1975b), 'Nash Equilibrium Strategies for the Problem of Armament Race and Control', *Management Science* 22, pp. 96–105.

Taylor, J.G. (1979), 'Recent Developments in the Lanchester Theory on Combat', in *IFORS Proceedings*, K.B. Haley (ed.), Amsterdam: North-Holland, pp. 773–806.

Whitmore, W.F. (1953), 'Edison and Operations Research', *Journal of the Operations Research Society of America* 1, pp. 83–5.

Wright, Q. (1942), *A Study of War*, Chicago: University of Chicago Press.

6. The evolution of Wicksell's concept of capital

Bo Sandelin

Knut Wicksell's (1851–1926) scientific work extended over approximately three decades, from the beginning of the 1890s until his death in 1926. A gradual change in his economics can be seen to have taken place. In this chapter we will concentrate on the evolution of Wicksell's concept of capital. This means that we do not accept the view that his capital theory, including the concept of capital, is exhaustively shown in the second and third editions of his *Lectures on Political Economy*.

We shall find that in his analysis in his early works – 'Kapitalzins und Arbeitslohn' (1892), *Value, Capital and Rent* (1893) and *Zur Lehre von der Steuerincidenz* (1895) – he was strongly influenced by the the old wage fund theory; capital was essentially treated as a fund of subsistence means. In *Interest and Prices* (1898), intermediate goods receive attention along with subsistence means, and we learn that capital is saved-up labour and saved-up services of land. In *Lectures on Political Economy* (1901), the emphasis is almost fully shifted to intermediate goods that embody saved-up labour and saved-up services of land.

This shift is, however, mainly verbal. Mathematically, Wicksell uses the same kind of capital equations throughout, from 'Kapitalzins und Arbeitslohn' (1892) to 'Real Capital and Interest' (1923). Capital is usually isolated on the left-hand side, and wages (and sometimes rent) are the central variables on the right-hand side. Differentiating the system of equations, he ultimately considers capital as an exogenously determined magnitude (i.e. equivalent to a given wage fund), with respect to which the differentiation is performed.

Wicksell's verbal abandonment of the wage fund, and his inability to abandon it mathematically, could be seen as a not wholly successful attempt to modernize the concept of capital. While he was only partially successful in relation to the concept of capital, he did well in other respects: around the turn of the century, he replaced simple interest by compound interest in his main calculations. In his famous wine example in the second edition of *Lectures* (1911), he replaced flow input-point output with point input-point output. This made it possible to get rid of the problems connected with the cumbersome concept of average period of investment, since the average period of investment now collapsed into the period of production. It also contributed to making the presentation simpler and clearer.

The changes were evidently a result of Wicksell's own 'learning by doing'. There is hardly any indication that he had been inspired by other, new economists. His main sources of inspiration throughout are Böhm-Bawerk, and, to a lesser extent, Jevons and Walras.

If any general hypothesis can be generated from this, it is: the longer a scholar works on a specific problem, the simpler and clearer his approach will become.

Background
As a capital theorist, Wicksell is usually classified among the Austrian school, whose capital theory was founded mainly by Böhm-Bawerk. When Wicksell in his first book *Value, Capital and Rent* (1893) begins the section called 'The New Theory of Capital', he does not conceal his principal source of inspiration: 'Throughout this chapter I shall use as fundamental the excellent works of Böhm-Bawerk, especially his *Positive Theorie des Kapitals*, which, I may be allowed to assume, is known to most readers' (Wicksell, 1893, p. 97).

Even though Wicksell's capital theory was influenced by Böhm-Bawerk's, Wicksell was more than simply an interpreter. He was influenced by other authors as well. Thus, it is usual to regard Wicksell's capital theory as a combination of Böhm-Bawerks' capital theory and Walras's general equilibrium system; Jevons's significance is also often mentioned (cf. Lutz, 1967, p. 30; Hayek, 1941, pp. 43–4; Uhr, 1985). In some regards, for instance concerning the concept of capital in his early works, Wicksell reminds one more of Jevons than of Böhm-Bawerk.

But he had his own ideas as well, and in several respects he was critical of his precursors. The fact that his approach to capital is successively modified, is one sign of his emancipation from his forerunners.

Wicksell's discussions of the concept of capital can be found in at least three places in his texts. First, in the sections which are explicitly devoted to the concept of capital. For Wicksell's generation, a detailed discussion of concepts was natural;[1] economic theory was at an early stage of development, and Wicksell and his contemporaries had no mature theory with fixed concepts and terms to adopt as their own.

A second discussion of the concept of capital is found in Wicksell's verbal discussion in his analytical sections. The third discussion is implicit in the definitions used in his mathematical models.

As Brisman (1912b) points out in a polemic against Wicksell, a complicating fact is that Wicksell, like other authors, uses the word capital 'to denote at least four different economic phenomena' even in a single book such as the

Lectures. Nevertheless, there are main uses and secondary uses, and here we are primarily interested in the evolution of Wicksell's main concept of capital.

Early 1890s

In *Value, Capital and Rent*, about ten pages are devoted exclusively to the concept of capital (Wicksell, 1893, pp. 97–106), and, in addition, comments on concepts and terms are dispersed throughout the book. Wicksell points out that originally, capital denoted the principal of a loan, but that it later on took on a wider meaning, and is now almost equivalent in meaning to fortune (Wicksell, 1893, p. 98). However, for scientific purposes, a more precise delimitation is required. Wicksell discards the distinction between private and social capital that was drawn by Smith and Böhm-Bawerk, and distinguishes between capital in a wider sense and capital in a narrower sense.

Capital in the *wider* sense comprises all interest-bearing material goods. Goods that are highly durable, are then termed rent-goods, 'whether they are products themselves, or, like virgin soil, goods furnished by nature itself' (Wicksell, 1893, p. 105).[2]

The rest, i.e., consumption goods and intermediate goods that have short durability, is capital in the *narrower* sense, provided they are in the hands of the capitalists. This non-durable, or little durable capital remains a concern of Wicksell's mathematical models until in 1923 he tackles Åkermans dissertation.

What about the subsistence fund, or wage fund, or wage and rent fund? In *Value, Capital and Rent*, Wicksell more or less takes for granted that the reader is acquainted with the old conception of wages (and rents) as advanced subsistence goods. Thus, 'free capital, by its very nature, consists of a sum of means of subsistence, i.e. consumption goods which are advanced to the workers and the owners of the forces of nature by the capitalists during production; that is to say, they are exchanged for labour and services of land' (Wicksell, 1893, p. 115; cf. p. 36).

The means of subsistence may be interpreted as means of production in a certain sense – capital from a subsistence fund which the capitalists can invest in the workers and the land-owners in order subsequently to obtain a completed product; how much later depends on the length of the period of production.

Wicksell seldom uses the word fund in *Value, Capital and Rent*. He speaks about subsistence means that are advanced rather than about a subsistence fund. When the word 'fund' is found, Wicksell is usually commenting on older authors. He probably uses the word sparingly because he wants to indicate something new, Böhm-Bawerks 'New Theory of Capital', which among other things implies a different capital equation than the old wage fund theory.

As several authors have observed (e.g. Lutz, 1967, pp. 31, 35–6; Ferguson, 1972; Blaug, 1985, p. 559) Wicksell is, nevertheless, bound to a type of given fund in his formal models on capital theory. In 1895 he seems to become more willing to use the word 'fund' in his own reasoning concerning the same model as that in *Value, Capital and Rent*. However, the fund is of a special kind, because all of the means of subsistence which compose the fund are not available at the same point of time.

This has already been observed in 'Kapitalzins und Arbeitslohn' (1892), where he says that the productive capital is 'in nature a sum of subsistence means, but those subsistence means are not at any given moment available. Only afterwards when one surveys the whole period of production, a certain capital has gradually entered in the form of wages or means of subsistence. Its value will not be replaced until the end of the period of production, by the selling of the finished products' (Wicksell, 1892, p. 867).

Mid 1890s
On May 29th 1895, Knut Wicksell defended his doctoral thesis *Zur Lehre von der Steuerincidenz* in Uppsala. It was a short thesis of only 75 pages, which was subsequently included as the first part of *Finanztheoretische Untersuchungen nebst Darstellung und Kritik des Steuerwesens Schwedens* (1896). His reasoning on capital theory in *Finanztheoretische Untersuchungen* is mainly carried out in the section which constituted his thesis. Here he puts forward essentially the same view on capital as before. Nevertheless, let us point to a few details.

An assumption which had earlier been implicitly included, at least in the mathematical analysis, is now formulated in the following way: '... it is assumed that the whole social capital, from an economic point of view, consists of a single homogeneous mass, from which any piece may be used in any of a wide range of productive purposes' (Wicksell, 1896, p. 21). Here Wicksell shows a view of capital which is similar to that which is found in Knight's (1944) Crusonia plant, Samuelson's (1962) 'jelly', and Phelps' (1963) and others' 'putty'.

Second, Wicksell now seems to be more inclined to use the word 'fund' in his own analysis. For instance, he talks about 'the annual wage fund' and 'the true meaning of the much discussed wage fund theory' ('den wahren Inhalt der vielbesprochenen Lohnfondstheorie') (Wicksell, 1896, p. 34) in relation to equations which he uses himself.

A third difference, compared with *Value, Capital and Rent*, is that he now provides a more thorough, critical examination of the old wage fund theory. This may be considered surprising, as the book actually is about taxes. It is difficult to find reasons for including a discussion of the wage fund in this context other than that by this time he had pondered further on the question.

According to Wicksell, the real problem with the old wage fund theory is that the wage fund represents in reality only a part of the entire productive capital. Besides, its share is undetermined. (It is true that he had already mentioned those things in passing in *Value, Capital and Rent*.) This is an interesting observation, because it is in contradiction to his mathematical models.

Usually, the wage fund can be identified 'with the "circulating" part of capital, in contrast to the "more or less fixed part" – both, by the way, not well defined concepts' (Wicksell, 1896, p. 25). We know that Wicksell would classify highly durable goods such as buildings and roads as land rather than as capital. He included tools and machines in the concept of capital, as they must be replaced from time to time (Wicksell, 1896, p. 28–9).

Thus, the concept of capital in Wicksell's theses and *Finanztheoretische Untersuchungen* includes, as in *Value, Capital and Rent*, finished consumption goods, raw materials, tools and machines. In the verbal discussion, but not in the formal analysis, he draws a distinction between tools and machines on the one hand and 'true' circulating capital on the other. Now, he does not hesitate to use the word 'fund' in connection with this capital.

Late 1890s

In *Interest and Prices* (1898), which is essentially a book on macroeconomic theory, it is possible to discern a stronger emphasis than before on viewing capital as saved-up labour (and land) services.

Wicksell emphasizes that it is possible to reconcile Jevons's concentration on the means of subsistence and Böhm-Bawerk's conception of capital as saved-up labour and land services. In a stationary state, the consumption goods (except the goods which are consumed in the form of interest by the capitalists) which are produced during a certain period of time may be regarded as capital in its *free* form, or, as a fund for the payment of wages and rents. (Thus, in this case the fund seems to be a flow rather than a stock.) This fund – Jevons's capital – represents the demand for labour and land services, and is paid to the workers and the land-owners. Next, an equivalent amount manifests itself in the output of labour and land, and is added to the *invested* capital of the country. This Böhm-Bawerkian capital takes different forms in the process of production: tools, machines, raw material, intermediate goods. Finally, finished consumption goods are obtained, which means that the capital once again appears in its free form, i.e. Jevons's form.[3]

The main part of the capital in the economy, 'indeed all of it, if we adopt a more accurate or more ideal point of view', appears, at a certain point of time, as *invested* capital at different distances from the beginning and the end of the process of production. 'But if a "lengthwise section" were taken, it would', instead, 'be seen that each individual piece of capital travels, slowly or rapidly as the case may be, around a circular path, and that both at the beginning and at the end it takes the form of free capital, that is to say, of consumption goods' (Wicksell, 1898, p. 126).

Thus, the essence of capital becomes almost a phantom which changes its guise time after time during its walk along the roundabout path of production. In this sense, capital is continually changing even in a stationary state. This becomes more evident in *Interest and Prices* than before. This view also appears in later works. For instance, in an obituary on Böhm-Bawerk in the *Ekonomisk Tidskrift* in 1914, Wicksell talks about the 'more or less viscous part of the capital's general stream'. Moreover, concerning monetary capital, 'every öre of this capital must *pass* [italics added] through the stage of labour and wages; otherwise, it could not be invested anew' (Wicksell, 1914, p. 325).

Turn of the century: a posthumous manuscript
Knut Wicksell left about a hundred unpublished manuscripts. Most of them were intended for the debate in the daily press, lecture notes, etc. But there is at least one advanced manuscript that contains a theoretical model on capital. It has recently been published with a comment by Hedlund-Nyström, Jonung and Sandelin (1987). A translation is found in the Appendix to Hedlund-Nyström, Jonung, Löfgren and Sandelin (1993).

The manuscript is unfinished and undated. Its content indicates that it is written after *Interest and Prices* (1898), but before an article 'On the problem of distribution' in the *Ekonomisk Tidskrift* 1902; the arguments are given in the above-mentioned comment.

Nothing is said in the manuscript about means of subsistence, nor about a wage and rent fund. Such words are missing completely. Instead, Wicksell uses expressions like: '*K* represents the national wealth, or its productive part, less the actual value of land, etc'. We should also note that Wicksell now consistently uses compound interest rather than simple interest.

1901: First edition of *Lectures*
In 1901 the first Swedish edition of the first volume of *Lectures on Political Economy* appeared. The two volumes of this book are certainly the best known of Wicksell's books among general economists. Five Swedish editions have appeared, of which the third (1928) has been translated into English and is the last one which contains any changes in the main text.

A characteristic feature of *Lectures* is how strongly the conception of capital as the materialization of 'previously-done' labour and services of land is maintained. It is repeated, over and over again, that capital is 'saved-up labour and saved-up land'. Consequently, different capital goods have the same kind of origin: 'All capital-goods, however different they may appear, can always be ultimately resolved into labour and land' (Wicksell, 1928, p. 149 (E), 176 (S)).[4]

In comparison with the discussion in Wicksell's early writings, the emphasis now seems to have moved ahead. Capital in the form of intermediate goods at different stages of the process of production are the focus of attention. Although Wicksell mentions that 'provisions and other commodities' for the support of labour should be included in capital, they play an unimportant role in the actual analysis, i.e. in his presentation of his modified variant of Böhm-Bawerk's theory of capital (p. 147–66 (E), 174–92 (S)). However, they are mentioned, together with other questions, in a subsequent section on 'controversies concerning the theory of capital' (p. 185–195 (E), 192–202 (S)).

1911: Second edition of *Lectures*

The most interesting novelty in the second edition of *Lectures* (1911) is a new section called 'Alternative treatment of the problems of interest and distribution'. The wine storing problem which is presented and solved there, is undoubtedly the best known feature of Wicksell's writings in capital theory.

The starting-point is a society that only produces wine.[5] After harvesting, society's labour produces grape juice which is stored for a number of years, and matures into wine fit for consumption. During this period of storage, no labour input is required. Other commodities are provided by trade with other countries. Thus, 'the whole of the circulating capital of that society will consist of stored wine, though it can at any time be wholly or partially converted into money' (Wicksell, 1911a, p. 173 (E), 178 (S)).

Capital appears in the model simply as goods in the process of production on their way to finished consumption goods. In the new section, there is no talk about the means of subsistence or a wage and rent fund. Wicksell seems to have left those older concepts completely.

This is evidently a deliberate step, which can be explained in the light of his article 'Böhm-Bawerk's Theory of Capital' in the *Ekonomisk Tidskrift* 1911. There he praises:

> the brilliant suggestion that the capitalistic process of production – 'the adoption of wisely chosen roundabout methods of production' – should be regarded as the *primary* concept, and capital itself as the *secondary*: 'essentially the intermediary products brought into existence at particular stages of the time-consuming roundabout process of production' (Wicksell, 1911b).

This, he says, renders superfluous all further discussion on the limits and extent of the concept of capital. However, Böhm-Bawerk had not been fully consistent, 'for in his account of the basis of the quantitative determination of the rate of interest on capital, he reverts, probably for didactic reasons, to the earlier Jevonian conception that national capital is a "Subsistence fund", an aggregate of (potential) wages, so that capital once more becomes the primary concept and the capitalistic process of production to some extent a secondary, derived concept'. (Wicksell, 1911b, p. 178–9 (E), 42 (S)).

Then, in a footnote he makes the following interesting statement: 'I have endeavoured to develop Böhm-Bawerk's original idea more directly in my published lectures, especially in the new edition of them which I hope will appear shortly.' In the second edition we actually find the lines quoted above, almost word for word (Wicksell, 1911a, p. 168 (E), 173–4 (S)). It is quite evident that Wicksell tried to move away from the old wage fund theory.

However, there are other signs which indicate that he was still influenced by the older outlook. As in the wage fund theory, capital is treated as a magnitude whose size is given. In the wine example, we read something that may seem contradictory to the idea that the stock of maturing wine constitutes the capital, and this makes us wonder about the *real* essence of capital. The grape juice from each year's harvest is stored for a number of years: 'How *long* it will be stored depends, as we shall soon see, exclusively upon the amount of the existing capital, which, on our assumption of a closed economy, can neither be increased by additions from outside nor diminished by export' (Wicksell, 1911a, p. 173 (E), 178 (S)). Here 'capital' evidently denotes something other than the stock of maturing wine, something of a given total amount.

The second edition of *Lectures* was the last published during Wicksell's life. The third edition, edited by his successor to the chair at Lund, Emil Sommarin, and published in 1928, two years after Wicksell's death, had a number of minor changes and additions which had been prepared by Wicksell himself. However, the revision did not alter Wicksell's concept of capital.

Debate with Brisman, 1912

When the second edition of *Lectures* had been published, *docent* Sven Brisman published three articles in *Ekonomisk Tidskrift* 1912. The second was directed towards Wicksell's treatment of the concept of capital and the rate of interest. Wicksell gave a reply which was followed by a third contribution from Brisman.

Brisman does not like the word capital to denote intermediate products, and he criticizes Wicksell for giving '6 or 7, partly inconsistent definitions of the concept of capital'. Furthermore, Wicksell used the word capital 'to denote at least four different economic phenomena' (Brisman, 1912b, p. 158).

Wicksell agrees that he uses the word capital in different senses. In some cases, he does so 'deliberately, and this should seldom cause any misunderstanding' (Wicksell, 1912, p. 312). Sometimes a distinction would be impractical; in other cases the concepts of capital coincide. However, Wicksell concludes that it is very important to distinguish between real capital and money, although he realizes that many economists 'have not been able to maintain this distinction' (Wicksell, 1912, p. 311). One could add that Wicksell himself is not always clear on this point.

On a few points, the discussion makes Wicksell's concept of capital clearer. Brisman is critical of Wicksell's principal definition, according to which 'capital is saved-up labour and saved-up services of land'. Instead, Brisman says, 'capital goods are *products* of, among other things, saving (saved-up labour and saved-up services of land)' (Brisman, 1912b, p. 164).

Wicksell replies that Brisman's proposal hardly means an improvement. A house may be the product of two years' labour, 'but many decades shall pass before this labour can be regarded as completely consumed or used up, and in *this* sense it remains saved' (Wicksell, 1912, p. 315).

How comestibles should be considered, was, as we have noticed before, an issue among Wicksell's contemporaries, and it turns up in the debate between Wicksell and Brisman, too. Both seem to agree that comestibles should be regarded as capital as long as they belong to the producers or the dealers. 'However', Wicksell says,

> if they have passed into the hands of the consumers, their remaining visible existence – at least concerning the consumption of the urban population – is usually limited to a few hours, when eating at a restaurant only a few minutes; and if they are, or are not, still reckoned as capital during this short period of time is completely unimportant.

Furthermore:

> Therefore, I have always been of the opinion that the question whether especially the workers' subsistence goods should be included in capital or not is fundamentally simply a dispute about mere words and should be removed from the agenda (Wicksell, 1912, p. 313).

The last sentence is hardly in agreement with the idea that one gets reading his early works, especially *Value, Capital and Rent*. Considerable space is devoted there to a discussion of how the subsistence goods of workers should be treated. The discussion in *Value, Capital and Rent* commences: 'But more important is the question of what is to be done with the "means of subsistence of workers"' (Wicksell, 1893, p. 101).

1920s: Durable capital

Wicksell's (1923) review of Gustav Åkerman's doctoral thesis *Realkapital und Kapitalzins* (1923) is particularly interesting.[6] The mathematical addendum to this review has, no doubt, been given greater attention then the thesis.

Like Böhm-Bawerk and Jevons, Wicksell had earlier concentrated on circulating capital. Walras, his third source of inspiration, had dealt with durable capital, but Wicksell had already criticized him in 'Kapitalzins und Arbeitslohn' (1892), and in subsequent works, for not having treated durability as a variable.

With a few limited exceptions, Wicksell had not dealt with durable capital in his *formal* models before his review of Åkermans thesis.[7] In his *verbal* discussions on the concept of capital, he had briefly touched upon it. However, he had hardly said more than that very durable capital goods should be reckoned as land.

In his review of Åkerman's thesis, he points to what he considered to be the greatest problem when analysing the role of durable capital: 'We cannot, at least without further analysis, apply the celebrated principle that capital is or corresponds to a certain amount of "previously-done labour", i.e. the accumulated saved-up, or invested, resources of labour (or land)' (Wicksell, 1923, p. 260). A new machine no doubt represents a certain amount of such labour, says Wicksell, but if it has been used for a number of years, so that only a part of the originally invested amount of labour remains, it is quite impossible to determine how much of the original labour that is still 'stored-up' in the machine. To determine how much of the original labour that is invested in a certain 'annual use' – which would be necessary in order to determine how much is left – is just as absurd 'as to try to find out what part of a pasture goes into wool and what part into mutton' (Wicksell, 1923, p. 260).

We may agree with Wicksell on this point. However, the problem that he raises is important only for the possibility of making an exact mathematical analysis of the role of capital. It is of little or no consequence for the concept of capital itself; it is still possible to imagine capital as 'saved-up' labour, even if one cannot determine how much of the originally invested labour is still left.

Although Wicksell did not thoroughly set about the theory of durable capital until he reviewed Åkerman's thesis, he obviously considered this a very important area – more important than the theory of circulating capital which is consumed immediately after having reached maturity. In the article 'Zur Zinstheorie' (1928), he declares that Böhm-Bawerk's 'simplest hypothesis' (about circulating capital) is abstract and often difficult to regard even as a first approximation of reality. The typical pattern of production is instead characterized by durable capital co-operating with labour and land.

It is evident that Wicksell's postponement of the analysis of durable capital was due to the inherent difficulties of the question. He used comparative statics in his mathematical analysis of Åkerman's problem, but thought that he would need a dynamic approach to explain the intricate phenomenon of the so-called Wicksell effect. In 'Zur Zinstheorie', too, he indicates that the analysis of durable capital would need a dynamic approach (Wicksell, 1928, p. 209). However, that was a step that he left to subsequent generations.

Conclusion: The same concept of capital?

We have now scrutinized what Wicksell wrote on the concept of capital. His verbal discussions preceeding his mathematical analyses have been our main source. He presents a concept of capital that remains largely, but not completely, unaltered. There is a clear shift in emphasis, from the subsistence means of the workers, to labour and services of land saved-up in goods in process.

In *Value, Capital and Rent* (1893) nothing is said about saved-up labour and services of land. There, the great problem seems to be to separate capital from land, and to treat the subsistence means of the workers in an appropriate way. If anything shall be considered the main definition of capital, it is the following: 'Consumable or quickly exhausted production or consumption goods, so long as the latter are not yet in the hands of consumers, I shall call capital-goods or capital in the narrower sense' (Wicksell, 1893, p. 105).

In *Lectures* (1901) there are several statements that may be interpreted as definitions, as Brisman says. 'Capital is saved-up labour and saved-up land' (Wicksell, 1901, p. 154 (E), 180 (S), Brisman considers the main definition, and this is evidently in accordance with Wicksell's intention, because on the previous line Wicksell says: "We thus arrive at the following simple definition'.[8] The definition is in line with the substantial space that Wicksell devotes in *Lectures* to setting out the idea that labour and services of land are, so to say, stored up in real capital.

In Wicksell's presentation of his formal models, too, a shift is noticed over time. In the central mathematical model in *Value, Capital and Rent* (1893), capital explicitly consists of 'the cost of maintaining the workers' (Wicksell, 1893, p. 121). In his later writings, this aspect is suppressed in the verbal comments on the models.[9]

Our statement that Wicksell modified his concept of capital, and tried to leave the wage fund theory, is consistent with the statement that he makes in a footnote to 'Zur Zinsteorie': 'In my printed *Lectures*, ... I have tried to follow the original idea of Böhm-Bawerk to regard capital as intermediate goods (saved-up labour), more closely than he does himself' (Wicksell, 1928, p. 208).

However, in his mathematical models, Wicksell is in reality hardly successful in avoiding the subsistence or wage fund approach. Throughout his career, he treats the amount of capital as an exogenously determined magnitude, i.e. like a given subsistence fund. His capital equation contains on the right-hand side, wages (and sometimes rents). Although he had verbally left the subsistence fund, the capital equation in his later works are modified only to the extent that is required by the assumption of compound interest instead of simple interest, and of point input instead of flow input.[10]

When Wicksell in the second edition of *Lectures* (1911) inserts a section in which he claims that 'Böhm-Bawerk was not entirely consistent, since in his account of the quantitative factors determining interest he reverts ... to the earlier Jevonian conception of capital as a *subsistence fund*, a sum of (potential) wages' (Wicksell, 1911a, p. 168 (E), 174 (S)), one is tempted to make the remark that one could charge Wicksell's mathematical models with a similar criticism for implicitly including the wage fund idea.

In sum, Wicksell's view on capital became more 'modern' as time went on. One indication of this is that he ceased talking about a wage or subsistence fund. However, his ambition was larger than his technical capability; in his mathematical models, capital remained an exogenously determined magnitude.

Another indication of the modernization is that in 1923, he introduced durable capital in a mathematical model. Other elements of the same kind, mentioned only in passing in this chapter, are his replacement of simple interest by compound interest around the turn of the century, and in the famous wine example in the second edition of *Lectures* (1911), his replacement of flow input by point input, which made it possible to dispose of the unwieldy concept of average period of investment.

Wicksell evidently learnt from his own work and gradually modified his approach to obtain greater clarity. There are hardly any indications that new authorities were behind this evolution.

Notes

1. For instance, Böhm-Bawerk uses 102 pages in *Positive Theorie des Kapitales* for the 'Begriff und Wesen des Kapitales'.
2. The reason that these goods are treated as land is that after some time, their cost of production does not influence the income generated in the form of, e.g., housing rent or freight charge; nor does remote income significantly influence the present capital value or yield (Wicksell, 1893, p. 118–19).
3. It seems that Wicksell tends to overstate the difference between Böhm-Bawerk and Jevons on this point, and that the difference is mainly verbal. Jevons says, 'I would not say that a railway *is fixed capital* but that *capital is fixed* in the railway. The capital is not the railway, but the food of those who made the railway' (Jevons, 1879, p. 239). This way of conceiving the process of capitalistic production is clearly common to Jevons, Böhm-Bawerk and Wicksell, although Jevons defined the concept of capital in a narrower manner than the other two usually did.
4. The reference means: p. 149 in the English edition (which builds upon the 3rd Swedish edition), p. 176 in the 1st Swedish edition. In references without (E) and (S), the page

number relates to the English translation, if such a translation is mentioned in the list of references at the end of this chapter.

5. One may ask why Wicksell chose 'the laying down of wine' or 'the planting of trees on barren land' (p. 172 (E), 176 (S)) as illustrative examples. Probably he got the idea from Jevons who used the same examples (Jevons, 1879, p. 236).
6. The review is translated and included as Appendix 2 in the English edition of the first volume of *Lectures*.
7. One exception is a section in *Finanztheoretische Untersuchungen* (Wicksell, 1896, p. 29–30) where he tried to determine the average period of investment in a point input–flow output model for a durable good. However, he made a fatal algebraic approximation which made him erroneously conclude that the average period of investment was longer than the average space of time between the point of investment and the different points of income generated by that investment (see Sandelin, 1990.) The fact that he was at that time acquainted only with models of circulating capital may explain the lack of intuitive reaction to this conclusion. A second exception where Wicksell mathematically deals with durable capital is found in a section in his, until recently (1987), unpublished manuscript.
8. In the second and the following editions 'simple' was deleted.
9. It is interesting to note that Wicksell himself found a shift in Böhm-Bawerk's *Positive Theory of Capital*, but in the opposite direction. At the beginning, Wicksell found a conception of capital as intermediate goods or saved-up labour; at the end of the book he found that Böhm-Bawerk returned to the older idea of capital as a subsistence fund. In 'Zur Zinstheorie' Wicksell says that he had asked Böhm-Bawerk about the reason for this discrepancy when they met once in Vienna in 1911. (The episode is also mentioned in a footnote in Wicksell [1914].) Böhm-Bawerk's answer may be surprising. The reason, he said, was that he had been in such a great hurry to get the book published, that the first half of it was at the printers before the manuscript of the second half was finished. One has to agree with Wicksell that 'bei einer solchen Arbeitsweise ist es wohl unvermeidlich, dass sich Diskrepanzen und Wiedersprüche grösserer oder geringerer Bedeutung gegen den Willen des Autors hier und da einschleichen.'
10. Thus, if we denote capital by K, the number of workers by L, the wage rate by w, and the period of production by T, two representative examples of his capital equations are:

$$K = \frac{LwT}{2} \tag{6.1}$$

and

$$K = w\int_0^T e^{rx}dx. \tag{6.2}$$

Equation (6.1) is from *Value, Capital and Rent*, and belongs to a flow input - point output model with simple interest. Equation (6.2) belongs to the wine model in *Lectures*, a point input – point output model with compound interest.

References

Blaug, Mark (1985), *Economic Theory in Retrospect*, 4th edn, Cambridge: Cambridge University Press.

von Böhm-Bawerk, Eugen (1921), *Positive Theorie des Kapitales*, 4th edn, Jena: Verlag von Gustav Fischer.

Brisman, Sven (1912a), 'Kapitalet och kapitalräntan', *Ekonomisk Tidskrift*, **14**, pp. 89–121

Brisman, Sven (1912b), 'Prof. Wicksells framställning af kapitalet och kapitalräntan', *Ekonomisk Tidskrift*, **14**, pp. 157–70.

Brisman, Sven (1912c), 'Ännu några ord om kapitalet och kapitalräntan', *Ekonomisk Tidskrift*, **14**, pp. 399–416.

Ferguson, Charles E. (1972), 'The Current State of Capital Theory', *Southern Economic Journal*, **39**, pp. 160–76.
Hedlund-Nyström, T., Jonung, L. and Sandelin, B. (1987), 'Opublicerat manuskript av Knut Wicksell med en kapitalteoretisk modell', *Ekonomiska Samfundets Tidskrift*, **40**, pp. 123–26, correction on p. 221.
Hedlund-Nyström, T., Jonung, L., Löfgren, K-G. and Sandelin, B. (1993), 'Knut Wicksell on Forestry: a Note', in Jonung, L. (ed.), *Swedish Economic Thought. Explorations and Advances*, London: Routledge.
Hayek, Friedrich A. (1941), *The Pure Theory of Capital*, 3rd impression 1952, London: Routlege & Kegan Paul.
Jevons, W. Stanley (1871, 1879), *The Theory of Political Economy*, Pelican Classics, 1970.
Knight, Frank H. (1944), 'Diminishing Returns from Investment', *Journal of Political Economy*, **52**, pp. 26–47.
Lutz, Friedrich A. (1967), *Zinstheorie*, 2nd edn, Zürich: Polygraphischer Verlag; Tübingen: J.C.B. Mohr (Paul Siebeck).
Phelps, Edmund S. (1963), 'Substitution, Fixed Proportions, Growth and Distribution', *International Economic Review*, **4**, pp. 265–88.
Samuelson, Paul A. (1962), 'Parable and Realism in Capital Theory: The Surrogate Production Function', *Review of Economic Studies*, **39**, pp. 193–206.
Sandelin, Bo (1990), 'The Danger of Approximation: Wicksell's Mistake on the Average Period of Investment', *History of Political Economy*, **22**, pp. 551–55.
Uhr, Carl G. (1985), 'Wicksell and the Austrians', *Research in the History of Economic Thought and Methodology*, **3**, pp. 199–224.
Wicksell, Knut (1892), 'Kapitalzins und Arbeitslohn', *Jahrbücher für Nationalökonomie und Statistik*, **59**, pp. 852–874.
Wicksell, Knut (1893), *Über Wert, Kapital und Rente nach den neueren Nationalökonomischen Theorien*, Jena: Verlag von Gustav Fischer. Translated 1954 as *Value, Capital and Rent*, London: George Allen & Unwin.
Wicksell, Knut (1895), *Zur Lehre von der Steuerincidenz*, Upsala.
Wicksell, Knut (1896), *Finanztheoretische Untersuchungen nebst Darstellung und Kritik des Steuerwesens Schwedens*, Jena: Verlag von Gustav Fischer.
Wicksell, Knut (1898), *Geldzins und Güterpreise. Eine Studie über die den Tauschwert des Geldes bestimmenden Ursachen*, Jena: Verlag von Gustav Fischer. Translated 1936 as *Interest and Prices. A study of the Causes Regulating the Value of Money*, London: The Royal Economic Society.
Wicksell, Knut (1901, 1911a, 1928), *Föreläsningar i nationalekonomi*, del 1, Lund: Gleerup. Third edition translated 1934 as *Lectures on Political Economy*, vol. 1, London: George Routledge & Sons.
Wicksell, Knut (1902), 'Till fördelningsproblemet', *Ekonomisk Tidskrift*, **4**, pp. 424–33. Translated as 'On the Problem of Distribution' in Wicksell, Knut (1958), *Selected Papers on Economic Theory*, London: George Allen & Unwin.
Wicksell, Knut (1911b), 'Böhm-Bawerks kapitalteori och kritiken däraf', *Ekonomisk Tidskrift*, **13**, pp. 39–49. Translated as 'Böhm-Bawerk's Theory of Capital' in Wicksell, Knut (1958), *Selected Papers on Economic Theory*, London: George Allen & Unwin.
Wicksell, Knut (1912), 'Kapital – und kein Ende! (Svar till doc. Brisman)', *Ekonomisk Tidskrift*, **14**, p. 309–22.
Wicksell, Knut (1914), 'Lexis och Böhm-Bawerk', I–II, *Ekonomisk Tidskrift*, **16**, pp. 294–300, 322–34.
Wicksell, Knut (1923), 'Realkapital och kapitalränta', *Ekonomisk Tidskrift*, **25**, pp. 145–180. Translated as 'Real Capital and Interest', Appx. 2, in Wicksell, Knut (1934), *Lectures on Political Economy*, vol. 1, London: George Routledge & Sons.
Wicksell, Knut (1928), 'Zur Zinstheorie (Böhm-Bawerks Dritter Grund), *Die Wirtschaftstheorie der Gegenwart*, Hrsg. von Hans Mayer in Verbindung mit Frank A. Fetter und Richard Reisch, vol. 3, Vienna.
Wicksell, Knut (1987), 'Ett opublicerat manuskript av Knut Wicksell', *Ekonomiska Samfundets Tidskrift*, **40**, pp. 127–36, corrections on p. 221.

PART III

ECONOMICS
BETWEEN THE WARS

7. From Marxism towards neoclassicism: on the decline of Dutch Marxist political economy in the inter-war period[1]

Frank Kalshoven

Introduction

From a Marxist point of view this is a sad story because it deals with the decline of Marxism in the Netherlands during the inter-war years. The unhappy ending is particularly dramatic because of the promising developments in the preceding period when Dutch Marxism flourished, notably in the theoretical journal *De Nieuwe Tijd* (I. 1896 – XXV. 1921). The promise these developments entailed for the next period was not kept. From a more general historical point of view the developments in the Netherlands are simply intriguing because Marxists tried to integrate what they called 'subjectivist' and 'objectivist' theories of value. The link between the two was provided by Bolzmann's explanation of entropy through statistical mechanics. Among other things this implied the introduction of mathematical economics at the expense of literary economics, denigratingly referred to as 'economic prattle' (*praateconomie*) from the 1920s onwards. But even from the more general point of view some sadness remains. The developments in the inter-war years meant a sharp break with the past. The good things of 'economic prattle', particularly the writings of J. Saks, were thrown away with the trash.

In this chapter I will discuss a series of methodological articles from the hand of Jacob van der Wijk (1921) in which he discussed statistical mechanics and argued for the application of its methods to economics. In the 1920s and 1930s both he and his lifelong friend Sam de Wolff tried to apply this methodology to different economic subjects, such as income distribution and population. I will then discuss one of the applications: De Wolff's (1925) attempt to derive Marx's 'law of value' – exchange at labour-values – from utility-maximizing behaviour of individuals in a society in which individuals confront each other as the producers of different commodities. I will argue that his results hinge on a number of stringent assumptions. Relaxing these turns his analysis into a standard neoclassical one. While looking for a deeper *Begründung* of Marxism, he found that Marxist economics was a special case of neoclassical economics (even if De Wolff himself was not aware of this).[2]

Marxism hardly existed in the Netherlands in the nineteenth century. Compared with other European countries, the Dutch were late with regard to both political and theoretical developments. The SDAP, the Social Democratic Labour Party, was founded as late as 1894; *De Nieuwe Tijd* (The New Era), the theoretical journal, was founded in 1896. Frank van der Goes is generally regarded as the spiritual father of the SDAP and the most important theorist of the 1890s. His theoretical work in this period (of which his 1894 work is the most important) is a blend of Marxism and social Darwinism. Van der Goes's lack of insight in Marxist economics comes to the fore in a discussion about value with J. Saks in *De Kroniek* (1899–1900). The young Saks, who would become one of the most important theorists of the 1900–1916 period, makes it painfully clear that Van der Goes, who had just been appointed as *privaat docent* (university teacher) at the University of Amsterdam, does not understand Marxist economics. In the course of the discussion Van der Goes has to admit that 'To whom it may concern I gladly declare that until a few months ago I had not cut, let alone read Marx II and III (*De Kroniek*, 7 January 1900).[3]

A massive Marx-critique by M.W.F. Treub (1902–3) stimulated the development of Marxism in the Netherlands. Treub's critique covers Marxist theory (almost) completely: philosophical foundations, historical materialism, the theory of value, crises, and the derived laws of motion of capitalist society. The editors of *De Nieuwe Tijd* counter-attacked Treub collectively. They all chose a subject and asked others to contribute articles on their specializations. This collective action resulted in a number of careful expositions on different subjects. The tenor of the anti-critiques was twofold: first, Treub misrepresents Marxism, and second his criticism is merely an overview of the well-known international literature. The second point is not entirely correct, and the first tells us more about Dutch Marxism than about Treub. Elsewhere (1993), I argue that Dutch Marxism developed distinct positions in at least three important theoretical fields: philosophy (especially the work of Pannekoek, the astronomer), the theory of value (Saks's contributions), and business cycle theory (Saks, Van Gelderen on the long wave, and especially De Wolff). If therefore Treub's criticism is not applicable to Dutch Marxism, this is not a criticism of Treub but a tribute to Dutch Marxists.

These distinct positions would not be developed any further after the War. World War I and the Russian Revolution led to confusion, discussion and conflict among Marxists and socialists as in other European countries. In the Netherlands, where the political organization had already broken up in 1909, the differences of opinion with respect to these international events further splintered the 'left'. In the pre-war years the left (the Social Democratic Party) had been the base for most theorists. Furthermore, many important theorists of the pre-war period redirected their attention to other fields. Finally, the SDAP founded a new theoretical journal, *De Socialistische Gids*

(The Socialist Guide) in 1916. After the party split in 1909 the SDAP had no theoretical journal of its own. The editors of the new journal opposed the views of the prewar theorists.

During the inter-war years a new generation of theorists came to the fore. They considered themselves to be *socialists* (defending their socialism, if at all, on ethical grounds) but not Marxist economists. Instead they tried to use 'modern economic analysis' to defend their socialist views. As Tinbergen put it in his 1928 article on the contract curve of the Edgeworth box:

> I want to show first and foremost that (and how) views which have been defended by socialists, and have been attacked by liberal economists using the theory of marginal value [*grenswaardeleer*], can, instead, be *derived* from that framework. (Tinbergen, 1928, p. 431; see Boumans, 1992 on this article and Tinbergen's work before World War II in general)

On a more ideological level, Van Gelderen 'denied positively that a consistent socialist view of life and society cannot accept modern subjectivist economics' (Van Gelderen, 1930, p. 878). This new generation of theorists tried to use *neoclassical*, rather than Marxist, economics to defend their socialist political views.[4] They did not explain why they no longer used Marxist economics.

De Wolff and, to a lesser extent, Van der Wijk are the exceptions to this rule. Van der Wijk calls himself a 'Marxist with respect to the sociologico-political (*'t sociologisch-politieke*)' (Van der Wijk, 1932, p. 288), even if his economics isn't Marxist at all. De Wolff always considered himself to be a Marxist economist. In his view the neoclassical theory of individual behaviour could give Marxism a more solid foundation.

Van der Wijk on methodology
J. van der Wijk, who studied chemistry at the University of Amsterdam in the 1890s, deliberately tried to redirect economics towards social physics. He lay down his research programme in a series of philosophical articles in the *Socialistische Gids* in 1921 (cf Van der Wijk, 1932). After a series of articles in 1923 on marginalist theories of value which illustrate his methodological position, he applied his methodological viewpoint to income-distribution (Van der Wijk, 1928; 1931). In this section I will focus on his 1921 article which contains the methodology De Wolff used to give Marxism a *tiefere Begründung*.

Boumans (1992) shows the importance of Ludwig Boltzmann's statistical mechanics for the methodology of Jan Tinbergen. He discusses the developments in physics and Tinbergen's acquaintance with them in some detail. Tinbergen was not the only Dutch 'imperialist' physicist for whom Boltzmann is important. Kohnstamm, in his *Warmteleer* (the theory of heat) (1915), the founding father of Dutch pedagogy, and Van der Waals had already discussed the general philosophical implications of entropy and Boltzmann's theoretical incorporation of it in mechanics. Their interpretation of it had been fiercely attacked by the Marxist Pannekoek (1917). In fact entropy in general, and Boltzmann's theory of it in particular, were generally discussed between about 1915 and the early 1920s.[5] Van der Wijk is the first theorist to discuss in some detail the implications of these developments in physics for social theory, particularly economics.

Van der Wijk published his series of articles under the title *Wetmatigheid in Natuur en Maatschappij* (Laws in Nature and Society). It consists of three parts: a discussion of the concept of law in physics, an investigation into the question whether or not this concept can also be applied to biology (in particular to evolution), and, third, a similar discussion concerning social theory, particularly economics.

The laws of physics
Mirowski (1989, pp. 59–66) provides an account of the international developments in physics which form the background to Van der Wijk's attempt to construct a new economics. Very briefly the story runs like this. Heat was a problem for mid-nineteenth-century physics. Physical deterministic theories rested upon the assumption of reversibility of processes, whereas real world processes in many cases showed the opposite. In 1865 Clausius tried to solve this problem by constructing a quantity called entropy, a variable of state in a reversible system.

> With this formulation [of entropy], Clausius managed to found the science of thermodynamics on two laws: the first, that the energy of the universe is a constant, and the second, that the entropy of the universe increases to a maximum. (Mirowski, 1989, p. 61)

Mirowski argues that Clausius's conception of entropy was dissonant with the general framework of the energy concept within physics. Regardless of whether Mirowski is correct, of more concern to us is Bolzmann's 1872 attempt to reconcile entropy and mechanics, which Van der Wijk considered successful. Bolzmann ascribed probability functions to the different characteristics (such as speed) of particles. He showed that entropy, which is the variable of state of the *system*, could be derived from the probability distributions of the characteristics of the *particles*. An example may help to illustrate the argument. If a drop of ink falls in a glass of water the ink will eventually mix with the water. Once this state has been reached, nothing much will change. If we compare two states of this closed system (the glass) – for instance, State 1 in which the inkdrop is concentrated in the middle of the water and State 2 in which the ink is mixed with the water – the latter state is the most likely one, provided that our only information is that a number of water-molecules and a drop of ink are both in a glass. This procedure solves the problem of reversibility and irreversibility. We can now argue that the most likely direction of change will be from State 1 to State 2: it is possible also to go from a state with high entropy (State 2) to a state with a lower entropy (State 1) but such a movement is highly unlikely. Whether or not this procedure solves the problem of the direction of time is unclear. It may be argued that the problem is circumvented because we simply compare two states, regardless of time. Van der Wijk takes a different standpoint. He argues that Boltzmann's theory does introduce the concept of time in physics and that, more generally, laws in physics are always dynamic laws which describe development in time.[6] After his discussion of Boltzmann's theory of statistical mechanics Van der Wijk concludes, 'we now understand the existence of all sorts of irreversible operations, and therewith understand the continuously increasing entropy, without this being inconsistent with theoretical mechanics' (Van der Wijk, 1923, p. 552). Certain assumptions have to be made before an argument such as the one in my example can be made. Van der Wijk is well aware of this. He mentions first, everything should take place in a closed system (the glass in our example); second, the system should consist of a large number of particles (water and ink particles); third, the changes in the state of these particles should be 'coincidental'. On this latter point he observes

> This (3. above) does not mean [...] that there is no cause for these changes; on the contrary, it means that there are many causes operative, but, because these causes operate simultaneously and counteract each other's operation, they are not observable. (Van der Wijk, 1921, p. 551)

I will come back to these assumptions below in my discussion of laws in economics.

Having observed that other fields in physics are also increasingly explained in terms of probability theory (referring for instance to Planck) Van der Wijk draws his conclusion:

> *There are laws in nature which seem to bear an absolute character but in reality they are valid only in approximation.* Seemingly necessities, they are *in truth the outcome of blind chance* [*toeval*], the coincidental cooperation of an enormous quantity of incoherent units. (Van der Wijk, 1921, p. 554)

Or, stated somewhat differently, '*The laws of nature are – or most of them are – statistical laws. They are special forms of the qualitative and quantitative applications of the law of large numbers to the phenomena of nature'* (Van der Wijk, 1921, p. 554).

The laws of physics and evolution

Before discussing economics we turn first to evolution. Evolution is import-ant for Van der Wijk because the direction of development of evolution seemingly contradicts the direction of development in statistical mechanics.[7] With the latter the direction of development is from 'the differentiated to-wards the undifferentiated' (Van der Wijk, 1921, p. 716), from a concentra-tion of ink particles in the middle of a glass towards an equal distribution of ink over the water. Evolution on the other hand is a development towards specialization and differentiation.

Narrowing down his discussion still further to the evolution of mankind, Van der Wijk argues that evolution has become a group phenomenon because functioning in a group has become a precondition for individual variation (a professional violin player needs a butcher, a baker, a house etc). In other words, the group had become the relevant evolving unit. This implies, he argues (Van der Wijk, 1921, p. 723) that evolution has been transformed from a strictly biological to a social phenomenon. And this is the point at which Boltzmann comes in: '[I]f our thesis is correct [...] evolution, *that is, if it is a "coincidental" evolution*, will show the same picture as the "distributions of states" [*toestandsverdeelingen*] we investigated in our discussion of Boltzmann's theory of entropy' (Van der Wijk, 1921, p. 807). The beauty of this distribution is that 'we can expect an absolute increase, but a relatively strong decrease of the extremes, when in the course of history the number of individuals in the group increases, and a concentration around the mean, that is, the group levels' (Van der Wijk, 1921, p. 807). This means that the binomial distribution (which underlies Boltzmann's statistical mechanics) takes on the shape of a normal 'Quetelet' distribution if the number of 'trials' is increased.[8]

Van der Wijk immediately applies this general result to phenomena such as political parties, democracy, women's liberation and wages. He further ob-serves that in many areas of society people consciously level society by means of standardization (e.g. the metric system) and normalization. Hence, the direction of development of the evolution of mankind is identical to the direction of development in statistical mechanics: towards the most likely state, the state with the highest entropy.

Micro and macro and laws in economics

So far, the implications for sociology (and economics) seem limited in scope. The discussion up to this point suggests that one should be able to find normal distributions in data-sets of social and economic variables. But isn't this exactly what Quetelet had already argued years earlier? The new feature of Van der Wijk's methodology is to be found at the level of explanation. Van der Wijk's discussion of explanation emerges from a hypothetical objection to applying a physicist's methodology to the social sciences, that is, the objection that 'individuals' differ from 'atoms' in that atoms are independent units whereas individuals are not. Van der Wijk distinguishes two opposing positions:

> The analyses of Marx and marxists usually begin with a – naturally fictional – society in which the 'summation and integration' of individuals has taken place so completely that the bridge between the individual and society can be safely ignored. (Van der Wijk, 1921, p. 927)

Marx (and for instance Max Adler) stresses the social character of the individual to such an extent that individuals as individuals disappear from the analysis; they are regarded as mere bearers of social relations. The subjectivist theories of value on the other hand start from atomic individuals and 'society is thought of as a group of units' (Van der Wijk, 1921, p. 928).

With respect to the theory of value this has led people to believe that subjectivist and objectivist theories are mutually exclusive. Hilferding, for instance, argues that:

> The commodity is a unity of use value and value, but we can regard that unity from two different aspects. As a natural thing it is the object of a natural science; as a natural thing it is the object of a natural science; as a social thing it is the object of a social science. The object of political economy is the social aspect of the commodity, of the good, so far as it is a symbol of social interconnection. On the other hand, the natural aspect of the commodity, its use value, lies outside the domain of political economy. (Hilferding (1904, p. 9) cited in Van der Wijk, 1921, p. 927)

Van der Wijk argues that in statistical mechanics the opposition between subjectivist and objectivist theories does not exist. In statistical mechanics some notions are only applicable to the system as a whole, the macro-state. But these notions can be explained from the behaviour of the individual particles. The notion of pressure, for instance, is pointless at the level of the individual particle, but, by making assumptions about the behaviour of the individual particles (e.g. concerning speed and mass) the macro notion of pressure can be explained. Hence in physics:

> the explanation and calculation – in terms we use in economics – will sometimes be 'objectivist' sometimes 'subjectivist. [...] [T]here is no fundamental contradiction between subjectivists and objectivists in physics, as we find in economics. On the contrary, Boltzmann formulated his purely 'subjectivist' theory of entropy in

order to remove certain objections from the objectivist theory of Clausius. (Van der Wijk, 1921, p. 926)

Economics, van der Wijk continues, should be constructed just like physics; objectivist and subjectivist theories can and should be used together. He argues that subjectivist theories can be characterized as genetic, describing the emergence of value, and objectivist theories as essential, describing its existence. Thus

> In our view every social theory that wants to be more than a tautology will have to have an objectivist structure, but it will need subjectivist elements for its construction and development. Marxism is no exception to this rule. (Van der Wijk, 1921, p. 929)

In his 1923a article Van der Wijk elaborates on this point with respect to the theory of value. He disagrees, he writes, with Böhm-Bawerk's formulation (1921, p. 161) that subjective value can in principle be used as a tool in order to determine objective exchange value. According to Van der Wijk this is not necessary, and not *per se* a good idea. His preference for objectivist theory follows from the following consideration:

> Like all the other social phenomena, they [economic relations] are of course resultants of the actions of individuals, and in principle one should be able to trace them back to those actions, thereby creating a 'purely subjectivist' foundation for economics. But I think that Marx takes not only the easier, but even the more reliable path in his theory of value by assuming a stationary equilibrium for the collective and by putting laws of economic relations and social development quite simply deduced from this to the test of experience, rather than getting the same results by induction that starts from what we know of the individual. (Van der Wijk, 1923a, p. 789)

Van der Wijk is confirmed in his view by the conviction that 'the behavior of one individual is completely different from that of another' (Van der Wijk, 1923a, p. 789). Later in this chapter we shall see that De Wolff tried to deal with this problem of subjectivist economics by assuming identical marginal disutility functions for all individuals.

The economics Van der Wijk had in mind, then, consists of two steps. The first is to apply the law of large numbers to social and economic phenomena. This, he thought, would generate constants. These constants could be summarized in mathematical relationships. The second step is to explain these relationships in the way we have just discussed.

He fancied that the first step would still give some trouble in most social sciences. Remember from our discussion above that Boltzmann's theory of entropy requires three assumptions. We need a closed system, a large number of particles and coincidental changes. The closed system Van der Wijk has in mind is an independent economic group, such as an autarkic country. But he is not very clear about it. The same goes for the other assumptions. His worries seem to concentrate on the number of particles he could get for most problems. His worries were much less for the application of the law to economic phenomena because 'exchange is *the* cause for levelling society' (Van der Wijk, 1921, p. 1024). Whereas in other social sciences the method could only be used to formulate questions, the law of large numbers could make economics (and demography) into a science. He gives a number of statistics on different economic phenomena and is able to construct a normal distribution out of the figures (either out of the figures themselves or their deviations from the mean). He concludes:

> Social phenomena are to an important and growing extent phenomena of groups. The law of large numbers applies qualitatively, and in many cases quantitatively. Therefore the laws [*wetmatigheid*] of society approximate those of nature, the methodology of social science approximates that of physics. Applicable to economics in particular is the conclusion: the objectivist way of analyzing and mathematical formulation are on the road and nothing will stop them. (Van der Wijk, 1921, p. 1039)

And 'In *this* stage of levelling the questions are open to the treatment which has already for centuries shown its superiority over the "chatter"-method in physics' (Van der Wijk, 1921, p. 1023).

De Wolff's attempt to apply Van der Wijk's methodology to the theory of value

De Wolff, who had been working on growth and business cycle theory almost exclusively prior to his 1925 articles on the theory of value, found all the elements he needed for his discussion waiting for him in Van der Wijk's articles of 1921 and 1923. Van der Wijk's influence was not restricted to methodology. In his 1923a article he had discussed J.B. Clark's *The Distribution of Wealth* (1899) and had given his blessing to the concept of disutility of labour. He argued that, unlike the Austrian school, the American school accepts that the sellers' utility is based on profit. As a result:

> the element of effort and costs enters into price-theory [...], for which the American school uses the name 'disutility'. [...] With Clark *et al.* one can take the argument a step further. Unlike Böhm-Bawerk, one can argue that the *indirect* ('substitution') value, as determined by production and exchange, also holds for the buyers on the market. (Van der Wijk, 1923, p. 1046)

With Böhm-Bawerk Van der Wijk considers it unlikely that individuals are able to weigh things like that. He therefore develops the argument into the

direction of labour-supply and labour-demand, which I will not discuss here.[9]
De Wolff on the other hand did try to use this 'substitution value' as we shall
see below.

De Wolff's exposition on method in his 1925 article is completely in line
with Van der Wijk's (1921).[10] He adds to Van der Wijk's views a notion of a
good theory. He gets this notion from Pierre Duhem's *La Théorie physique,
son objet et sa structure* (1914): 'What is a *theory* in its highest form? *Such a
theory is a system of mathematical tenets which are deduced from a small
number of principles and aimed at describing a group of empirically found
laws as simply, completely and accurately as possible*'. (De Wolff, 1925, p.
352)

De Wolffs's analytical argument consists of three parts. The first is devoted
to the determination of the distribution of labour over different uses in the
case of an atomic individual, an everyman named Robinson, 'as good a
technician as he was a mathematician and an experimental psychologist' (de
Wolff, 1925, p. 766). The second part deals with exchange under the assumption of given endowments. In the third part De Wolff combines the two
preceding steps into a model of a simple competitive economy without capital. De Wolff's aim was twofold. First of all he wanted to show that Marx's
objectivist theory of value could be derived from a subjectivist base. Given
the two principles of maximization and decreasing marginal utility, he wanted
to show that the 'Marxist theory of value is not at all destroyed: on the
contrary, it refuses to lie down and towers over everything socialists and non-
socialists today consider to be a theory of value' (De Wolff, 1925, p. 346).
His second aim was to solve what he called the 'economic' problem which he
opposed to 'rationality problems'. He argued that constrained maximization:

> cannot be the basic principle of economic science, because neither the 'result' nor
> the 'means' can be treated as given, for these are the very things we have to
> establish. [...] One only acts economically if and when the difference of revenue
> and costs is as big as possible, if it is a 'maximum'. In all other cases one may act
> rationally, but not economically. (De Wolff, 1925, p. 476)

It is not completely clear what De Wolff is aiming at. His more detailed
formulation of the 'economic problem' shows that his grudge against rationality problems is that the analyses of production and exchange are separated
(cf Tinbergen's (1929, p. 852) review of De Wolff, 1929). The economic
problem, then, is the following:

> What are the laws of a society in which production is aimed at exchange? The
> volume of production, the prices, the quantity of each commodity every indi-
> vidual has before and after the act of exchange, all this can be derived solely from
> the psychological utility and disutility functions of the members of that society.

However, one may only assume [...] that all members of society pursue a maximum utility-balance. (De Wolff, 1925, p. 671)

This is an ambitious programme. Let us follow De Wolff's three-step argument and see if he gets were he wants to go.

Robinson

Robinson wants two commodities the value of which is represented by means of a utility function $U = f(x_1, x_2)$. To get the commodities he has to work. The disutility this brings him is valuated in the disutility function $D = g(x_1, x_2)$. The unit that is being valued in the utility function is not number of products, but 'the average quantity of labour required for the production of a given unit of these products' (De Wolff, 1925, p. 567). However, using the explicit utility function for Commodity 1 (fish), $U = 20x - x^2$, he explains 'This means that an hour of average labour of fishing on a certain day, gives him a product, which gives him a utility of 19 units' (De Wolff, 1925, p. 567).

It seems that De Wolff wants to have a mixture of a production function (stating the relation between hours worked and number of commodities produced) and a utility function (stating the relation between the number of commodities and the utility this brings Robinson). The disutility function is measured in the same unit. The difficulty is resolved (pragmatically), for the present purpose only) if we separate the production and utility functions, and assume that the production function $[X(x_1, x_2) = h(l_1, l_2)]$ has constant returns to scale for both commodities. 'Average hours of labour' (l_1, l_2) produce outputs x_1, x_2; the outputs are now valuated in the utility function in the usual unit, i.e. quantities of commodities. The disutility of labour can be measured in the same unit, because there is a one to one relation between the 'average quantity of labour' and the number of commodities.

Robinson maximizes his total utility function (De Wolff uses separate, explicit, quadratic utility functions and a lot of numerical examples – this example is a reconstruction):

$$\max_{x_1, x_2}: \quad f(x_1, x_2) - g(x_1, x_2) \tag{7.1}$$

by taking the first derivatives to x_1 and x_2 and setting them equal to zero.

$$\frac{\partial f}{\partial x_1} - \frac{\partial g}{\partial x_1} = 0 \tag{7.2}$$

$$\frac{\partial f}{\partial x_2} - \frac{\partial g}{\partial x_2} = 0 \tag{7.3}$$

Hence 'The balance of marginal utility and marginal disutility is zero for every product' (De Wolff, 1925, p. 584).

This result is obtained through maximization, but without imposing constraints; furthermore production and 'exchange' relations are determined simultaneously. The number of hours worked can be found by substituting the number of commodities in the production function.

Exchange

De Wolff discusses exchange as a rationality problem (with given endowments), not as an economic problem. He starts with two individuals (A and B) who have utility functions for two commodities ($f_1 = f(x_1, x_2)$ for individual A; $f_2 = f(x_1, x_2)$ for individual B). Both individuals have endowments. De Wolff uses the same symbol as in Robinson's case but here x denotes a number of commodities.

In equilibrium the slopes of the utility functions of the two individuals are equal.

$$\frac{\frac{\partial f_1}{\partial x_1}}{\frac{\partial f_1}{\partial x_2}} = \frac{\frac{\partial f_2}{\partial x_1}}{\frac{\partial f_2}{\partial x_2}} \tag{7.4}$$

De Wolff is aware that this does not provide him with enough information to solve the exchange problem. He adds the condition that 'the exchange relation x_1/x_2 must be chosen in such a way that *neither individual wants to exchange any part of his holidays for any other commodity after this exchange relation has emerged*' (De Wolff, 1925, p. 659).

He does not explain how this exchange relation comes about; it merely fixes a point on the contract curve.[11] It supplies him with:

$$\frac{\frac{\partial f_1}{\partial x_1}}{\frac{\partial f_1}{\partial x_2}} = \frac{x_2}{x_1} \tag{7.5}$$

and hence, in equilibrium:

$$\frac{\frac{\partial f_2}{\partial x_1}}{\frac{\partial f_2}{\partial x_2}} = \frac{x_2}{x_1} \tag{7.6}$$

$$\frac{\dfrac{\partial f_1}{\partial x_1}}{\dfrac{\partial f_1}{\partial x_2}} = \frac{\dfrac{\partial f_2}{\partial x_1}}{\dfrac{\partial f_2}{\partial x_2}} = \frac{x_2}{x_1} \tag{7.7}$$

or as De Wolff puts it himself correctly:

> Our new condition implies the law that in equilibrium, both for individual 1 and individual 2, the marginal utility of the second commodity stands to the marginal utility of the first commodity as p, i.e. is equal to the relation in which commodity x_1 is exchanged for commodity x_2. (De Wolff, 1925, p. 660)[12]

Production for the market
In combining the two preceding steps De Wolff makes a number of critical mistakes which render his argument invalid. His main result however can be derived without much difficulty from the extension of the first step of the argument.

De Wolff combines the two preceding steps without any further ado. He wants to show that in equilibrium prices are related as marginal disutilities. The conclusion from the first part was that the 'balance of marginal utility and disutility is zero for every product'. In his Robinson discussion De Wolff uses separate and additive utility and disutility functions for every product (f_1 and f_2 are Robinson's utility functions for commodities x_1 and x_2; g_1 and g_2 his disutility functions). Hence:

$$f(x_1, x_2) = f_1(x_1) + f_2(x_2) \tag{7.8}$$

$$g(x_1, x_2) = g_1(x_1) + g_2(x_2) \tag{7.9}$$

His version of our Equations 7.2 and 7.3 is therefore:

$$\frac{\partial f_1}{\partial x_1} - \frac{\partial g_1}{\partial x_1} = 0 \tag{7.2*}$$

$$\frac{\partial f_2}{\partial x_2} - \frac{\partial g_2}{\partial x_2} = 0 \tag{7.3*}$$

He – illegitimately – concluded that he could substitute the identical terms of Equations 7.2* and 7.3* in Equation (7.7), which gave him the equilibrium results of exchange. His notation is sloppy: in Robinson's case, subscripts, e.g. f_1, refer to commodities, whereas in the exchange equations the subscripts refer to different individuals. The difficulty resolves once we assume that the two individuals from our exchange problem have identical marginal utility and marginal disutility functions. Although at this point of the argument he denies this, he does assume equality at a later stage; there he starts working with a representative individual. Let us assume therefore that Robinson and Friday have the same (marginal) utility functions. In that case the legitimate substitution amounts to

$$\frac{\dfrac{\partial f_1}{\partial x_2}}{\dfrac{\partial g_1}{\partial x_1}} = \frac{\dfrac{\partial g_2}{\partial x_2}}{\dfrac{\partial f_2}{\partial x_1}} = \frac{p_2}{p_1} \qquad (7.10)$$

The next step is to argue that when individual A switches from the production of x_1 to the production of x_2, his 'balance of utility-intensity and disutility-intensity' would still be zero. Hence,

$$\frac{\partial g_1}{\partial x_2} - \frac{\partial f_1}{\partial x_2} \qquad (7.11)$$

and

$$\frac{\partial g_2}{\partial x_1} - \frac{\partial f_2}{\partial x_1} \qquad (7.12)$$

and, substituting Equations (7.11) and (7.12) in Equation (7.10) gives the result that prices relate as marginal disutilities.

$$\frac{\dfrac{\partial g_1}{\partial x_2}}{\dfrac{\partial g_1}{\partial x_1}} = \frac{\dfrac{\partial g_2}{\partial x_2}}{\dfrac{\partial g_2}{\partial x_1}} = \frac{p_2}{p_1} \qquad (7.13)$$

De Wolff's conclusion is that:

With *rational* exchange relative prices equal relative marginal utilities: with *economic* production, which implies rational exchange, this rule still holds, but at the same time relative prices equal the relation of marginal utility and disutility: with *economic production in equilibrium* relative prices also relate as the marginal disutilities. (De Wolff, 1925, p. 771)

If we also assume, as De Wolff did, that marginal utilities are identical, and that disutility is measured in socially necessary labour-time,[13] then the prices relate as labour-embodied value.

A few remarks will conclude this section. First, it is clear that De Wolff adopted Van der Wijk's methodology, and that this methodology accounts for the structure of his argument. De Wolff tries to prove an 'objective law' – exchange at labour-values – by explaining it with a minimum of subjectivist assumptions concerning the characteristics of individuals (cf De Wolff, 1925, p. 774).

Second, De Wolff could have obtained his result much more easily if he had thought more thoroughly about the first step of his argument. Remember that the unit in which he wanted to measure Robinson's utility and disutility was 'the average quantity of labour required for the production of a given unit of these products' (De Wolff, 1925, p. 567). We could write this as $g(l_x)$ which indeed has the desired property of relating production of commodity x by means of labour l to disutility of labour g. The first derivative with respect to x is

$$\frac{\partial g}{\partial x} = \frac{\partial g}{\partial l}\frac{\partial l}{\partial x} \tag{7.14}$$

Assuming constant returns to scale sets $\partial l/\partial x$ equal to unity. Labour disutility now corresponds with expended labour-time. Using the knowledge that Robinson will produce commodities x_1 and x_2 until the relation of marginal utilities equals the relation of marginal disutilities, it follows that Robinson's optimum can be described by:

$$\frac{p_1}{p_2} = \frac{x_2}{x_1} = \frac{\dfrac{\partial f}{\partial x_1}}{\dfrac{\partial f}{\partial x_2}} = \frac{\dfrac{\partial g}{\partial x_1}}{\dfrac{\partial g}{\partial x_2}} = \frac{\dfrac{\partial g}{\partial l_1}\dfrac{\partial l_1}{\partial x_1}}{\dfrac{\partial g}{\partial l_2}\dfrac{\partial l_2}{\partial x_2}} \tag{7.15}$$

If we depict Robinson as the representative individual,[14] it follows that Equation (7.15) equals the relative prices in a competitive economy. Then it is true that since the quantities exchanged are expressed in units of average social labour, this means that with *economic production in equilibrium exchange takes place according to quantities of average social labour* (De Wolff, 1925, p. 772). The third remark is that De Wolff's 1925 model does not analyse a capitalist economy, which is in line with his argument that 'real scientific research starts with analysis of the simplest relations' (De Wolff, 1925, p. 767). However he does claim that his 'views remain basically valid in capitalism', admitting that 'proof of this [...] can only be given by a further examination' (De Wolff, 1925, p. 784). This further examination is given in his 1929 book (on which see Plasmeijer, 1988, and Kalshoven, 1993).

Concluding remarks

De Wolff's attempt to apply the new methodology to the theory of value was laborious. What I find intriguing about his attempt is that he manoeuvred himself into a no-win situation. Even if he had succeeded in convincing people that he had shown that an embodied labour theory of value is consistent with neoclassical price-theory, he would at best have been able to show that an embodied labour theory of value is a special case of neoclassical price-theory. This would have been a success for neoclassical theory, not for Marxism.

Marxist economics disappeared in the course of the inter-war years. Most socialist economists did not discuss it at all; and the socialist economists who did consider themselves to be Marxist economists, De Wolff and, to a lesser extent, Van der Wijk, ended up working on their own versions of neoclassical economics. However, we cannot conclude that De Wolff was not a Marxist economist. He considered himself to be just that, and in historical analysis Marxism should be defined as whatever Marxists make of it.

It may seems strange, however, that De Wolff and Van der Wijk took over the neoclassical 'tool kit' so readily. I can think of four complementary explanations. First, they wanted to transform economics from 'prattle' into an exact, mathematical science like physics. In their view this required finding statistical laws and describing and explaining these laws mathematically. They therefore needed mathematical economics – and the only mathematical economics available was neoclassical economics. Second, neoclassical mathematical economics had the quality of providing a theory of individual behaviour. Since the application of statistical mechanics to economics would have to bridge the gap between subjectivist and objectivist theories, and Marxism lacked a theory of individual behaviour, this was a quality De Wolff and Van der Wijk appreciated. Third, most Dutch socialist economists subscribed to the fundamental tenets of neoclassical theory, and some of them in passing made critical remarks on Marx's theory of value. De Wolff therefore had a strategic interest in convincing his fellow-socialists that Marx's theory of value can be derived from neoclassical assumptions. Fourth, historically the Austrian school, particularly Böhm-Bawerk, was regarded as the theoretical (as well as ideological) enemy. This stems as much from Böhm-Bawerk's own continuous criticism of Marxism as from the fact that most critics of Marx in the Netherlands were Austrians. As long as it wasn't Austrian, Dutch Marxists could live with marginalism.[15]

Notes

1.   This chapter was presented as a paper at the HES annual meeting, June 1 1992 (Fairfax, Virginia). I would like to thank the participants and especially my referent Gilles Dostaler for their stimulating questions and criticism. Furthermore I would like to thank Alexander

van Altena, Marcel Boumans, Phil Mirowski, Geert Reuten and Boe Thio for useful comments on an earlier draft.

2. This chapter is part of a larger project, which will result in a book covering the history of Dutch Marxist political economy in the period between 1883 and 1939 (Kalshoven, 1993). What follows is a taste of the developments before World War I, so as to illustrate the larger perspective of the developments in the Netherlands.

3. All quotations in this article are translated from Dutch. As far as I know none of them has ever been translated before.

4. 'Neoclassical' is of course a post World War II conception. The socialists who defended 'neoclassicism' at the expense of Marxist economics used the terms 'subjectivism', 'marginalism', 'modern economic analysis' and also 'official economics'. Whenever I use the term 'neoclassical', it refers to these descriptions.

5. See, for example, J. de Jager (1920); J.P. Wibaut (1920), both in the *Socialistische Gids*.

6. In 1923 Van der Wijk uses this argument to criticize the different schools of marginalism which consider a static economy, and he praises Marshall for incorporating time in the shape of his supply curves.

7. A further reason why biology is important for Van der Wijk is that biology and physics were contrasted at that time, by Bergson (1914) for instance, as the sciences of 'living' and 'dead' nature. This distinction was considered fundamental, that is, it was held that this difference of the object of research implied that different methods had to be used to research them. Since the same argument can be made in contrasting physics and social science, biology was a convenient intermediary step for Van der Wijk (1921, p. 715 et seq.).

8. Van der Wijk (1921, p. 546 et seq.) explicitly discusses probability. By means of examples he shows how binomial probabilities converge to a normal distribution.

9. See Van der Wijk (1923a, p. 1047 et seq.). In his book published in 1929, De Wolff would come back to the problem of labour supply. Plasmeijer (1988) suggests influence from Jevons in this respect. Compare Kalshoven (1993).

10. See for instance De Wolff (1925, p. 357) where he discusses the alleged contradiction between subjectivism and objectivism: 'O reader, have you not learned from Van der Wijk's (1921) magnificent study that *real* science is "subjective" and "objective" at the same time?' Plasmeijer (1988) has a different opinion of De Wolff's views on method.

11. In his *Mathematical Psychics* (1881) Edgeworth showed that the problem of two individuals, two commodities has a range of solutions. He called this range the contract curve. Through the condition De Wolff imposed the contract curve is reduced to a point. A few years after De Wolff (1925), Tinbergen (1928) tried to solve the indeterminateness of the contract curve by means of imposing organizational principles. De Wolff's condition is identical with Tinbergen's first 'form of exchange', in which both individuals have the same bargaining strength (see Boumans, 1992).

12. De Wolff (1925, p. 665 et seq.) also derives supply and demand functions. Since this is not relevant for the present argument I will not discuss it here.

13. Van Gelderen (1930, p. 659) strongly opposes this unit of measurement. He considers it to be a trick to turn an otherwise neoclassical argument into a Marxist one. Cynically he says: 'This [measuring disutility in socially necessary labour-time] bring us back home to Marx, taking with us only the empty shell of disutility, which is imported from an entirely different theoretical construction'.

14. De Wolff did not consider this to be an unwarranted assumption. Using Van der Wijk's 1921 article as a reference De Wolff argues that increasing mechanization of the production process levels labour disutility. Furthermore, capitalism cause 'group enlargement'. And as groups grow larger 'the events take a course in accordance with a priori probabilities' (Van der Wijk, 1921, p. 1012, cited in De Wolff, 1925, p. 773).

15. Rudolf Kuyper is an exception to this rule in the sense that he *did* hold the Austrian theory of value to be correct. He argued, as early as 1902–3, that the Austrian and Marxist theories of value are not incompatible. I have argued elsewhere (Kalshoven, 1992) that his attempt to show this failed (compare Kalshoven, 1993).

References

Bergson, H. (18th ed. 1914), *L'Evolution créatrice*, Paris.
Boltzmann, L. (1872), *Theoretical physics and philosophical problems*, reprinted in B. McGuinness (ed.) (1974), *Selected writings of Ludwig Boltzmann*, Dordrecht/Boston: Reidel Publishing.
Boumans, M. (1992), *Jan Tinbergen (A Case of Limited Physics Transfer)*, Amsterdam: thesis publishers, forthcoming.
Buiting, H. (1989), *Richtingen- en partijstrijd in de SDAP (Het ontstaan van de Sociaal-Democratische Partij in Nederland)*, Amsterdam: IISG
Clark, J.B. (1899), *The distribution of wealth* (a Theory of Wages, Interest and Profits), New York: Macmillan.
Duhem, P. (2nd ed. 1914), *La Théorie physique, son objet, sa structure*, Paris.
Edgeworth, F.Y. (1881), *Mathematical Psychics*, London.
Ehrenfest, P. and T. (1912), 1990), *The conceptual Foundations of the Statistical Approach in Mechanics*, New York: Dover.
Gelderen, J. van (1930), 'Verdieping van het marxisme?' in *De Socialistiche Gids* (XV), pp. 561–76, 652–72, 799–810, 869–78.
Goes, F. van der (1894), *Organische ontwikkeling der maatschappij*, Amsterdam: Poutsma.
Goes, F. van der (1900), 'Ten Slotte', *De Kroniek*, 7 January, pp. 4–5.
Hilferding, R. (1904), 'Böhm-Bawerk's criticism of Marx', in P. Sweezy (ed.) (1949, 3rd ed. 1973), *Karl Marx and the Close of his System by Eugen von Böhm-Bawerk & Böhm-Bawerk's Criticism of Marx by Rudolf Hilferding*, New York.
Jager, J. de (1920), 'Religieus-socialistische oriëntering', in *De Socialistiche Gids* (v), pp. 754–67.
Kalshoven, F. (1992), 'The development of the theory of value', in M. van der Linden (ed.), *Die Verbreitung der Werke von Karl Marx und Friedrich Engels in den Niederlanden*, Amsterdam: IISG.
Kalshoven, F. (1993), 'Over marxistische economie in Nederland (1883–1939)', Amsterdam: Thesis Publishers/IISG, forthcoming.
Kohnstamm, P.A. (1915), *Warmteleer*, Amsterdam.
Kuyper, R. (1902–3), 'Over Waarde', in *De Nieuwe Tijd* (VII and VIII), reprinted in R. Kuyper, *Marxistische Beschouwingen* [four vols], 1920–1922, vol. I.
Mirowski, P. (1989), *More Heat than Light [Economics as Social Physics, Physics as Nature's Economics]*, Cambridge: Cambridge University Press.
Pannekoek, A. (1917), 'Twee natuuronderzoekers in maatschappelijk-geestelijke strijd', in *De Nieuwe Tijd* (XXII), pp. 300–14; 375–92.
Plasmeijer, H. (1988), 'Overschatting en onderwaardering (over de politieke economie van Sam de Wolff (1878–1960))', in H. Plasmeijer (ed.), *De theoretische grondslagen van economisch beleid*, Groningen: Wolters Noordhoff, pp. 51–69.
Saks, J. (1905–1907), 'De minderwaardigheid der meerwaardetheorie', in *De Nieuwe Tijd* (X), pp. 68–80; 233–44; 383–96; 546–68; 678–700; continued in *De Nieuwe Tijd* (XI), pp. 77–92; 220–36; 437–56; 520–32; 797–812; 892–904; continued in *De Nieuwe Tijd* (XII), pp. 461–80.
Tinbergen, J. (1928), 'Opmerkingen over ruiltheorie', in *De Socialistiche Gids* (XIII), pp. 431–45; 539–48.
Tinbergen, J. (1929), 'Het ekonomiese getü' (review of De Wolff, 1929) in *Socialistiche Gids* (XIV), pp. 1011–24.
Treub, M.W.F. (1902–3), *Het wijsgeerig-economisch stelsel van Karl Marx* [two vols], Amsterdam/Haarlem: Scheltema en Holkema/Tjeenk Willink.
Wibaut, J.P. (1920), 'Natuurwetenschappelijk overzicht', in *De Socialistiche Gids* (V), pp. 916–31.
Wijk, J. van der (1921), 'Wetmatigheid in natuur en maatschappij', in *Socialistiche Gids* (VI), pp. 539–55; 715–23; 803–14; 921–32; 1019–54.
Wijk, J. van der (1923a), 'De Oostenrijksche of averechtse waardeleer', in *De Socialistiche Gids* (VIII), pp. 769–90; 908–28; 1038–54.

Wijk, J. van der (1923b), 'Het bevolkingsvraagstuk', in *De Socialistische Gids* (VIII), pp. 20–39; 219–36; 315–41; 428–50.

Wijk, J. van der (1928), 'De Gemiddeldewet', in *De Economist* (76), pp. 565–90.

Wijk, J. van der (1931), 'Psychisch inkomen en psychisch vermogen', in *De Economist* (79), pp. 112–40; 232–43; 305–19.

Wijk, J. van der (1932), 'Wetmatigheid in de maatschappij', in *De Socialistische Gids* (XVII), pp. 275–93.

Wolff, S. de (1925), 'Beschouwingen over de waardeleer', in *De Socialistische Gids* (X), pp. 346–61; 472–88; 566–85; 648–71; 765–86.

Wolff, S. de (1929), *Het economisch getij [bijdrage tot de verklaring van het conjunctuurverschijnsel]*, Amsterdam.

8 Mainstream economics and uncertainty in the inter-war period[1]

Emiel F.M. Wubben

> Uncertainty was the new strand placed gleamingly
> in the skein of economic ideas
> in the 1930s.
> (Shackle, 1967, p. 6)

Introduction

Credit for being the first economist to distinguish between risk and uncertainty usually goes to Frank Hyneman Knight (1885–1972). His *Risk, Uncertainty, and Profit*, published in 1921, is widely acknowledged as a major contribution to economic theory (Mitchell, 1922, p. 274; Buchanan, 1968, p. 425) especially for introducing the concept of uncertainty into economics.

However, is Shackle correct to argue that, after the 1930s, economic theory was trying to explain scarcity and uncertainty (Shackle, 1967, p. 6–7)? Or is it rather the case that economic theory during the inter-war decades studiously avoided the problem of uncertainty (Rowley and Hamouda, 1987, p. 45)? How was the theme of uncertainty treated in the inter-war years following Knight's celebrated publication? Did the connotation and meaning of uncertainty remain the same throughout this period? These are the questions addressed in this chapter. In treating this subject I will define uncertainty as the intuition-based range of outcomes deemed possible for the situation under scrutiny.

This chapter will restrict itself to tracing trends in the treatment of uncertainty within the neoclassical school of economics, in particular to the inter-war period and as far as connected to its introduction by Knight. The following topics will feature prominently: first, the meaning and connotation of the concept of uncertainty and its implications for economic theory; second, the differences between risk and uncertainty; third, the relationship between uncertainty and the theory of economic development; and fourth, the consequences of uncertainty for decision-making. The chapter will only touch upon such related topics as co-ordination failures, psychological aspects or policy implications.

Risk, uncertainty and profit

Knight's *Risk, Uncertainty and Profit* can be read as 'tackling one of the most fundamental problems of epistemology and ethics' (Gordon, 1974, p. 572), that is, uncertainty. Knight's search for a valid theory of profit places the problem of uncertainty and risk in competition in the centre of discussion. 'But Uncertainty must be taken in a sense radically distinct from the familiar notion of Risk, from which it has never been properly separated' (Knight, 1921, p. 19). According to Knight, uncertainty is a neglected theme, 'which we propose to put in its rightful place' (Knight, 1921), p. 231).

Uncertainty is defined as the 'fact of ignorance and necessity of acting upon opinion rather than knowledge' (Knight, 1921, p. 268). Knight considers the decisive factor separating risk and uncertainty to be measurability. The term uncertainty must be restricted 'to cases of the non-quantitative type' (Knight, 1921, p. 20), that is when there 'is *no valid basis of any kind* for classifying instances' (Knight, 1921, p. 225). No sufficiently homogeneous groups can be formed in such cases to make possible an empirical determination of the occurrences of alternatives. 'The conception of an objectively measurable probability or chance is simply inapplicable' (Knight, 1921, p. 231).

In economic life the fundamental uncertainties are first, the errors in predicting the future, and second, in making adjustments to future conditions (Knight, 1921, p. 259). The concept of uncertainty, as used by Knight, clearly has negative connotations.

Knight discusses uncertainty in relation to the third of the following three different ideal types of probability situations/cases:

1. A priori probabilities can be calculated from general principles. An example is the a priori or *real* probability of getting a six in throwing dice. This type of probability is practically absent in economic behaviour (Knight, 1921, p. 215).
2. Statistical probabilities are probabilities derived from past experiences, with the aid of applying statistics to actual instances, and ending up with empirically determined classifications of instances. The example of the chance of a specific house burning down fits this category. Statistical probabilities are *extremely common* in business (Knight, 1921, p. 215).
3. Estimates or guesses are inevitable whenever a valid homogenous basis for a classification of alternative outcomes is non-existent. The uniqueness of the situation will, in general, mean the absence of a distribution of outcomes (Knight, 1921, pp. 226, 233). For example, the profitability of an investment in producing a totally new product is uncertain, because no relevant experience has yet been acquired (Knight, 1921, pp. 209–32).

Both a priori and statistical probabilities enable us to know the distribution of the outcomes in a certain group of instances. The first two of three types of probability situations can be combined under the term risk (Knight, 1921, pp. 216–25, 233; Orlean, 1987, p. 10–11).

The absence of uncertainty is, according to Knight, a prerequisite enabling the scientist to use the assumption of perfect competition. Under perfect competition demand and supply can be represented respectively by the laws of diminishing utility and of diminishing returns. In fact, when uncertainty is absent, there are no deliberate decisions being made: men will act like automatons. In an efficiently operating economy you will not find any profits when there are only risks, because risks can be insured against. Risks result only in extra costs, with inputs being paid according to their capacity. In the absence of uncertainty, the rate of return must be equal in all directions. The introduction of time will not result in imperfect competition and profits. Predictable future changes in supply and demand by themselves will not result in profits, losses or managerial problems (Knight, 1921, p. 268). Consequently, profits and losses are conditioned on the presence of uncertainty. Uncertainty forms the basis for a valid theory of profit and, outside monopoly considerations, appears to underly the difference between 'the conditions which theory is compelled to assume and those which exist in fact' (Knight, 1921, p. 51).

The forward-looking character of the economic process is at the bottom of the uncertainty problem, and consists of two kinds of foresight: first, objective final quantities and qualities of production must be estimated in advance of any production, and second, the future demand which the producer is striving to satisfy with his products must also be estimated beforehand (Knight, 1921, pp. 237–8).

Knight stresses the point that the relation between change and profit is indirect. Profit is the effect of our imperfect knowledge of the future, itself 'a consequence of change' (Knight, 1921, p. 198). Lasting profits can result only from those changes for which first, the law of change is not known, second, there is no knowledge of what actual changes are about to occur, and third, there is no knowledge of the probability of any particular occurrence (Knight, 1921, Chapters 2 and 7). 'At present we are concerned only to emphasize the fact that knowledge is in a sense variable in degree and that the practical problem may relate to the degree of knowledge rather than to its presence or absence *in toto*' (Knight, 1921, p. 199).

Our powers of dealing with our total environment through knowledge are highly inadequate, making perfect knowledge of, and anticipation for, future developments impossible. 'The existence of a problem of knowledge depends on the future being different from the past, while the possibility of the solution of the problem depends on the future being like the past' (Knight,

1921, p. 313). Therefore when scientists treat changes as following known laws, they explain uncertainty by explaining it away (Knight, 1921, p. 313).

An action under uncertainty hinges on two separate exercises of judgement: the formation of an estimate of the probable outcome of any proposed course of action; and a subjective estimation of the amount of confidence held in the conclusion reached (Knight, 1921, pp. 226–7). For example, an entrepreneur will use the best estimate he can form of the outcomes of his actions. Knight disagrees with Irving Fisher, who stated that there is only the estimation of the subjective feeling of probability itself. A person may also estimate the correctness of his estimates:

> The action which follows upon an opinion depends as much upon the amount of confidence in that opinion as it does upon the favorableness of the opinion itself. The ultimate logic, or psychology, of these deliberations is obscure, ... we must simply fall back upon a *capacity* in the intelligent animal to form more or less correct judgments about things, an intuitive sense of values. (Knight, 1921, p. 227)

Nevertheless, Knight lists six ways to reduce economic uncertainty (Knight, 1921, pp. 238–63, 347). In practice they are mixed, and mixed differently with different situations:

1. *Consolidation* Uncertainties are often less prominent in groups. Statistical and a priori uncertainties, measurable risks, tend to disappear with the enlargement of co-ordinated situations. The institution of insurance serves as an example, converting determinate uncertainties of single situations into effective certainty (Knight, 1921, pp. 46–7). Even when we cannot find a valid basis for classification, that is, in the case of real uncertainty, we often observe some tendencies toward regularity. An example is the institution of free enterprise itself.
2. *Specialization* Due to different attitudes towards uncertainty, we are able to specialize the function of risk-bearing. This point intermingles with that of consolidation, because specialization involves concentration, which involves consolidation. Speculation and the separation of aspects of enterprises into a new enterprise are examples of this specialization.
3. *Control of the future* The use of advisers and the promotion of better management makes better control of the future possible.
4. *Increasing power of prediction* Gathering, digesting and disseminating information enhances the quality of the resulting predictions. Better estimates of probable future changes and outcomes can be made by enlarging the quantity of related information.
5. *Exposing separable economic areas to risk.* The diffusion of consequences has a further implication, a point of its own: the chance of losing

a small fraction of total resources is less troublesome than the chance of
losing a larger part.
6. *Steering production towards less uncertain lines*   By concentrating on
    production which gives more certain results than other lines of produc-
    tion, one reduces uncertainty.

Consolidation, the first economic means of reducing uncertainty just mentioned, is the most important. What individuals may regard as uncertain, but
which actually involve known risks, can be reduced to any desired limit by
developing organizations, such as insurance companies, in order to combine
a number of cases.

Enlarging the quantity of related experiences will transform situations of
uncertainty into situations of risk. Under uncertainty, re-adjustments will be
carried out by trial-and-error methods under the motive to better oneself (Knight,
1921, p. 272). In an stabilized economy insurance and competition will cancel
out losses and profits. In real life situations, however, no objective line can be
drawn between profits and other incomes, because economic life always involves economic changes and imperfections of competition. With uncertainty
present, we find that the market brings labour and property services into the
comparative value scale. All payments have some relation to uncertainty.

The presence of uncertainty brings about important characteristics of social organization. For instance, consider the production for a market, and the
concentration of direction and control of production: 'The fundamental principle underlying organized activity is therefore the reduction of the uncertainty in individual judgments and decisions by grouping the decisions of a
particular individual and estimating the proportion of successes and failures,
or the average quality of his judgments as a group' (Knight, 1921, p. 293 see
also p. 268). The principle of consolidation is applied here. Effective institutions, within a *government of law* will spontaneously arise. Yet, the result
cannot be calculated from general principles or past experience, but inevitably involves estimates or guesses.

The existence of the enterprise is a direct result of uncertainty. In business
situations we find many unique problems regarding the future of the company,
partly as a consequence of technological innovation. 'It is this *true uncertainty*
which by preventing the theoretically perfect outworking of the tendencies of
competition gives the characteristic form of *enterprise* to economic organization as a whole and accounts for the peculiar income of the entrepreneur'
(Knight, 1921, p. 232). But Knight does not explain how the social organizations that deal with uncertainty in capitalism differ from the comparable social
organizations in the preceding era (Arrow, 1951, pp. 408–9).

The specialization of what Knight calls the function of 'responsible direction', combining the two elements of responsibility and control, is in his

opinion the essence of enterprise: 'Any degree of effective exercise of judgment or making decisions, is in a free society coupled with a corresponding degree of uncertainty-bearing, of taking the responsibility for those decisions' (Knight, 1921, p. 271). In principle, management is not different from routine work. A manager will become an entrepreneur, however, when his judgements are open to errors, and when he has responsibility for others.

The presence of uncertainty introduces specific problems in the field of hiring labour power. 'With uncertainty present, doing things, the actual execution of activity, becomes in a real sense a secondary part of life; The primary problem or function is deciding what to do and how to do it' (Knight, 1921, p. 268). Climbing up the hierarchy of a company we may observe that a large part of the job consists of judging, more or less intuitively, the knowledge, opinions and capacities of others. The crucial factor becomes our knowledge of another man's capacity to deal with a problem, not his knowledge of the problem itself (Knight, 1921, pp. 270–1, 295–6, 309).

Uncertainty drives a fourfold inclination to the selection of men and the specialization of functions: first, it concerns man's adaptation to occupations on the basis of knowledge; second, a similar adaptation takes place on the basis of degree of foresight; third, there will be an hierarchical specialization within groups; and finally, those with confidence in their judgement will specialize in risk-taking (Knight, 1921, p. 270).

Knight considers it problematic to link neoclassical concepts to evolving real life situations, where man is liable to error, and may adjust his opinions. Because of uncertainty, there results a contrast between the scientific concept of knowledge and the convictions and opinions upon which conduct is based. Often, one notices differences in the conclusions (Knight, 1921, p. 230). Time and time again Knight stresses the unpleasant, but unavoidable, surprises implicated in discussing the concept of uncertainty. Problems are brought about by terminological ambiguities (Knight, 1921, pp. 19, 232), the probability paradox (p. 218), the uniqueness of the instances involved (p. 226), the contrast between logically distinct types and our compounded reality (p. 224), our intuitive activities without scientific deliberation (p. 230), and so on. Our world is full of contradiction and paradox (Knight, 1921, pp. 217, 224, 313). 'In any case we *do* strive to reduce uncertainty, even though we should not want it eliminated from our lives' (Knight, 1921, p. 238). Knight acknowledges that some further foundation would be useful, but he explicitly stops short at intuitive judgement or 'unconscious induction', and the mystery of life; 'We are so built that what seems to us reasonable is likely to be confirmed by experience, or we could not live in the world at all' (Knight, 1921, p. 227).

Knight concludes with a paradox: action in the face of uncertainty involves the 'apparent theoretical impossibility of solution. But like a host of impossible things in life, it is constantly being done' (Knight, 1921, p. 298). This unsatisfactory link between his economic theory of uncertainty and economic practices clearly hampered Frank Knight, the economist as philosopher (Buchanan, 1968, p. 425). For example, he concedes that, in practice, all gradations but the extremes of perfectly homogeneous groups and absolutely unique situations exist. Hence, according to Knight, the element of uniqueness of any typical business decisions applies to most decisions. In some cases uncertainty prevails more than in other cases. No experience is absolutely unique, any more than any two things are absolutely alike. 'Yet it is true, and the fact can hardly be over-emphasized, that a judgment of probability is actually made in such cases' (Knight, 1921, p. 226). In all sorts of situations, men form opinions as to their judgemental capacities. Even more, one is perfectly well aware of the vagueness of the border separating statistical probabilities from estimates or guesses. But then one may feel puzzled to find stated that the theoretical distinction between situations of risk and uncertainty is of the greatest importance, and is clearly discernable in nearly any instance of the exercise of judgement (Knight, 1921, pp. 226–9). Knight did not solve this puzzle satisfactorily. He would later be criticized for mistakenly concentrating on a clear-cut distinction between the two extremes of a continuous sequence (see, for example, Little, 1938, p. 39n2).

A key to solving some of the problems just mentioned may be found in the probability theory chosen. First of all, it is unclear which of the alternative probability theories has been used in Knight's typification of probability situations. Furthermore, when discussing uncertainty, neoclassical economists tend more and more to concentrate on its statistical manifestations. This leads us to the question of the contemporary developments in the theory of probability and Knight's place in it.

Probability theory
While probability theory first emerged around 1660 (Hacking, 1990, p. 9) it was widely discussed in the nineteenth century by, among others, A.-A. Cournot, L. Ellis and J. Venn, paralleling a society-wide rise of interest in classification and enumeration (Hacking, 1990, p. 3). The probabilistic laws were applied as a physical property, and associated with the laws of gravity. The concept of probability was thus drawn towards a deterministic perspective. This classical theory of probability was considered inadequate by about 1900: in 1912, Poincaré expressed doubt whether a satisfactory definition of probability could be given (Mises, 1928, 1957, p. 67).

In the first decades of this century, the dominant classical theory of probability was displaced first by the subjectivist theory of probability, and then by the frequentist theory of probability. The subjectivist theory was proposed and elaborated by John Maynard Keynes in *A Treatise on Probability*, published in 1921. Richard von Mises provided a philosophical foundation for the frequency theory of probability, which is best described in his *Probability, Statistics, and Truth*, first published in German in 1928 (Mises, 1928, 1957, p. 224). The explicit break with the classical probability theory, together with an unprecedented growth in the mathematics of probability, gave rise to a circle of virtuosi in the development of probability theory. In this period, probability coexisted with the idea of personal freedom. It was taken that free will dominates within a collectively determined flow of events (Hacking, 1990, p. 116).

Laplace developed the following classical definition of probability: 'Probability is the ratio of the number of favourable cases to the total number of equally likely cases' (Mises, 1928, 1957, p. 67). This theory had been used primarily for binominal distributions, also called simple alternatives. Deduced from a priori probabilities, it could be applied to little more than simple cases. An imagined ideal coin, a die, or a can with balls are often used as clarifying means. An economic example might be the number of profitable transactions out of a total number of transactions.

The classical theory was vulnerable on several grounds. First, the Poisson or the first law of large numbers using the classical definition of probability, does not lead to any statements about relative frequency and its probability. This theorem is no more than a statement about purely arithmetic regularities, not about empirical entities (Mises, 1928, 1957, pp. 104–109, 115, 116). Second, undue emphasis is put on the importance of the a priori equality of the possibilities of different cases, also called the principle of indifference (Mises, 1928, 1957, pp. 69–71, 78, 79). Closely related to this element is the criticism that the classical theory omits important practical problems, such as life insurance problems. The complexity of such problems is too high for classical probability theory to handle. To summarize, the classical theory of probability cannot deal satisfactorily with distributions of outcomes and probabilities.

Mises defines probability as a Kantian synthetic proposition. Probability is 'the limiting value of the relative frequency with which this attribute recurs in the indefinitely prolonged sequence of observations' (Mises, 1928, 1957, p. 221). It is important to note that the subject matter of the frequency theory is the study of observable mass phenomena and repetitive events, not of individual observations (Mises, 1928, 1957, pp. vii, 102).

Probability can acquire a precise meaning only within a neatly restricted collective (Mises, 1928, 1957, pp. 18, 103, 221). A collective appropriate to the application of the theory of probability must fulfil two conditions: the relative frequencies must possess limiting values; and the limiting values must be independent of place selection. This second condition is the principle of randomness (Mises, 1928, 1957, pp. 24–5, 28–9). In cases where the collective cannot be easily constructed, it is incorrect to employ the word probability (Mises, 1928, 1957, p. 20).

Although widely acclaimed and commonly used, the frequency theory of probability is not without drawbacks. First of all, the condition of randomness, the absence of place selection, can be proved neither in practice, nor in theory. The reason is that the notion of a countable infinite sequence of observations is in no way logically definable (Mises, 1928, 1957, p. 85). This notion is necessarily based on randomness itself, for we are unable to list and test all possible place selections (Mises, 1928, 1957, p. 91). We may quite possibly end up using a probability distribution of outcomes, in a case of a perfectly deterministic sequence of outcomes. Second, in a test situation, we have to face the problem of the missing memory of the object. It is not illogical to find an infinity of tails when tossing a *perfect* coin. Mises, therefore and rightfully so, defines his law of large numbers as the *almost certain* inclination of the observed frequencies to tend to the unknown real values (Mises, 1928, 1957, p. 131). But what more than intuition can ultimately justify the presumption of neat distributions of outcomes around the real values and the x per cent reliability interval? In their search for constants or tendencies in economic activities, scientists inevitably use the hidden assumption that the data are generated by a research object that has a memory of the already produced data.

A related criticism concerns the condition of possessing limiting values. This condition can only be applied satisfactorily in an ergodic world, under the actuality of the uniformity of nature. Most economists, including Knight (Knight, 1921, pp. 204, 230, 313; Knight, 1935, p. 114) take it for granted, but neglect the consequences: first, we are faced with the probability paradox – we have to meet the logical problem that with real identity in things we have 'uniformity and not probability in the result' (Knight, 1921, p. 218); and second, under this condition of possessing limiting values, scientists cannot deal with cases of non-ergodicity. Real changes must be considered impossible. In the social sciences, by contrast, we are faced with results that change fundamentally after a period of time. It is the lack of relevant history that makes it necessary to estimate the result. It is here that Knight places economic uncertainty, the necessity to fall back on estimates, and the interesting business problems. And it is here that Mises renounces the use of probability theory.

To return to Frank Knight: we remember that on the one hand, Knight discusses a priori probabilities; they can be computed on general principles, and have the status of mathematical propositions (Knight, 1921, pp. 214, 224). On the other hand, the statistical probabilities are based on an empirical classification and the evaluation of resulting frequencies (Knight, 1921, pp. 214, 225). But neither a priori calculations nor empirical studies are of any use when discussing the cases of estimates. 'This form of probability is involved in the greatest logical difficulties of all, and no very satisfactory discussion of it can be given' (Knight, 1921, p. 225). We are bound to favour numerical probabilities in such cases, and supplement them with an estimate of how much trust to put in this ratio.

Knight's formulation is open to criticism. First, Knight tried to link his different theoretical concepts to a heterogeneous mass of real life situations. He suggested three different probability concepts: the classical, the frequency, and the subjectivist. Next, he stated that in the economy we have only mixed cases of the three types of probability situations. But how should we deal with situations where the basis for classification is equivocal? Knight is unable to show how to link the irreducible, ideal–typical probability concepts to the broad range of empirical situations.

A second criticism concerns the probability theory actually prevailing in his 1921 book. Frank Knight had his roots in the classical theory of probability. We may find numerous characteristic passages in which he does not discuss a distribution of outcomes, but rather the reliability of one outcome (Knight, 1921, pp. 212, 216–17, 220, 226–9, 231, 234–7, 293). For example, practically all decisions are supposed to rest upon opinions 'which on scrutiny easily resolve themselves into an opinion of **a** probability' (Knight, 1921, p. 237; emphasis added). Or, the degree of subjective uncertainty is a product of the estimate of the objective probability ratio and the degree of confidence (Knight, 1921, p. 237).

In contrast to using the classical theory of probability, Knight also applies ideas related to the frequency theory of probability. The six possible means to reduce uncertainty derive from the frequency theory of probability. For example, the discussion on consolidation and specialization suggests the use of the distribution of the different outcomes from a group of instances. And yet, we do not find any statements on another axiom of frequency theories: namely the summing up of probability to unity.

Knight's original, but in fact hybrid, classificatory scheme of probability cases characterizes his 1921 book as being written in a transformation phase. But would this mixture of elements from subjectivist, frequentist, and classical theories, taste better when only one of these theories had been used? The answer to that question is necessarily negative. If we consider the frequentist and classical theories, uncertainty would first of all always have to be quantifiable. This is an unrealizable condition, for non-reducible qualitative elements will pop up and materialize sooner or later. Besides, Knight's definition of uncertainty excludes the construction of the neutral collective and the application of the frequency theory to changes. If uncertainty finds its origin in unpredictable changes, and is as prevalent as Knight presumes it to be, then we are unable to approximate the possible economic consequences of uncertainty by using the frequency theory of probability.

Following the publication of Knight's book we may trace two main lines of thought in the discussion on economic uncertainty. First, as already mentioned, a change took place in the techniques chosen to *model* uncertainty and risk, and frequency theory took the lead. Second, uncertainty, the fact of ignorance and necessity for acting upon opinion, as it was defined by Knight, soon became scientifically side-tracked. Moreover, the idea of distinguishing uncertainty and risk aroused discussions, but resulted in remarkably few critical or elaborative writings.

Uncertainty linked to risk

During the inter-war period, economic theory became increasingly rigorous, inspired by the ghost of Marshall. In his search for tendencies and realism he had left economists with a heritage suited for determinate theory. It was the orthodox economist, Frederick Lavington (1881–1927), who in the first few decades of this century, elaborated on Marshall's writings in the direction of uncertainty. Lavington aimed at no more than clarifying his hero Marshall, as is reflected in one of his favourite dicta: 'It is all in Marshall, if you'll only take the trouble to dig it out' (Withers, 1927, p. 504). He had published three relevant articles, which taken together may illustrate the development of economic thought on uncertainty.

Lavington related economic uncertainty to the rate of interest in his *Economic Journal* article of 1912. There, he stated that uncertainty is a form of ignorance about the amount of one's potential gains or losses (Lavington, 1912, p. 398). With perfect foresight the normal rate of return is equal to the net rate of interest and to the so-called *actuarial value*. But changes in the future environment can only be foreseen imperfectly. In general the return on an enterprise is uncertain. The larger the felt uncertainty, the larger the spread of prospective rates of returns. This is due to the state of knowledge, the rate of social change, and the degree of immobility of resources (Lavington, 1912, p. 398). As a consequence, readjustments are no more than a succession of approximations. The result precludes the close investment of capital. A closer investment of capital presupposes a reduced financial insecurity for the owners of resources, who in general require a compensating addition to the rate of payment.

Lavington distinguishes three categories within the social machinery for dealing with the important social consequences of what he calls the 'evil of Uncertainty' (Lavington, 1912, pp. 401, 409). First, we have the methods of prevention. Examples may be the reduction of ignorance by investment in intelligence, and the institution of law and police which eliminates certain kinds of changes. Second, those who bear the results of uncertainty may transfer the effects, either by dissipating the effects over a large number of capitalists, or by compounding its effects directly or via insurance companies. The result of the latter method of transfer is not the reduction of uncertainty of any event, but is claimed to reduce the amount of reserves which must be held against eventualities (Lavington, 1912, p. 401). Third, conceivably the most important category of methods for dealing with uncertainty links up with the holding of reserve funds adequate to eliminate the residual effects of uncertainty. The organizations engaged in the marketing of capital, such as the stock exchange and the banking system, reduce the cost of this provision (Lavington, 1912, p. 407). The banking system implicitly supplies capital on demand, which corresponds to the explicit contract of an insurance company, and is based on the same principle. In fact banks offer insurance against financial emergency, because their readiness to lend reduces the necessity for business men to hold reserves against emergencies. Furthermore banks reduce the cost of a cash reserve, which is due to the loss of interest by substituting investments for this stock of resources (Lavington, 1912, pp. 404–9). In this article the consequences of the withdrawal of the assumption of completely mobile resources is highlighted. The removal of the assumption of a stationary state or the perfect calculability of the product of these resources is emphasized in two articles published in the 1920s (Lavington, 1926, pp. 196–7).

In 1925–6, in a series of two publications, Lavington elaborates on a theory of business risks. Emerging from these publications is the judgement that the real costs of risks are far heavier than the real costs of uncertainty. Surprisingly, there were no references to Knight in this work. Note also that the word uncertainty is prominent in the 1912 article, while the word risk is dominant in the two publications in the 1920s. Furthermore it is stated that both costs are intimately related and have a common origin (Lavington, 1925, pp. 198–9). The common origin is the condition of incalculability of the results of the activities. This incalculability is due to the 'immense complexity of the processes by which the future grows out of the present' (Lavington, 1925, p. 187). It creates a tendency to error at least in the short run (Lavington, 1926, p. 199) and impairs the close adaptation of means to ends.

These real costs arising from incalculability are peculiar in two, not equally important respects. The first peculiarity of real costs is the fact that they fall into two parts: the real costs of risks and those of uncertainty. The former part relates to the expectation of loss due to the misdirection or imperfect use of resources. The latter, that is, real costs of uncertainty, relates to the likely error of the just mentioned expectation of loss. Such errors result in an incalculable irregularity in individual incomes, and call for the holding of reserves. The real costs involved are caused by the less complete satisfaction of one's economic wants, and by the personality of the individual, who is usually unwilling to bear uncertainty (Lavington, 1925, pp. 192–3). The second characteristic of incalculability is that the related costs arise from our imperfect understanding of the condition in which we work. If we may believe Lavington, the second characteristic is much more important than the distinction between risk and uncertainty (Lavington, 1926, p. 195).

Still according to Lavington, business men charge prospective payments for accepting the forementioned two real costs of incalculability. Theoretically speaking there are three distinct charges: first, the reduction in the efficiency of productive resources which is caused by its misdirection, the related charge is called the amortization charge; second, as the possible future fluctuations in individual income, called the reduced efficiency of individual incomes (Lavington, 1925, pp. 192–4) may result in a charge for uncertainty-bearing, this 'reduction in the efficiency of income' (Lavington, 1926, p. 194) ordinarily becomes part of profits; and third, the acceptance of risk results in a demand for organizing faculties needed to deal with perpetual readjustments which generate costs. The charges are the earnings of management. Together, the (individual) expectation, not the (actuarial) probability, of loss arising from the occurrence of these three real costs together is defined as *risk*. The *risk charge* is the total of prospective payments just sufficient to induce a business man to accept a given risk, and it enters into the price of the output (Lavington, 1926, p. 194).

In the short run, both the magnitude and the distribution of the realized losses resulting from taking some risks is lawless or arbitrary. In the short run, there is no necessary relation between individual losses and the losses falling on society as a whole. However, experience is supposed to have a corrective influence in the long run. The tendency will be on conforming the average realized loss to the average amortization charge (Lavington, 1926, pp. 194–9).

When reading these two articles it is clear that there is no vital distinction between risk and uncertainty (Lavington, 1925, p. 199). The difference in importance of the two characteristics of incalculability is reaffirmed by the following corollary to his argument on the definition of the term risk: 'If its general drift were agreed to, it would seem possible to simplify the definition of Profits, in particular by avoiding the logical need for a separate factor of production – Uncertainty-bearing – and to bring the scope of the term more nearly into line with the meaning given it in America' (Lavington, 1926, p. 194). This quotation illustrates a conflict over whether the consistency of theory itself or the correspondence of theory with economic practices should be of primary importance. Moreover, the direct link between uncertainty and profit, which was stressed by F. Knight, is downgraded to one of mere logical importance. We may conclude that Lavington blurred the distinction between risk and uncertainty.

In the early 1930s, Knight shifted his opinion on production and capital (Knight, 1921, pp. xxxvi–xlii): 'I also recognised that the change of view called for a restatement of my theory of risk and uncertainty' (Knight, 1921, p. xli). The more vague circumscription of uncertainty, which he is emphasizing in the new introduction of the reprint, delineates uncertainty as a lack of anticipation to 'the *indefinite* future, in effect, to infinity' (Knight, 1921, p. xxxviii; see also Knight, 1935, pp. 79–80n, 92).

Put otherwise, I might say that Knight considers uncertainty to depict the open future: while uncertainty may be an important characteristic of a decision-making situation, it cannot be used as a causal factor. Of course, we could try to predict the sometimes major economic consequences of uncertainty, but it is useless to pretend to be able to predict the emergence of the underlying changes themselves.

How did economists react to Knight's 1921 publication? W.C. Mitchell was clearly impressed by it, and advised economists to taste the book. 'For the distinction between risk and uncertainty is not less valid to the realistic economist than to the pure theorist' (Mitchell, 1922, p. 175). Did economists get excited by this taste, or was it soon put aside?

Uncertainty and profit
Hicks's *The Theory of Uncertainty and Profit* (1931) is one of the few papers commenting directly on Knight's distinction between risk and uncertainty. Hicks, who had been asked by Lionel Robbins to lecture on risk and uncertainty at the London School of Economics (LSE), acclaimed that *Risk, Uncertainty, and Profit* broke the deadlock in the development of the theory of profit. It was Frank Knight who finally got the skeleton out of the cupboard. Around 1930, the prevailing theory of profit resembled Knight's theory (Knight, 1934). 'At the very least, that work has laid securely the first foundation on which any future theory of profits must rest – the dependence of profits on uncertainty' (Hicks, 1931, p. 170). But there the praise ends, and the criticism begins. Hicks comments that Knight gave us a theory of profit based on metaphysics and psychology. The theory of profit should be based on economics, supplemented with some simple assumptions, for example, about the application of probability to economics (Hicks, 1931, p. 171).

Knight and Hicks disagreed about the importance of uncertainty in economic activities. Knight, according to Hicks, had not justified why true uncertainties should claim such a large part of our attention (Hicks, 1931, p. 171). Perhaps, however, it is almost impossible to prove the extent of uncertainty, because it seems to be open for judgement only by analysing its possible yet unforeseeable consequences. Moreover, how can we ever distinguish profits/losses between the consequences of uncertainty and the imperfect working of competition that is due to other reasons?

Another part of the disagreement seems to concern the different models of classification. Knight proposed three ideal types, and discussed them. He started with uncertainty and risk, and analysed accordingly. Because of this classification, he is obliged to pay attention to uncertainty-type situations, and analyse economic cases with his ideal types. Following Knight, uncertainty is an aspect of almost every practical situation.

In contrast to Knight, Hicks takes practical situations, and classifies and discusses them. He distinguishes between four groups of probability situations: first, the cases considering a large number of identical partial operations; second, the cases which are separable into identical partial operations; third, all those cases in which there are only small deviations from the norm; fourth, true uncertainties or unmeasurable risks. He gives the principal characteristics of each of these four groups. But, unlike Knight, he does not aim at tracing the essentials behind this classification. Hicks believes that the problem of the heterogeneity of situations is of little practical importance for economic analysis. Risk theory is a good enough method. Thus, part of the disagreement about the importance of uncertainty is resolved by taking different analytical methods.

The equivalence in the used probability theory is not without significance. First of all, both Knight and Hicks use the classical theory of probability. This enables Hicks to elaborate on a point already hinted at by Knight (Knight, 1921, p. 237). Hicks comes up with the idea of an ordinal uncertainty curve, relating the amounts of incurred uncertainty to the expected result. For both supply and demand of the resources one can draw uncertainty curves; different for dissimilar terms and resulting in an ordinal equilibrium probability ratio or chance (Hicks, 1931, pp. 173–9). The forms of the uncertainty curves are dependent upon, and will change with, the given technique, the scale of production, and the used means and ends of production. For example, one may use complementary types of production in order to reduce an unstable production, or use electricity instead of oil to diminish the risk of fire. This idea probably enhanced belief in the containment of uncertainty.

Furthermore Hicks writes about the reduction, instead of the elimination, of risk. The extent to which risk changes, and the exact direction of such changes, may often be found only by empirical research (Hicks, 1931, pp. 174, 178). He thereby facilitates application of the theory of profit in most cases, as long as they are imperfectly homogeneous (Hicks, 1931, pp. 171, 175n).

Hicks did not follow Mises, who restricted himself to discussing groups of operations. The application of the frequency theory to single instances is prohibited by Mises (Mises, 1928, 1957, pp. 9, 11, 15). Hicks, however, considers repetitive situations, using the law of large numbers, and derives from the results conclusions for individual cases (Hicks, 1931, pp. 173–4). According to Hicks, we can discuss the chance of a particular result in a particular situation. Such a chance is 'the ratio of the number of cases in which that result occurs to the total' (Hicks, 1931, p. 171).

However these are not cases of Knightian uncertainty. Under uncertainty it is the impossibility of finding relevant data that causes the problems. Knight does not so much view often repeated situations, but those situations in which unpredictable changes take place (Hicks, 1931, p. 175). We see, then, that the absence of the word *risk* in the title of Hicks's paper, together with the previous discussion, indicates a change in the prevalent meaning of the word 'uncertainty'.

Did Frank Knight change his opinion about the need to discuss separately the forward-looking character of the economic process? No, not really, although he no longer elaborated on the ensuing problem of uncertainty itself. Knight would remain dissatisfied with the application of the marginalist analysis to economic developments. 'The case is somewhat like that of a river and its channel; for the time being the channel locates the river, but in the long-run it is the other way' (Knight, 1935, p. 142).

In the 1920s, dynamic economics had already become a term referring to the limitations of static analysis, 'a sort of catch-all for stressing changes in given conditions' (Knight, 1935, p. 167). On the one hand, economics has no place for relations between force (motive), resistence (ignorance, prejudice, etc.), and movement (social processes). On the other hand, in mechanics 'mass and energy are *really* neither created nor destroyed' (Knight, 1935, p. 167). Furthermore Knight would like to answer differently, but is inclined to a negative conclusion when considering the usefulness of relativity theory in economics (Knight, 1935, pp. 162–7).

Knight considers the question whether the forces acting under given conditions tend to produce an equilibrium to be more important than the question about the equilibrium itself. Economics lacks such a study of the laws of motion, 'the kinetics of economic changes' (Knight, 1935, p. 141). In order to support this statement he first of all distinguishes between four levels in the stability of data:

1. The price situation at the moment, that is, in a speculative market.
2. The more or less stable production period, e.g., of crops.
3. Longer periods of approximately a decade, with roughly constant total productive powers, populations, habits and techniques. Disturbances and maladjustments are due primarily to uncertainty or ignorance of the future.
4. The long period, within a fairly stable set of cultural values. It is here that we must locate the problem of growth and change.
    (Knight, 1930, 1935, pp. 170–80; Knight, 1935, pp. 140–5)

Accumulating processes, such as the growth of population, the growth of capital, the concentration of ownership and the expansion of wants, cannot be treated properly with the notion of a tendency toward equilibrium (Knight, 1930, 1935, pp. 177–84). 'Probably we must go further and reject entirely the use of the mechanical analogy, the categories of force, resistance, and movement, in discussing basic historical changes' (Knight, 1930, 1935, p. 185). Unfortunately, Knight did not elaborate on what alternative he might have had in mind.

Back to basics
In his acclaimed essay on the subject-matter of economics (Robbins, 1932, 1935) Lionel Robbins confronts scientists with the difficulty in trying to work out and apply relatively simple, static models. Consequently Robbins renounces the scientific status of the study of economic development, once so forcefully propagated by Schumpeter. Economics was better off reduced to the study of the equilibrium and what were euphemistically called equilibrating tendencies. Thus, fundamental change and uncertainty became marginalized research subjects. How could this happen? Was Robbins not 'the main expositor of Knight's views at LSE' (Coase, 1988, p. 20)? Two arguments in Robbins's essay push uncertainty to the periphery of economics.

First, according to Robbins, economists cannot treat uncertainty scientifically since they lack stable economic elements. The economic system functions without predictable future production functions and without permanently stable elasticities of supply and demand. Robbins acknowledges that the economic system is *open* if only because some resources are devoted to marketing and research, transforming tastes and technological knowledge respectively (Robbins, 1932, 1935, p. 129). We may be able to explain changing relationships due to changes in individual values, but we cannot explain changes in the data itself (Robbins, 1932, 1935, p. 127), because 'there are certain things which must be taken as ultimate data' (Robbins, 1932, 1935, p. 135). In spite of the fact that everyone is free to speculate about legal and political changes, or venture guesses on changes in techniques and in the supply of demand, 'economic analysis can have little to do with it' (Robbins, 1932, 1935, p. 133). The theory of profit is an 'analysis of the effect of uncertainty, with regard to the future availability of scarce goods and scarce factors' (Robbins, 1932, 1935, p. 77). This is the main postulate of the theory of dynamics. Robbins restricts the field of dynamic theory to planning for the future (Robbins, 1932, 1935, p. 79). In line with Robbins's devotion to high theory is his interest in Knight's 1921 book on perfect competition (Coase, 1988, p. 20). It precedes the extensive discussion on risk and uncertainty.

Second, Robbins suggested that the difficulties to be confronted in our search for the laws of equilibrium and equilibrating tendencies should make us humble. A scientist must necessarily start with the most convenient assumptions. Perfect foresight and perfect rationality are examples of such assumptions with an 'essentially arbitrary nature', but which are convenient for economic analysis (Robbins, 1932, 1935, p. 57). Uncertainty is clearly not one of them, for it would complicate scientific research tremendously.

The popularity of Robbins's book, with its preference for the choice of convenient concepts, rigorous analytical research and for the revealing of theoretical deficiencies by means of empirical studies, illustrates and affirms the popularity of the mathematical approach and the rejection of 'theoretical quibbling'. It presents another effort in the direction of offsetting the unpleasant surprises involved in discussing uncertainty.

Uncertainty versus perfect expectations

The publication, in 1938, of T.W. Hutchison's *The Significance and Basic Postulates of Economic Theory*, marks the start of the positivist epoch in economics (Caldwell, 1982, p. 1), and the beginning of a fierce debate with Knight (Knight, 1940; Hutchison, 1941; Knight, 1941). Paradoxically however, the arguments which Hutchison presents in this debate are very much in line with Knight's *Risk, Uncertainty, and Profit*. The central role uncertainty plays in his work is present in many of his early writings (e.g. Hutchison, 1937a; Hutchison, 1937b; Hutchison, 1938).

Hutchison states that uncertainty is essentially the singular factor that causes problems of conduct (Hutchison, 1937b, p. 652). Furthermore Hutchison, like Knight, considers the analytic distinction between absolute certainty and absolute uncertainty to be fundamental: 'where the consequences of all decisions can be perfectly foreseen, the maximum principle clearly works itself out in a very special way, which must be fundamentally distinguished from the only way in which it can work itself out when there is any uncertainty present, that is under conditions where people cannot conceivably *know* or *calculate* but can only more or less vaguely *guess*, which out of many possible lines of conduct will lead to the fulfilment of the principle' (Hutchison, 1937b, p. 638; see also Hutchison, 1938, p. 87).

Empirically this distinction presents us with a complicated question, because the distinction between *certain choices* and *uncertain choices* does not correspond with any clearcut distinction in choices among goods (Hutchison, 1937a, p. 73). Most actual choices are mixtures of the two extremes. Nevertheless, a large number of choices, especially investment choices, must be located near the uncertainty extreme (Hutchison, 1937a, p. 72). 'In a *dynamic* economic world many decisions cannot be simply *calculated* but must be based more or less on *intuition*' (Hutchison, 1938, p. 182).

In the presence of uncertainty, the neoclassical assumption of rational conduct can no longer be the starting point for economic analysis. Economic agents are supposed to act according to their expectations. The term rational is usually added to these expectations, or to the process of arriving at the expectations. But men are not acting like automatons, because risk, uncertainty, and more or less correct expectations about the future pervade all action, economic or otherwise (Hutchison, 1937b, pp. 638, 640). Under absolute uncertainty all alternatives are of equal standing, and there remains little more than guesswork. Besides, in such cases it is irrelevant how choices are actually made, and terms like *rational* and *irrational* lose their meaning (Hutchison, 1937b, p. 638). Therefore 'apart from the pure pleasure in gambling for its own sake– ... –*there is no advantage or significance at all in being free to make it oneself as against having it made for one*' (Hutchison, 1937a, p. 72).

Hutchison and Knight disagree on the necessity and sufficiency of the perfect expectation postulate for equilibrium theory. According to Knight, the postulate of perfect expectation is unnecessary for equilibrium theory: 'the assumption of practical omniscience on the part of every member of the competitive system' (Knight, 1921, p. 197). The omniscience about the future is what Hutchison denotes by perfect expectation (Hutchison, 1937b, p. 645). Knight states that uncertainty cannot be linked with perfect expectations, and therefore neither with equilibrium theory.

Hutchison asserts that uncertainty and equilibrium theory can be combined, because equilibrium theory can do without the perfect expectation postulate (Hutchison, 1937b, p. 642). In this, he agrees with Knight. Perfect expectations are, according to Hutchison, only compatible with optimal markets under competitive conditions. Real world problems resulting from uncertainty are thus often excluded from research (Hutchison, 1937b, p. 644; Hutchison, 1938, p. 162).

The assumption of perfect expectations is incompatible with an interdependent economic system. Profit maximization together with adjusting one's conduct under perfect expectations of another man's conduct is logically impossible. Moreover, with perfect expectations of one another's expectations a game could not be played (Hutchison, 1937a, p. 73; Hutchison, 1938, pp. 97–100, 163).

Assuming that people tend to fulfil the maximum principle is not enough. For instance, one might not perceive that he had achieved a maximum position (Hutchison, 1937b, p. 638). The conclusion must be that activities under less than perfect competition are dependent on necessarily imperfect expectations about the conduct of others.

Hutchison disagrees with Knight, in so far as theorizing on economic behaviour under uncertainty within an equilibrium theory is concerned. The validity of the theory does not depend on why people behave in a certain way. What is necessary, however, is simply that they do so behave. (Hutchison,

1937b, p. 642). It is not the knowledge which led people to certain actions that is important, but the actions and conditions of an individual or community.

Hutchison argues against the postulate of perfect expectations, and in favour of the postulate of correct expectations. Correct expectations are expectations with the right relations between actions and outcomes. Under correct expectations one may remain unaware of certain, possibly more profitable, opportunities. Economists might use the concept of correct, undisappointed, expectation, but not the concept of perfect expectations (Hutchison, 1938, p. 101).

According to Hutchison, uncertainty is influenced by learning, the period of production, and competition. Uncertainty rises with the lengthening of the processes of production. Likewise, the more oligopolistic markets are, the more important is uncertainty. As long as we do not have data on economic prognoses, the question whether the countervailing power of learning ultimately results in more correct prognoses or not remains an open and unimportant problem (Hutchison, 1937b, p. 648).

Consequently equilibrium is better defined as the 'optimum maximum' condition (Hutchison, 1937b, p. 646). Moreover, in the presence of uncertainty, economic theorizing requires an extra principle in addition to rational conduct; for example, action directed by habits (Hutchison, 1937b, p. 648). The actions and conditions of an individual or community are important for finding out existing economic relations and outcomes, which are below the optimum maximum. There is no need to search for any psychological imperatives behind them. Hutchison declares himself a positivist. Economic principles do not have to be explained in psychological terms, because we can observe economic relations in reality. Testing is necessary in order to be able to split metaphysics, based on intuitions and convictions, from science. Therefore what is claimed to be described must at least be testable. Propositions should, in principle, be reducible to testable statements. He acknowledges that, contrary to the laws of physics, the conformity of actual behaviour to economic principles cannot be verified. Economic magnitudes are at most estimated. 'The fact that human behavior is affected by error ... necessarily means that there is a divergence between the formula or positive law which describes economic behavior and that which describes its purpose, motive or intent' (Knight, 1941, p. 752). But he argues that, if economists are to agree among themselves, the only way open is to adopt the methods of the more advanced sciences, that is, by constant testing of their propositions (Hutchison, 1941, pp. 742–3).

Hutchison considers statistics to be the problem solving instrument in economics. Although cautious about the multitude of interrelated factors and the difficulty of collecting accurate data, he persists in defending the fact that more data results in better tests of economic postulates (Hutchison, 1941, p. 741). In the preface of the 1960 edition Hutchison acknowledges his formerly rather optimistic view on this point.

We may presume that Hutchison, by taking the hypothetic–deductive approach, facilitated the profession's avoidance of questions of uncertainty. He is clearly a neoclassical theorist working with a hypothetic–deductive model. That is to say, the primary interest of economic principles is to describe an ideal, not reality. Economic principles may be submitted to testing, under the agreement of reasonable men. To illustrate the problems involved, recall Knight's statement that all gradations but the extremes of perfectly homogeneous groups and absolute unique situations exist. The classification could not be based directly in reality.

Testing propositions as quickly as possible, as propagated by Hutchison, would sooner or later confront economists with the consequences, and with the non-quantifiable nature, of changes and uncertainties in economic life. With the dominance of discussions concentrating on methods and choosing concepts instrumentally, any discussion with regard to the intricate problem of uncertainty remains a marginal affair. Because of the prevalence of uncertainty about the future, it is a useless affair to deduce implications from some fundamental assumption within a static analysis. The formation of expectations must be incorporated in any model that claims to deal with uncertainty. The only way to obtain this goal is 'to look and see' (Hutchison, 1937b, p. 652).

Is this uncertainty?

What was the dominant attitude towards uncertainty in economic practices and theories around 1940? *Anticipations, Uncertainty, and Dynamic Planning* (Hart, 1940), provides us with a good example of the prevailing approach to uncertainty among economists at that time. What became a bestseller 'was part of the rather substantial literature this approach produced between 1935 and 1940' (Hart, 1940, p. v). A.G. Hart (1909–), who became economics professor at Columbia University, had just finished his study at Harvard and Chicago, when he wrote the book. His well-considered viewpoint was an assimilation of ideas from the writings, teaching, discussions and guidance of economists such as F.H. Knight, J.R. Hicks, N. Kaldor, an K.E. Boulding. This systematic and accurate monograph concentrates on the analysis of anticipations as the starting point for building a formal dynamic theory of the business firm. It is in line with Robbin's restriction of the theory of dynamics to the planning for the future (Robbins, 1932, 1935, p. 79). As stated earlier, it would imply that only the most convenient assumptions must be made the basis of any economic model.

While both Knight and Hart may be labelled 'literary pure theorists' (Knight, 1921, pp. 5–6n), Hart is the more rigorous of the two in applying the hypothetical–deductive way of theorizing. The advantages of taking this methodological strategy of augmenting details in an initially uncomplicated, ideal model are prominent; featuring standardized terminology, straightforward argumentation and convenient explanation.

As a result a major difference exists between Knight (1921) and Hart (1940) with regard to the logical rigor applied. Knight uses a discursive way of writing, combining theory and practice, while Hart is more of a stringent logician, discussing problems in a more *technical* economic language (Hart, 1940, p. 4), in what may be called economic shorthand. To illustrate, in his 1921 work, Knight devotes three chapters (146 pages) to defining and analysing perfect competition, while summarizing economic theory, discussing premisses, implications and arguments. Because economic phraseology and terminology became standardized by the end of the inter-war period, Hart is able to write with economy. For example, 'in the *timeless* enterprise theory of the textbooks the *data* with which the entrepreneur is confronted are market situations (under perfect competition, fixed buying-prices and selling-prices; under monopolistic competition, supply curves and demand curves) and technical input-output relations' (Hart, 1940, p. 9). Likewise, the word 'convenience' is used numerous times to the advantage of a clear argument. Nevertheless, the logical rigor applied comes at the expense of realistic properties.

It will be clear from the above that during the inter-war period the treatment of uncertainty changed dramatically. Hart and, to a lesser extent, Hutchison, use 'uncertainty' in a sense in which Knight would have used 'risk'. Uncertainty is circumscribed as 'the dispersion of anticipations around the expectation' (Hart, 1940, p. 65). In the given definition of uncertainty, the elements 'singularity of outcomes' and 'estimation of future events', stand out as crucial. The ability to clarify the essential features of uncertainty or risk is called for. 'Estimates about any future event which is not regarded as certain may involve either uncertainty or risk. The event viewed in isolation is always uncertain. But viewed as a member of a group of events so related that their joint outcome is more certain than the individual events in the group, it is a risk' (Hart, 1940, p. 51).

Hart refers to Knight (1921) for further discussion on the difference between risk and uncertainty, but does not himself develop the distinction (Hart, p. 1940). Moreover, risk and uncertainty are considered to indicate no more than different levels of a pyramid, distinguished by the level of aggregation. Uncertainty loses its characteristic of unmeasurability. To summarize, risk and uncertainty differ only according to the dimension of the number of cases under scrutiny.

Risk and uncertainty reflect, if we may believe Hart, merely different levels of aggregation. Risk situations exist in firms, that is, an organization of productive resources for business purposes under one financial control (Hart,

1940, p. 2), only when the firms carry on separate and comparable operations with independent outcomes. A reduction of the degree of uncertainty is defined as a decrease in the dispersion of market anticipations (Hart, 1940, p. 65). Insurance can take away uncertainties with regard to specific unfavourable contingencies.

This meaning fits the Knightian definition of risk. It has nothing in common with the estimates or guesses that are relevant in cases of uncertainty. Hence, it seems that uncertainty has become encapsulated in risk theory. The open future is reduced to denoting no more than points in isolation, taken from a probability distribution.

In the absence of uncertainty and risk, applying rationality to economic decisions boils down to what Hart calls 'operating on the marginal principle' (Hart, 1940, p. 4). He cuts short the fundamental and practical problems involved in the acquisition of information, the formation of rational estimates and the establishment of rational plans, by simply assuming, 'business plans are explicit and rational in the light of explicit estimates' (Hart, 1921, p. 5).

According to Hart, the introduction of the dimension of time by itself is not enough to leave behind the static extrapolation of optimizing techniques. Under certainty about future developments, it remains balancing *at the margin*. It is analogous to finding the optimum of the firm in static analysis: the quantities of various components must be alternated in order to find the optimum plan in time (Hart, 1940, p. 18).

Hart states that, in the presence of uncertainty, one can talk about a distinction between less and more reliable data, at respectively lower and higher costs. Costs are involved in both the gathering of data, and in the processes of estimation and planning. To be able, *ex ante*, to tell accurately how profitable extra information is, 'involves an accurate forecast both of the final estimate and of the event – which obviously cannot be made on the basis of the preliminary inquiry'. Information about future markets will always remain incomplete and unreliable. 'Unfortunately it must remain eternally a matter of guesswork just where the margin of profitable estimation and planning lies' (Hart, 1940, p. 81).

The main reactions to uncertainty are the use of unspecialized equipment, the buying of insurance and the maintenance of liquidity (Hart, 1940, pp. 72, 25). These reactions enlarge the adaptive capacity of the firm in order to react in due time to new developments and to allow it to take advantage of yet unknown opportunities. The prime entrepreneurial means of meeting uncertainty is the postponement of decisions until more information comes in, that is, 'the preservation of flexibility in his business plan' (Hart, 1937, p. 286).

Flexibility will have a minor role to play in planning under certainty. When losses are not expected, no insurance will be taken. Similarly, calculations for cash balances and inventories will render reserve holdings redundant. However, flexibility in plant and organization may offer better results in the case of a prospective varying rate of output. Likewise, in the case of variable sales, costs for production flexibility must be weighed against storage costs (Hart, 1940, pp. 25–7).

Whenever it is expected that situations with more scattered outcomes are the more profitable, it will be recommended to build a more flexible system of production. Hart regards flexibility to be foremost a requirement because of uncertainty and consequent capital-market imperfections (Hart, 1940, p. 25). This introduction of flexibility as a response to uncertainty is considered to be Hart's principal contribution to economics (Blaug, 1986, p. 376).

With regard to the planning problem, Hart uses the frequency theory of probability, and favours the use of both the expected value and the distribution of outcomes. It may be contrasted with Knight's approach. Knight used the classical theory of probability, and discussed the estimate of a specific outcome. Furthermore, he was well aware of the essential role in economic behaviour played by intuitive opinions, next to measurable information.

Hart, however, explicitly uses cardinal probabilities, summing up to unity. He asserts that the use of ordinal probabilities is considered insufficient for decision-making. Moreover, cardinality must enter somewhere in decision-making, e.g., on evaluating the fairness of insurance premiums (Hart, 1940, pp. 53–4). The use of the expected value of a probability distribution, together with knowledge about the width of the distribution of outcomes, makes the discussion of flexibility a clear outflow of the pragmatic discussion on uncertainty. Hart criticizes economists who use only the expected value; such an attitude would result in unjustifiably static recommendations.

The following two reasons may be found in favour of the expectation cum distribution view towards expected outcomes. First, the entrepreneur may be non-neutral towards risks. The author considers both risk aversion and uncertainty to be of quantitative importance in economic behaviour (Hart, 1940, p. 74). Second, planning at t_0 for *all* present and future activities of the firm is considered to be unnecessary and foolish business policy. The combination of an open future and the costs of estimation and planning limit the economic horizon of the entrepreneur. Estimates of the near future may be more definite and detailed than estimates of the remote future, whereas fuller information will become available with the passage of time. 'The very core of the uncertainty situation is the expectation of knowing more about the future as it draws in toward the present. In short, anticipations include the expectation that anticipations will change' (Hart, 1940, pp. 83–4).

And yet this viewpoint carries with it the following crucial drawback: A necessary condition is the narrowing of the range of the distribution of estimates through time: 'The t_1 estimates must recognize no possibilities for later dates not contemplated at t_0. And some ... must have dropped out of consideration' (Hart, 1940, p. 85). Thus, the unexpected appearance of once written off or yet uncontemplated possibilities is not allowed to take place. A surprise is impossible; there is always an encompassing basis for classifying all possible instances, and probabilities can be added to them.

Consequently Hart states that estimates and plans must be less detailed and concentrate more and more on decisions about durable equipment, when projecting further away from the present. The reason is that relevant developments become more indefinite in time. Anticipations are considered to change more often or over a larger distance, as the element under scrutiny gets further away into the future. However at t_0 a one-shot optimization takes place covering all contingencies, balancing all costs and all benefits, and plans accordingly the optimal timing of specific decisions.

Under what Hart calls uncertainty there will exist a zone of schedules, a probability-linked set of possible receipts from sales in time. This zone will widen through time. Or as Hart stated in 1937, 'estimates for the near future will normally display less diffusion than estimates for more remote dates' (Hart, 1937, p. 286). Among the schedules one will rank the most probable. From these schedules one may derive the expectation schedule, weighing all estimated receipt schedules by the estimated probability of the contingency, and summing up the results for each date.

The simple case of sales uncertainty can be expanded to discussing the existence of several types of output, and for uncertainty of technology, of buying prices, and of interest rates. Each of these elements should result in plans that leave adequate room for changes (Hart, 1940, pp. 59–60).

Buying-market uncertainty and selling-market uncertainty are almost symmetrical. The latter makes it profitable to keep down holdings of durable inputs, to avoid long-term buying contracts, to produce unspecialized intermediate goods capable of storage, to keep short production periods and to plan for a quick switching of production. The former favours plans under which substitution of inputs is simple, input reserves are held and prompt production rises are possible (Hart, 1940, pp. 60–5).

According to Hart, an important practical consequence of uncertainty is the existence of a *stepped* capital market. Capital market institutions differ to a large extent because of uncertainty. 'The institutions of the capital-market are deeply affected by the investor's uncertainty' (Hart, 1940, p. 40). Any entrepreneur is confronted with the following four sources of capital: own capital; outside equity participations (limits are determined largely by investment banking practices); borrowing via investment middlemen, such as bankers and insurance companies (securities are commonly exacted); and renting capital goods (this source would make no difference under a free capital market).

Capital rationing, i.e., the limits set fall short of the volume of capital the firm would choose to carry on if free (Hart, 1940, p. 34), is an effect of uncertainty. The causes are the possible dishonesty of the borrower and the uncertainty for the entrepreneur and/or others, of business prospects (Hart, 1940, p. 43).

When you want to borrow via investment middlemen, security is commonly exacted for two reasons: to engender confidence in the ultimate investor, the savers; and to eliminate the need for expensive investigations. Certain types of inventories or real estate, and certain ratios, function as doorsteps to enter markets for capital. 'Hence investment specialists [...] have built up systems of more or less arbitrary rules, which are followed also by many private investors' (Hart, 1940, pp. 40–9).

The entrepreneur obtains capital on this stepped market, each with own interest rates, its own rules of thumb, and fairly definite quantitative limits. Capital market imperfections induce a modification of plans in the direction of the enlarging respectability of the company. The holding of larger idle cash balances is induced by more uncertain interest forecasts, more risk aversion, and more uncertainty about the availability of capital in capital markets (Hart, 1940, p. 71). Cash balances and insurances may serve the function of increasing borrowing power or reducing interest rates. This is true, irrespective of the individual entrepreneur's feelings of uncertainty (Hart, 1940, p. 50).

The following conclusion may be drawn with regard to the development of economic thought on uncertainty: ignorance is no longer seen to necessitate the acting upon an intuition-based range of possible outcomes. In spite of contemporary scientists taking the opposite stance, Hart regards ignorance to be relatively unimportant (Hart, 1940, pp. 84–7). The word uncertainty is no longer used in the meaning given by Knight. I would argue that this abandonment of the Knightian concept of uncertainty is caused by the prevalence of the *technical* approach. Support may be found in Hart's preface to the 1951 edition. The sequence analysis offered in the book in essence presents 'formally a *mechanical dynamics*, with an *expectational dynamics* between the lines' (Hart, 1940, p. viii). The approach presumes that we know the distribution of probable outcomes.

Since the inter-war period, neoclassical economists commonly interpret uncertainty as denoting the negation of certainty or, rather, the assumption of closed sets of outcomes. When studying economic behaviour under uncertainty, they, in fact, assume a world of risk. Probabilities are attached to presumed different and mutually exclusive possible future states of the world. Probability is believed to be a property of knowledge or beliefs (Hey, 1979). It has been justified by talking about subjective probabilities which will make a convergence to the *real* or a priori probabilities, when more information becomes available and may be used for the formation of these subjective probabilities (Hart, 1940, 60). It has resulted in rational expectations theory, which is a stochastic form of perfect foresight (Arrow, 1987, p. 210).

The submergence of Knightian uncertainty

The question posed in the introduction can now be answered. In tracing trends in the treatment of uncertainty in neoclassical economics, following its introduction into economics by Knight, I have found two major trends. First, during the inter-war period the Knightian concept of uncertainty was restricted to the field of profit theory; later, it became a side issue; and finally it was written out of the script. Uncertainty, as Knight defined it, was submerged, due partly to the prevalence of theoretical ambitions, and partly to the multi-faceted problem of providing a useful concept of uncertainty. During this period uncertainty changed meaning, that is from unmeasurable outcomes to unknown chances. Throughout this period, the negative connotation prevailed. But its connotation changed, however, in another respect: The dynamic approach offered by Schumpeter and Knight, acknowledging the importance of changing patterns of economic behaviour, was overtaken by the viewpoint of a one-shot optimization.

Second, the change in techniques, stimulated by a change in the probability theory used, facilitated the straightforward modelling of economic activities. Uncertainty became conveniently encapsulated in probability distributions. A terminological veil of so-called uncertainties has been draped around the combination of determinism and probabilism. Of Knight's ideas on uncertainty there remains little more than a single event conforming to irreducible (Hacking, 1990, pp. 181–2) statistical laws which govern phenomena. The intricate problem of merging numerical data with possibly unmeasurable or unpredictable outcomes could thus be ignored. But, this so-called stochastic determinism is unable to take account of major changes. You may recall that Knight actually warned against what had evolved out of related discussions during the inter-war period; When scientists treat changes as following known laws, they explain uncertainty by explaining it away (Knight, 1921, p. 313).

When we restrict ourselves to the neoclassical school of economics, I am inclined to reject the quotation taken from Shackle. After the inter-war period, economics was not so much coping with uncertainty as an intuition-based range of outcomes deemed possible, but with sets of *ex ante* defined outcomes, each having a specific probability of occurrence. Neoclassical economics is unable to deal with situations which are unique to a high degree. The developments may best be summarized by the following citation,

> One characteristic of changes in economic theory during these two decades identifies the initial awareness of complexity, the gradual use of probability to represent complexity, and the ultimate summary of probability distributions by means and standard deviations so that analytical convenience is enhanced [...] It seems appropriate to describe this development as the *avoidance of uncertainty*. (Rowley and Hamouda, 1987, p. 45)

Furthermore this chapter sustains the conviction that the laws of nature are probabilistic, thereby safeguarding individual freedom. 'Probability is, then, *the* philosophical success story of the first half of the twentieth century' (Hacking, 1990, p. 4). Although it is impossible to prove, I have made a strong case to support the conclusion that as a consequence of this success story, the word 'uncertainty' changed meaning and became a side issue.

Note

1.   I am indebted to T. Vandevelde, J. Paelinck, R. Emmett, P. Groenewegen, B. Bateman and other participants to the HES-1992 annual meeting.

References

Arrow, K.J. (1951), 'Alternative Approaches to the Theory of Choice in Risk-Taking Situations', *Econometrica*, **19**, 404–37.

Arrow, K.J. (1987), 'Rationality of self and others in an economic system' in Hogarth, R.M. and M.W. Reder (eds), *Rational Choice. The contrast between economics and psychology*, Chicago: University of Chicago Press, 201–15, reprinted from *The Journal of Business*, (1986), **59** (4).

Blaug, M. (1986), *Who is Who in Economics. A biographical Dictionary*, London: Wheatsheaf Books.

Buchanan, (1986), 'Knight, Frank H.' in Ellis, D.L. (ed.), *International Encyclopedia of the Social Sciences*, 8, London: Macmillan Press, 424–8.

Caldwell, B. (1982), *Beyond Positivism: Economic Methodology in the Twentieth Century*, London: Allen & Unwin.

Clark, J.B. (1893), 'Insurance and business profit', *Quarterly Journal of Economics*, **7**, 40–54.

Coase, R.H. (1988), 'The Nature of the Firm: Meaning', *Journal of Law, Economics, and Organization*, **4** (1), 19–32.

Coats, A.W. (1983), 'Half a century of methodological controversy in economics: as reflected in the writings of T.W. Hutchison' in Coats, A.W. (ed.), *Methodological Controversy in Economics: Historical Essays in Honor of T.W. Hutchison*, Greenwich, Conn.: JAI Press.

Gordon, S. (1974), 'Frank Knight and the Tradition of Liberalism', *Journal of Political Economy*, **82** (3), 571–7.

Hacking, I. (1990), *The Taming of Chance*, Cambridge, Cambridge University Press.

Hart, A.G. (1937), 'Anticipations, Business planning, and the Cycle', *Quarterly Journal of Economics*, **LI**, 273–97.

Hart, A.G. (1940, 1951), *Anticipations, Uncertainty, and Dynamic Planning*, New York: A.M. Kelly.

Hawley, F.B. (1901), 'Enterprise and Profit', *Quarterly Journal of Economics*, **15**, 75–105.

Haynes, J. (1895), 'Risk as an economic factor', *Quarterly Journal of Economics*, **9**, 409–49.

Hey, J.B. (1979), *Uncertainty in Economics*, Oxford: Martin Robertson.

Hicks, J.H. (1931), 'The Theory of Uncertainty and Profit', *Economica*, **11** (4), 170–89.

Hopkins, W.S. (1933), 'Profit in American economic theory', *The Review of Economic Studies*, **1**, 60–6.

Hutchison, T.W. (1937a), 'Note on Uncertainty and Planning', *The Review of Economics Studies*, **4**, 72–4.

Hutchison, T.W. (1937b), 'Expectation and rational conduct', *Zeitschrift für Nationalökonomie*, **8**, 636–53.

Hutchison, T.W. (1938, 1960), *The Significance and Basic Postultates of Economic Theory*, New York: A.M. Kelly, Inc.

Hutchison, T.W. (1941), 'The Significance and Basic Postultates of Economic Theory; A Reply to Professor Knight', *Journal of Political Economy*, **49**, 732–50.

Keynes, J.M. (1921), *A Treatise on Probability*, London: Macmillan.

Knight, F.H. (1916), 'Neglected factors in the problem of normal interest', *Quarterly Journal of Economics*, **XXX**, 279–310.

Knight, F.H. (1921, 1948), *Risk, Uncertainty and Profit*, Boston: Houghton Mifflin.

Knight, F.H. (1930), 'Statics and Dynamics. Some queries regarding the mechanical analogy in economics', *Zeitschrift für Nationalökonomie*, **2**, 1–26, reprinted in Knight, F.H. (1935), Chapter VI.

Knight, F.H. (1934), 'Profit' in Seligman, E.R.A. (ed.), *International Encyclopedia of the Social Sciences*, 480–6

Knight, F.H. (1935, 1936), *The Ethics of Competition and Other Essays*, London: Allen & Unwin.

Knight, F.H. (1940), '"What is Truth" in Economics?', *Journal of Political Economy* , **48**, (1) 1–32.

Knight, F.H. (1941), 'A Rejoinder', *Journal of Political Economy*, **49**, 750–3.

Lavington, F. (1912), 'Uncertainty in its relation to the net rate of interest', *Economic Journal*, **22**, 398–409.

Lavington, F. (1925), 'An approach to the theory of business risks', *Economic Journal*, **XXXV**, 186–99.

Lavington, F. (1926), 'An approach to the theory of business risks (II)', *Economic Journal*, **36**, 192–203.

Little, L.T. (1938), 'Economics and Insurance', *The Review of Economic Studies*, **5**, 32–52.

Mises, R. von 1928 (1957), *Probability, Statistics and Truth*, London: Allen & Unwin.

Mitchell, W.C. (1922), 'Risk, Uncertainty, and Profit. A Review', *American Economic Review*, **12**, 274–5.

Orlean, A. (1987), *Heterodoxie et incertitude*, Paris: INSEE.

Robbins, L. (1932, 1935, 1969), *An Essay on the Nature and Significance of Economic Science*, London: Macmillan.

Rowley, R. and Hamouda, O. (1987), 'Troublesome probability and economics', *Journal of Post-Keynesian Economics*, **10**, (1), 44–65.

Schumpeter, J.A. (1911, 1934, 1980), *The Theory of Economic Development*, Oxford: Oxford University Press.

Shackle, G.L.S. (1967), *The Years of High Theory*, Cambridge: Cambridge University Press.

Tuttle, C.A. (1927), 'The entrepreneur function in economic literature', *Journal of Political Economy*, **35** (4), 501–21.

Withers, H. (1927), 'Frederick Lavington (obit.)', *Economic Journal*, **37**, 503–5.

PART IV

JOHN MAYNARD KEYNES

9. The locus of Keynes's philosophical thinking in *The General Theory*: the concept of convention

John B. Davis

I have argued elsewhere (Davis, 1989, 1991a, 1991b) that the criticisms addressed to Keynes's earlier philosophical thinking as initiated by Frank Ramsey, together with his own sense of the limitations of his earlier philosophy, led Keynes to reformulate his understanding of the central concept of his early philosophy, namely, the concept of intuition. This conclusion follows from Keynes's later philosophical statements and claims, first in his assessment of his early philosophy in 'My Early Beliefs', and second in his comments on economic method in letters to Harrod, where Keynes's earlier conception of the individual and society is extended and redeveloped to include a new emphasis on convention and a new understanding of intuition and judgement. On this new view, intuition and judgement are dependent upon and function within a system of interdependent belief expectations in which individuals find themselves embedded, so that it is no longer sufficient to explain the content and character of a particular individual's judgements and decisions in terms of a pure, unmediated intuition, but rather necessary to account for the manner in which a particular individual's judgements reflect different individuals' similar or like judgements in similar circumstances.

These conclusions flow directly from consideration of Keynes's philosophical development. Yet clearly what dominated Keynes's intellectual development in the years subsequent to his initial concern with philosophy was his struggle with the problems of economic theory and policy. This conceptual terrain was almost entirely removed from the language and interests of his early philosophy, and indeed philosophy in general, so that it cannot be said that Keynes's philosophical development was directly focused upon matters of philosophical significance, as would have been the case had his intellectual career taken the path upon which it had originally embarked. Keynes's philosophical development, thus, proceeded at two removes from the natural objects and preoccupations of philosophy. It did not make the traditional problems of philosophy its primary vehicle, and it also required translation from a different set of issues and a different way of thinking that occupied an increasing share of his intellectual activity. What this implies is that though one can trace the outlines of Keynes's later philosophical development by marking its occasional signposts in his occasional philosophical comments, to fully understand this development it is necessary to read off its expression in theoretical matters of a quite different nature, namely, Keynes's economics. The task of those who seek to explain Keynes's philosophical thinking, therefore, is to demonstrate how Keynes resolved problems specifically in economics as a philosophically self-conscious thinker. Practically speaking, this is to explain the philosophical commitments of Keynes's later economics in a manner consistent with Keynes's own philosophical interests and history of philosophical thinking. Yet as a matter of emphasis, it is not to attach Keynes's later economics to his philosophy, as does the most recent literature that favours his early views (Carabelli, 1988; O'Donnell, 1989), but rather to find out how Keynes's philosophical commitments evolved with his economics and largely in their service.

To proceed on this score is to turn attention to *The General Theory*. Only after an examination of the philosophical dimensions of this work will it make sense to further discuss Keynes's later philosophical thinking. As preparation for that larger project, in what follows Keynes's conception of the workings of the economy in *The General Theory* will be set forth, with special attention to his emphasis upon the concept of convention. The concept of convention is both central to the argument of *The General Theory* regarding equilibrium unemployment, and was also singled out after the publication of *The General Theory* by Keynes in 'My Early Beliefs', as his chief later philosophical concern. Moreover, its elaboration in the locations in *The General Theory* in which the concept appears, bears strong connection to Keynes's comments to Harrod about economic method. The discussion below first summarizes Keynes's general argument in *The General Theory*, and then turns to an analysis of the role of convention in this argument.

The argument of *The General Theory*

In recent years there have been many good accounts of Keynes's argument in *The General Theory* (e.g., Chick, 1983; Kahn, 1984; Amadeo, 1989; Rogers, 1989; Asimakopulos, 1991). Keynes himself summarizes his argument in Chapter 18, 'The General Theory of Employment Re-stated'. He starts out by explicitly identifying the factors that are given, the independent variables, and the dependent variables. The 'ultimate independent variables' are:

> (1) the three fundamental psychological factors, namely, the psychological propensity to consume, the psychological attitude to liquidity and the psychological expectation of future yield from capital assets, (2) the wage-unit as determined by the bargains reached between employers and employed, and (3) the quantity of money as determined by the action of the central bank (Keynes, VII, pp. 246–7).

These variables determine at any one time an economy's national income and its quantity of employment, the dependent variables whose explanation is the primary object of *The General Theory*. They are also variables that Keynes says are susceptible to influence and in some instances subject to deliberate control or management by central authorities to promote full employment levels of national income and output. Keynes summarizes his argument as follows (Keynes VII, pp. 247–9).

Focusing upon new investment as the crucial form of expenditure, Keynes notes that new investment proceeds to the point at which the supply price of each type of capital asset, taken together with its expected yield in the future earnings it is likely to generate, makes the marginal efficiency of capital equal to the rate of interest. This immediately presupposes states of activity for three of the independent variables noted above, the 'psychological expectation of future yield from capital assets', or as Keynes also describes it, the 'state of confidence' (Keynes VII, p. 248) concerning prospective yields, the psychological attitude to liquidity, and the quantity of money as determined by the actions of the central bank, which together thus determine the rate of new investment. New investment then brings forth new consumption, yet, according to the marginal propensity to consume, another of Keynes's independent variables, in an increment less than the increment to income stemming from the new investment. The ratio of new investment to additional income is termed the investment multiplier; by regarding it as equivalent to the associated employment multiplier, the increment to employment attendant upon the new investment can be established. Higher income then raises the schedule of liquidity preference by increasing the demand for money, which, given the quantity of money as determined by actions of the central bank, raises the rate of interest until new investment is halted.

The position of equilibrium, with values for national income and employment, need not of course be a full employment equilibrium. Indeed, in Keynes's view, the capitalist economic system is 'capable of remaining in a chronic condition of sub-normal activity for a considerable period without any marked tendency either towards recovery or towards complete collapse' (Keynes VII, p. 249). This state of affairs derives from the levels achieved by the independent variables Keynes isolates, or more specifically, from the state of activity exhibited by the psychological propensities or attitudes he believes of central importance. But what does it mean to say that a particular psychological propensity or attitude, for example, the psychological attitude toward liquidity, exhibits a particular state of activity? In determining equilibrium income and employment this question does not arise, since the levels of the independent variables, and the state of activity of each psychological propensity, are taken as given for that purpose. Yet *The General Theory* does more than demonstrate that unemployment may exist in equilibrium; it also considers how this state of affairs is tied to the development of a monetary economy that has made the psychological propensities Keynes isolates the chief determinants of income and employment. From this historical perspective, the question of how the psychological propensities isolated achieve their respective states of activity becomes important. Indeed, Keynes asserted that his selection of independent variables was in part motivated by a conviction that these particular psychological propensities and attitudes were potentially subject to influence by central authorities. More needs to be said, then, about the nature of the psychological propensities and attitudes that underlie the argument of *The General Theory*, and more in particular about Keynes's philosophical understanding of the concept of a psychological propensity.

To begin, it helps to emphasize that Keynes's summary view of his argument, with its focus upon new investment expenditure, gives primary attention to two of the three 'fundamental' factors he identifies, the psychological attitude toward liquidity and psychological attitude toward or state of confidence concerning the future yields from capital assets. These attitudes, it should be noted, are also the subject of Keynes's most emphatic statements in *The General Theory* about the conventional character of economic behaviour. In his discussion of the incentives to liquidity Keynes asserts, '[i]t might be more accurate, perhaps, to say that the rate of interest is a highly conventional, rather than a highly psychological, phenomenon. For its actual value is largely governed by the prevailing view as to what its value is expected to be' (Keynes VII, p. 203). In discussing long-term investment expectations, Keynes states that the valuation of investments cannot be accomplished solely through mathematical calculation, but depends upon a convention in organized investment markets that 'the existing state of affairs will continue indefinitely, except in so far as we have specific reasons to expect a change' (Keynes VII, p. 152). The chief psychological propensities at issue in Keynes's view of the economy, then, are thought to require explanation in terms of the notion of a convention. Keynes's (Chapter 18 summary) view of the operation of the capitalist market economy, accordingly, itself needs to be understood in this way. How is this to be done?

In *Macroeconomics After Keynes*, Victoria Chick asserts that at an important point in the transition from his thinking in the *Treatise on Money* to that in *The General Theory* Keynes came 'to the astonishing conclusion that the chief cause of unemployment is not so much that the real wage is too high, but that the rate of interest is too high' (Chick, 1983, p. 10). That the rate of interest could be too high meant for Keynes that the array of empirical, psychological, and institutional factors (such as bank policy, lenders' and borrowers' attitudes toward risk and liquidity, etc.) which determined the rate of interest possessed a configuration relative to the configuration of those empirical, psychological, and institutional factors (such as employers' and employees' bargaining strengths, relative wages, etc.) which determined the wage-unit that left income and output below full employment levels. Put differently, that there existed unemployment was ultimately to be explained by the inertial evolution of conventional attitudes and predispositions regarding finance and the labour market that locked the interest rate and the real wage in non-market clearing relations to one another. As emphasized by Colin Rogers (1989), for Keynes the Wicksellian notion that there exists a real or natural, long rate of interest that constitutes the ultimate anchor to which all other variables ultimately freely adjust is without foundation and intellectually naïve. It is market forces, rather, which the historical evidence demonstrates are constrained to adjust to conventional non-market, historically and socially determined institutional arrangements, and it is these, in fact, that thus constitute the centre of gravitation for the economic system as a whole. Should, then, the demand for liquidity as determined by such forces be especially high, it is because of institutional and psychological developments in the historical evolution of financial markets that, given long-standing, conventionally established levels for real and relative wages, leave the interest rate too high to justify the new investment needed for full employment.

Income and employment are then determined by the level of effective demand this state of affairs permits. Here Keynes's argument and its view of market forces in the labour market is familiar.

> The propensity to consume and the rate of new investment determine between them the volume of employment, and the volume of employment is uniquely related to a given level of real wages – not the other way round. If the propensity to consume and the rate of new investment result in a deficient effective demand, the actual level of employment will fall short of the supply of labor potentially available at the existing real wage, and the equilibrium real wage will be *greater* than the marginal disutility of the equilibrium level of employment (Keynes VII, p. 30).

The principle of effective demand, by way of the dependence of investment upon conventional attitudes toward liquidity and prospective yield, is thus in significant degree detached from the logic of market forces. Indeed, when entrepreneurs determine their offers of employment in light of their (short-term) expectations of sales and earnings, they put aside concern with the effects of possible wage changes on desired output, and focus their primary concern simply upon the level of expected sales. Relatedly, from the perspective of the economy as a whole, Keynes often emphasized that any economy-wide wage deflation might well negatively affect effective demand. In combination, then, the attitude toward liquidity, with its effect on the interest rate, and the attitude toward prospective yields, with its impact on long-term expectations, jointly serve to determine income and employment, and both behaviours, clearly, are for Keynes pre-eminently conventional in nature.

That Keynes's argument in *The General Theory* takes this form is not always well appreciated. No doubt this is partly due to the fact that the short-period equilibrium focus of the book makes investigation of the further determinants of the argument's independent variables, or what might explain the states of activity the different psychological propensities and attitudes exhibit, a less immediate objective. But surely also important is the fact that this latter investigation is largely an historical-social one that lacks the well-defined, formal character of the income determination argument. As Keynes emphasized to Harrod, economics is an art or way of thinking that makes unusual demands upon the economist, and '[g]ood economists are scarce, because the gift for using "vigilant observation" to choose good models, although it does not require a highly specialised intellectual technique, appears to be a very rare one' (Keynes XIV, p. 297). Here, the successful exercise of this 'art or way of thinking' is taken to require a deeper understanding of the psychological attitudes and propensities Keynes believes central to the determination of income and employment, and 'vigilant observation' in choosing such models to depend upon grasping the precise role that conventions play in establishing the state of activity of these attitudes and propensities. More can be understood about Keynes's own thinking in this regard by turning to own analysis of average expectation and the structure of convention.

Convention and average expectation in Keynes's argument
For Keynes, conventions are responsible for determining the general level or state of activity displayed by the psychological propensities and attitudes at work in the economy. Yet psychological propensities and attitudes manifest themselves in varying degrees in different individuals, and thus it is more useful and more informative to say that Keynes's interest in conventions was ultimately directed toward explaining how conventions act to structure different individuals' psychological propensities and attitudes in relation to one another – alternatively how conventions relate the degrees to which psychological propensities and attitudes operate across different individuals. This is borne out most clearly in Keynes's often-cited Chapter 12 explanation of the role convention assumes in determining long-term investment expectations. It can readily be seen, however, that Keynes's analysis there is quite general, and as such, applies in similar fashion to his treatments of the differences between individuals regarding the attitude toward liquidity, the propensity to consume, relative wages, and entrepreneurial behaviour in the short-period. How, then, does Keynes understand convention in his account of long-term expectations?

Perhaps this question is best approached by first asking why it should be the case that the convention governing investment valuation – 'that the existing state of affairs will continue indefinitely, except in so far as we have specific reasons to expect a change' (Keynes VII, p. 152) – assumes the form that Keynes says it does. Why is it the case, that is, that organized investment markets tend to preserve the status quo – 'the existing state of affairs' – rather than, say, constantly challenge it? Keynes's characterization of the convention that operates in investment markets has as its background a number of important statements he makes regarding the origins of speculative activity in equity markets and stock exchanges. Chief among these is his statement that at the end of the nineteenth century, capital markets were not nearly so highly developed as they came to be in the first decades of the twentieth century when there emerged a significant separation between ownership and management in the typical business firm. Prior to that separation – when 'enterprises were mainly owned by those who undertook them or by their friends and associates' (Keynes VII, p. 150) – close involvement with the affairs of a business, and with the fundamentals of its operations, typically meant a steady commitment to that firm's growth. 'Decisions to invest in private business of the old-fashioned type were [...] decisions largely irrevocable, not only for the community as a whole, but also for the individual' (Keynes VII, p. 150). This decentralized, atomistic world of business, in which individuals had little interaction with one another in regard to decisions to invest and grow, was largely displaced by the emergence of a more mobile and versatile form of capital ownership, which permitted the daily transfer of wealth from one investment to another, and which threw investors together on centralized stock exchanges in their common pursuit of speculative gains. In this change in the site and character of investment activity, investors lost both their former isolation from one another, and their former hands-on knowledge of the operations of business. They gained the opportunity to daily compare their judgements and those of others, so that the modern investment process made investors far more interdependent, though at the same time less well acquainted by past standards with those considerations specific to particular firms' investment strategies.

In these circumstances, Keynes tells us, what constituted a good or bad investment came to be 'governed by the average expectation of those who deal on the Stock Exchange as revealed by the price of shares, rather than by the genuine expectations of the professional entrepreneur' (Keynes VII, p. 151). While one might be tempted to think that the reference to good or bad investment implies that the 'energies and skill of the professional investor and speculator' are to be largely devoted to acquiring a better knowledge than widely available, so as to permit 'superior long-term forecasts of the probable yield of an investment over its whole life', in Keynes's view the investor's 'energies and skill' are rather almost entirely devoted to 'foreseeing changes in the conventional basis of valuation a short time ahead of the general public' (Keynes VII, p. 154). Thus, while 'the social object of skilled investment should be to defeat the dark forces of time and ignorance which envelop our future [...] the actual, private object of the most skilled investment to-day is "to beat the gun", as the Americans so well express it, to outwit the crowd, and to pass the bad, or depreciating, half-crown to the other fellow' (Keynes VII, p. 155). Average expectation regarding the worth of various investments is thus not only removed from an informed acquaintance with the underlying facts relevant to those investments, but really represents no more than an average opinion of their worth – or, more accurately, Keynes asserts, an opinion of 'what average opinion expects average opinion to be' (Keynes VII, p. 156).

Nonetheless, in such circumstance, or 'under the influence of a mass psychology' as not surprisingly develops when average opinion seeks to determine average opinion, the professional investor's 'behaviour is not the outcome of a wrong-headed propensity', but rather the inevitable 'result of an investment market organised along the lines described' (Keynes VII, p. 155). This average expectation of an investment's prospective yield, of course, subsumes different individual expectations of prospective yields both above and below that average. Different individuals accordingly have different views of the value of any given investment, and their taking action in regard to any particular investment opportunity depends upon their recognizing how their particular expectations differ from the average. Different individuals might thus be said to position themselves in investment markets relative to average opinion in those markets, though, despite the importance of this distribution for the daily play of trade between different investors, in the final analysis it is average expectation – and end-of-the-day mean result of any given distribution of individual investors acting upon their different, particular expectations – that is always visible to investors *en masse* in the form of the final price that clears the market.

The historical background to Keynes's treatment of convention, then, emphasizes the role of average expectation as a force in determining long-term expectations. How are the 'daily, even hourly, revaluations of existing investments carried out in practice? In practice, we have tacitly agreed, as a rule, to fall back on what is, in truth a *convention*. The essence of this convention [...] lies in assuming that the existing state of affairs will continue indefinitely, except in so far as we have specific reasons to expect a change' (Keynes VII, p. 151–2). More accurately, the convention in place regarding investment behaviour is that average expectation is fairly taken to be correct, except in so far as particular individuals find their own special circumstances give them reason to think otherwise. Alternatively, any standing or broadly accepted interpretation of the existing state of affairs is correct as representing the best, general knowledge or understanding available, and incorrect to the extent that particular individuals have special knowledge associated with their own individual circumstances which justifies their thinking otherwise. Put in these terms, a convention effectively combines two different forms of knowledge – general and individual – both of which individuals utilize to plan their different courses of action.

These two sorts of knowledge conventions deserve further comment. The general sort of knowledge or understanding that average expectation represents acquires its credibility from the fact that, because investors are less and less able to interpret the fundamentals of firms' operations, a knowledge of these firms' average performance gains in relative importance. The weakness of this sort of knowledge or understanding is that, as but a summary form of thinking, average expectation naturally subsumes a variety of individual opinions, some of which, no doubt, represent a more accurate estimation of the value of various investments. In contrast, the sort of understanding the special knowledge particular individuals often possess has as its strength the greater possibility of being better founded on the true determinants of an investment's value. The weakness of this sort of knowledge or understanding derives from the fact that, with the separation of ownership and management, this sort of individual knowledge or understanding is still deficient by comparison with the standard of close, in-house acquaintance with firm operations that explained individual knowledge before the modern separation of ownership and management.

Despite their comparative disadvantages – or better, precisely because of them – these two sets of counterbalancing considerations together dictate the way in which the conventional valuation of investments is established. Thus, on the one hand, we recognize that average expectation is ever-changing, and accordingly do not 'really believe that the existing state of affairs will continue indefinitely. We know from extensive experience that this is most unlikely' (Keynes VII, p. 152), and this reminds us that average expectation at best approximates a good knowledge of an investment's worth. At the same time, nonetheless,

> We are assuming, in effect, that the existing market valuation, however arrived at, is uniquely *correct* in relation to our existing knowledge of the facts which will influence the yield of investment, and that it will only change in proportion to changes in this knowledge; though, philosophically speaking, it cannot be uniquely correct, since our existing knowledge does not provide a sufficient basis for a calculated mathematical expectation. (Keynes VII, p. 152)

That is, average expectation is still fairly taken to be 'correct' – despite its evident deficiency – on account of the fact that that standard by which it might be discounted, namely, 'calculated mathematical expectation', is not typically available to us on 'our existing knowledge'. Indeed, a 'calculated mathematical expectation', were it to be possible or appropriate, would at the very least reflect an individual knowledge of the specific facts surrounding a particular investment. Yet since the separation of ownership and management, the in-house acquaintance with firm operations necessary for this knowledge and such a calculation rarely exists for most investors. Ironically, with this separation, the method of mathematical expectation gains in reputation with investors who, now distant from particular facts in their firm-specific contexts, seek a technique of judging the significance of collections of the various facts available to them that will improve on average expectation. As a result of this overall state of affairs, investment valuation becomes the product of an uneasy balance between an average expectation that is invariably wrong yet accepted and each individual's specific judgements which lack firm foundation yet offer at least the promise of doing better than average thinking. It is this combination that makes it necessary to regard a convention as a structure of expectations, a structure, it should still be emphasized, that is always rooted in a specific historical setting.

A conventional valuation of investments – indeed convention generally in *The General Theory* it can be argued – is thus constituted out of a structure of diverse opinion that bears a complex relationship to average opinion as its central reference. In this structure, it is the significance of average expectation as a central reference that explains why conventions favour the status quo. More will be said about the nature of the complex relationship between average and individual expectation that produces this result in the following section in regard to investment valuation. Here it should be emphasized that a convention in the sense set out here is a form of practical interaction that exercises a regulative effect on individuals via their recognition of the significance of average opinion, while at the same time accommodating action that departs from this central reference. Such a structure is normative in the most general sense in that it imposes an orientation upon individual behaviour without at the same time making that orientation binding. This is reflected in the fact that the content of ruling conventions typically change over time. What a particular investment is worth may generally be agreed upon to be one thing on one occasion, and yet generally agreed upon on another occasion to be something quite different. Convention seen from this perspective is a dynamic structure; in essence, the competing rationales that average and individual expectation offer guarantee regular change in the content of any convention, and this places a considerable premium upon 'vigilant observation' as central to the economist's craft.

Keynes of course addressed the important topic of the dynamics conventions exhibit in regard to the issue of their stability and precariousness.

Fundamental in this is his emphasis on the role played by the state of confidence, which, with the decline in 'the element of real knowledge in the valuation of investments' attendant upon the separation of ownership and management (Keynes VII, p. 153), emerges as a factor 'to which practical men always pay the closest and most anxious attention' (Keynes VII, p. 148). In these circumstances, ephemeral and insignificant matters often disturb an investment community's attachment to the notion that average opinion genuinely represents a reasonable valuation of a particular investment. That is, confidence emerges as significant with the very emergence of average expectation as a central reference in investment valuation. Thus, as it is increasingly average opinion seeking average opinion that characterizes such markets, a 'conventional valuation [...] established as the outcome of the mass psychology of a large number of ignorant individuals is liable to change violently as the result of a sudden fluctuation of opinion due to factors which do not really make much difference to the prospective yield' (Keynes VII, p. 154). In this ever more insubstantial world, even the more skilled individual, 'who, unperturbed by the prevailing pastime, continues to purchase investments on the best genuine long-term expectations he can frame' (Keynes VII, p. 156), is likely to be a casualty of the general change in character of the modern investment process, which more and more makes for the outsider '[i]nvestment based on genuine long-term expectation [...] so difficult to-day as to be scarcely practicable' (Keynes VII, p. 157).

The state of confidence regarding any given investment option, then, is not impressive by comparison with the full play and expression of animal spirits that characterized the past era of enterprise. Though entrepreneurs in the past undoubtedly also acted on the assumption that what obtained in the past was an important guide for their decisions about the future, this was 'business as a way of life' (Keynes VII, p. 150), where life in business was embedded in lifelong commitments to particular firms. Average expectation lacked meaning in this historical context, so that the state of confidence also lacked significance. In short, investment markets assume a different complexion as speculation and the pursuit of short-term gain come to dominate both enterprise and the long-term project of forecasting the prospective yields of assets. Perhaps this is nowhere more sharply expressed by Keynes than in his comparison of the investment process and a newspaper beauty contest.

[P]rofessional investment may be likened to those newspaper competitions in which the competitors have to pick out the six prettiest faces from a hundred photographs, the prize being awarded to the competitor whose choice most nearly corresponds to the average preferences of the competitors as a whole; so that each competitor has to pick, not those faces which he himself finds prettiest, but those which he himself thinks likeliest to catch the fancy of the other competitors, all of whom are looking at the problem from the same point of view. It is not a case of choosing those which, to the best of one's judgment, are really the prettiest, nor even those which average opinion genuinely thinks the prettiest. We have reached the third degree where we devote our intelligences to anticipating what average opinion expects average opinion to be. And there are some, I believe, who practice the fourth, fifth and higher degrees. (Keynes VII, p. 156)

The professional investor neither asks what might be intrinsically the 'prettiest' or best investment, nor even what average opinion will take to be the 'prettiest' or best investment, but rather what other investors believe other investors believe to be the 'prettiest' or best investment. In these circumstances, investors' expectations display a flimsy attachment to their central reference in average expectation – the necessary, though hardly all-dominating moment in a structure of interdependent beliefs regarding good investments. In such circumstances, the state of confidence is inevitably a changing phenomenon, and long-term investment commitments are often and easily abandoned, with the result that the level of investment is generally lower than would likely be the case were the spirit of enterprise more dominant.

Given, then, that '[t]hese tendencies are a scarcely avoidable outcome of our having successfully organised 'liquid' investment markets' (Keynes VII, p. 159), Keynes concludes that the modern world faces a dilemma.

The spectacle of modern investment markets has sometimes moved me towards the conclusion that to make the purchase of an investment permanent and indissoluble, like marriage, except by reason of death or other grave cause, might be a useful remedy for our contemporary evils [...] But a little consideration of this expedient brings us up against a dilemma, and shows us how the liquidity of investment markets often facilitates, though it sometimes impedes, the course of new investment. For the fact that each individual investor flatters himself that his commitment is 'liquid' ... calms his nerves and makes him much more willing to run a risk. If individual purchases of investments were rendered illiquid, this might seriously impede new investment, so long as *alternative ways* in which to hold his savings are available. This is the dilemma. So long as it is open to the individual to employ his wealth in hoarding or lending *money*, the alternative of purchasing actual capital assets cannot be rendered sufficiently attractive. (Keynes VII, p. 160)

The liquid character of investment markets enhances investment activity, while the availability of money investments that are comparatively attractive hampers it. It is true, as Richard Kahn has noted (1984), that Keynes's account here does not clearly distinguish between decisions regarding real capital formation and decisions taken on stock exchanges, so that there is some ambiguity in his thinking concerning just how decisions made in the latter case come to affect decisions made in the former. Keynes's general view, nonetheless, is clear. The increasing importance of speculative activity pursuant upon the historic separation of ownership and management had, and was likely to continue to have, decidedly negative effects on the level of investment expenditure.

This could well be seen as being a matter of the diminished role remaining in economic life for the full play and exercise of 'animal spirits', that 'spontaneous urge to action rather than inaction' (Keynes VII, p. 161) that was more fully in evidence in that earlier period when business enterprise was more dominant. Speculation, in contrast, with its greater emphasis upon the immediate, foreseeable return, places heavy weight upon the estimation of probable gain. Yet because the consequences of so many of the long-term projects business contemplates are fundamentally uncertain – as Keynes puts it, really no clearer at the outset in their ultimate upshot than 'an expedition to the South Pole' (Keynes VII, p. 162) – the occasions available for 'calculated mathematical expectation' are rare, so that the increasing role for speculation changes the character of the investment process for the worse. Long-term investment, where uncertainty about the future is inescapable, makes it clear that 'individual initiative will only be adequate when reasonable calculation is supplemented and supported by animal spirits' (Keynes VII, p. 162) and the 'spontaneous optimism' (Keynes VII, p. 161) they manifest.

From this perspective, chronic unemployment results from the interest rate being too high, because the short-term gains available to those whose wealth is ready and liquid sustains a demand for money that keeps interest rates high relative to the marginal efficiency of capital and investor animal spirits. In this conception, interdependent expectations are formed around both long-term investment and around the long rate of interest. Clearly in Keynes's thinking these two sets of expectations are related, since individuals with investible wealth may substitute between financial and real investment. Keynes nonetheless treats the two underlying psychological attitudes involved, that toward liquidity and that toward prospective yield, as separate independent variables, and consequently founds his equilibrium income determination analysis upon the interaction of these two sets of interdependent expectations through the income adjustment process. This must be regarded as a concession to the need to define the income model in determinate terms, since any collapsing of these two independent variables would render Keynes's insight regarding the too-high level of the interest rate difficult to explain. Yet from the deeper perspective involved in investigating the social-historical determinants of these independent variables – that investigation which has been initiated here in an explication of the levels of activity of these psychological attitudes via their constitution in conventional structures of interdependent activity – it will ultimately not be possible to avoid treating the linkage between financial and real investment and their associated systems of interdependent expectation.

What role, then, does convention play in Keynes's income and employment analysis? We have seen that investors' attitudes toward prospective yields are structured around average expectation so as to tend to sustain the past valuation of investments, albeit given the forces for change embodied in individual expectations. The level and volume of this investment, however, is influenced by the level of the rate of interest, which is also conventionally determined for Keynes. Attitudes toward liquidity should also be seen to be structured around an average expectation of the interest rate, much as attitudes toward prospective yields on investments are structured around their average expectation. In the case of the interest rate, 'its actual value is largely governed by the prevailing view as to what its value is expected to be. *Any* level of interest which is accepted with sufficient conviction as *likely* to be durable *will* be durable; subject, of course, in a changing society to fluctuations for all kinds of reasons round the expected normal' (Keynes VII, p. 203). Any particular interest rate, that is, reveals a balance of expectations across individuals with different views of the value of money, a balance which manifests itself in an average, central reference value in terms of which individuals form their respective expectations regarding the value of money. The reigning interest rate, accordingly, is conventional in that it is expected to obtain unless there are reasons to expect otherwise. And like investment expectations, the average expectation of the interest rate 'is not rooted in secure knowledge', is not rooted in any objective understanding of the true value of money, and thus 'may fluctuate for decades about a level which is chronically too high for full employment' (Keynes VII, p. 204).

Keynes's general conception of the economy, thus, is one in which these two fundamental sets of psychological attitudes, the attitude toward prospective yields and the attitude toward liquidity, are structured as dynamic, interactive systems of interdependent belief. In each case, an average expectation, though changeable in content, reigns as a conventional, central reference for the range of particular expectations different individuals form regarding prospective yields or future interest rates respectively. The state of average expectation in the money market relative to the state of average expectation regarding future yields determines the interest rate relative to the determination of firms' investment demand schedules, and jointly they determine the level of effective demand, income, and employment. Should the actual contents of these two conventions change relative to one another, then demand, income, and employment will change. A condition of chronic unemployment, further, is the result of a particular balance between these two, key sets of psychological attitudes in particular circumstances at a particular point in history. Specifically, the manner in which individuals' psychological attitudes are structured in recent experience is such that the desire for liquidity is strong relative to the confidence in prospective yields. A full explanation of the existence of chronic unemployment, therefore, incorporates an historical–institutional analysis of the structuring of these two, key sets of psychological attitudes to account for the particular balance these two, conventional systems of interdependent beliefs have attained in modern economies.

Keynes's underlying vision in *The General Theory*, then, partakes of both insights into the social–psychological dimensions of the economy and sensitivity to the evolving historical framework of the economy. In the first connection he develops an analysis of those psychological attitudes central to the understanding of monetary economies that explains economic outcomes in terms of a systematic organization of the beliefs and choices that derive from these attitudes. In his attention to the structure of interdependence these beliefs assume, he further characterizes a formal connection between these beliefs and attitudes that has the specific advantage of being determinate yet open-ended. That a convention reigns is explained by the significance a perceived average expectation possesses. Yet that average expectation can assume any content means that the logic of average expectation can accommodate an historically diverse experience. Convention, for Keynes, is thus a formal yet instantiable concept, and this is crucial to the incorporation of his historical insights, the latter dimension to his particular vision. On this score, it cannot be too much emphasized that Keynes's historical diagnosis regarding the shift from enterprise to speculation is crucial to his overall project of explaining unemployment. It is crucial in that, on the one hand, it enables him to say how chronic unemployment came about, and on the other hand, it creates opportunities for investigating unemployment's potential remedies.

Convention as a structure of interdependent expectations

More needs to be said, however, about Keynes's emphasis upon the nature of interdependent expectations to explain his later philosophical thinking, and here the attention needs to be directed to the issue of just how individuals come to form their particular expectations. Recall that when writing to Harrod about the nature of economics as a moral science after completing *The General Theory*, Keynes had also emphasized that the subject matter of economics is neither 'constant' nor 'homogeneous', and that this is due to the fact that it dealt with individuals' 'motives, expectations, [and] psychological uncertainties' (Keynes XIV, p. 300). We now see that he might well have added that individuals' 'motives, expectations, [and] psychological uncertainties' are variegated and diverse, and that this stems from the fact that individuals invariably find themselves in very different circumstances when it comes to such things as their respective views regarding the prospective yields on various investments and perceptions of the relative desirability of holding money. It is interesting that this point did receive special attention in *The General Theory* discussion of 'bulls' and 'bears' in the money market (a treatment which recalled a similar analysis in the *Treatise on Money*), and

that Keynes thought this analogous to his account of long-term expectations
and the marginal efficiency of capital.

> Just as we found that the marginal efficiency of capital is fixed, not by the 'best'
> opinion, but by the market valuation as determined by mass psychology, so also
> expectations as to the future of the rate of interest as fixed by mass psychology
> have their reactions on liquidity-preference; – but with this addition that the
> individual, who believes that future rates of interest will be above the rates
> assumed by the market, has a reason for keeping actual liquid cash [...] whilst the
> individual who differs from the market in the other direction will have a motive
> for borrowing money for short periods in order to purchase debts of longer term.
> The market price will be fixed at the point at which the sales of the 'bears' and the
> purchases of the 'bulls' are balanced (Keynes XIV, p. 170).

A structure of individual expectations, then, not only has average expectation
as its central reference, but also, as this passage emphasizes, somehow achieves
a balance between divergent individual expectations. This particular emphasis, which gives less weight to the gravitational aspects of average expectation as a central reference, invites us to further investigate the principles that
govern the distribution of individual expectations about the mean. Clearly, in
a market system these principles will go beyond the simple arithmetical
concept of a mean, since average expectation, as a reigning value in a single
price market, emerges from a non-arithmetical market logic of offers and
counter-offers. This proposition is perhaps best examined by thus taking a
closer look at individual expectation in relation to average expectation.

Following the treatment above, it will be helpful to retain the focus upon
investors' attitudes toward prospective yields. In the equity market, the average expectation of a particular stock's value emerges from a trading process
between buyers and sellers of that stock. Different traders' initial offers to
buy and sell a stock range over a variety of values, and bargaining between
them each day brings about a market-clearing exchange at a single value that
involves adjustment in asking price on the part of some and entry to and exit
from the market on the part of others. The average expectation of a particular
stock's value in this sense subsumes a variety of individual views regarding
that stock's potential value on the part of the market's participants. As the
quoted price or reigning value, it constitutes a central reference for buyers
and sellers, both because, as already noted, it reflects the collective wisdom
of the market regarding the value of any particular stock, yet also because it
represents a point of departure for offers to buy and sell at the start of each
successive trading day. On this analysis, average expectation is more than
simply a mean value of individual offers, since it represents the outcome of
individuals' dealings with one another in light of the daily re-determination
of a reigning value.

The convention that 'the existing state of affairs will continue indefinitely, except in so far as we have specific reasons to expect a change' thus means different things to different individuals according to their different perspectives on how they believe average expectation is likely to change. When individuals have 'specific reasons to expect a change' in average expectation based on their own particular circumstances, views, and information, they act upon those 'reasons' in making offers to buy and sell stocks, and in the process help to determine a new average expectation of these stocks' values. In this, individuals most definitely hope that it will not be the case that 'the existing state of affairs will continue indefinitely', since they optimistically believe that their particular, special perspective on the market will put them in a position 'to outwit the crowd, and to pass the bad, or depreciating, half-crown to the other fellow' (Keynes XIV, p. 155). Individuals, that is, are principally interested in changes in average expectation, just because they believe that the individual insight embodied in their individual expectations is superior to the collective wisdom represented by average expectation.

How is it the case, however, that individual traders judge as justified offers that depart from average expectation which they and others make, when the collective wisdom average expectation embodies must always weigh against an individual buyer or seller entertaining an expectation different from the average? That an individual hopes 'to outwit the crowd' hardly implies he or she can do so. Yet individual traders invariably look upon the reigning price produced by average expectation as a point of departure in the pursuit of gain. Individual expectation must, then, have its own ground of legitimacy. Of course, entertaining the expectation of a stock's value different from its reigning value generally depends upon being in the possession of some special information or view not widely distributed among those in the market. The distribution of individual expectations about the average is thus in the first instance a function of the differential possession of information or knowledge about the market on the part of different individuals. Being in such possession, while nonetheless necessary, is not sufficient to explain how individuals judge offers departing from average expectation as justified, since information or views not widely distributed must for that very reason also appear suspect relative to the consensus understanding represented by average expectation. Indeed, since average expectation already comprehends differential or unevenly distributed information and views, being in the possession of special information cannot by itself provide sufficient incentive for making offers that depart from average expectation.

Keynes, however, provides an additional explanation for the distribution of individual expectations around average expectation. In his account of the development of speculation and the decline of enterprise, he argues that the professional investor comes less and less to be concerned with the underlying fundamentals of an investment, and more and more with anticipating the psychology of the market surrounding that investment. Indeed in his metaphor of the newspaper beauty contest, the goal of the professional investor is not merely to estimate average opinion, but rather to estimate 'what average opinion expects the average opinion to be' (Keynes XIV, p. 156). From this perspective, investors judge the desirability of offers to buy and sell that depart from average expectation according to their views of the psychology of the market regarding average opinion. In the context of the discussion here, transactions between particular traders turn upon these individuals' mutual opinions of each other's individual expectations – in effect, their opinions of each other's psychology – since it is these individual expectations that embody views of what average opinion is likely to be. This implies that when individual traders actually go ahead to complete transactions with one another at prices that depart from reigning values, they share a confidence in the justifiability of such transactions that itself adds to their prior reasons for effecting it based on special information or knowledge. Confidence, then, specifically a confidence distributed and shared differentially across potential traders, is Keynes's additional condition for explaining observed trading behaviour.

This notion of a shared confidence, it should be noted, is linked to Keynes's discussion of introspection and value judgements as methods employed in economics understood as a moral science. Previously (1991b) I have argued that these methods Keynes believes important for economic science are equally at the disposal of individuals in the economy. Transposing Keynes's views on economic method to the behavior of economic agents implies that individuals form interdependent beliefs expectations when they reciprocally consult their own cases to judge the likely opinions of others by analogy with their own. In *The General Theory*, Keynes's reference to 'what average opinion expects the average opinion to be' displays a preoccupation with essentially just this same sort of interdependence. Professional investors consider offers to buy and sell that depart from quoted prices, and in important degree determine the desirability of acting upon those offers according to the perceived interest and willingness of those with whom they transact to do so as well. From the moral science emphasis on introspection and analogical reasoning process, each individual trader attempts to ascertain the motives of those with whom he or she would transact by a consideration of what his or her own motives would be in a like situation. If the imputed motives and reasoning appear defensible, trade at a price away from the reigning or quoted price begins to acquire a plausibility that supplements a trader's own original rationale for considering such a price based on differential information. That this process of evaluation occurs reciprocally adds further potential support to possible transactions between traders, both in that two traders rather than one may compare initial own reasoning with the reasoning of another, and in that each may also take the other's opinion of his or her own reasoning as further validation of that initial reasoning. This sort of interdependent reasoning and formation of individual expectations, therefore, allows for the possibility that individual traders may supplement their differential possession of information with a sufficient degree of shared confidence that enables them to resist the pull of average expectation.

How, then, does this reciprocal interaction of judgements actually occur? Each individual attempts to understand the thinking of the other by reference to what he or she imagines would be his or her own thinking in the other's place. Yet each trader is also aware that just as he or she is attempting to replicate the reasoning of another, so the other is simultaneously attempting to do the same. This means that to properly understand the thinking of the other each must also attempt to replicate the other's attempt at replication, so that, in addition to estimating the other's reasoning, each must also estimate how his or her own reasoning appears to the other. Higher-order replications may be imagined, but they do not add materially to the basic conception of interdependence at hand. On this conception, interdependent decision-making contexts are essentially much like what a more recent literature explains as game-theoretic coordination problems (e.g., Lewis, 1969). In this framework individuals making independent yet interdependent decisions are said to be capable of co-ordinating their separate and conflicting objectives (here, traders' different goals in buying and selling to one another) by arriving at a system of concordant mutual expectations of first and higher orders regarding each other's aims and thinking. They are, however, only potentially able to do so, since the dominance of individual interest and perspective implicit in the notion of an interaction between separate individuals makes co-ordination failures the general premise of the analysis. As for Keynes, then, the principal issue that confronts this more modern literature concerns specification of those conditions that make such co-ordination possible.

In the game theoretic literature, this issue is sometimes characterized in terms of the idea of salient solutions (Schelling, 1960). If difficulty in communication constitutes an obstacle forestalling co-ordination of independent plans, individuals may avail themselves of co-ordination equilibria that stand out from other courses of action in virtue of their conspicuousness. The salient or conspicuous solution need not be uniquely good or have any other particularly remarkable characteristics. It need only be something that enables interacting individuals to expect each other to expect each other to detect some particular solution to their coordination problem. Precedent, in particular, counts as an important source of salience and means of achieving co-ordination. Individuals possessing a similar experience with some particular regularity similarly extrapolate this regularity into the future to hit upon a means of co-ordinating their respective actions and separate intentions. In the broadest sense, a precedent is only some past, commonly recognized pattern, external to the immediate interaction of individuals, that guides their individual expectations. Precedents may thus be institutionally embedded or merely shared perceptions.

Put in this light, the special attention Keynes devotes in *The General Theory* to the state of confidence indicates less a concern that investors lacked the will or the needed quantity of animal spirits to commit themselves to long-term investments in the age of speculation, and more a conviction that investors are less and less able to discover sufficient precedents for co-ordinating their individual investment plans. In these circumstances, average expectation gains in significance at the expense of individual expectation, and investors accordingly reduce the extent of their commitments demanding prolonged neglect of average expectation. In effect, the historical development of the investment process produces a structure or distribution of individual expectations that is increasingly compact around average expectation. Yet note that because the possibility of profit (and loss) derives from pursuing offers to buy and sell that depart from reigning prices, an investment activity increasingly compact around average expectation must as a whole become less profitable. This produces a chronic stagnation of investment expenditure which itself depresses aggregate demand. Put in terms of Keynes's important emphasis upon uncertainty, the increasing difficulty investors find in establishing a shared confidence regarding potential transactions reflects an increasing uncertainty regarding their expectations of one another. It is, therefore, not so much the essential indeterminacy of the future that explains uncertainty (which, it should be emphasized, is no less a reality in times when investment is extensive), but rather the changed state of confidence within the community of investors, who find it increasingly difficult to establish concordant expectations regarding transactions that depart from average expectation, that explains uncertainty. In this respect, it would be misleading to say that for Keynes uncertainty is an inescapable, existential dilemma. More appropriately, for Keynes uncertainty is chiefly a social relation; a social relation, moreover, that is tied to a specific history to which we must turn if we are to explain the state of activity of animal spirits, as reflected in Keynes's independent variables.

Concluding comments

The historical transition from the era of enterprise to the age of speculation, it might finally be noted, produces an ironic reversal in the relationships between individuals involved in the investment process. When business was a 'way of life', individuals worked for extended periods for one firm. They were close to the fundamentals of firm operations, and detached from any mass market psychology regarding long-term investment. This enabled them to disregard average expectation (to the extent that it was at all tangible in such an era), and project individual expectations regarding the firm's expansion that had clear precedent for outside investors in lengthy involvement with firm operations. Moreover, the decision in a firm to offer equity shares or sell bonds was also the product of discussions between firm owners and managers that addressed just these fundamentals. Thus, though firms acted atomistically in investment markets in virtue of the unique character of their respective underlying fundamentals, they did so by establishing an internal shared confidence among themselves regarding their firm's individual investment expectations that constituted a precondition for the shared confidence established between the firm and its outside investors.

In contrast, the separation of ownership and management that gave speculative activity a predominant role in investment markets produces precisely the opposite state of affairs. When investors found that they must attend to the psychology of the market rather than to the underlying fundamentals of firm operations, they lost that atomistic relation to one another as buyers and sellers of investments that prevailed when ownership was united with management. At the same time, however, their detachment from firm fundamentals made it increasingly difficult for investors to achieve a shared confidence over transactions at prices departing from average expectation. Removed from the setting of the firm, investors thus found themselves cast together in their common concern with average opinion, yet at the same time less able to reach agreements with one another that would potentially earn them profits. This changed horizon is important for understanding Keynes's long-term policy perspectives regarding investment, since these depend upon restoring the lost past balance between the private and public aspects of character in the investment process.

In this reversal, then, we see Keynes's ultimate philosophical concern with the broad categories of individuality and sociality. *The General Theory* takes us beyond this framework as previously advanced in its incorporation of an understanding of the historical development in capital markets and the economy. On the broad philosophical level, Keynes's thinking requires a general explanation of the interrelated nature of individuality and sociality. On the historical plane, the way in which interdependent expectations link individuals together depends upon the institutions that exist in the economy. Keynes came to recognize this when he discovered the importance of convention. In his early philosophical thinking, in contrast, individuality had been balanced by a commonality of human nature. However, Keynes came to believe this inadequate on account of his difficulties in explaining the play of intuition, and thus, as he insists in 'My Early Beliefs', determined that individuality was balanced by convention. The treatment of convention in

The General Theory, as a structure of interdependent individual expectations having average expectation as a point of reference, gives concrete expression to this balance.

References

Amadeo, E.J. (1989), *Keynes's Principle of Effective Demand*, Aldershot: Edward Elgar.

Asimakopulos, A. (1991), *Keynes's General Theory of Accumulation*, Cambridge: Cambridge University Press.

Carabelli, A. (1988), *On Keynes's Method*, London: Macmillan.

Chick, V. (1983), *Macroeconomics After Keynes*, Cambridge, MA: MIT.

Davis, J.B. (1989), 'Keynes on Atomism and Organicism', *Economic Journal*, **99** (389), pp. 1159–73.

Davis, J.B. (1991a), 'Keynes's critiques of Moore: philosophical foundations of Keynes's economics', *Cambridge Journal of Economics*, **15**, pp. 61–77.

Davis, J.B. (1991b), 'Keynes's View of Economics as a Moral Science', in B.W. Bateman and J.B. Davis (eds), *Keynes and Philosophy*, Aldershot: Edward Elgar.

Kahn, R. (1984), *The Making of Keynes's General Theory*, Cambridge: Cambridge University Press.

Keynes, J.M. (1971–1989), *The Collected Writings*, ed. D.E. Moggridge, London: Macmillan.

Lewis, D.K. (1969), *Convention: A Philosophical Study*, Cambridge, MA: Harvard.

O'Donnell, R.M. (1989), *Keynes: Philosophy, Economics and Politics*, London: Macmillan.

Rogers, C. (1989), *Money, Interest and Capital*, Cambridge: Cambridge University Press.

Schelling, T.C. (1960), *The Strategy of Conflict*, Cambridge, MA: Harvard.

10. Two perspectives on Keynes in *The General Theory* and after[1]

John E. Elliott

Introduction

In a classic motion picture, *The Three Faces of Eve*, Joanne Woodward portrays the ambiguities and tensions associated with multiple personalities within an individual: the very proper Eve White, the very naughty Eve Black, and, guided by the psycho-analytic prowess of actor Lee J. Cobb, the emergent, middle-of-the road Eve Gray.

Similarly, many scholars have noted elements of ambiguity and tension in Keynes's interpretations of economic life. These include not only differences between Keynes's *Treatise on Money* (1930) and *The General Theory of Employment, Interest and Money* (1936, hereinafter *GT*), (Leijonhufvud, 1968; Shackle, 1967), but incongruities within the *GT* itself (Minsky, 1975) and additional differences between the *GT* and post-*GT* articles, notably Keynes's own restatement of the *GT* (1973) provided in his critique of Jacob Viner's (1936) review (Shackle, 1967).

A useful, albeit somewhat exaggerated, way of examining these themes is by depicting Keynes's views, in and after the *GT*, as if they were embodied in (at least) two distinguishable 'models' – herein designated as 'Keynes I' and 'Keynes II' – instead of simply two sets of facets of one overall theory. For this exaggeration, we beg the reader's indulgence. First, explicating and clarifying the more intellectually radical aspects of Keynes's writings is an important task, beyond tidying up this particular corner of our discipline's intellectual history. Second, extricating an under-recognized and under-appreciated Keynes II from the more familiar Keynes I, is a useful device to sharpen our understanding of the more intellectually radical components of Keynes's mature writings and thereby enhance our analysis of contemporary economic problems.

By 'intellectually radical' in this context, we mean those aspects of Keynes's economic theory that are least concordant with the main ingredients of what has come to be called the neoclassical-neo-Keynesian 'synthesis' (Samuelson, 1967). It is argued both that the content of Keynes's comparative statics was broader and more interesting than 'synthesis' formulations of 'Keynesian' analyses and that Keynes's argument contains significant, expressly dynamic elements.

The chapter begins with an overall characterization and interpretation of this topic. This is followed by an identification of those aspects of Keynes's *GT* which are foundational to and most concordant with neoclassical-neo-Keynesian modelings of Keynes, which we dub 'Keynes I'. We then turn to an alternative interpretation of Keynes or 'Keynes II', distinguishing it not only from 'textbook Keynesianism' but from Keynes I as well. Next, we examine Keynes's theory of economic expansion, focusing on the theme of continued expansion versus equilibrium. Finally, we consider Keynes's ideas on crises and their aftermath, and why, according to Keynes, contractions may be self-amplifying rather than automatically self-correcting, or even equilibrating at less than full employment.

Tensions and ambiguities in the *General Theory*
The *GT* contains alternative, and partly conflicting, patterns of thought. Notably, it contains a focus on equilibrium, albeit at less that full employment, and moderate instability. But it also embraces notions of disequilibrium, uncertainty, and severe economic fluctuations. One explanation for this incongruity is suggested by Keynes's self-appraisal in the Preface to the *GT*. There, Keynes notes his own 'long struggle of escape [...] from habitual modes of thought and expression' [*GT*, p. viii] and his own 'lack of emancipation from preconceived ideas' [GT, p. vi] prior to the *GT*. By extension, one might argue that, within the *GT* itself, Keynes was in some instances more successful, in others less successful, in escaping from 'the confines of the orthodox economic theory' (Minsky, 1975, p. x). And, just as Keynes differentiated the *GT* from the *Treatise*, so too commentators have differentiated such post-*GT* articles as Keynes's 1937 restatement of the *GT* from the *GT*. In the *GT*, Minsky states, Keynes 'never clearly differentiated' between more traditional and more radical dimensions of his argument (Minsky, 1975, p. x). In what Shackle (1967, pp. 135–6) calls Keynes's 'third edition', that is, his 1937 critique of Viner's review of the *GT*, however, Keynes, in Isaiah Berlin's colourful choice of language, focused on 'one big thing': the dynamic process of investment under conditions of fundamental uncertainty. Viner's review had 'tied Keynes's new theory into the old, and Keynes quite explicitly denied the validity of Viner's interpretation' (Minsky, 1975, p. x), thereby more clearly characterizing the economic process as fundamentally dynamic rather than equilibrating.

Another interpretation of the tensions and ambiguities in Keynes's analysis is suggested by the 'wine and bottles' analogy. Using this analogy, Keynes may be said to have proposed 'new wine', notably his propositions that unemployment was the rule and full employment the exception, rather than the other way around, and that movement, through market processes and without the right kind of stimulus by an activist government, from an under-employed to a fully employed economy, was neither automatic nor likely.

But, continuing with the analogy, Keynes was confronted by a strategic problem of intellectual choice. Should he pour the new wine into 'old bottles' (equilibrium analysis) or 'new bottles' (dynamic analysis)? The choice was fraught with dangers. If he chose an expressly dynamic framework ('new bottles'), his orthodox colleagues could accept his work, but undermine its influence by characterizing it as merely one of a long line of neoclassical business cycle theories, leaving the basic framework of full employment equilibrium essentially intact. If he chose a comparative statics framework ('old bottles'), he would both unduly narrow the scope of his contributions and, as it has turned out, be in danger of having his analysis reabsorbed back into a slightly modified variant of neoclassical theory.

Keynes (perhaps tacitly) broke the Gordian Knot by doing both. He provided a (primary) argument within the framework of equilibrium theory. But he also provided, sometimes in the same or an adjacent paragraph, a (secondary) argument, broader and more explicitly dynamic than the first. It is this latter, insightful, albeit secondary, perspective that we want to explicate and contrast with the former.

Keynes I

Thus, one may suggest there are two intellectual souls contending for dominion in the *GT* (and associated post-*GT* articles, notably Keynes's 1937 restatement). One, christened here as Keynes I, focuses on equilibrium at less than full employment and essentially sets aside disequilibrating processes, crises, and severe fluctuations.

Significant textual evidence supports this common interpretation of Keynes. First, when Keynes differentiates between his 'general' theory and the 'special' theory of 'classical' economics in the insouciantly brief, and misleading, Chapter 1 of the *GT*, he (unduly) restricts his critique of received doctrine. On the one hand, he claims that traditional theory 'assumes' a 'special case only', that is, that of full employment, and not 'the general case', that is, levels of output which include the possibilities of both involuntary unemployment and full employment. On the other, he opines that the 'characteristics of the special case assumed by the classical theory happen not to be those of the economic society in which we live, with the result that its teaching is misleading and disastrous if we attempt to apply it to the facts of experience' (*GT*, p. 3).

Later (in Chapter 21 of the *GT*, pp. 292–3), Keynes condemns the 'false division' between the theory of value and distribution and the theory of money and prices, the latter presented in 'Volume II, or more often in a separate treatise'. He then proposes a 'right dichotomy' between a theory of firm and industry with a 'given quantity of resources' and a theory of output and employment '*as a whole*' (italics in original).

Keynes's indictment of 'classical' theory for assuming the 'special case' of full employment is closely allied with his (unduly) restricted critique of Say's Law for assuming that aggregate demand always equals aggregate supply. Keynes's criticism of classical theories of the labour market (Chapter 2), saving-investment relationships (Chapter 14), the demand for money (Chapter 15), and wage-price relationships (Chapter 19) makes it clear that his qualifications about Say's Law are actually based on fundamental, theoretical argument. But what Keynes expressly objects to in Say's Law early in the *GT* is not the theoretical proposition ('Say's Equality', in contemporary terminology) that competitive markets, through downward price flexibility, in principle, will stimulate sufficient demand to match full employment. Instead, he limits his objection to opposing the view ('Say's Identity' in current parlance) that the 'whole of the costs of production must necessarily be spent in the aggregate [...] on purchasing the product' [*GT*, p. 18]. Or, as Keynes expresses it in Chapter 3, Say's Law holds that aggregate demand equals aggregate supply 'for all volumes of output' [*GT*, p. 26], not that they tend to become equal through market processes of price (and wage, and so on) adjustments.

In these various kinds of critical comments, Keynes challenges the scope and assumptions of his colleagues. In effect, their argument '*assumes* full employment'. Thus, a 'whole dimension of affairs', that is, study of the scale of output and level of employment as a whole, 'has been neglected'. How, then, 'could it offer any hint or hope of a theory to explain unemployment'? (Shackle, 1967, p. 146, italics in original).

Guided by Chapter 1 of the *GT*, therefore, one would suppose that the single most important point Keynes wishes to make is to distinguish between the practical, real-world experience of unemployment and the 'special' assumption of full employment, without any reference to crises or cyclical instability. Indeed, Keynes's explicit discussion of cyclical fluctuations is postponed and essentially restricted to a single chapter late in the *GT* [Chapter 22].

Keynes continues his focus on a practical, as distinguished from theoretical, critique of prevailing orthodoxy in his discussion of policy issues in the concluding Chapter 24 of the *GT*. If criticism of the accepted theory, he states, lies 'not so much' in 'logical flaws in its analysis' as in the fact that its 'tacit assumptions are seldom or never satisfied', it 'cannot solve the economic problems of the actual world' (*GT*, p. 378). By contrast, 'if our central controls succeed in establishing an aggregate volume of output corresponding to full employment as nearly as is practicable, the classical theory comes into its own from this point onward' and 'no objection' need be raised against the dominant microeconomic orthodoxy concerning its choice-theoretic and equilibrating analyses of resource allocation and income distribution (*GT*, pp. 378–9). Thus, hints of a 'grand neo-classical synthesis' (Samuelson, 1967, p.

361), wherein mainstream microeconomics is allotted the theoretical task of explicating how competitive markets allocate resources and foster equilibration (including labour markets) and Keynesian macroeconomics is given the assignment of assembling the practical reasons explaining unemployment and, as a corollary, justifying expansionary monetary and fiscal policy, finds some foundations in Keynes's *GT* itself.[2]

The impression of an acyclical Keynes is reinforced by Keynes's placement of his distinction between levels of full employment versus unemployment in the context of the concept of equilibrium. In Chapter 1, Keynes describes the classical view of full employment as being 'a limiting point of the possible positions of equilibrium' (*GT*, p. 3). This then contrasts with the Keynesian alternative, so often cited in the textbook literature, of 'equilibrium with less than full employment' (*GT*, p. 243). Several sets of notions undergird this concept: first, Keynes's argument, in Chapter 11, that investment 'will be pushed to the point on the investment-demand schedule where the marginal efficiency of capital is equal to the market rate of interest' (*GT*, pp. 136–7); second, Keynes's conclusion, in Chapter 8, that in 'a given situation', the propensity to consume is 'fairly stable' [*GT*, p. 95]; third, Keynes's analytic decision not to consider or take 'into account the effects and consequences of changes' in underderlying foundations of aggregate supply (*GT*, p. 245); fourth, Keynes's explanation of equilibrium income and employment in terms of interactions of aggregate demand and supply (or investment and saving); fifth, Keynes's explanation of the multiplying effects of changes in investment on changes in income and employment as dependent on a stable multiplier rooted in a stable propensity to consume.

Keynes's early summary of the *GT* in terms of aggregate demand [*D*] and supply [*Z*] analysis, in Chapter 3, is in this mode:

> Thus, given the propensity to consume and the rate of new investment, there will be only one level of employment consistent with equilibrium; [...] But there is no reason in general for expecting it to be *equal* to full employment. [...] Thus, except on the special assumptions of the classical theory [...] the economic system may find itself in stable equilibrium with *N* [employment] at a level below full employment, namely at the level given by the intersection of the aggregate demand function and the aggregate supply function. [...] (*GT*, p. 28, italics in original)

This exposition, taken by itself, encourages a view of Keynes as an equilibrium theorist. As one commentator puts it, Keynes's model, in contrast to the 'noise' which surrounds it,

> is essentially an exercise in comparative statics, with some dynamic glosses, purporting to deny the classical and neoclassical view that a competitive economy tends automatically to generate full employment. [... The] central message [of the

GT is that] saving and investment are brought into equality, not by variations in the rate of interest, but by variations in income and that aggregate equilibrium in this sense is typically achieved at income levels below those of full employment. (Blaug, 1987, pp. 666, 671)

Moreover, Keynes concludes a summary of his theoretical ideas, in Chapter 18, by citing certain 'special characteristics' of his core analytic relationships which, although not logically necessary, may be generalized from actual experience. Among these empirical factors, two may be noted here. On the one hand, Keynes believes that the marginal propensity to consume, and hence the multiplier, is relatively small. Therefore, changes in investment will generate only moderate alterations in income and employment. On the other, because of the 'increasing cost of producing a greatly enlarged output from the existing equipment, [...] moderate changes in the prospective yield of capital or in the rate of interest will not be associated with very great changes in the rate of investment' (*GT*, pp. 250, 252). The practical consequence of these 'conditions of stability' is that capitalist market economics in practice can remain in a 'chronic condition of sub-normal activity for a considerable period without any marked tendency either towards recovery or towards complete collapse' (*GT*, pp. 249–50).

Keynes II versus Keynes I
Thus, Keynes I criticizes neoclassical theory as limited in scope (to microeconomics), by assumption (to full employment), and in analytic imagination (to Say's Identity). This Keynes provides a macroeconomic supplement or complement to neoclassical economics, assumes as a 'general' case that employment levels may as easily be those involving unemployment as full employment, and sets Say's Law aside. This Keynes also provides the broad contours of a static, and comparative static, equilibrium model of national income and employment. Equilibrium occurs when $D = Z$, given the level of investment and a 'fairly stable' propensity to consume; changes in equilibrium occur when aggregate demand shifts by a given amount, again given the propensity to consume. When, for largely dynamic reasons beyond the scope of the equilibrium model *per se*, the level of investment is or becomes sufficiently low, such an equilibrium is perfectly compatible with (greater or smaller amounts of) unemployment. These leading ideas of Keynes I are found largely, though not exclusively, in Chapters 1, 3, 8, 11, 14, 18, and 24 of the *GT*; conversely, these chapters are devoted largely, though by no means exclusively, to the kinds of propositions just summarized. As thus characterized, it is fair to identify Keynes I as the 'founding father figure' of textbook Keynesian economics. The reason why Keynesian analysis is so discordant with Keynes's work is not because the latter has not influenced the former. It has – and profoundly so. The discordance stems from the failure to

incorporate some of the more analytically radical elements from Keynes (that is, those from the as yet to be systematically identified Keynes II) and the concomitant need, therefore, to incorporate ad hoc notions antithetical to, or at least not literally found in, Keynes II in order to yield the conclusion of unemployment.[3]

Keynes II recognizes that full employment emerges as a conclusion from neoclassical theory, but challenges that theory. For example, Chapter 2 of the *GT* examines and rejects Pigou's theory of the labour market, based on traditionally-perceived supply and demand functions, wherein equilibrium, and therefore full, employment occurs when 'the utility of the marginal product balances the disutility of the marginal employment' (*GT*, p. 6). Whereas Keynes I assumes money wages to be 'constant', though only as a 'simplification, [...] introduced to facilitate the exposition', Keynes II fulfills the promise to dispense with this assumption, and provides a theoretical exposition, in Chapter 19, intended to demonstrate that the 'essential character of the argument', that is, the proclivity toward unemployment, is 'precisely the same whether or not money-wages, etc., are liable to change' (*GT*, p. 27). Specifically, Chapter 19 characterizes money wages and prices as freely flexible, but criticizes the theory that such flexibility fosters full employment equilibrium. It then offers a radically different theoretical view in which a reduction in money wages, instead of raising aggregate demand and thereby employment to full employment levels, actually may cause greater economic contraction.

Tacitly, in the light of this more fundamental theoretical critique, Keynes's indictment of Say's Law now takes a different form from his initial comments early in the *GT*. Instead of claiming that classical and neoclassical versions of Say's Law presuppose that *D* and *Z* are 'necessarily' equal, Keynes critically evaluates the theory that *D* and *Z* tend to become equal at full employment through the operation of the price system.

Put somewhat differently, because the Keynes I critique of neoclassicism is an 'external' one, restricted to its scope, assumptions, and policy conclusions, the Keynes I theory – that is, notions of stable equilibrium characterized by $D = Z$ – complements and supplements orthodoxy. One can honestly be a neoclassicist on Monday, Wednesday, and Friday, and a (Keynes I) Keynesian on Tuesday, Thursday, and Saturday, without logical inconsistency, simply by modifying one's assumptions. A representative textual account (Crouch, 1972, p. 163) put this proposition clearly: neoclassical and 'neo-Keynesian' (that is, Keynes I-based) economists 'both accept the same basic theoretical apparatus', including neoclassical labour supply and demand functions, 'differing only in the assumptions they make before they operate it'. Notably, neoclassicists assume perfect wage and price flexibility while neo-Keynesians assume perfect wage and price rigidities.

By contrast, the Keynes II critique is an 'internal' one. It challenges neoclassicism on its own theoretical grounds and accuses it of errors of commission, not merely omission. As a corollary, an alternative (Keynes II) theory is both needed and feasible. Through this perspective, Keynes may be seen as rendering his theory less vulnerable to counter-attack, and protecting its analytic integrity from the argument that he has simply substituted alternative assumptions.

If the core idea of Keynes I is equilibrium income and employment, analysed in terms of interaction of given D and Z (or, alternatively expressed, investment and saving) functions, Keynes II explains why investment (and thereby aggregate demand) is low and/or subject to upward or downward shifts, indeed to collapses. In Keynes I, shifts in investment are introduced, in effect, as a *deus ex machina*. The real focus of attention is on equilibrium and the equilibrating process. In Keynes II, the focus is on the causes and consequences of disequilibration. Thus, Keynes I explains how unemployment is consistent with (a certain kind of) equilibrium if D is insufficient. Keynes II, notably by explaining the bases for investment, illuminates why a money-using, capitalist, market system is not automatically self-regulating at full employment and thus why unemployment emerges endogenously and is inherent in the system.

As Minsky aptly puts it, for Keynes (II), capitalism is 'inherently flawed' because it is 'intractably cyclical'. Such an economy 'cannot by its own processes sustain full employment' (Minsky, 1975, p. 57), not, as in Keynes I, simply because aggregate demand may be insufficient, but because the financial system, which translates 'animal spirits' into investment, 'contains the potential for runaway expansion, powered by an investment boom'. Such a runaway expansion is halted because 'accumulated financial changes render the financial system fragile, so that not unusual changes can trigger serious financial difficulties'. Consequently, 'even if policy succeeds in eliminating the waste of great depressions, the fundamental financial attributes of capitalism mean that periodic difficulties in constraining and then sustaining demand will ensue.[4]

Although what we are here calling Keynes II incorporates a richer and more variegated body of comparative static analysis than does Keynes I or textbook Keynesian models based on Keynes I, it is also openly dynamic. Keynes makes his intentions clear in the preface to the *GT*, where he states that in his earlier *Treatise*, he 'failed to deal thoroughly with the effects of *changes* in the level of output'. The 'dynamic development, as distinct from the instantaneous picture, was left incomplete and extremely confused.' The *GT*, by contrast, 'has evolved into what is primarily a study of the forces which determine changes in the scale of output and employment as a whole ...' Or, as Keynes put it elsewhere (Keynes, 1937, p. 221), 'This that I offer is, therefore, a theory of why output and employment are so liable to fluctuation'.

Keynes then defines a 'monetary economy' as 'essentially one in which changing views about the future are capable of influencing the quantity of employment and not merely its direction,' and, as a corollary, describes his method as one of 'analysing the present under the influence of changing ideas about the future' (*GT*, p. vii). Later, in Chapter 21, after identifying a 'right dichotomy' between the theory of firm and industry and that of output and employment 'as a whole,' he proposes another division, between:

> the theory of stationary equilibrium and the theory of shifting equilibrium – meaning by the latter the theory of a system in which changing views about the future are capable of influencing the present situation. *For the importance of money essentially flows from its being a link between the present and the future.* (*GT*, p. 293; italics in original)

One prominent reaction to these stated dynamic elements in the *GT* (and elsewhere) is to identify (Keynes I) comparative static equilibrium theory as the core of Keynes's 'model' and to deny a comparable cohesion or theoretical status to other (Keynes II) arguments. Thus Blaug, as already noted, describes these other aspects of the *GT* as 'dynamic glosses' and 'noise'. Writing to an earlier generation of economists, in 1947, Williams loftily refers to non-equilibrium components of Keynes's *GT* as mere '*obiter dicta*'. Early Keynesians often also adopted at least an overlapping view. Samuelson, for example, warns the 'young and innocent [...] away from Book I', which includes the rejection of standard labour market theory in Chapter 2 as well as 'the difficult Chapter 3' (1946, p. 149), and urges readers of the *GT* to focus on the positive contributions of Parts III and IV (the propensity to consume and the marginal efficiency of capital) and Chapter 24 (the policy conclusions).

Both textbook Keynesianism and its neoclassical critics assigned a 'privileged' position to Keynes I, thus 'aborting' the Keynesian Revolution contained in Keynes II (Minsky, 1975, p. 12). Among other factors, this was probably derivative, at least in part, from methodological preferences for comparative static modeling combined with an abiding faith in the efficacy of competitive market pricing processes.[5] Because Keynes holds neither of these two positions, it seems misplaced to privilege Keynes I and to reject Keynes II out of hand.

John R. Hick's success, through his early (1937) review of the *GT*, in formalizing and simplifying what became the dominant 'Keynesian' model, was also no doubt substantially important in 'aborting the Keynesian Revolution'. Hicks substituted first, a conceptualization of the demand for money as an inverse function of the interest rate for Keynes's notion of the impact of current interest rates in relation to expected rates; second, an exogenous for an endogenous money supply; third, a stable, given, investment demand schedule for a volatile one and thereby a view of investment as regulated primarily by changes in interest rates rather than by alterations in expected profitability. In this instance, simplification constituted (serious) modification. The spirit of Keynes I was popularized by sins of commission concerning Keynes II, not only by those of omission.

There are also several positive arguments which support the legitimacy of a Keynes II interpretation of Keynes. First, the constituent propositions which differentiate Keynes II from Keynes I – a theoretical critique of prevailing orthodoxy, a richer specification of functional relationships, and an identification of underlying causes of dynamic changes in expected profitability in relation to interest rates – are conceptually cohesive and logically connected. They thereby form a whole greater than the result of the mere listing of the several parts.

Second, the Keynes II perspective 'matters'. Theoretically, there is a world of difference between an explanation of unemployment based on *ad hoc* rigidities and one resting on a fundamental, critical theory. There are also significant policy differences.

Next, what we have called Keynes II does not consist only of occasional comments. Much of Chapters 2, 12, 15, 17, 19, and 22 can be more readily associated with Keynes II than Keynes I. The exposition in these chapters is too full-bodied and carefully constructed to be characterized as mere 'intuition' or unsystematic flashes of insight.

In addition, Keynes II ideas have been unusually fruitful in affecting the subsequent course of the discipline. Foremost among these influences was that of Keynes on Keynes. In the preface to the *GT*, as noted earlier, Keynes admits to his own 'long struggle of escape [...] from habitual modes of thought and expression' [*GT*, p. viii]. In several post-*GT* articles in the late 1930s, evidence of this struggle continues and the ratio of Keynes II to Keynes I is expanded. Keynes's 1937 review article is only the most celebrated example. In that essay, residual elements from Keynes I survive (for example, the notion of a relatively stable propensity to consume). But the paramount focus there is on the crucial role of uncertainty, as shall be adumbrated in the next section.

Another example is the work of such early Keynesians as Hicks (1950) and Hansen (1951), when they depart from overall summaries of the Keynesian system. In Hansen's argument, for example, the economic process is perceived as essentially cyclical, not equilibrating (Hansen, 1951, Chapter 24). The single most compelling cause of crises and failure to establish stable equilibrium thereafter is collapse of and contraction in short run marginal efficiencies of capital. These phenomena are not simply assumed, but are explained as arising endogenously, out of the processes of change in capitalist market economies.

Shackle provides a final, vivid example. He claims that Keynes's 1937 review article (with Chapter 12 of the *GT* serving as a kind of prelude) reveals the 'ultimate meaning' of Keynes's project. According to this interpretation of Keynes, the 'ultimate ground' of massive unemployment is uncertainty concerning profit expectations. Rational expectation 'being unattainable, we substitute for it first one and then another kind of irrational expectation'. Thus, unemployment theory is 'inescapably' a theory of 'disorder' (Shackle, 1967, pp. 129, 133–4).

Carried to an extreme, this 'fundamentalist' vision of the Keynesian project, based on comprehensive and pervasive uncertainty, Coddington argues is 'consistent but analytically nihilistic' (Coddington, 1983, pp. 61–2). A 'root and branch' application of radical 'subjectivism' is analogous to 'an outbreak of Christian Science among the medical profession, or a passion for telekinesis among airline pilots'. Keynesian 'fundamentalism' rejects Keynes I as firmly as the standard interpretation rejects Keynes II. Both viewpoints differentiate 'good (true) Keynes' from 'bad (false) Keynes' in a way analogous to that of Harvard–Radcliffe students and other patrons of the Brattle Street Theatre of the 1970s, who distinguished between 'Good Bogey' (The Maltese Falcon, Sam Spade) and 'Bad Bogey' (The African Queen, Treasure of the Sierra Madre).

As we shall illustrate in the next sections, Keynes's commitment to dynamic change does not lead him to abandon equilibrium conceptualizations. Although juxtapositions of one with the other are occasionally confusing, Keynes uses both kinds of argument to make his points. Moreover, Keynes refuses to separate static and dynamic elements into two unconnected bodies of thought. To the contrary, some of his most interesting and insightful ideas concerning crises and contractions pertain to circumstances in which formerly stable relationships become destabilizing. As Minsky observes, Keynes's short-run equilibria are 'transitory', in the sense that 'relations are built up which transform the way in which the economy will behave' (Minsky, 1975, p. 57). As the economy moves toward equilibrium,

> endogenously determined changes occur which affect the set of system variables toward which the economy tends. [...] Each state, whether it be boom, crisis, debt-deflation, stagnation, or expansion, is transitory. During each short-run equilibrium, in Keynes' view, processes are at work which will 'disequilibrate' the system. Not only is stability an unattainable goal; whenever something approaching stability is achieved, destabilizing processes are set off. (Minsky, 1975, p. 61)

Thus, Keynes II supplements and complements Keynes I rather than supplanting it, and 'Good Keynes' is Keynes I + Keynes II (plus, of course, other interpretations of Keynes beyond the scope of this chapter, rather than Keynes I alone.

Expansion and equilibrium

Once cyclical recovery succeeds depression or low-level equilibrium, 'the manner in which it feeds on itself and cumulates is obvious' (*GT*, p 319). As long as the marginal propensity to consume exceeds zero, 'when there is an increment of aggregate investment, income will increase by an amount which is *k* times the increment of investment' (*GT*, p. 115). Increased 'employment for investment must necessarily stimulate the industries producing for consumption and thus lead to total increase in employment which is a multiple of the primary employment required by the investment itself' (*GT*, p. 118). As long as investment continues to increase, unless the propensity to consume were to shift down sufficiently to overpower the rise in investment, *D*, and thereby income, consumption, and employment, will also continue to expand and, to some extent, will do so in a cumulative and self-amplifying manner. Keynes simplifies his argument by supposing, as noted earlier, an essentially stable propensity to consume and an investment essentially independent of the current level of income and employment. 'The fact that an increase in consumption is apt in itself to stimulate this further investment,' he adds in 1937 (Keynes, 1937, pp. 220–1), 'merely fortifies the argument'.

In the special circumstances where expansion carries the economy to full employment, an emendation is needed. Keynes provides two variants. At a given moment in time, full employment insures that rising *D* 'produces no further increase in output'. Therefore, 'any attempt to increase investment still further will set up a tendency in money-prices to rise without limit' and a state of 'true inflation' will have been reached (*GT*, pp. 118–19, 303). Over time, presuming expansion has proceeded until full employment, further 'change and progress', in response to rising investment, 'would result only from changes in technique, taste, population and institutions' (*GT*, pp. 220–1), that is, from changes in the underlying determinants of *Z* that Keynes does not claim to take 'into account' in his theory (*GT*, pp. 245). Hence, a growth rate in investment larger than that in potential *Z* would yield expansion in both real output and prices. Similarly, even before full employment is reached, such factors as diminishing returns, 'bottlenecks' and short run supply inelasticities, and money wage increases will cause 'increasing output [to] be associated with rising prices' (*GT*, p. 300). But whether expansion is non-inflationary, purely inflationary, or somewhere in between, and whether growth occurs in the process of moving toward full employment or under full employment conditions, its foundational stimulus is investment. For Keynes, rising investment generates an expanding economy; an expanding economy presupposes rising investment.

According to Keynes, the marginal propensity to consume tends 'to diminish as employment [and] real income increase' (*GT*, p. 120). He cites two specific reasons. One is that expansion primarily raises the income of the re-employed. As the unemployed become employed, their former acts of negative saving tend to disappear. Thus, consumption rises by less than what would have occurred 'from an equal increase in the community's real income accruing in different circumstances'. Another reason is that price increases, rooted in higher costs because of diminishing returns, tend to increase 'the proportion of aggregate income which accrues to the entrepreneurs, whose individual marginal propensity to consume is probably less than the average for the community as a whole' (*GT*, p. 121). A decrease in the overall marginal propensity to consume, however, although it would tend to reduce the extent of expansion in income and employment associated with any particular increase in investment, does not necessarily trigger a crisis or even a cessation of the expansion. To the contrary, the same redistribution of income from workers to entrepreneurs brought by higher prices presumably raises the proclivity to invest. If so, expansion continues, even if the cumulative magnitude of multiplier effects from higher investment decreases.

For investment, and hence expansion, to continue according to Keynes's analytic framework, the schedule of the marginal efficiency of capital must be (sufficiently) 'high' relative to the average level of interest rates and/or cyclical fluctuations in short run relationships between profit expectations and interest rates must temporarily raise the ratio between them sufficiently to sustain expansion for a time despite the 'low' average relationship.

Keynes's assessment of the longer-run relationships is grim. Dynamic growth factors in the nineteenth century, he holds, together with the propensity to consume, were sufficient to create a schedule of the marginal efficiency of capital high enough to allow 'a reasonably satisfactory average level of employment to be compatible with a rate of interest high enough to be psychologically acceptable to wealth-owners' (*GT*, p. 307). As noted earlier, Keynes believes the relationship between long run profit expectations and the rate of interest is 'much lower' in the twentieth century.

Keynes identifies a second reason why long run profit expectations are low. Physical capital, he argues, generates a net 'yield' above replacement cost in value terms because capital goods are scarce. As the stock of capital becomes more abundant in a wealthy society, net yields, and hence profitable opportunities for further investment, decline. In principle, it is conceivable that the capital stock could become so abundant that its net yield of income above production costs, and therefore the marginal efficiency of capital, would be reduced 'approximately to zero' (*GT*, p. 220). Of course, an increase in the stock of capital raises potential output and, therefore, consumption. But as long as the marginal propensity to consume is less than one (and

we abstract from both dynamic growth factors affecting autonomous investment and the effects of income on induced investment), increases in the
capital stock above a 'full investment' (*GT*, p. 324) position is untenable. In
general, an increased capital stock will occur only if 'future expenditure on
consumption is expected to increase. Each time we secure today's equilibrium by increased investment, we are aggravating the difficulty of securing
equilibrium tomorrow' (*GT*, p. 105). This aggravation would become insurmountable if capital were to become so abundant as to reduce its net yield to
(even approximately) zero.

Low-level marginal efficiency of capital schedules would not necessarily
constitute insurmountable barriers to continued expansion if the average rate
of interest, around which short run interest rates fluctuate, were lower. In fact,
Keynes believed, the opposite is true. Keynes elaborates the bases for this
interpretation in Chapters 15 and 17 of the *GT*. In principle, any asset, he
states, has its 'own' rate of interest, composed of three attributes: yield,
carrying costs, and liquidity premium, or $q - c + l$. If an asset is to be newly
produced, its rate must attain (or exceed) the level of the highest rates of all
other assets; that is, that asset whose 'own-rate of interest' is the largest,
notably because it falls more slowly than all others as the stock of assets
increases and 'eventually knocks out the profitable production of each of the
others,' and thereby 'rules the roost' (*GT*, pp. 223, 229).

The 'peculiar significance' of the rate of interest on money in limiting the
expansion of output and employment, for Keynes, arises from money's 'special characteristics' which render its own-rate of interest 'more reluctant to
fall as output increases than the own-rates of interest of any other assets' (*GT*,
p. 229). Keynes identifies three such characteristics:

1. Money has a 'very small elasticity of production', that is, money cannot
    be easily expanded by employing more labour to produce it when it is in
    great demand.
2. Money has a virtually zero elasticity of substitution, that is, there is no
    inexpensive substitute capable of 'doing money's duty equally well'.
3. Under certain conditions, 'demand may be predominantly directed to
    money'

(*GT*, pp. 230, pp. 234).

Money is demanded, *inter alia*, as a store of wealth, 'we are told without a
smile on the face'. True, money's carrying costs, *c*, are low; but because it is
'barren,' its yield, *q*, is zero. Why, then, should 'anyone outside a lunatic
asylum' want to hold money? Essentially, Keynes replies to his own question, in an economy in which uncertainty about the future is systemic, our
desire to hold money 'is a barometer of the degree of our own calculations

and conventions concerning the future'. Money's liquidity, l, 'lulls our disquietude, and the premium which we require to make us part with money is the measure of the degree of our disquietude' (Keynes, 1937, p. 216). Given, at any particular moment, generally accepted views about what interest rate, i, is 'safe', any reduction in i 'increases the risk of illiquidity' by decreasing the actual rate relative to the 'safe' rate and decreases the 'current earnings from illiquidity'. As the costs of illiquidity go up and its benefits drop, speculators increasingly turn to money. The greater intensity of demand for money at low rates makes it increasingly difficult to achieve further reductions in long run or average rates of interest, either by expansionary monetary policy or through the effects of decreases in prices (that is, the so-called 'Keynes Effect'). Keynes describes this phenomenon as 'perhaps the chief obstacle to a fall in the rate of interest to a very low level' (*GT*, p. 202), although it is reinforced by the 'intermediate costs of bringing the borrower and the ultimate lender together' and the 'lender's risk' which must be added to the 'pure rate of interest' (*GT*, pp. 144, 208).

As observed earlier, the low average relationship between profit expectations and interest rates may be temporarily offset by a higher short run relationship. Indeed, a short run recovery of marginal efficiency of capital schedules is essential, and short run reductions in interest rates are contributive, to cyclical expansion after a depression. But for Keynes, crises are both immanent and imminent in the expansionary process. The expansion in income, employment, and prices in itself raises transactionary, and thereby overall, demands for money. The resulting increase in the interest rate restrains investment 'unless the monetary authority takes steps to the contrary' (*GT*, p. 199). Meanwhile, because of the 'increasing cost of producing a greatly enlarged output from the existing equipment', replacement costs of capital assets rise and expected rates of profit, r, fall (*GT*, p. 252).

Under these circumstances, the best that can be hoped for is an anemic expansion which ends ignominiously in a 'stable equilibrium' at less than full employment where $r = i$. Given the 'low' level of long run marginal efficiencies of capital, the 'high' level of long run interest rates, and the proclivity of short run interest rates to rise and short run profit rates to fall during cyclical expansion, 'an insufficiency of effective demand may, and often will, bring the increase of employment to a standstill *before* a level of full employment has been reached' (*GT*, pp. 30–1; italics in original).

Crisis and contraction

Such an equilibrium is only 'stable' temporarily, however. If $r = i$ (a necessary condition for equilibrium), the slightest upward jiggle in i or drop in r will cause investment to fall, a crisis (defined by the insufficiency of D relative to Z) to ensue, the economy to reverse itself, and income and employment to decrease. If, however, the expansion is weak, the ensuing crisis and contraction is unlikely to be catastrophic. Tepid fluctuations 'tend to wear themselves out before proceeding to extremes and eventually to reverse themselves'. In this event, the system is 'not violently unstable' (*GT*, pp. 249, 251).

By contrast, when an expansion is robust and its later stages take on the qualities of a 'boom', then the crisis is likely to be sharp and severe. It is customary, Keynes observes, to attribute crises primarily to rising interest rates, caused by an increased demand for money 'both for trade and speculative purposes'. In some instances, he states, this process plays 'an aggravating and, occasionally perhaps, an initiating part'. But the 'typical' crisis is caused, not primarily by rising interest rates, but by a 'sudden collapse' in the marginal efficiency of capital (*GT*, p. 315).

'Collapse' in expected profitability is usually preceded by 'optimistic expectations as to the future yield of capital-goods sufficiently strong to offset their growing abundance and their rising costs of production and, probably, a rise in the rate of interest, also' (*GT*, p. 315). The 'whole object' of wealth accumulation through capital investment, Keynes states (1937, p. 214), is to yield prospective results 'at a comparatively distant, and sometimes *indefinitely* distant, date'. Such knowledge of the future is 'fluctuating, vague, and uncertain'. Uncertainty concerning future interest rates, prices, yields, and costs of capital assets are matters about which 'there is no scientific basis on which to form any calculable probability whatever. We simply do not know'.

Uncertainty in this sense is endemic in a market capitalist economy. Saving is:

> not a substitution of future consumption-demand for present consumption-demand, [...] but a desire for 'wealth' as such, that is for a potentiality of consuming an unspecified article at an unspecified time. [...] The only radical cure for the crises of confidence which afflict the economic life of the modern world would be to allow the individual no choice between consuming his income and ordering the production of the specific capital-asset which, even though it be on precarious evidence, impresses him as the most promising investment. (*GT*, pp. 161, 211)

But this 'radical cure' is beyond the scope of a monetary, capitalist, market economy, characterized by systemic uncertainty. Investors try to cope with the uncertain and precarious nature of the future in various ways. First, they assume that the present is a more illuminating guide to the future than the past has been to the present, the existing state of opinion correctly previsages the future, and the conventional judgement that collective or average behaviour is better informed than any particular individual. Therefore, expansion tends to breed expansion through 'waves of optimistic [...] sentiment', which are 'unreasoning', yet 'legitimate', when 'no solid basis exists for a reasonable calculation' (*GT*, p. 154).

Second, the development of organized equities markets makes it possible for individuals to revise their investment decisions and change their investments. Although there is no investment liquidity for 'the community as a whole', the appearance of liquidity for any given individual 'calms his nerves and makes him much more willing to run a risk'. As long as 'we can rely on the maintenance of the convention' – that 'the existing state of affairs will continue indefinitely, except in so far as we have specific reasons to expect a change' – this sense of liquidity 'often facilitates, though it sometimes impedes, the course of new investment' (*GT*, pp. 152, 155, 160).

Third, much investment activity depends on 'spontaneous optimism' and 'animal spirits' rather than on a 'mathematical expectation' (*GT*, p. 161). A short run shift toward greater business optimism can reduce both 'lender's risk' and 'entrepreneur's risk'. Thus, profits can be buoyed up relative to interest rates (which, if not lowered, may rise by less than they otherwise would) by an optimistic 'state of confidence' which later, more sober, calculation comes to regard as greater than warranted. Alternatively put, if expansion elicits a heightened state of business confidence, subjective opinions about expected yields and interest rates may raise the prices of capital assets relative to their costs; investment may then increase by more than it otherwise would have, business confidence again improves, and the expansion cumulatively reinforces itself.

Keynes's analysis of wage–price–interest rate relationships focuses on downward flexibility. But his argument may be reversed to give greater specificity to his view of expansion and crisis. First, Keynes believes that wage increases tend to be smaller than price increases during expansions. Unemployment serves to constrain increases in money wages, while rising production costs caused by diminishing returns plus other reasons elicit some price increases even before full employment is reached. Moreover, because of uncertainty derivative from the absence of overall co-ordination of wages and employment in a capitalist market economy, workers fear that money wage cuts in one sector may well not be accompanied by similar cuts elsewhere. Focusing on relative wages, they vigorously (and sensibly) resist money wage reductions. By contrast, it would be 'impracticable to resist every reduction in real wages' caused by a decrease in purchasing power 'which affects all workers alike', and thus 'no trade union would dream of striking on every occasion of a rise in the cost of living' (*GT*, pp. 14–15). As noted above, although the resulting redistribution of income from workers to entrepreneurs may reduce somewhat the marginal propensity to consume, it may stimulate investment and react favourably on business confidence. Even if wages do rise more rapidly than prices, which becomes more likely as full employment is approached, the resulting increase in real wages will not cause a break in the expansion as long as technological progressivity and new capital investments raise productivity sufficiently to maintain or extend current profitability and thereby reinforce optimistic expectations about future profit rates.

Increases in prices during expansions may amplify the expansionary process. Among the several factors Keynes discusses, the following are especially notable. One is that an increase in prices decreases the burden of debt and thereby tends to stimulate investment. Moreover, if prices rise more rapidly than wages (and interest rates), as Keynes supposes they will, then bankruptcies will decrease, strengthening marginal efficiencies of capital. The accompanying redistribution of income from rentier to entrepreneurs, on balance, should be favourable to the propensity to consume although this may be offset in part by adverse real balance effects.

The adverse Keynes Effect presupposes that the quantity of money 'is virtually fixed'. If this were so, then interest rates would rise more or less along with prices and income. But if the quantity of money 'is itself a function of the wage and price-level', increasing as they do, then the expanding money supply will constrain increases in interest rates, raise capital asset prices, and foster higher profit expectations, thus reinvigorating the expansion which stimulates the endogenous increase in the money supply (*GT*, p. 266). Also, to apply Keynes's argument to the expansionary case, when a more optimistic view is taken concerning profitability, 'that is no reason why there should be an [increased] propensity to hoard'. To the contrary, the 'same circumstances' – improvements in business optimism and reductions in both entrepreneur's and lender's risks – which cause increases in expected profit rates 'are apt to [decrease] the propensity to hoard' (Keynes, 1937, p. 218).

Now, the practical consequence of these kinds of considerations is that if expansion, based on short run, subjective increases in the ratio r/i (or demand prices of capital assets/replacement costs), is extended significantly beyond that which would be warranted based on more prudent calculations of long run profitability, expansion's foundation is 'flimsy' and 'subject to sudden and violent changes'. The false sense of certainty and security 'suddenly breaks down'. The 'forces of disillusion may suddenly impose a new conventional basis of valuation'. All the 'pretty' calculi 'collapse', and it becomes clear that 'vague panic fears and equally vague and unreasoned hopes are not really lulled but lie a little way below the surface' (Keynes, 1937, p. 215). In short, when 'disillusion falls on an over-optimistic and over-bought market, it may fall with sudden and even catastrophic force' (*GT*, p. 316).

Expansions are precarious and prone to interruption by crises, Keynes believed, for a second reason, beyond fundamental uncertainty concerning expectations of future profit rates and interest rates. In Chapter 12 of the *GT*, turning to 'a different level of abstraction from most of this book', Keynes differentiated between the proprietary, atomistically competitive capitalism of the nineteenth century and the big business, corporate capitalism of the twentieth. In the former circumstances, 'enterprises were mainly owned by those who undertook them', businesses were conducted 'as a way of life', and investment decisions were 'largely irrevocable' (*GT*, pp. 149–50).

With the emergence of the 'separation between ownership and management' and 'organized investment markets' of the twentieth century, the investment process has changed in such a way as to add 'greatly to the instability of the system' and to create 'no small part of our contemporary problem of securing sufficient investment' (*GT*, pp. 150–1, 153). Thus, uncertainty is rooted in an historical shift in socio-institutional relationships, not merely in lack of knowledge about the future in general (Davis, 1992).

First, 'real knowledge in the valuation of investments by those who own them or contemplate purchasing them has seriously declined'. Second, ephemeral, day-to-day profit fluctuations having little effect on long run profits 'tend to have an altogether excessive, and even an absurd, influence' on equities markets. Third, based as they are on the 'mass psychology' of many individuals, conventional valuations are 'liable to change violently as a result of a sudden fluctuation of opinion'. Hence, continued vigorous expansion is extremely precarious because, in the absence of a 'solid basis' for 'reasonable calculation', optimistic sentiment can easily and rapidly shift to pessimism. Fourth, speculators and professional investors are 'mainly occupied' not with superior forecasts of long run investment profitability, but in anticipating changes 'in the conventional basis of valuation a short time ahead of the general public', that is, in 'what average opinion expects the average opinion to be'. Fifth, speculation is based significantly on borrowed funds, the provisioning of which depends strategically on the 'confidence of the lending institutions' in speculators. Thus, a 'collapse' in equities prices causes 'disastrous reactions' on interest rates as well as on profit expectations (*GT*, pp. 153–4, 156, 158).

According to Keynes, the magnitude and severity of contraction is profoundly affected by the extent and intensity of the preceding expansion. Suppose that the expansion, propelled primarily by a straightforward multiplier process based on a fairly stable propensity to consume, dead-ends in a position of stable equilibrium at less than full employment, with little upward revision of r/i ratios (or ratios of capital asset prices to replacement costs) and therefore little cumulative reinforcement of the expansion. In this event, the downturn (triggered by a mild downward readjustment of r/i) would be succeeded by a metaphorical 'glide to a soft landing'. Because both the initiating decrease in investment and the multiplying secondary reductions in consumption are relatively small (given a fairly stable propensity to consume and assuming a relatively small marginal propensity to consume), the decline in income and employment is also likely to be moderate.

In these circumstances, contraction is constrained by two properties of the consumption function. First, the motive to satisfy 'immediate primary needs' generally outweighs proclivities to accumulate, which 'only acquire effective sway when a margin of comfort has been attained'. This typically leads to 'a greater [lesser] proportion of income being saved as income increases [decreases]'. Whereas the average gap between income and consumption rises during expansions, hence raising the proportion of investment to income required to sustain the expansion, that gap falls during contractions, reducing the investment as a percentage of income needed to constrain the cumulative contractionary process. The relative stability and higher average resilience of the propensity to consume when employment falls thus works to restrain the magnitude and length of downswings just as its stability and lower average potency works to limit upswings. Second, one's 'habitual standard of life usually has first claim' on one's income, and adjustments of consumption to changes in income will occur only imperfectly in short periods of time. Thus, 'a rising income will often be accompanied by increased saving, and a falling income by decreased saving, at a greater scale at first than subsequently'. Indeed, a decrease in income because of a reduction in employment may stimulate considerable dissaving, by both individuals and governments (for example, to provide unemployment relief). Consequently, the average propensity to consume is also likely to rise (and the marginal propensity to consume to fall) during mild contractions, at least in short periods of time. If the short run propensity to consume did not exhibit these properties, Keynes concludes, 'a fall in employment and income, once started, might proceed to extreme lengths' (*GT*, pp. 97–8).

Moreover, the milder and shorter the contraction, the greater the likelihood that wage–price–interest rate reductions will be benign. On the one hand, a mild contraction plausibly strengthens certain favourable effects of wage and price cuts. For example, if the mildness of the contraction and the early tendency to stabilize at an equilibrium level elicits the view that the recession will be short, the dominant emergent expectation by businesses may well be that money wages are being cut now relative to future wages. This can both 'produce an optimistic tone in the mind of entrepreneurs' and encourage them to employ more workers now rather than to postpone re-employment decisions. Similarly, if the downturn has been characterized by only mild reductions in profit expectations, then the tendency for lower prices to release money from transactionary balances and thereby, *ceteris paribus*, 'reduce the rate of interest and thus prove favourable to investment', will be strengthened (*GT*, pp. 263–4).

On the other hand, if contractions are mild, several adverse consequences of wage and price reductions will be minimized. For instance, speculative downward wage and price spirals are less likely, as are 'labour troubles'. Sharp upward shifts in the propensity to hoard are less likely to occur and thereby to offset the favourable effect of price reductions, through interest rates, on investment. Moderate price decreases will cause fewer bankruptcies than large ones. And bankers will be less inclined to reduce loans and thereby the money supply (*GT*, p. 264).

In any event, the milder the contraction, the less pressure on wage and prices to fall in the first place. In fact, wages (and, consequently, prices) are 'relatively sticky in terms of money'. This is not caused by monopoly or other market imperfections, but is rooted in those qualities that make money liquid, that is, that make the 'excess of liquidity-premium over carrying-costs [...] greater for money than for any other asset'. Money's low elasticities of production and substitution and low carrying costs 'raise the expectation that money-wages will be relatively stable'. And because money wages are relatively sticky downward, so too are money prices. Consequently, the potentially powerful adverse effects of price reductions are lower in practice than they would be under conditions of 'perfect downward wage and price flexibility' (*GT*, pp. 232, 237, 239, 303–4).

By contrast, consider the case, described in the *GT*, Chapters 12 and 22, and in Keynes's 1937 review article, where expansion feeds on itself through short run upward revisions of expected yields and capital asset prices. Under these conditions, disillusion falls 'with sudden and even catastrophic force', and the crisis is severe and large. Here, the force initiating the contraction is much more powerful. First, there is the 'sudden collapse' in marginal efficiency of capital schedules and consequent large-scale reductions in investment, described earlier. It is this which 'renders the slump so intractable'. Later, reductions in interest rates will be a 'great aid' to cyclical recovery and, 'probably, a necessary condition of it'. But at the outset of the contraction, the collapse in profit expectations may be 'so complete that no practicable reduction in the rate of interest will be enough' (*GT*, p. 316). Next, when

> a more pessimistic view is taken about future yields, that is no reason why there should be a diminished propensity to hoard. Indeed, the conditions which aggravate the one factor tend, as a rule, to aggravate the other. For the circumstances which lead to pessimistic views about future yields are apt to increase the propensity to hoard. The only element of self-righting in the system arises at a much later stage and in an uncertain degree. (Keynes, 1937, p. 218)

Thus, the increased uncertainty and pessimism accompanying the collapse in profit expectations 'naturally precipitates a sharp increase in liquidity-preference – and hence a rise in the rate of interest', thereby dealing investment a doubly repressive blow (*GT*, p. 316). This is reinforced by the fact that bankers, confronted by increased 'lender's risk' and afflicted with the same increased desire for liquidity that others are, reduce credit creation and thereby the money supply.

A 'serious fall' in marginal efficiencies of capital 'also tends to affect adversely the propensity to consume'. As profit expectations are revised downward, stock market prices undergo a 'severe decline'. This exerts a 'very depressive influence' on investors, 'especially if they are employing borrowed funds', because such individuals' expenditures are perhaps 'even more influenced' by changes in 'the value of their investments than by the state of their income' (*GT*, p. 319). To sum up: the collapse in profit expectations interacts with an increased propensity to hoard, credit destruction, and a downward shift in the propensity to consume to initiate a massive decline in aggregate demand.

This initial reduction in aggregate demand (and income and employment) also generates, through amplifying decreases in consumption, additional contraction via the multiplier process. Because the initial decrease in demand is large, so, too, will be the total contraction, even if the marginal propensity to consume is small. However, because of the greater severity and duration of depression, the marginal propensity to consume may become larger than in a shorter and milder recession. Consequently, the severity of the contraction may become greater.

Under these conditions, the adverse (favourable) consequences of money wage and price cuts presumably would be larger (smaller). Although cuts in commodity prices, taken by themselves, raise the real value of monetary wealth and thereby consumption, stock market collapse, reductions in asset values, and redistribution of wealth from entrepreneurs to rentier, normally would swamp such effects. Thus, in a severe depression, where profit expectations have collapsed, 'those who believe in the self-adjusting quality of the economic system must rest the weight of their argument' on the tendency for wage and price cuts, via reductions in the demand for money, to decrease interest rates. But in a serious depression, wage cuts are more likely than in a mild contraction to yield the expectation, indeed the 'serious possibility, of a further wage reduction'. The 'most unfavourable contingency' likely under 'free wage bargaining', is where money wages 'are slowly sagging downwards'. This will diminish profit expectations and 'will lead to the postponement of both investment and consumption'. These reactions by themselves 'may offset the decline in the rate of interest' elicited by reduced prices. In any event, if 'the quantity of money is itself a function of the wage and price level, there is indeed, nothing to hope in this direction' of the effect of wage and price cuts on the transactionary demand for money (*GT*, pp. 232, 263–5).

Once the endogeneity of the money supply is acknowledged, another self-amplifying element in the contractionary process must be recognized. Price reductions increase the burden of debt and thereby have a 'depressing influence' on investment. If the magnitude of price cuts is large, and interest rates do not fall sufficiently to compensate, heavily indebted entrepreneurs may 'soon reach the point of insolvency, – with severely adverse effects on investment' (*GT*, p. 264). Thus, price cuts may cause bankruptcies and restrictions on money and credit, which elicit further price cuts and thereby another round of bankruptcies and reductions in money and credit, and so on. Because profit expectations are determined by 'the uncontrollable and disobedient psychology of the business world, [...] they are insusceptible to control in an economy of individualistic capitalism'. Hence, 'slumps and depressions are exaggerated in degree', and 'recovery requires the revival of both', that is, eventual upward revisions of marginal efficiencies of capital based on long run growth factors, depreciation of fixed capital, running-down of inventory stocks, and restoration of confidence, as well as reductions in interest rates (*GT*, pp. 158, 160, 317).

Fortunately, money wages and prices are, in practice, relatively 'sticky' and resistive to reductions. Instead of serving as an impediment to recovery, this may actually reduce the severity of contractions. If 'money-wages were to fall without limit' in the event of reductions in aggregate demand, income, and employment, 'there would be no resting-place below full employment until either the rate of interest was incapable of falling further or wages were zero'. Every 'small fluctuation' in demand would cause money prices 'to rush violently between zero and infinity'. Because of the downward 'violent instability' in wages and prices, 'there might be no position of stable equilibrium except in conditions consistent with full employment' (*GT*, pp. 239, 253, 303–4). In an economic environment in which interest rates are relatively high and slower to fall than money wages and prices, marginal efficiencies of capital are subject to large-scale collapses and may be adversely affected by depressionary psychology and the burden of business debt and bankruptcies, and endogenous reductions in money and credit depress investment, wage and price decreases may make the situation worse rather than better. If, as is likely in a severe contraction, adverse effects outweigh favourable ones, wage and price cuts, by helping to plunge the economy into deeper depression, may easily be 'too large' rather than 'too small'. Moreover, once the assumption of 'perfect instanteneity' (wherein wage and price reductions occur simultaneously and once-and-for-all throughout the entire economy) is dropped, reduced 'imperfection' in downward flexibility of wages and prices may well have destabilizing effects on income and employment (DeLong and Summers, 1986, p. 1042).

The general conclusion derivative from the preceding discussion of Keynes's analysis of crises and contraction (as well as the implications of expansions for crises and succeeding downswings) is that Keynes provides a fundamental, theoretical critique of classical and neoclassical economics and a rich and variegated explication of dynamic and cyclical processes in money, finance, and market-using capitalist economics.

Notes

1. The author would like to thank Gary Dymski, Robert Pollin, and Tracy Mott for helpful comments on earlier drafts of this chapter.
2. It should be recalled, however, that Keynes's hints of the forthcoming 'synthesis' owe more to his reading of Alfred Marshall than of Leon Walras. Indeed, traces of the Marshallian influence may be found in the ideas of Keynes II as well as Keynes I (see Marshall, 1952, pp. 710–11).
3. These include such propositions as the liquidity trap, the interest inelasticity of investment, the 'inconsistency' between full employment saving and investment, and downward rigidity in money wages and prices. See Ackley (1961) and Crouch (1972) for classic expositions. What is problematic about these *ad hoc* features of 'Bastard Keynesianism' is not only that they constitute an impoverished narrowing of Keynes's argument, which does not rely on them, but that it places in jeopardy Keynes's original project itself, (see Elliott, 1992).
4. As a policy corollary, expansionary fiscal and monetary policy are not enough to foster stable, full employment. A 'somewhat comprehensive socialization of investment' (*GT*, p. 378) is needed, which shifts 'the weight of public and private demand toward the public sectors, so that the potential for evil from the instability of financial markets and private investment is reduced' (Minsky, pp. 11–12).
5. Minsky suggests several additional reasons. These include: confusing comingling of old and new ideas in the *GT*; Keynes's failure to participate significantly in ensuing debates over the *GT*; Keynes's immersion in issues of wartime finance as a governmental adviser; the overly optimistic beliefs by post-war Keynesian economists that 'endogenous business cycles and domestic financial crises were a thing of the past, now that the secrets of economic policy have been unlocked'; the apparent scientific advances of new–old theories of market equilibrium via elegant formal proofs, albeit under highly restrictive assumptions; the apparent policy success of post-war Keynesian economics; and the substitution of the simplified Hicksian LM–IS model for Keynes's own ideas, as noted in the main body of the text (Minsky, 1975, pp. 12–17).

References

Ackley, Gardner (1961), *Macroeconomic Theory*, New York: Macmillan.

Blaug, Mark (1987), *Economic Theory in Retrospect*, New York: Cambridge University Press.

Chick, Victoria (1983), *Macroeconomics After Keynes: A Reconsideration of the General Theory*, Cambridge: The MIT Press.

Coddington, Alan (1983), *Keynesian Economics: The Search for First Principles*, London: George Allen & Unwin.

Crouch, Robert L. (1972), *Macroeconomics*, New York: Harcourt Brace.

Davis, John (1992), 'Keynes' Philosophical Thinking in the General Theory', Milwaukee: Working Paper.

DeLong, J. Bradford and Summers, Lawrence H. (1986), 'Is Increased Price Flexibility Stabilizing?' *American Economic Review*, **76** (5), December, pp. 1031–44.

Elliott, John E. (1992), 'Keynes' Critique of Wage Cutting as Anti-Depressionary Strategy', in Warren A. Samuels, (ed.), *Annual Research in History of Economic Thought and Methodology*, Greenwich: JAI Press.

Hansen, Alvin H. (1951), *Business Cycles and National Income*, New York: W.W. Norton.

Hicks, John R. (1950), *A Contribution to the Theory of the Trade Cycle*, Oxford: Oxford University Press.

Hicks, John R. (1937), 'Mr Keynes and the Classics: A Suggested Interpretation', *Econometrica*, **5**, April, pp. 147–59.

Keynes, John M. (1930), *Treatise on Money*, London: Macmillan.

Keynes, John M. (1936), *The General Theory of Employment, Interest and Money*, New York: Harcourt Brace.

Keynes, John M. (1937), 'The General Theory of Employment', *Quarterly Journal of Economics*, **51**, pp. 209–23.

Leijonhufvud, Axel (1968), *On Keynesian Economics and the Economics of Keynes: A Study in Monetary Theory*, New York: Oxford University Press.

Marshall, Alfred (1952), *Principles of Economics*, Eighth (1924) edition, New York: Macmillan.

Minsky, Hyman (1975), *John Maynard Keynes*, New York: Columbia University Press.

Modigliani, Franco (1944), 'Liquidity Preference and the Theory of Interest and Money', *Econometrica*, 12, January, pp. 45–88.

Patinkin, Don (1965), *Money, Interest, and Prices*, New York: Harper & Row.

Rogin, Emil (1956), *The Meaning and Validity of Economic Theory*, New York: Harper & Row.

Samuelson, Paul A. (1967), *Economics*, New York: McGraw-Hill.

Samuelson, Paul A. (1952), 'The General Theory', in Seymour E. Harris (ed.), *The New Economics*, New York: Knopf.

Shackle, G.L.S. (1967), *The Years of High Theory: Invention and Tradition in Economic Thought, 1926–1939*, New York: Cambridge University Press.

Viner, Jacob (1936), 'Mr. Keynes on the Causes of Unemployment', *Quarterly Journal of Economics*, **51**, November, pp. 147–67.

Williams, John H. (1947), 'An Assessment of Keynesian Economics', *American Economic Review, Papers and Proceedings*, May.

11   Keynes on mensuration and comparison[1]

Anna Carabelli

Interest in the problems of the measurement and comparison of magnitudes is a constant throughout Keynes's intellectual career. In his 1938 'My Early Beliefs', Keynes remembers how in his youth for him and his Bloomsbury friends,

> the problems of mensuration in which we had involved ourselves, were somewhat formidable. It was all under the influence of Moore's method, according to which you could hope to make essentially vague notions clear by using precise language about them and asking exact questions. It was a method of discovery by the instrument of impeccable grammar and an unambiguous dictionary (*CW* X, p. 440).

However, in 1938 he also notes 'though it is a comfort to-day to be able to discard with a good conscience the calculus and the mensuration and the duty to know *exactly* what one means and feels' (*CW* X, p. 442).

This chapter shows how Keynes's analysis of the measurement and comparison of *probability* provides the link between these two opposite positions on mensuration and calculation. In particular, *A Treatise on Probability* (1921) is the work in which Keynes's transformation comes about, passing from his early Moorean position of 1903 to the mature one of 1938. In this work he criticizes Moore's method (as well as Russell's) and develops his own original method.[2] In the early 1907 version of *TP Principles of Probability*, (henceforth *PP*) Keynes already stops dealing with the vague and imprecise concept of probability as if it were precise and calculable, thus abandoning Moore's scholasticism and his Benthamite 'highly problematical calculus' (*CW* X, p. 445).[3] He argues that common sense and ordinary language are the proper domain of probability.

Probability: measurement and comparison

To show Keynes's attitude to the measurement and comparison of probability, I shall start from his manifesto in *TP*. Keynes has a three-fold conception of probability:

> I maintain, then, in what follows, that there are some pairs of probabilities between the members of which *no* comparison of magnitude is possible; that we can say, nevertheless, of some pairs of relations of probability that one is greater and the other less, although it is not possible to measure the difference between them;

and that in a very special type of case, to be dealt with later, a meaning can be given to a *numerical* comparison of magnitude. (*TP*, p. 36)

Reversing Keynes's order, I call the first case, CASE-III; the second, CASE-II and the third, CASE-I. Hence:

CASE-I: numerically comparable probabilities
CASE-II: quantitatively comparable probabilities in terms of equal, more or less (unequal)
CASE-III: non-comparable comparison of probabilities

CASE-I deals with numerically comparable or cardinal (univocally numerical) probabilities. Most of the interpreters of Keynes's concept of probability agree substantially on the extremely limited role which this case plays in *TP* and in his economic writings. Therefore I only mention it but in section 2 I will come back and consider the conditions which Keynes fixes to secure numerical comparison. Here I dwell upon the two remaining cases.

CASE-II deals with quantitatively, not non-numerically, comparable probabilities. Comparison is quantitative when we can say that 'the degree of our rational belief in one conclusion is either equal to, greater than, or less than the degree of our belief in another' (*TP*, p. 37). In this case, we can also speak of ordinal comparison between probabilities.

Quantitative comparison requires that each degree of probability can be arranged in an order. Note however that the contrary is not always true. In examining CASE-III, we will see that, when *different* orders of probability exist, the ordering of probabilities does not guarantee, in general, the quantitative comparison between any two probabilities.

For the moment, let us limit ourselves to the existence of just one order of probability. A series of quantities of probability is ordered if between every pair of its members there is a relation of more or less (a relation of 'between'), so that we can affirm that a probability increases or decreases but not by how much:

In these instances we can, perhaps, arrange the probabilities in an order of magnitude and assert that the new datum strengthens or weakens the argument, although there is no basis for an estimate *how much* stronger or weaker the new argument is than the old. (*TP*, p. 31)

For the ordering it is necessary that the relation of 'between' hold between certainty, the quantities of probability under investigation and impossibility:

in such a case a relation seems clearly to exist between the two [probabilities] in virtue of which one lies *nearer* to certainty than the other. Several types of argument can be instanced in which the existence of such a relation is equally apparent. (*TP*, p. 38)[4]

The relation of 'between' is compared by Keynes to the relation of order of colours or to likeness between objects. A colour or an object supply the standard of reference for ordering. They are similar to certainty in the order of probability:

> When we describe the colour of one object as bluer than that of another, or say that it has more green in it, we do not mean that there are quantities blue and green of which the object's colour possess more or less; we mean that the colour has a certain position in an order of colours and that it is nearer some standard colour than is the colour with which we compare it ... But the closest analogy is that of similarity ... We say that one argument is more probable than another (i.e. nearer to certainty) in the same kind of way as we can describe one object as more like than another to a standard object of comparison. (*TP*, p. 38–9)[5]

Keynes holds that orders of degrees of probability are not, in general, continuous. So, it is not true that every pair of probabilities belonging to an order should have a probability 'between them' (*TP*, p. 41). The function of probability, if it exists, is not necessarily continuous. Poincaré's conventionalist hypothesis – by which it is tacitly assumed that probability is 'a regular, continuous function and with continuous differential coefficients' – is rejected by Keynes as theoretically unacceptable (*TP*, pp. 52–3). Furthermore, an order is not necessarily complete.

The real problem for a quantitative comparison of probabilities is *how* and *when* it is possible to order the different degrees of probability, certainty and impossibility. That is, how and when we can speak of ordered series for probability. In *TP* Keynes's problem is '*how* we are to know when two probabilities are equal or unequal' (*TP*, p. 44). He wants to know: '*how and in what circumstances* such orders can be established' (*TP*, p. 41).

Two observations are to be made before answering this crucial question. First, Keynes thinks that the ordering of probabilities should never be tacitly assumed:

> we can only build up these ordered series in special cases. If we are given two distinct arguments, there is no general presumption that their two probabilities and certainty can be placed in an order. The burden of establishing the existence of such an order lies on us in each separate case. An endeavour will be made later to explain in a systematic way *how and in what circumstances* such orders can be established ... For the present it has been shown to be agreeable to common sense to suppose that an order exist in some cases and not in others. (*TP*, p. 41; my italics)

Secondly, the ordering of probability is not possible in general. Degrees of probability can be arranged in an order only for *a few types* of probability relative to particular propositions and arguments (*TP*, p. 58). Further, this can be done only in *restricted circumstances*. Quantitative characteristics of probability can be considered only in situations represented by '*more reason* for one conclusion than for the other'. This is a preliminary condition for ordering:

> We must look, then, at the quantitative characteristics of probability in the following way. Some sets of probabilities we can place in an ordered series, in which we can say of any pair that one is nearer than the other to certainty, – that the argument in one case is nearer proof than in the other, and that there is *more reason* for one conclusion than for the other. (*TP*, p. 40, my italics)

In CASE-III we will see that ordering is possible in situations where the *reasons* (or the grounds or the evidence, as Keynes also calls them) are expressible in terms of *more or less*. This will require homogeneity of reasons (grounds or evidence). On the contrary, in situations where the reasons are *different or heterogeneous*, the ordering and hence the quantitative comparison of probabilities is not possible.[6]

The philosophical premises of probability
Keynes's discussion of '*how* and *in what circumstances* such orders can be established' (*TP*, p. 41), covers no less than two chapters of the 1921 version of *TP*, i.e. Chapters 4–5, and is then briefly summed up in Chapter 9. There, Keynes discusses the problem of how we are to know when one probability is equal to, greater or less than another, i.e. the problem of the knowledge of the equality or inequality of probabilities. Hence this problem is central in *TP* and represents the core of Keynes's own philosophy of probability. Its importance can be also inferred from the plan of Chapters, 4–5, which Keynes puts forward quite clearly at the beginning of Chapter 4:

> In the last chapter it was assumed that in some cases the probabilities of two arguments may be *equal*. It was also argued that there are cases in which one probability is, in some sense, greater than another. But so far there has been nothing to show *how* we are to know when two probabilities are equal or unequal. The recognition of equality, when it exists, will be dealt with in this chapter, and the recognition of inequality in the next. (*TP*, p. 44)

Its importance can be equally inferred from the beginning of Chapter 5, where Keynes again outlines the content of the chapter: 'We will enquire first in *what circumstances* we can expect a comparison of more or less to be theoretically possible' (*TP*, p. 70).

In the 1907 version of *TP* the discussion is dealt with by Keynes in Chapter V under the significant title: 'The problem of premises in probability, and the Principle of Non-Sufficient Reason'. In this chapter, as too in Chapters 4–5 of the final version, Keynes discusses the *philosophical premisses* for the ordering of probabilities. Or better, he makes *explicit* the philosophical premisses of probability which, in his opinion, are always kept tacit.

These philosophical premisses for ordering are also at the base of the calculus of probability. In fact, for Keynes, the equality of probabilities is necessary for numerical calculus;[7] whereas inequality (in terms of greater or less) is necessary for quantitative comparison and then for logical-quantitative calculus. These premisses should therefore be interpreted as *necessary conditions* for calculus in general, be it numerical or quantitative.

The investigation of the premisses of calculus is fundamental in Keynes's approach to probability in *TP*. Consider the opening passage of Chapter V of the 1907 version:

> The problem to be attacked in this Chapter ['The Problem of premisses in probability, and the Principle of Non-Sufficient Reason'] must be, in a sense, the crux of any philosophy of probability. It is the metaphysic of the subject. Up to this point it has been assumed that knowledge concerning the probability of propositions is *possible*. It has been supposed that certain probabilities are known to be equal or unequal to certain others, and the argument has been concerned with the manipulation of these given quantities. The more ultimate problem of providing the material for the logical calculus has been tacitly ignored.
>
> There is warrant for this in the ordinary practice of logicians. The discovery of premisses they leave to the metaphysicians. Their province is to manipulate *given* premisses, and to discover what conclusions are related to these premisses by way of inference. Their logical processes cannot rid themselves of a hypothetical element, or of themselves tell us what is true. In the same way the logic of probability cannot tell us unaided *what* is probable. (*PP*, pp. 69–70; see also *TP*, p. 86)

In the first Part of *TP*, Keynes sets himself two main tasks: to make explicit the tacit premisses of calculus and to investigate the characteristics of the material of probability. These tasks cover what we have called Keynes's philosophy of probability. He maintains that the premisses of probability should have precise characteristics to support calculus and that not all the material of probability reflects those characteristics.

In particular, calculus can never be developed without making explicit its tacit premisses: 'But probability is not yet on so sound a basis that the formal or mathematical side of it can be safely developed in isolation' (*TP*, p. 86). Actually, the investigation of the tacit premisses of calculus aims to show that it has *limited application*.

The premisses of calculus which Keynes brings to light in this part of *TP* are the direct judgements of indifference and relevance. He shows that calculus, even when applicable, always depends on these direct judgements, whose nature is intuitive. In Keynes's opinion, the rules of calculus are not self-sustaining. They are always grounded on direct judgements and intuition. In 1907 he writes:

> It is clearly useless to approach the problem of premises in probability in the hope of discovering a method by which individual probabilities may be determined without any assistance from intuition or direct judgement. Just as probability cannot be completely defined in terms of other notions, so individual probabilities cannot be derived from considerations of other kinds alone ... The statement of probability in its final form may be the resultant of a direct judgement of a peculiar kind and of certain logical rules and principles. (*PP*, pp. 103–4)

In fact, in Part II of *TP* Keynes deals with calculus stressing the hypothetical nature of the premises (*TP*, p. 145). Keynes's stress on the way in which calculus depends upon its philosophical premises emerges clearly from the structure of argument used in Chapter 12 of Part II. His whole argument is formulated in terms of 'if'.

Keynes's discussion of the philosophical premises of calculus also brings to light the contrast between 'reasoning' and 'calculation', between the principles of reasoning and the rules of calculus which is a constant in his general method.[8] This is a general attitude which he also adopts in his economic discourse. In his critique of the classical theory, he makes its tacit hypotheses explicit to show that the theory is not general and has limited validity. He also points out the paradoxes, logical fallacies and contradictions in reasoning which arise when the theory or the theoretical tools do not reflect the nature and the characteristics of the material under investigation. In economics, Keynes detects the fallacies of composition and *ignoratio elenchi* (Carabelli, 1991).[9]

Case-III: non-comparable probabilities

CASE-III of our classification is the most complicated. Non-comparable probabilities emerge in two situations, which I shall call CASE-III(i) and CASE-III(ii):

> CASE-III(i): when probabilities, though not quantitatively comparable, can be arranged in an order of magnitude
> CASE-III(ii): when probabilities cannot even be arranged in an order of magnitude

CASE-III(i) considers situations in which *different* orders of probability exist:

Some probabilities are not comparable in respect of more and less, because there exists more than one path, so to speak, between proof and disproof, between certainty and impossibility; and neither of two probabilities, which lie on independent paths, bears to the other and to certainty the relation of 'between' which is necessary for quantitative comparison. (*TP*, pp. 37–8)

It is not easy to grasp *why* quantitative comparison among different orders is impossible. Later in this chapter, an interpretation in terms of incommensurability of magnitudes and dimensions will be suggested. For the moment, I will follow Keynes's description, which draws an analogy with the relations of orders of likeness between objects. Keynes utilizes a diagram which is useful here (*TP*, p. 42):

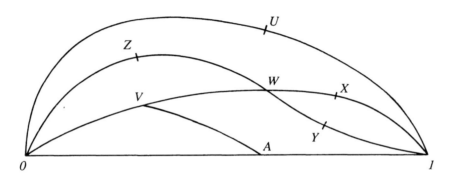

Figure 11.1   Non-comparable probabilities – Keynes's diagram

In CASE-II, we have seen that, if we can arrange each degree of probability in an order, we can compare probabilities belonging to the same order. In this CASE-III(i), we cannot compare, in general, probabilities belonging to different orders: probabilities *U* and *V* in the diagram are of this type. Quantitative comparison of probabilities belonging to different orders is possible only if the different orders cross each other: in the diagram, probability *V* is quantitatively less than *X* and *Y*. A same degree of probability can, therefore, belong to more than one order, as does probability *W*. In fact, the two orders cross each other at that point.

In CASE-III(ii) the quantitative comparison of probabilities is not possible because the degrees of probability cannot even be arranged in an order (Carabelli, 1982 p. 100; 1988 p. 49). This case has been neglected by other interpreters of Keynes's view of probability, save recently by Meeks (1991, p. 146).[10] Dardi (1991, pp. 68–9) denies its very existence.[11] I first consider how Keynes puts the problem, then comment on it. In 1921, he asks himself:

In these instances we can, perhaps, arrange the probabilities in an order of magnitude ... But in another class of instances is it even possible to arrange the probabilities in an *order* of magnitude, or to say that one is the greater and the other less? (*TP*, p. 31 Keynes's italics)

He gives two examples where probabilities cannot even be arranged in an order. The first is relative to inductive arguments:

Consider three sets of experiments, each directed towards establishing a generalisation. The first set is more numerous; in the second set the irrelevant conditions have been more carefully varied; in the third case the generalisation in view is wider in scope than in the others. Which of these generalisations is on such evidence the most probable? There is, surely, no answer; there is neither equality nor inequality between them. We cannot always weigh the analogy against the induction, or the scope of the generalisation against the bulk of evidence in support of it. If we have *more* grounds than before, comparison is possible; but, if the grounds in the two cases are quite different, even a comparison of more and less, let alone numerical measurement, may be impossible. (*TP*, pp. 31–2, Keynes's italics)

Keynes's second example which I will jokingly call the 'umbrella dilemma' is:

Is our expectation of rain, when we start out for a walk, always *more* likely than not, or *less* likely than not, or *as* likely as not? I am prepared to argue that on some occasions *none* of these alternatives hold, and that it will be an arbitrary matter to decide for or against the umbrella. If the barometer is high, but the clouds are black, it is not always rational that one should prevail over the other in our minds, or even that we should balance them, – though it will be rational to allow caprice to determine us and to waste no time on the debate. (*TP*, p. 32)

In reading the first example, the reader should take note of Keynes's italics. If we have '*more* grounds than before', the ordering of probabilities in terms of equal, more or less is possible; if, on the contrary, the 'grounds are quite *different*' (my italics), it is impossible.

In discussing the previous CASE-II, I have briefly referred to Keynes's preliminary condition for the ordering of probabilities as that of having '*more* reasons for a conclusion rather than for another' (*TP*, p. 40). In Keynes's first example, this condition, instead of being expressed in terms of more reasons, is expressed in terms of *more grounds*. In other parts of *TP*, Keynes also refers to more evidence. The three terms are actually equivalent.

We can now fully grasp why the *quantitative* characteristics of probability can be considered only when we are in situations represented by *more* or *less* reason (grounds or evidence). And why this is impossible in situations represented by *different* reasons (grounds or evidence). In fact, the arranging of reasons in terms of more or less requires, as a preliminary condition, that these reasons be *homogeneous*. In situations of heterogeneity of reasons, we cannot say that we have more or less reason for a conclusion rather than for another. Then, the ordering of probabilities is impossible.

In Keynes's second example it is clear that the motive for the impossibility of ordering is due to heterogeneity of reasons. 'High barometer' and 'black clouds' are clearly heterogeneous and opposite reasons.

It is therefore this heterogeneity of reasons which is at the base of the impossibility of ordering and then of quantitatively comparing probabilities.

At this point we can tackle Keynes's detailed analysis of the conditions for ordering probabilities.

In examining CASE-II, I have anticipated that Keynes, in Part I of *TP*, thoroughly investigates '*how and in what circumstances* such orders can be established' (*TP*, p. 41). This analysis represents his search for the *necessary conditions* to avoid paradoxes, fallacies and contradictions in probable reasoning (*PP*, p. 104). In *TP*, the discussion of these *conditions* for ordering is quite complex. Here I shall synthetize it, following the 1907 version which is simpler than the final one.

Keynes analyses *three* conditions which guarantee the possibility to establish orders, i.e. to know either the equality or the inequality (in terms of greater or less) of probabilities. He examines first the conditions to establish equality; then those for inequality.

The *first condition* considers the working of the 'Principle of non sufficient reason'. For Keynes, through the exercise of equiprobability judgements, this fundamental principle of probable reasoning allows the application of numerical calculus to probability.

In Keynes's opinion, the principle should be reformulated in more precise terms as 'the principle of indifference': 'The meaning and object of the three principal conditions will now be explained. The first condition is simply the principle of non sufficient reason made more precise' (*PP*, p. 117). The precision Keynes requires consists in making explicit the role of direct judgements in the working of the principle. As we have seen, these judgements are also the philosophical premises of probability:

> our first object must be to make the principle itself more precise by disclosing how far its application is mechanical and how far it involves an appeal to logical intuition.
>
> Without compromising the objective character of relations of probability, we must nevertheless admit that there is little likelihood of our discovering a method of recognizing particular probabilities, without any assistance whatever from intuition or direct judgement ... Let us seek to distinguish between the element of direct judgement and the element of mechanical rule in the principle of indifference ... the appeal to intuition is not as explicit as it should be. (*TP*, pp. 56–7)

The *second condition* aims to exclude cases where the principle is not a sufficient condition: 'The second condition excludes a number of cases in which the principle of non sufficient reason is not a sufficient condition' (*PP*, p. 118). The principle is not a sufficient condition when we do not know if the classes of magnitudes under investigation are finite or if the entities under investigation belong to a specific class of magnitudes or if the qualities we are dealing with are single qualities or classes of qualities. Keynes's conclusion is: 'If we are without this knowledge the probabilities are not equal but incommensurable' (*PP*, p. 119). I shall return to this problem of the incommensurability of probabilities.

The *third condition* considers cases where the propositions (which, let us remember, are the material of Keynes's probability) are not pairs of equally probable propositions (*PP*, pp. 123–4). These probabilities are relative to propositions such as: 'This book is red' and 'This book is not red'; or 'This proposition is true' and 'This proposition is not true'. Keynes maintains that: '"red" and "non red" are not fair or equivalent alternatives ... For the number of contraries to any proposition on any evidence is always infinite' (*PP*, p. 91).

In these cases, propositions are characterized by infiniteness and incompleteness. It is these characteristics of the material of probability which give rise to the paradoxes in probable reasoning:

> The examples in which the principle of non sufficient reason breaks down evidently have very much in common ... The paradoxes and contradictions have, in each case, arisen when the areas, which we have called equal in probability, are actually unequal in extent. (*PP*, p. 104)

In brief, the third condition requires that 'our alternatives must deal with infimae specie ... our alternatives deal with entities that are actually incapable of further subdivision' (*PP*, p. 94).

These three conditions for the equality of probabilities are then extended by Keynes, without substantial modifications, to the analysis of inequality between probabilities. When these conditions are not fulfilled, the method is inapplicable or, as Keynes writes, 'breaks down':

> The establishment ... of inequalities between probabilities follows at once on similar principles. If condition (i) is fulfilled, and one class contains more members than the other or composes a greater stretch, then the alternative involving the class is the more probable; and in some cases the probabilities of the alternatives are numerically comparable. Again in the application of condition (i), if for every known proposition relevant to one alternative, there is a corresponding proposition relevant to the other and *more too* which increase its probability, and if condition (ii) is fulfilled, then the latter is the more probable.

The method breaks down when there are known relevant propositions on each side, which are not identical in form and corresponding. (*PP*, p. 125)

To sum up, the conditions to establish the equality or inequality between probabilities require that the material of probability have characteristics of homogeneity. Otherwise problems of incommensurability arise.

In CASE-II of our classification, the quantities of probability are homogeneous; so they can be arranged in an order and then quantitatively compared within the order. In CASE-III, these conditions cannot be fulfilled. The different quantities of probabilities are heterogeneous and, for this reason, are, in general, quantitatively incomparable. In CASE-III(i) incomparability is due to heterogeneity in the orders of probability whereas in CASE-III(ii) incomparability is due to the impossibility of ordering probabilities because reasons are themselves heterogeneous.

At this point, we can affirm that our CASE-III represents the case where the above *conditions* to establish the equality or inequality of probabilities *do not* exist. So, CASE-III covers the 'discarded' situations of CASE-II, i.e. it represents the awkward situations where probabilities are *neither equal nor unequal*. Note that the calculus of probability cannot be applied to these 'discarded' cases because the conditions for it do not exist. The appropriate tools for these cases are ordinary language and common sense.

CASE-III: its relevance and generality
For Keynes, these 'discarded cases' are neither few nor irrelevant. In the 1907 *PP*, at the end of his discussion of the three conditions for ordering, he indeed states that these cases comprise the greater part of the judgements of probability which are used in practice: 'These cases unfortunately comprise the majority of the judgements of probability with which we are in practice concerned' (*PP*, p. 125).

In his approach to probability in *TP*, Keynes considered our CASE-III of incomparable and non orderable probabilities as the most general.[12] The other cases, CASE-II and CASE-I, represent the working of limited conditions.

CASE-III is not only the most general case in *TP*, but is also the most relevant for the interpretation of Keynes's economics. It represents Keynes's own view of probability, upon which he grounds his notion of economic expectations and uncertainty and also his approach to the measurement and comparison of economic magnitudes.

The neglect of this as a *general case* is at the base of the misinterpretation of Keynes's view of probability and rationality advanced by some other interpreters, particularly by O'Donnell (1989). In his opinion, Keynes in *TP* would hold a view of strong rationality based on known probabilities, only later to move in the *GT* to a more radical concept of uncertainty and weak rationality based on unknown probabilities. He suggests that there is an internal shift of emphasis after Ramsey's criticism. The 'indeterminate domain' and the weak rationality which has a marginal role in *TP* is increasingly widened to become dominant in the *GT*.

Actually, Keynes's uncertainty does *not* depend on whether probabilities are known or unknown, or whether or not expectations are reducible to probabilities. In *TP*, two parallel domains for probabilities, the one determinate and the other indeterminate, do not exist.[13] There exists, on the contrary, a general case which includes all the other cases as sub-cases which can be obtained only under restricted conditions. While in the general case *the conditions for calculus do not exist*, in the sub-cases (our CASE-II and CASE-I) quantitative and numerical calculus, respectively, can be developed.

It is equally untenable, as Dardi (1991, p. 69) suggests, that Keynes's theory of probability has nothing to say if orders or quantitative comparison of probabilities cannot be established, i.e. when probabilities are *neither equal nor unequal* (our CASE-III).

Furthermore, in this case the situation is *not* of total indeterminacy as O'Donnell (1991, p. 15) maintains. Keynes still allows the working of direct judgements or the playing of various rules of choice between these non-orderable or incomparable probabilities.

Certainly, in these cases, the choice is arbitrary and we are not in such situations where the rules for ordering or for quantitative or numerical comparison (always backed by the direct judgements of indifference or relevance made explicit) guarantee the calculation of probability. But determinacy of choice does not imply for Keynes calculation. Keynes's conception of rationality is therefore not to be interpreted as that of the calculating reason.

Neither does arbitrariness mean irrationality. Keynes maintains that in these situations of non orderable and incomparable probabilities, it is rational to allow *direct judgements* – and even caprice, as we will see – to play a role. These choices have, in comparison with the others, an element of arbitrariness and the impossibility of computation; but they are not, for these motives, considered by Keynes irrational. Lack of computation does not mean irrationality of choice.

Keynes admits that, in these cases, human action becomes even more fallible than in the fortunate cases where ordering, quantitative or numerical comparison is possible. But, note, human action is equally fallible even in these fortunate cases, because uncertainty is never exorcized by Keynes. Referring to the above mentioned 'discarded cases' of CASE-II, he writes in 1907:

> These cases unfortunately comprise the majority of the judgements of probability with which we are in practice concerned. But these cases are not for that reason

beyond the pale, or outside the control of our logic. There too we may apply our direct judgements and draw direct conclusions from the evidence with which we are presented. We have not in these cases those checks and controls that might otherwise aid and correct us, and in all such conclusions we are more than ordinarily liable to error and delusion. (*PP*, p. 125)

In the final version of *A Treatise on Probability*, Keynes again stresses that these arbitrary choices among non orderable or incomparable probabilities are not at all irrational. In Keynes's example of the 'umbrella dilemma', where the conditions for ordering do not exist, rationality is represented by caprice: 'it will be an arbitrary matter to decide for or against the umbrella ... it will be rational to allow caprice to determine us and to waste no time on the debate' (*TP*, p. 32).

In Keynes's conception of probability, the exercise of caprice in the choice between non-orderable or incomparable probabilities falls within the application, in general, of direct judgements in probable reasoning. We are not to be astonished by the central role which Keynes gives to these judgements in *TP*. We have already seen that he continuously stresses their role even when the *conditions* for calculus *exist*. Direct judgements of indifference and relevance are always to be made explicit, if one does not wish to fall into paradoxes, mistakes and fallacies of probable reasoning. In Keynes's concept of probability, direct judgements – and the intuition behind them – operate nonetheless, though at different levels of analysis (*TP*, p. 57). Keynes maintains that direct judgements have a fundamental role in reasoning, whether we be calculating or not. Nay, they are at the base of the calculus itself. Actually, he thinks that we reason even when we do not calculate or when we have no basis for calculation.[14]

In my opinion, our CASE-III is also the situation which best characterizes Keynes' conception of uncertainty in *GT*: a situation where the *conditions* for calculus, that is ordinability and comparability (either numerical or quantitative) between the quantities of probability, *do not exist*. But where a choice between these quantities is to be made, in whatever manner. In 1936, Keynes writes that 'the *basis* for making such calculations *does not exist*' (my italics). In 1921, the determinacy of choice is secured by caprice. In 1936, by 'animal spirits' or by 'whim, sentiment or chance'. It appears that these two situations are more similar than not:

We are merely reminding ourselves that human decisions affecting the future, whether personal or political or economic, cannot depend on strict mathematical expectation, since the basis for making such calculations does not exist; and that it is our innate urge to activity which makes the wheels go round, our rational selves choosing between alternatives as best we are able, calculating where we can, but often falling back for our motive on whim or sentiment or chance. (*GT*, *CW* VII, p. 162)

To speak of 'non-probabilistic uncertainty' as O'Donnell (1991, p. 20) has recently done, is as equally unacceptable as his old interpretation. He suggests that when there is no numerical or quantitative comparison, then there are no quantities of probability at all not even vague and imprecise ones; or, if they do exist, they are unknown. So they have no domain, not even in ordinary language. This misunderstanding leads to the introduction of a further false distinction between probability and expectations. In my opinion, what he calls 'low weight uncertainty' is nothing else but the incomparability of the joint judgement of probability and the weight of argument, which will be considered in the next section. What he calls 'irreducible uncertainty' is not due at all to unknown probabilities, as he suggests. Keynes's 1937 sentence 'we simply do not know' does not mean, as suggested by O'Donnell, that we do not know the probabilities. It means that we do not know the calculable probabilities. In fact, Keynes writes: 'there is no scientific basis on which to form calculable probabilities whatever' (*CW* XIV, p. 114). Finally, what O'Donnell calls 'unrankable uncertainty' is merely the case of the incomparability of the joint judgements of probability and goodness – considered in the next section under CASE-III*.

CASE-III*: non-comparable joint judgements

A new case of incomparability is to be introduced to complete our analysis of Keynes's attitude to the measurement and comparison of probability. As it does not easily come under our CASE-III, I shall call it, CASE-III*.

Until now judgements of probability alone have been considered. We shall now consider situations where these judgements are associated with other judgements to form joint judgements: joint judgements of probability and the weight of argument; joint judgements of probability and goodness.

The weight of argument allows quantitative comparisons between arguments on the basis of a valuation which is different from that of probability. It is attentive to the absolute amount of relevant knowledge:

> it seems that there may be another respect in which some kind of quantitative comparison between arguments is possible. This comparison turns upon a balance, not between the favourable and the unfavourable evidence, but between the *absolute* amounts of relevant knowledge and of relevant ignorance respectively. (*TP*, p. 77)

In the 1907 *PP*, Keynes also calls these judgements, judgements of the intensity of probability; in 1936 *GT* they become judgements of confidence. He maintains that, as for probability, numerical and quantitative comparisons of the weight of argument are limited to restricted cases:

> The measurement of evidential weight presents similar difficulties to those with which we met in the measurement of probability. Only in a restricted class of cases can we compare the weights of two arguments in respect of more or less ... Where the conclusions of two arguments are different, or where the evidence for the one does not overlap the evidence for the other, it will often be impossible to compare their weights, just as it may be impossible to compare their probabilities. (*TP*, pp. 77–8)

Difficulties of comparison build up when joint judgements of probability and the weight of argument are considered. There are first the difficulties of ordering probability and the weight of argument respectively. Apart from these difficulties, however, the new joint judgement of probability and goodness is not strictly dependent on the two separate orders, even when these orders can be established. In particular, the new direct joint judgement does not depend on the sum or the product of the quantities of the two different orders. It is a new direct and organic judgement on the situation as a whole. In 1907, Keynes further maintains that most of the judgements we use in practice are actually joint and organic judgements of these two orders of reasoning and not judgements of probability alone:

> Finally, may not the direct and instinctive judgements of probability by which we are guided in practice be no judgements of probability at all but joint and organic judgements of probability and intensity? This is by no means impossible. The element of intensity may seldom affect the final order of magnitude ... But on fundamental points the difficulty in discovering a logical development of pure probability, which is in conformity with the direct and instinctive judgements of commonsense, may easily be due to the fact that it is not really with judgements or pure probability that commonsense is ordinarily concerned. (*PP*, pp. 129–30)

It is this type of joint judgement which represents Keynes's notion of uncertainty in Chapter 12 of *GT*:

> it would be foolish, in forming our expectations, to attach great weight to matters which are very uncertain ... The state of long-period expectation, upon which our decisions are based, does not solely depend ... on the most probable forecast we can make. It also depends on the *confidence* with which we make this forecast ... The state of confidence ... is a matter to which practical men always pay the closest and most anxious attention. But economists have not analysed it carefully. (*GT*, p. 148)

Let us now consider joint judgements of probability and goodness.[15] If we are in situations where we cannot even order the degrees of probability, the incomparability of the joint judgement again derives from this basic difficulty. More interesting is the discussion of situations where we have two *different orders* of probability and goodness. Keynes maintains that difficulties of quantitative comparison can arise even in this more favourable situation. For the investigation of this case a considerable amount of material is available covering over forty years of Keynes's intellectual career. This material covers both the early (1907–1921) and the mature (1938–1944) periods, apparently without solution of continuity in his approach to the quantitative incomparability of such a joint judgement.

The existence of the two different orders of probability and goodness is typical of the fundamental case considered in ethics, that of 'right conduct' or 'duty' in human action. This is also the case which is the most relevant for the interpretation of Keynes's theory of economic action.

Let us start from his words in 1907, in the opening passage of Chapter XVI of *PP* ('The Relation of Probability to Ethics, and the Doctrine of Mathematical Expectation'). This is necessary to fix the background of his notion of reasonable action in economics and of his refusal of the Benthamite calculus. Let us recall that, for Keynes, economics is a moral science:

> I do not know of any passage in the ancient philosophers which explicitly points out that the pursuit of good is only a duty in proportion to the agent's reasonable expectations of attaining them. It is, perhaps, part of the explanation of the supposed relativity of good, that this distinction has not been clearly made. The quantity, which figures, when we decide upon our duty, is doubly relative, relative to our powers and relative to our information. This quantity is a complex and a product, one of whose factors is quantity of goodness, but whose relativity is due to the presence of the other factor [i.e. the quantity of probability]. (*PP*, p. 347; see also *TP*, p. 339)

First, the passage shows how the quantity upon which right conduct or duty depends is *relative* to the amount of information or limited knowledge upon which, in Keynes's own conception, probability depends.

Second, it shows how the problem of right conduct or moral duty in ethics is by Keynes, so to speak, dissolved into that of reasonable action. His 1907 position is in line with his earlier (23 January 1904) critique of Moore's theory of action in 'Ethics in relation to conduct'.[16] Right action or duty is simply reasonable action. Keynes maintains that what matters is the reasonableness, not the absolute rationality of action. Reasonableness is relative to contingent and changeable cognitive circumstances. It is a sort of historical rationality. Keynes's notion of reasonableness is comparable to 'phronesis', Aristotle's practical reason in *Nichomachean Ethics*.[17]

Third, it shows how the quantity upon which reasonable action depends is 'a complex and a product' of the quantity of goodness and of the quantity of probability. This quantity is therefore the result of a joint judgement. As such, it can raise difficulties of quantitative comparison.

In particular, difficulties arise if probabilities are not numerically measurable or, at least, quantitatively comparable. This gives rise to the incomparability of the products of the quantities of probability and goodness: 'A further difficulty arises from the admission that not all probabilities are numerically or even quantitatively comparable among themselves. For it follows from this that not all products of magnitudes of probability and goodness are comparable' (*PP*, p. 353).

These difficulties of comparison arise not only because probabilities are not, in general, numerically measurable or, at least, quantitatively comparable. In 1907, he also raises doubts on the numerical measurement of goodness:

> It may be remarked in this connection that the question, whether *every* pair of goods are numerically comparable even in respect of goodness, has not received a proper consideration. Many such questions of the greatest importance have hitherto escaped attention, on account of the generally received opinion that *all* magnitudes, of the same kind *prima facie*, must necessarily be capable of numerical comparison. (*PP*, p. 354; see also *TP*, pp. 345, 349)

It is this difficulty of quantitative comparison of products which lies fundamentally at the base of Keynes's critique of Moore's doctrine of mathematical expectations and of his acceptance of the Benthamite calculus.[18] This thesis is fully elaborated in 1907. Keynes holds it firmly at least until 1944, the last year from which material is available on this point.

In this case, as in those considered above of the incomparability of probabilities and of joint judgements of probability and the weight of argument, reasonable action is not univocally determined. In 1907 and in 1921 respectively, Keynes wrote:

> It must be admitted, I think, that the question of right action is not, under all circumstances, a determinate problem, even if perfect logical and intuitive power be pre-supposed. (*PP*, pp. 353–4)

> We must accept the conclusion that, if one good is greater than another, but the probability of attaining the first less than that of attaining the second, the question of which it is our duty to pursue may be indeterminate ... It may be remarked, further, that the difficulty exists, whether the numerical indeterminateness of the probability is intrinsic or whether its numerical value is, as it is according to the frequency theory and most other theories simply unknown. (*TP*, p. 345)

Again, arbitrariness and indeterminacy in choice do not mean unreasonableness of action, nor does it always imply indeterminateness in action. Although the choice between the incomparable products of the quantities of probability and goodness is arbitrary, the final decision depends on new direct synthetic judgements of the situation as a whole and not on mechanical rules of comparability between the previous orders. Other rules of choice or direct judgements play a fundamental role and are considered no less rational by Keynes:

> The judgement of goodness and the judgement of probability both involve somewhere an element of direct apprehension and both are quantitative. The question at issue is whether the magnitude of the 'oughtness' of an action can be in all cases directly determined by simply multiplying together the magnitudes obtained in the two direct judgements. The alternative, I propose to this, is a new direct judgement of the magnitude of the 'oughtness' of an action under given circumstances. This third direct quantitative judgement would not bear any simple and necessary relation to the two former.
>
> This supposition appears to me highly doubtful. But it may represent our actual practice more closely than the abstraction of 'mathematical expectation'. For in practice we do not, I think, make the two former judgements and then deduce the third. We fly direct to the third as a result of our general survey of the situation. (*PP*, pp. 357–8; see also *TP*, pp. 348–9)

Actually, the possibility of applying direct joint judgements to the situation as a whole transforms the indeterminate action into a determinate one: 'the question of which it is our duty to pursue may be indeterminate, unless we suppose it to be within our power to make direct quantitative judgements of probability and goodness jointly' (*TP*, p. 345).

To conclude the examination of our CASE-III*, we will consider Keynes's mature position in 1938–39 and 1944 which does not change substantially.

In his letters of 27 July 1938 and 7 December 1938 to Townshend, Keynes explicitly refers to his early position in *TP*. He deals with joint judgements of probability and goodness in a manner similar to our CASE-III(ii), i.e. where probabilities cannot be arranged in an order for the heterogeneity of reasons which back them (Keynes's 'umbrella dilemma'):

> But that still leaves millions of cases over where one cannot even arrange an order of preference. When all is said and done, there is an arbitrary element in the situation ... [I]n making a decision we have before us a large number of alternatives, none of which is demonstrably more 'rational' than the others, in the sense that we can arrange in order of merit the sum aggregate of the benefits obtainable from the complete consequences of each. To avoid being in the position of Buridan's ass, we fall back, therefore, and necessarily do so, on motives of another kind, which are not 'rational' in the sense of being concerned with the evaluation of consequences, but are decided by habit, instinct, preference, desire, will, etc. (*CW* XXIX, pp. 289, 294)

In a letter to Werner Stark (10 February, 1944), Keynes comments on Stark's article presented for the *Economic Journal* in which the author offers a Bergsonian critique of the foundations of orthodox economics. The methodological difficulty stressed by Keynes, in contrast with Stark, arises exactly when a particular economic decision is the result – as a whole and not as a sum or a product – of two different orders of preference, if the latter are not numerically measurable or, at least, quantitatively comparable. In Keynes's example, the two orders are, respectively, an order relative to the final results of the action and an order relative to their probabilities. The difficulty is devastating for the very possibility of economic calculus. No logical meaning can be attributed to the product of single quantities. The new order is not the result of the product of the quantities of the previous orders. It is a new direct judgement on the situation as a whole. As Keynes writes in this previously unpublished letter:

> I daresay it is true that economists have not paid as much attention to Bergson's criticism of their foundations as they ought, or rather as they should have when Bergson was first writing. For, as I mention below, Bergson is not really up to date in these matters on the lines of more recent thought.
>
> Bergson was pretty completely successful, I should agree, against Fechner or against the sort of things Edgeworth was putting forth when he wrote 'Mathematical Psychics' and 'Metretike'. But the modern psychologists know all this pretty well. Above all Bergson was not enough of a mathematician to appreciate the difference between a concept being quantitative and instances of it being capable of arrangement in an order of magnitude without quantitative relations. He was, of course, quite unacquainted with the modern mathematics of order. His arguments against attributing quantities to degrees of preference are not equally valid against the conception of ranging preferences in an order of magnitude, which is really what the modern economist would do if he were to give more attention to these fundamental matters than is at present the fashion.
>
> In my judgement, the real difficulty arises, and that is something which Bergson does not touch on, when some particular position is the resultant of two distinct orders of preferences, neither of which is strictly quantitative. For example, one can arrange one's preferences for the ultimate end results in an order of magnitude, and one can also range in an order of magnitude the probability or intensity of belief which, in one's judgement, attaches to attaining these end results. Clearly one's action ought to be so governed that the degree of preference multiplied by the degree of probability comes highest. The trouble is, however, that no logical meaning can be attached to this. The order of preference for the purpose of choice, which takes account both of the value of results and the probability of getting them, has, it seems, to be arrived at by quite a distinct direct process. All this, I agree, economists are in the habit of neglecting. But, if one is to tackle this subject, one has to tackle it, I think, on these lines rather than on what are to the modern mind the rather elementary and old-fashioned concepts of Bergson (Keynes, 1944)

The methodological difficulty pointed out by Keynes to Stark in 1944 is in line with his early position in 1907. Indeed, Keynes appears unusually modest. As seen, in 1907 his position is even more radical than in 1944. There he doubts the very possibility of ordering probabilities in general and of applying the 'mathematics of order' to quantities of probabilities relative to any arguments.

In the next section, we will see how Keynes's position is the outcome of his early critique of Bertrand Russell. In fact Russell's *Principles of Mathematics* (1903) is the starting point for the 'modern mathematics of order', to which Keynes refers in his letter to Stark. To clarify this aspect, however, we must re-read what has been said thus far on the measurement, comparison and ordering of probabilities from a different perspective, that of Keynes's own philosophy of measurement. This perspective is also needed to grasp Keynes's economics. He applies his philosophy of measurement not only to his notion of uncertainty, but also to the measurement and quantitative comparison of macroeconomic magnitudes such as the value of money, real output as a whole, aggregate capital, and utility.

Philosophy of measurement
The central problem in Chapter 3 of *TP* on the measurement of probability is the discussion of the *theoretical* possibilities of measuring probabilities irrespective of the practical possibilities of measuring it. The same critical exercise is carried out by Keynes for the measurement of economic magnitudes in his 1909 essay on index numbers (*CW* XI, pp. 49–156; Carabelli, 1992).[19]

Philosophy of measurement: probability
In Chapter 3 of *TP*, Keynes tackles the logical and theoretical difficulties of the measurement of probability, not the statistical–mathematical ones due to *our* inability to measure it. He raises the problem of the existence of a measure for probability, i.e. the existence of a general or 'natural' unit of measure and of quantity (*TP*, p. 33). For this reason, his discussion is more relevant to theoreticians (be they economists or not) than to applied scientists or statisticians: 'That such comparison is *theoretically possible*, whether or not we are actually competent in every case to make the comparison, has been the generally accepted opinion' (*TP*, p. 21).

In this regard he quotes a passage from Donkin where this distinction between theoretical and practical difficulties of measurement is made explicit:

> the difficulty of *ascertaining numbers* ... [and the] difficulty of *expression by means of numbers*. The former difficulty is real, but merely relative to our knowledge and skill; the latter, if real, would be absolute and inherent in the subject matter, which I conceive is not the case. (*TP*, p. 22)

Keynes's position is, however, the opposite of Donkin's. He maintains that the theoretical difficulty of numerical measurement is intrinsic and inherent in probability. Again, it is to be noted how this difficulty is equally intrinsic and inherent in macroeconomic magnitudes and does not depend on our inability to measure them (*CW* XI, pp. 52, 135).

He thinks that the current view by which probability is, in general, measurable is to be *limited* to a few restricted cases. Equally, in his critique of classical economists, Keynes limits the conditions of validity of the opposite theory, making its tacit premises and conditions explicit (Carabelli, 1991). He aims to reduce the generality of the classical theory, thus securing for his own theory (in probability or in economics) the true generality: 'It has been assumed ... that probability is ... measurable ... I shall have to limit, not extend, the popular doctrine' (*TP*, p. 21).

Now consider Keynes's philosophy of measurement proper. In the first version of *TP*, Keynes considers the contemporary status of the philosophy of measurement and, in particular, of the measurement of *relations*. His main interest is in the 'philosophy of magnitude', not in the mathematics of magnitude (*PP*, p. 119; see also *TP*, p. 37). He thoroughly analyses Russell's *Principles of Mathematics* (1903).

The general characteristics of Keynes's philosophy of measurement can be briefly outlined here. Probability is a relation between propositions, i.e. between premises and conclusions (*PP*, p. 8). Therefore, it falls within the problem of the measurement of relations. In particular, the probable relation is a quantity (*PP*, p. 52) and so Keynes writes of the magnitude of probability. In this connection, Keynes discusses Russell's question in the *Principles of Mathematics* as to whether there be any other relation having magnitude besides the relation of distance. He answers positively by showing that probability is a relation similar to Russell's relation of distance. He thinks that Russell uses this term to cover the relation between different shades of colour or between different moments of time, as well as between different points in space (*PP*, p. 53).

In his work, Russell distinguishes between extensive and intensive magnitudes. Extensive magnitudes are defined as magnitudes which are rendered amenable to numerical measure. By difference, all other magnitudes are intensive.[20] In particular, the class of divisibilities and of relations of distances belongs to extensive magnitudes.

In contrast, Keynes maintains that relations of probability, notwithstanding their similarity to Russell's relations of distance, do not belong to the same extensive magnitudes as Russell's class of relations of distances and divisibilities. In fact, for probability, Keynes also considers classes of quantities of probabilities relative to propositions for which equal intervals might not exist. He compares the quantity of probability to the quantity measured by specific volume or specific density. Consequently, Keynes's relations of probability belong, in general, to Russell's intensive rather than extensive magnitudes:

> I think that the classes of quantities, for which equal intervals are in the absence of contrary information equally probable, are those which Mr Russell calls 'dis-

tances' and 'divisibilities'. 'Intensive' quantities, on the other hand, to which measurement stands in a much less intimate relation, cannot be dealt with in this way. The quantity measured by specific volume or specific density is clearly 'intensive' in the technical sense in which that term is used here. (*PP*, pp. 119–20)

Keynes also criticizes Russell's notion of a *kind* of magnitude. He wants, as he writes, 'a new definition' of it:

it is upsetting to one's *prima facie* conception of the nature of magnitude. It is necessary to deny Mr. Russell's proposition that 'given any magnitude, those which are greater or less than that magnitude for a certain definite class, within which any two are one greater and the other less. Such a class is called *a kind* of magnitude'. For we may have two magnitudes, both of which are comparable with a given magnitude in respect of more or less, and yet which are not comparable with one another. A new definition of a kind of magnitude is required. (*PP*, p. 58; Keynes does not give the page of the quotation but it is from Russell, 1903, ed. 1937, p. 164)

Keynes points out that there are different kinds of magnitudes of probability relations: 'The magnitudes of probabilities are not all of the same kind. That is to say the relations of more or less do not hold between *any* pair of them' (*PP*, p. 57). So, the ordering and quantitative comparison of the magnitudes of probability relations are not possible between *any* pair of probabilities: some homogeneity in kind is required. He thinks that, if probabilities are of the same kind, they can always be compared (*PP*, p. 58).

It should be noted, however, that Keynes also thinks it possible quantitatively to compare probabilities which belong to different orders, i.e. which are of 'different kinds': 'At the same time the relations of more or less may hold between magnitudes of probabilities of *different* kinds' (*PP*, pp. 57–8). In fact, he writes: '*some* probabilities of different kinds will be comparable in respect of more or less' (*PP*, p. 58). Keynes, therefore, widens the possibility of quantitative comparison even between probabilities of 'different kinds'. This can happen in limited cases: only if the different orders cross each other, as we have seen in Keynes's diagram quoted above.

Numerical comparison requires a further condition. Only relations which are of the 'same kind' and which are further measurable in terms of *a common unit* are numerically measurable and then numerically comparable (*PP*, p. 62): 'others again seem to be capable of numerical measurement in terms of some common unit' (*PP*, p. 61).

Thus, probability relation is, in general, a non-numerically measurable quantity. Keynes points out that a quantity is not necessarily a number: 'The numerical view of probability is partly traceable to the frequent definition of probability as a number and not as a quantity' (*PP*, p. 56).

Furthermore, the ordering of probabilities does not guarantee, in general, numerical measurement:

> Probability is, then, a quantitative relation. It may or may not be measurable: that is to say it may or may not be possible to establish a one-to-one correspondence between its various magnitudes and all or some of the numbers. (*PP*, p. 57)

Using Georgescu-Roegen's terminology, we can say that Keynes clearly distinguishes between the ranking and the ordinal measurability of probabilities. The ordering of probabilities guarantees numerical comparison only if a common unit of measure and of quantity exists. This is in contrast with De Morgan's view:

> De Morgan held ... that, whenever we have differences of degree, numerical comparison *must* be theoretically possible. He assumes ... that all probabilities can be placed in an *order* of magnitude, and argues from this that they must be measurable ... Objects can be arranged in an order, which we can reasonably call one of degree or magnitude, without its being possible to conceive a system of measurement of the differences between the individuals. (*TP*, p. 22)

In fact, the existence of differences in degrees does not mean that we can always measure these differences numerically:

> We must bear in mind that our theory must apply to all probabilities and not to a limited class only, and that, as we do not adopt a definition of probability which presupposes its numerical mensurability, we cannot directly argue from differences in degree to a numerical measurement of these differences. (*TP*, p. 37)[21]

Probability relations are then similar to relations of likeness even as to numerical measurement: 'the greater the similarity the greater the probability of our conclusion. But we cannot in these cases *measure* the increase' (*TP*, p. 30).

Keynes maintains that probability relations have an intrinsic quantitative indeterminateness. The impossibility of a numerical measurement of probability is not ascribed to our incapacity, lack of knowledge or skill but to the nature of the case itself. In this sense, he writes of this impossibility as 'absolute and inherent in the subject matter' (*PP*, p. 65). The magnitudes of probability are indeterminate because there is no determinacy in the units of quantity. Their units belong to different kinds of magnitudes of probability:

> they are 'essentially' indeterminate ... I say 'essentially', because this indeterminacy is not simply relative to our knowledge or to a particular set of premises, but is absolute. We have to do with different kinds of the same species of quantity, whose units are essentially indeterminate in terms of one another, but which are sometimes comparable within certain limits. The case is not to be compared to

that of a real number π and a rational number … In these probability scales a new conception of relative indeterminacy of units of magnitude must be introduced. For although we can always express one unit in terms of another to *some* degree of approximation, there are strict limits to this and we cannot increase at will the closeness of the approximation. (*PP*, p. 65)

This intrinsic numerical indeterminateness is stressed again in the final version of *TP*. In fact, a general, or in Keynes's words, a natural unit of measure does not exist for probability:

It is not the case here that the method of calculation, prescribed by theory, is beyond our powers or too laborious for actual application. *No* method of calculation, however impracticable, has been suggested. Nor have we any *prima facie* indications of the existence of a common unit to which the magnitudes of all probabilities are naturally referrable. A degree of probability is not composed of some homogeneous material, and is not apparently divisible into parts of like character with one another … Probabilities do not all belong to a single set of magnitudes measurable in terms of a common unit (*TP*, pp. 32–3; on measurability in terms of a common unit see also pp. 35–6).

Given this intrinsic indeterminateness, a multiplicity of different units of quantity and of measure of probability relations exists. This variety of quantity and measure depends on the nature of the material under investigation: 'the magnitudes of probability relations must be measured in various units according to the particular case in question, these units being incommensurable among themselves' (*PP*, p. 67).

Philosophy of measurement: economic quantities

Keynes transfers this philosophy of measure and comparison of probabilities to macroeconomic magnitudes. His 1909 'Essay on Index Numbers' is the work in which this transfer takes place. In it he aims at 'a philosophical discussion of these ideas, postponing the mathematical difficulties of our subject but facing those which depend rather upon reasoning than upon calculation' (*CW* XI, p. 64). So, similarly to probability, he tackles the logical and philosophical difficulties of the measurement of economic magnitudes, not the mathematical ones. He clearly distinguishes between difficulties in reasoning and difficulties in calculating.

Keynes considers economic magnitudes such as uncertainty, income as a whole, aggregate capital and utility and the general price level, as similar to probability from the standpoint of the philosophy of measurement and quantitative comparison.

In his 1909 paper, it is his discussion on the measurement of national income which best shows the common roots of these two philosophies. The quantities of probability are of different kinds. The same goes for economic quantities. Further, both are characterized by three degrees of 'intimacy'. The lowest degree is represented by heterogeneous quantities – such as the quantities of a ton and of a mile – incomparable and incommensurable:

> Everybody recognises that there are different kinds of quantities. We do not suppose that, because a ton is a quantity and a mile is a quantity, we can therefore compare the magnitudes of a ton and a mile. There are also admitted instances of quantities between which there is an intermediate degree of intimacy; they are, that is to say, not as completely disparate as a ton is from a mile, and yet not capable of the numerical relation which exists between one mile and two miles. We may give the example of degree of similarity. A green octavo volume is more like a green folio than a red octavo is, but it would be evidently false to say that it is twice or any other number of times as like. We may say that a set of quantities are of the same *kind* when each of the set can be compared in respect of *more and less* with each of the others, and that they are in the same *unit* when *numerical* comparison is possible between every pair of the set ... A numerical comparison between two aggregates of utilities would only be possible if each of the utilities were strictly of the same kind and if the laws of arithmetic could be validly applied to their summation. This does not seem to be the case. (*CW* XI, pp. 53–4)

In the 1909 essay, even Keynes's words are the same as in his 1907 *PP*. The phrase 'three degrees of intimacy' he uses to indicate the three cases of numerical comparison, quantitative comparison and incomparability of economic magnitudes is actually borrowed from it:

> three possible degrees of intimacy between the magnitudes of any pair of probabilities. Some cannot be compared at all in this respect; between others the relations of more or less can be established; and others again seem to be capable of numerical measurement in terms of some common unit ... [The first ones] represent pairs of probabilities between which the lowest of the three degrees of intimacy exists; it is impossible to say of either that it is either less or greater than the other, or to compare their magnitude in any respect whatever. (*PP*, pp. 60–2)

And even Keynes's own definition of index numbers makes explicit the theoretical difficulties detected in his philosophy of the measurement of probability. He defines index numbers stressing the theoretical difficulties of their construction, not the practical ones. The series of quantities should have the *same kind of relation* to the different moments of time, space or class of objects considered. These quantities should be further measurable in terms of the same unit of measure:

> An index number is in itself no more than the measure of the magnitude of an object at one time or in one place in terms of the magnitude of the same or similar object at another time or in another place. If we are dealing with a series of quantities $f(t_1), f(t_2)$, each of which has the *same relation* to different moments of time or parts of space or classes of objects, and which are all numerically measur-

able in terms of a *common unit*, then the ratio [100 $F(t_2)/f(t_1)$] is defined as the index number of f for the time or place or class t_2 referred to its value for t_1 as base. (*CW* XI, pp. 51–2; my italics)

Moreover, his stress on the theoretical necessity of making explicit the system of 'weighing' in the building of index numbers shows a further striking parallelism with his attitude in probability: the necessity to make explicit the implicit direct judgements. The weighing of index numbers parallels direct judgements of relevance in probability. In fact, in *TP*, judgements of relevance are to a certain extent connected with the weight of argument.

Incommensurability of magnitudes

We have seen that, in his philosophy of measurement, Keynes defends a notion not of *a kind* but of *different kinds* of magnitudes. He thinks that only if magnitudes are of the *same kind* and if they are further measured in terms of a common unit can they be numerically compared (*PP*, p. 58). Therefore, numerical comparison of magnitudes requires homogeneity in kind and in measurement whereas quantitative comparison requires only homogeneity in kind. This means that Keynes considers heterogeneity in kind as the general case both for probability and economics. Thus, quantities of probability can be as heterogeneous as the quantities of a ton and a mile are.

Difficulties in the quantitative comparison of probabilities or in finding a common unit of measure and of quantity for the different kinds of probabilities depend on the fact that these quantities of probability are similar to quantities which can at the same time be characterized by an 'ensemble' or a complex of heterogenous attributes moving in different directions, for example by a class of qualities rather than by one single quality:

> the comparison of the probability of such propositions as 'This book is red', and 'This book is blue'. By 'red' not one single quality is meant, but a class of qualities. The book is to have one out of a class of qualities which we may call 'the reds'. (*PP*, p. 120)

The existence of different orders of probability relative to the different kinds of magnitudes is like the existence of different orders of similarity between two complex objects. Their different qualities move in different directions originating increasing and diminishing orders.

In these cases, it is impossible to compare quantitatively the two complex objects as a whole – and even less to compare them numerically: 'It is not possible to say of every pair of objects which of them is *on the whole* the more like a third object' (*TP*, p. 122; my italics).

So, can we speak of probability as a non homogeneous item? Or as a non-homogeneous complex characterized by heterogeneous attributes which move, in a non-proportional manner, in different directions, either in space or in time? Can we therefore apply to probability what Keynes says for output as a whole: 'a non homogeneous complex which cannot be measured ... except in certain special cases, as for example when all the items of one output are included in the same proportion in another output' (*GT*, p. 38)? Can we also apply to probability what Keynes says for real capital: 'a quantitative comparison of the eventual real capital after the elapse of an interval of time with the initial real capital ... would involve a problem, insoluble except in special cases, of the quantitative comparison of non-homogeneous items' (*CW* XIII, p. 471)?

Keynes's example in Chapter 3 of *TP* helps us to answer these crucial questions:

> For instance, a book bound in blue morocco is more like a book bound in red morocco than if it were bound in blue calf; and a book bound in red calf is more like the book in red morocco than if it were in blue calf. But there may be no comparison between the degree of similarity which exists between books bound in red morocco and blue morocco, and that which exists between books bound in red morocco and red calf. (*TP*, p. 39)

The objects in Keynes's example (two books in this case) are characterized by *different qualitative attributes* – such as the type and colour of the binding of the two books – which are not numerically measurable. If objects of this kind exist, then their quantitative comparison, as a whole, is impossible. A partial comparison between them is, however, possible if we concentrate – by some direct judgement of favourable or unfavourable relevance – on just one relevant attribute at a time: in Keynes's example, 'morocco-binding' and 'redness' respectively.

But it is, however, equally very difficult to make – so to speak – a second level of comparison between the degrees of the two already established orders of comparison (unless the two orders, by chance, intersect each other at some point, like point *W* in Figure 11.1, see p. 210). The situation is similar to that of trying to form a new joint judgement of similarity, starting from some already established orders of similarity, so bringing the two orders of similarity together *as a whole*: to establish a new order of similarity over the orders of similarity already established.

This is what happens in probability when we try to form a new joint judgement of probability starting from some already established orders of probabilities. Or, as seen, when we try to form a joint judgement of probability and the weight of argument, or, of probability and goodness together:

> As in the example of similarity, where there are different orders of increasing or diminishing similarity, but where it is not possible to say of every pair of objects

which of them is *on the whole* the more like a third object, so there are different orders of probability, and probabilities, which are not of the same order, cannot be compared. (*TP*, p. 122, my italics)

Incommensurability and incomparability due to heterogeneity in dimension. Manifoldness of magnitudes

At this point, an additional question can be raised: whether this heterogeneity in kind of the quantities of probability is due not only to the existence of an 'ensemble' of heterogeneous qualitative attributes (similar to the physical heterogeneity of the aggregate capital or output) but to the manifoldness of the quantities or orders of probability. In brief, the question is whether there is also heterogeneity in the *dimensions* of the quantities of probability, like those of beauty and goodness. In fact, the dimensions of beauty and goodness are heterogeneous; hence, their magnitudes are incommensurable and incomparable.

It is difficult to give a definite answer to this question. In the 1907 version of *TP*, Keynes maintains that the quantities of probabilities belonging to different orders – though heterogeneous in kind – are not completely in different dimensions like those of beauty and goodness:

> The most difficult point, which the diagram helps to bring out, is the relationship to one another of the units of the different strands ... Yet the base units of the different strands are not altogether in different dimensions, as, for instance, are those of beauty and goodness; for we may be able to say (e.g.) that seven times one unit is less than six times another. But they are *essentially* indeterminate in relation to one another; I say 'essentially', because this indeterminacy is not simply relative to our knowledge or to a particular set of premises, but is absolute. We have to do with different kinds of the same species of quantity, whose units are essentially indeterminate in terms of one another, but which are sometimes comparable within certain limits. I know of no analogous instance ... In these probability scales a new conception of relative indeterminacy of units of magnitudes must be introduced (*PP*, p. 65).

In the final version of *TP*, this view is absent. Keynes only refers to heterogeneity in dimension in three contexts:

1. Joint judgements of probability and the weight of argument. Keynes refers here to weight and probability as 'independent properties' of the argument (*TP*, p. 83) or 'as two independent dimensions in which the judgement is free to move' (*TP*, p. 85).
2. Joint judgements of probability and goodness. Keynes quotes a passage from Leibniz's *Nouveaux Essais* (Book II, Chapter xxi): 'in such judgements ... "as in other estimates disparate and heterogeneous and, so to speak, of more than one dimension, the greatness of that which is dis-

cussed is in reason composed of both estimates (i.e. of goodness and probability), and is like a rectangle, in which there are two considerations, viz. that of length and that of breadth"' (*TP*, pp. 340–1).

3. Lastly, when the measurement and comparison in space and time of the 'composite quantity' representing the value of money are discussed: 'where we seek to build up an index number of a conception, which is quantitative but is not in itself numerically measurable in any defined and unambiguous sense' (*TP*, p. 237). He considers explicitly the 'variations of different type' of the value of money (*TP*, p. 235). In this section of the 1921 *TP*, Keynes transfers part of his discussion in the 1909 essay on index numbers.

It is, however, in his economic writings that Keynes refers explicitly to the multidimensionality and manifoldness of economic magnitudes, due to heterogeneity in dimension. First, in his 1909 'Essay on Index Numbers'; later, in the 1930 *TM* and in the 1936 *GT*.

In the 1909 Essay, Keynes reports Bourguin's remark on the value of money:

> Le pouvoir de la monnaie n'est qu'un mot; il ne désigne pas une qualité, mais un *ensemble* de rapports qui n'ont rien de commun entre eux, n'étant pas des équations entre grandeurs de même espèce (CW XI, p. 67).

But it is in *TM* that we find the most explicit reference:

> This difficulty in making precise quantitative comparisons is the same as arises in the case of many other famous concepts, namely of all those which are complex or manifold in the sense that they are capable of variations of degree in more than one mutually incommensurable direction at the same time. The concept of purchasing power, averaged over populations which are not homogeneous in respect of their real incomes, is complex in this sense. The same difficulty arises whenever we ask whether one thing is superior in degree to another *on the whole*, the superiority depending on the resultant of several attributes which are each variable in degree but in ways non commensurable with one another. (*TM*, p. 88, Keynes's italics)

In this passage, he explicitly refers to his discussion of non-numerical measurement and non-quantitative comparison of probability in *TP* (*TM*, p. 88, fn. 2). He also refers to 'incommensurable directions', that is to manifoldness. See also the passage, 'we can give no meaning to a numerical comparison between the purchasing power of money to a poor man and its purchasing power to a rich man, the two things being, so to speak, in different dimensions' (*TM*, p. 87). And, lastly, he implicitly refers to heterogeneity and multidimensionality in *GT*'s famous passage of Chapter 4:

To say that net output today is greater, but the price level lower, than ten years ago or one year ago, is a proposition of similar character to the statement that Queen Victoria was a better queen but not a happier woman than Queen Elisabeth – a proposition not without meaning and not without interest, but unsuitable as material for differential calculus. (*GT*, p. 40).

This passage if read along the interpretation here suggested, i.e. in terms of manifoldness and heterogeneous dimensions, acquires a new light. In Keynes's example, the dimensions of happiness and goodness are heterogeneous. Thus, the two complex objects to be compared as a whole (the two queens – one better but unhappier than the other) are incommensurable and incomparable due to heterogeneity in dimension.[22]

New elements on the continuity in Keynes's methodological approach emerge. Neither in probability nor in economics is comparison *as a whole* (either numerical or quantitative) possible between complex objects characterized by an ensemble of incommensurable qualitative attributes moving in different dimensions at the same time.

This methodological continuity becomes even closer if we compare the above quoted *GT* passage on the two queens with the following one of the 1921 *TP*:

There are, however, many cases in which these rules furnish no means of comparison; and in which it is certain that it is not actually within our power to make the comparison. It has been argued that in these cases the probabilities are, in fact, *not comparable*. As in the example of similarity, where there are different orders of increasing and diminishing similarity, but where it is not possible to say of every pair of objects which of them is *on the whole* the more like a third object, so there are different orders of probability, and probabilities, which are not of the same order, cannot be compared. (*TP*, p. 122; my italics)

At this point, we can answer affirmatively to the rhetorical questions raised at the beginning of the section. Probability is a non-homogeneous object similar to the 'non homogeneous complex which cannot be measured ... except in certain special cases' (*GT*, p. 38) and to the 'incommensurable collections of miscellaneous objects' (*GT*, p. 39).

In fact, in 1921, Keynes writes of probability: 'A degree of probability is not composed of some homogeneous material' (*TP*, p. 32). Thus, probability too is intrinsically a non precise quantity, similar to the *GT* 'vague and non quantitative concepts' (*GT*, p. 40).

Non quantitative comparison of economic quantities. The problem of the units of time and economic dynamics

In Keynes's philosophy of the measurement and comparison of magnitudes, not only is numerical measurement and numerical comparison in question but also the very possibility of quantitative comparison.

In economics, Keynes refers to the difficulties of quantitative comparison and not only of numerical comparison in the famous passage on the organic interdependence of the economic material in his 1924 'Essay on Edgeworth': 'comparison of quantity fails us' (*CW* X, p. 262).

This explains not only his attention to the choice of units of quantity and measure in macroeconomics ('difficulties as to the definition of the physical unit of capital' (*GT*, p. 138; see also Carabelli, 1992)[23] but also his attention to the choice of the different units of time: the 'production period' which corresponds to the time necessary to produce investment goods; the 'accounting period' and the 'daily' period which are connected to the determination of employment.[24]

This further explains his scepticism on the possibility of quantitatively comparing economic magnitudes and of dealing with economic variations in time, i.e. his approach to economic dynamics and to historical time in economics: 'The problem of comparing one real output with another ... presents conundrums which permit ... of no solution' (*GT*, *CW* VII, p. 39). And, 'It does not enable us to make the comparison for communities as a whole, unless the change in the purchasing power of money ... is uniform for all the different levels of real income' (*TM*, *CW* V, p. 87).

Variation and change in economic variables are not mechanical but qualitative and organic. Time is not homogeneous and there is further organic unity through time. This empties all the naïve attempts of measuring and quantitatively comparing economic magnitudes through time.

Yet, again, as happens for incomparable probabilities where direct judgements, caprice or habits equally play a role, the same happens for incomparable economic quantities. Here too, arbitrariness in the choice does not imply total indeterminacy:

> The fact that two incommensurable collections of miscellaneous objects cannot in themselves provide the material for a quantitative analysis need not, of course, prevent us from making approximate statistical comparison, depending on some broad element of judgement rather than on strict calculation, which may possess significance and validity within certain limits. (*GT*, *CW* VII, p. 39)

This is also Keynes's position in Chapter 8 of *TM* ('The meaning of comparisons of purchasing power'). In his view, it is always possible to use the direct method of comparison by the application of direct judgements:

> This method ... is, in fact, the method which is most often employed by common sense. It depends on a commonsense judgement of degrees of well-being by persons who have a general acquaintance with the conditions of life in both of the two positions under comparison. (*TM, CW* V, pp. 89–90)

Indeed, common sense and ordinary language are not hostage to the incommensurability of magnitudes! This is why they are the fitting tools for the imprecise science of economics:

> What degree of precision is advisable in economics? There is the danger of falling into scholasticism ... A generalisation to cover everything is impossible and impracticable. Generalising in economics is thinking by sample, not by generalisation. There is no possible use of mechanical logic, you only have it for a sample case not a general case. Even mathematical thinking is not in terms of *precise* concepts but 'fluffy grey lumps' ... Many economists in making their definition so precise, make them too rigid. This is the danger of scholasticism – a generalised case is more often a sample than a real generalisation ... Another danger is that you may 'precise everything away' and be left with only a comparative poverty of meaning. There is a grey, fuzzy, woolly monster of imprecision in one's head. In a complicated subject like economics the thing to do is avoid woolliness on the one hand, and scholasticism on the other ... Even in mathematics, when it is a matter of original thought, you do not always think in precise terms. (Keynes's lectures 1932–35: 6 November 1933; in Rymes 1989, pp. 101–2).

Notes

1. The abbreviation *CW* stands for *The Collected Writings of J.M. Keynes* followed by volume and page number, *PP*, for *Principles of Probability* (1907), *TP* for *A Treatise on Probability* (1921), *TM* for *A Treatise on Money* (1930), *GT* for *The General Theory* (1936). I wish to thank Keynes Trustees and King's College, Cambridge for permission to quote from Keynes's manuscripts (*MSS*) (unpublished writings of J.M. Keynes copyright The Provost and Scholars of King's College, Cambridge, 1994) and The Royal Economic Society for permission to quote from *A Treatise on Probability*.
2. On Keynes and Moore, see also Davis, 1991 and Shionoya, 1991.
3. What Keynes means by scholasticism can be understood from his lecture given on 6 November 1933. Using a definition by Ramsey, Keynes explains that the essence of scholasticism 'is treating what is vague as what is precise' (Rymes, 1989, p. 101).
4. The quotation ends: 'But we cannot assume its presence in every case or in comparing in respect of more or less the probabilities of every pair of argument' (*TP*, p. 38). On this, see CASE-III(ii) below.
5. Orders of probability are also compared to orders of the cardinal numbers:

   > Another example is afforded by the cardinal numbers. We say that the number three is greater than the number two, but we do not mean that these numbers are quantities one of which possesses a greater magnitude than the other. The one is greater than the other by reason of its position in the order of numbers; it is further distant from the origin zero. One number is greater than another if the second number lies *between* zero and the first. (*TP*, p. 39)

6. In Keynes's conception, probability is a relation between propositions or arguments – i.e. between premises and conclusions. Therefore, the material of probability consists of

propositions. Consequently, reasons, grounds or evidence supporting the relation of probability are themselves propositions.

7. Keynes writes: 'We wish ... to have a numerical measure of degrees of probability. This is only occasionally possible. A rule can be given for numerical measurement when the conclusion is one of a number of equiprobable, exclusive, and exhaustive alternatives, but not otherwise' (*TP*, p. 122).

8. In *TP*, his critique on the usage of the method of correlation in statistical inference follows the same approach:

> The controversial side of the method of least squares is purely logical; in the later developments there is much elaborate mathematics of whose correctness no one is in doubt. What is important to state with the utmost possible clearness is the precise assumptions on which the mathematics is based; when these assumptions have been set forth, it remains to determine their applicability in particular cases. (*TP*, p. 233)

9. See also Keynes's critique of Tinbergen's method:

> the difficult logical problems involved in applying to economic data methods which have been worked out in connection with material of a very different character ... it leaves unanswered many questions which the economist is bound to ask before he can feel comfortable as to the conditions which the economic material has to satisfy, if the proposed method is to be properly applicable ... the next instalment should be primarily devoted to the logical problem, explaining fully and carefully the conditions which the economic material must satisfy if the application of this method to it is to be fruitful. (*CW* XIV, pp. 306–7)

10. Actually, in 1922 Edgeworth and Jeffreys had already acknowledged that in *TP* Keynes holds the view that probabilities cannot, in general, be arranged in an order, though Edgeworth found Keynes's thesis unconvincing. However, to find a thesis unconvincing implicitly means having recognized its existence and importance. Edgeworth writes:

> In short the issue is narrowed to the question whether it is always possible 'to arrange probabilities in an order of magnitude,' to say that one is greater or less than another ... Mr Keynes objects to even rough comparison between probabilities unless they are *in eodem genere* ... The case is illustrated by the degrees of *similarity* which cannot always be placed in an order of magnitude (p. 258) ... That probability in general presents gradations has not been disproved [by Keynes]. It seems equally possible to arrange probabilities relating to different cases, if *in eodem genere*, in an order of magnitude, to say that one is greater than another (p. 279), (Edgeworth, 1992, pp. 258, 279)

I will return to the '*in eodem genere*' condition for ordering probabilities while discussing Keynes's philosophy of measurement. In the meantime, it is to be noted that Keynes's 1926 essay on Edgeworth (*CW* X, pp. 251–66) with its famous passage on 'organic interdependence and comparison of quantity' (*CW* X, p. 262) can be read as an indirect answer to the 1922 criticism of *TP* by Edgeworth.

In his review of *TP*, Harold Jeffreys (1922, p. 132) writes:

> he [Keynes] denies not only that the probabilities of all arguments can be expressed by numbers, but also that they can be arranged in a one-dimensional series at all. Thus the probability of one argument may be neither greater than, equal to, nor less than that of another.

11. Dardi (1991, p. 69) writes: 'it is clear that there [in *TP*] he [Keynes] questions only the numerical, and not the intrinsically ordinal character of probability'.

12. CASE-III will soon be joined by a new CASE-III* concerning the incomparability of joint judgements of probability, the weight of argument and goodness together.
13. O'Donnell (1991, p. 15) maintains that in the *TP*'s indeterminate domain of weak rationality, expectations are not reducible to probabilities because these are unknown for want of reasoning power.
14. Hodgson (1988, p. 226) is wrong on this point: 'Keynes' theory involves the assumption that actions of economic agents are, as far as possible, governed by reason and calculation ... In his work, reason and calculation are highlighted; rational agency is over-stressed with a neglect of habits and institutions'.
15. Keynes also considers the difficulties of comparison of the joint judgements of probability, the weight of argument and goodness altogether: 'It seems doubtful ... whether a good whose probability can only be determined on a slight basis of evidence can be compared by means merely of the magnitude of this probability with another good whose likelihood is based on ampler knowledge' (*PP*, p. 357).
16. The dating of this essay is questioned by Moggridge 1992, pp. 131–6.
17. Carabelli (1988, p. 150). For Aristotle, 'phronesis' – i.e. prudence or wisdom in concrete situations, characterizes those decisions such as political action, where it is not possible to deduce from general and immutable principles as is possible in mathematical demonstrations where truth governs. In politics, we have to take a decision without knowing the truth, thus deliberating on the base of probability and likeness. Not for this, however, does the arbitrariness of political decisions imply indeterminacy and irrationality.
18. This difficulty adds to the other criticisms already raised in 'Ethics in Relation to Conduct': (*a*) the interpretation of probability in terms of frequency; (*b*) the overwhelming attention to the long run effects of action; the need for certainty rather than probability; the numerical measurement of probability.
19. Please note that the next section follows, albeit with slight changes, a part of my 1992 paper.
20. According to Russell, measurement requires two axioms: the axiom of Archimedes and the axiom of linearity. The first axiom, based upon Russell's notion of *a kind* of magnitude (to which we will return soon) asserts that, 'given any two magnitudes of a kind, some finite multiple of the lesser exceeds the greater'. The second asserts that 'a magnitude can be divided into *n* equal parts and forms part of Du Bois Reymond's definition of linear magnitude' (Russell, 1903, pp. 181–2).
21. If these differences in degrees can be measured numerically, the relation of probability is reduced to Russell's relation of distance: 'It is true of some types of ordered series that there are measurable relations of distance between their members as well as order' (*TP*, p. 39).
22. Here not only numerical comparison is in question, as Keynes's remark on the impossibility of differential calculus would suggest. Quantitative comparison is also in doubt.
23. It is impossible to define the natural unit of probability: we have no '*prima facie* indications of the existence of a common unit to which the magnitudes of all probabilities are naturally referrable' (*TP*, p. 32).
24. 'The importance of the accounting period lies in the fact that all decisions to employ labour depend on expectations covering this period; though some of these expectations depend in turn on expectations covering the longer period' (*CW* XXIX, p. 74). And: '*Daily* here stands for the shortest interval after which the firm is free to revise its decision as to how much employment to offer. It is, so to speak, the minimum effective unit of economic time' (*GT*, *CW* VII, p. 47).

References

Carabelli, A. (1982), 'Investimento' in Lunghini G. (ed.), *Dizionario di economia politica*, Turin: Boringhieri.

Carabelli, A. (1988), *On Keynes's Method*, London: Macmillan.

Carabelli, A. (1991), 'The Methodology of the Critique of the Classical Theory: Keynes on

Organic Interdependence' in Bateman, B.W. and Davis, J.B. (eds), *Keynes and Philosophy*, Aldershot: Edward Elgar.

Carabelli, A. (1992), 'Organic Interdependence and the Choice of Units in the *General Theory*' in Gerrard, B. and Hillard, J. (eds), *The Philosophy and Economics of J.M. Keynes*, Aldershot: Edward Elgar.

Dardi, M. (1991), 'Interpretazioni di Keynes: logica del probabile, strutture dell' incerto', *Moneta e Credito*, **173**, March.

Davis, J.B. (1991), 'Keynes's critiques of Moore: philosophical foundations of Keynes's economics', *Cambridge Journal of Economics*, **15** (1), March.

Edgeworth, F.Y. (1922), 'The Philosophy of Chance', *Mind*, **31** (123), July.

Hodgson, J. (1988), *Economics and Institutions*, London: Polity Press.

Jeffreys, H. (1922), 'The Theory of Probability', Review of Keynes's *A Treatise on Probability*', *Nature*, **109** (2727), 2 February.

Keynes, J.M. (23 January 1904?), 'Ethics in Relation to Conduct', unpublished manuscript, Cambridge: King's College Library.

Keynes, J.M. (1907), *The Principles of Probability*, unpublished manuscript, Cambridge: King's College Library.

Keynes, J.M. (1944), 'Letter to W. Stark (10 February 1944)', unpublished manuscript, Cambridge: King's College Library.

Keynes, J.M. (1971–89), *Collected Writings*, London: Macmillan.

Meeks, G. (1991), 'Keynes on the Rationality of Decision Procedures under Uncertainty: the Investment Decision', in *Thoughtful Economic Man*, Cambridge: Cambridge University Press.

Moggridge, D.E. (1992), *Maynard Keynes. An Economist's Biography*, London: Routledge.

O'Donnell, R.M. (1989), *Keynes: Philosophy, Economics and Politics*, London: Macmillan.

O'Donnell, R.M. (1991), 'Keynes on Probability, Expectations and Uncertainty', in *Keynes as Philosopher-Economist*, London: Macmillan.

Russell, B. (1903), *Principles of Mathematics*, London: Unwin.

Rymes, T.K. (ed.) (1989), *Keynes's Lectures 1932–35*, London: Macmillan.

Shionoya, Y. (1991), 'Sidgwick, Moore and Keynes: a Philosophical Analysis of Keynes's "My Early Beliefs"' in Bateman, B.W. and Davis, J.B. (eds), *Keynes and Philosophy*, Aldershot: Edward Elgar.

PART V

PROBLEMS OF MEASUREMENT

12. How the 'G' got into the GNP

Ellen O'Brien

Introduction

National income and product accounts largely circumscribe the macro-economist's object of investigation. Their purportedly objective status has helped to legitimate theoretical analysis and is to no small degree responsible for the perception that economics is scientific (Porter, 1991). The fact that nearly every principles text includes a chapter on national accounts attests to the power of the numbers. Given the important role of the numbers internal to the discipline as well as within policy circles, it is somewhat surprising that there is not more critical discussion of measurement practices. But unlike what goes on in other sciences, economists are seemingly disdainful of the data and prefer to remain a step removed from the 'dirty', day-to-day work of compiling the numbers. This distancing has even been described as a favourable outcome (one which helps to ensure the objectivity of the data) since national accountants are thought to be largely unconnected to any particular theoretical agenda.

While the view that the numbers are objective facts may be held by most economists, historians of national accounts have tended to argue that the data are theory-laden. Thus, it has been the task of historians to describe how accounting changes are made within the context of a theoretical framework, usually under the assumption that changes reflect improvement relative to some meaningful theoretical criterion. In a sense, then, this chapter is about deciding which of these two interpretations of how empiricism gets done is correct: the naïve empiricist view which interprets the data as objective and theory-free, or the view which locates the data in a theoretical scheme; or whether possibly a third view is needed. The third view, which is advocated in this chapter, is that both of these interpretations are too simplistic. Theories and facts are codetermined within, and emerge from, a particular historical context. The specific focus of this chapter is how the government product came to appear in US national income accounts. My aim is to show that the methods of national income accounting are highly contingent. While the identity $Y = C + I + G + X - M$ is rarely viewed as controversial or problematic, the history of the accounts reveals that a number of other categorizations could easily have appeared in its place. In particular, the isolation of a separate government product was not always thought to be necessary. Moreover, the exact content of 'G' was long a source of disagreement. The structure of accounts is also suspect since it becomes clear, when examined historically, that the final form of the accounts constitutes an uneasy compromise between functional and institutional categories. The social constructivist account given here seeks to show that the accounting change was not merely a straightforward application of any single theoretical criterion. Instead, the evolution of the national accounting framework should be understood as a process of construction which reflects the historical context from which it emerged.

Estimates of national income by type of expenditure are often said to be products of the Keynesian revolution. While it is true that official national income measurement practices were standardized in the post World War I period, the tendency to assume that accounting changes were prompted by theoretical developments is a case that has not been made in a convincing fashion. Why the Keynesian version of events is so easily accepted is not solely a function of ignorance of the actual history, but more importantly an effect of the fact that historians of thought are comfortable with the view that their practices are theory-driven. Moreover, the alternative version of events which interprets the changes in accounting practices as contingent upon particular historical conditions is far 'messier' than the Keynesian story.

My thesis is that Keynesian theory had little impact on US national income accounting. Simply arguing from chronology, the development of expenditure estimates preceded the Keynesian revolution and so cannot have been inspired by it. The groundwork had been laid in the early 1930s by Kuznets (1937)[1] and Warburton (1934), both of whom provided early estimates of gross national product by type of expenditure, and also by Currie and Krost (1936) of the Federal Reserve who had sought to assign a number to the net contribution of government to the national income. Further, while estimators at the US Department of Commerce were specifically accused of injecting Keynes into the accounts, the treatment of the government sector put in place in 1947 (which has remained standard practice in the US since that date) was initiated by estimators in order to assess the impact of the tremendous increase in war expenditures on the economy. While World War II may have focused attention on the role and finance of government spending, theoretical debates from the pre-war period continued through 1947 and were never fully resolved. Both the inclusion of total government expenditures in the national income and the establishment of a separate category for the government spending in the final demand estimates suggest an increasing emphasis on the government's role in the economy. It may be no coincidence, moreover, that the government sector became more important when the accounting was taken over by government bureaucrats. Accordingly, while Keynesian theory has be invoked as providing a stable referent for national income measurement, this is merely as *ex post* attempt to impose rationality on a very disorderly hodgepodge. To argue that Keynesian theory explains the accounting decisions is to ignore the complexities of those decisions.

Keynesian Accountancy?

The idea that momentum for the elaboration of national income statistics was provided by the Keynesian research programme is derived from the fact that national income accounting did not take off until after World War I and that its systematization occurred in the post World War II era. Therefore the nature of the relation between the two 'revolutions' (Patinkin, 1976) of the inter-war period – the Keynesian revolution in economic theory and the revolution in national income measurement – is held to be one of unidirectional causation from Keynes to the accounts. Those who take this position suggest that the timing of the developments in macroeconomic theory and national income accounting is more than coincidental. More substantial arguments invoked to establish the link between Keynesian theory and the accounts presume either that Keynes was directly involved or that the practising statisticians were interested in providing the empirical counterpart to Keynes's theoretical framework.

With respect to Keynes's direct role in shaping the British official accounts, Keynes is credited with appending Meade and Stone's early national income estimates to a paper he was writing on the analysis of war finance which was to be circulated as a White Paper with the British National Budget of 1941. He was sufficiently interested in the statistics that he supported continuation of the estimations at an official level, even advising Meade and Stone in their early work on British national accounts (Kendrick, 1970, Patinkin, 1976). One of the leading historians of national accounting suggests that Keynes's 'distinctions among the major sectors in terms of their motivations and behaviour patterns suggested the development of interrelated sectoral accounts' (Kendrick, 1970, p. 305), and that interlocking GNP accounts were worked out in the early 1940s by Meade and Stone 'with encouragement and detailed advice from Keynes' (Kendrick, 1970, p. 308). Thus, Keynes is given credit for making Government 'just another sector' (Boss, 1990). Keynes, however, was more likely concerned with the magnitudes arrived at and less concerned with the actual details of the construction of accounts or definition of the totals, perhaps because he had little faith in such aggregate estimates and believed his own intuitive judgements to be more reliable (Patinkin, 1976, p. 1113). One must be careful about placing too much emphasis on Keynes's personal interest in national income statistics, moreover, since he was suspicious of Colin Clark's figures and failed to advocate official estimation at an earlier stage with the 1931 report of the Macmillan Committee (Patinkin, 1976).

It need not be shown, however, that Keynes had a hand in or even an interest in national accounting in order to sustain the argument that accounts were shaped by Keynesian theory. It can reasonably be assumed that the national accountants were familiar with the *General Theory* and the theoretical framework that Keynes set out there. Indeed the common view is less of an argument about Keynes himself and more of an assertion that the statisticians were interested in making their work consistent with the theory. Sam Rosen's (1963) statements to this effect are representative. He argues that 'real momentum in establishing official and regular national income and product accounts began in the forties, doubtlessly because of wartime exigencies but even more because the theoretical groundwork had been prepared by Keynes in his celebrated *General Theory of Employment, Interest and Money*' (Rosen, 1963, p. 215). Perlman credits Keynes with providing a 'well-knit theoretical system' for national accounting that imposed order on an 'endless literature of historical generalizations' (Perlman, 1987, p. 140).

In the United States, Milton Gilbert is usually identified as the individual responsible for making the accounts Keynesian (Carson, 1971, p. 186; Perlman, 1987). Among those at the Department of Commerce in the 1940s, Gilbert, especially, is said to have been intent on developing a new blueprint that 'not only reflected the omnipresent specter of American defense preparations but also the Keynesian macro theoretical system, with its emphasis on postwar full-employment, compensatory government investment, and a federal program of income distribution' (Perlman, 1987, pp. 144–5).

The tendency to associate Keynesian theory with the national income accounts thus stems from the fact that the fundamental identity of national income accounting, $Y = C + I + G + X - M$, is attributed to Keynes. However, if one wants to assert that the accounts are Keynesian, the *General Theory* is not the place to turn for justification. The argument runs into trouble almost immediately, for when Keynes does provide a national income identity (in Chapter 6 of the *General Theory*) the one he produces is $Y = C + I$. There were no special categories to distinguish purchases by foreigners or by governments. Government consumption was included in C and government investment included in I. Thus, to the extent that the omnipresent identity is linked to Keynes, the proponents of this position would need to show that Keynes revised his beliefs concerning the types of expenditures which generate the national income. Since the presentation of existing expenditure estimates in both the US (Warburton, 1934) and the UK (Clark, 1932) took the form $Y = C + I$, the more compelling question is whether Keynes simply found it convenient to borrow a definition of national income from standard accounting practice, hence giving us an example of the opposite chain of causation from that which is usually said to characterize the theory – practice relation.

To justify establishing a category for government spending as an income-generating expenditure, it could be argued that the consumption and saving behaviour of government is quite different from the consumption of individuals and investment decisions of private enterprises and that spending ought to be divided according to different types of transactors (Tew, 1953). It is not clear that Keynes believed that the motivations and behaviour patterns of government were sufficiently different from private sector decisions to warrant a separate government sector. Keynes was concerned about types of expenditures; for his purposes consumption versus investment was a relevant distinction, a public/private dichotomy apparently was not, at least not until he considered policy issues in *How to Pay for the War.*

With regard to the latter, the breakdowns of national output that Keynes gives in his 1940 *How to Pay for the War* could provide the foundation for the claim that Keynes put *G* into the GNP since there he distinguishes a category for government expenditures. However, it seems as if Keynes could have gone either way since in the course of a short appendix on national income, he first isolates government expenditure as a component of national income, and subsequently absorbs *G* back into the measure of consumption (see Table 12.1).

Table 12.1   Keynes's Definition of National Output

p. 79 Keynes defines National Output as:

£ million

3,710	current value of private consumption excluding indirect taxation but including the cost of making good current depreciation
290	current cost of net new investment in buildings, plant, transport and stock, i.e., current capital outlay in excess of what is required to make good current capital depreciation
850	current cost of Government operations excluding 'transfer' payments to pensioners, holders of national debt, etc., expenditure out of which is already included in previous items
4,850	

p. 81 Keynes defines National Output as:

£ million

4,140	Private and Government consumption apart from making good wastage and depreciation
420	Making good wastage and depreciation
290	New investment
4,850	

Source: Keynes (1940) *How to Pay for the War*, Appendix I: The National Income

The distinction between the treatment of national income in the *General Theory* and the practical application of *How to Pay for the War* does not get made, however. This may be attributable to a reluctance on the part of historians to acknowledge any obvious decoupling of practical application from theory. Still, it is the common view that Keynes was responsible for putting *G* into the GNP. This belief must result from a lack of familiarity with the *General Theory*, the acceptance of some 'bastardized' version of the Keynesian model, or perhaps an assertion that Keynes's analysis on page 79 of *How to Pay for the War* provides the best indication as to how he would have structured national accounts.

The government controversy
To understand how *G* got into the GNP, we have to explain how what once was a functional division between *C* and *I* came to be transformed into an institutional categorization summarizing the working of the economy in terms of its constituent parts ($Y = C + I + G + X - M$). It did not simply become apparent to national income accountants that the economy should be viewed in terms of four distinct consuming sectors: Households, Business, Government and the Rest of the World. These institutional categories did not appear until quite late – the early 1940s in the US official estimates. One of the few who even makes mention of the change in accounting practice is Mark Perlman who writes that:

> 'By the mid and late 1930s the federal government's role in the economy had expanded and whether the Kuznets 1933 perception could have been implemented is now a moot question. In practice, the government's various roles in the economy were *sui generis*, and all its economic activities were segregated for accounting purposes.' (Perlman, 1987, pp. 144–5)

Paul Samuelson has argued that World War II was responsible for increasing government expenditures to such a degree that the 'peculiar Kuznets definition ... had become quite untenable, since at the wartime peak as much as a quarter of all GNP would have been excluded if one had stubbornly adhered to the definition' (Samuelson, 1975, p. 44).

Government bureaucrats may have been more interested in establishing a distinct measure of government product than was either Keynes or Kuznets. When Keynes and Kuznets did put *G* in separately, each was doing so in the context of using the national income statistics to understand the economic repercussions of World War II. As a consequence of the stabilization of measurement practices, the debates about how to measure the national income have long been forgotten. That is, once *G* gets put in as a separate number in the GNP the issue of whether it really belongs disappears. The question of why a government product is included in the national income, though, is one that does not permit an obviously correct answer. This is made apparent by the variety of treatments of the government product that have been suggested and implemented by practitioners of economic accounting at various points in the history of national income measurement. However, it is rare that someone suggests that the current treatment of the government product in national income is flawed[2] and it is nearly inconceivable that it would be suggested that a government product doesn't belong at all.

The fact that national income controversies have been forgotten is due in part to the nature of the debates. Even when practicing national accountants addressed contentious issues such as how to account for the government product, the debate was not outwardly about whether or not to include a government product in the national income. The issue of whether a government product even belonged in the national income was overshadowed by debates about how to value *G*. The appearance of agreement concerning the more fundamental issue was being negotiated through more technical debates over valuation, with the government's contribution to final product being considered in terms of the treatment of specific items: transfers, taxes, subsidies, government pensions, and interest on the government debt.

The government controversy initially manifested itself as a debate about whether the government should be considered a productive industry along side agriculture, manufacturing and mining and other productive pursuits. In the early estimates for the United States, there was no consistency of treatment of the government in the national income. In Charles B. Spahr's (1896) estimate of national income by industry, the government does not appear as a productive industry. In 1915, however, Willford King's first estimate does include government as productive industry. The contribution of the government to the national income is measured in terms of payments to employees. The National Bureau of Economic Research, having made the estimation of national income its first project in 1920, carried through King's practice of including a government product. Two 'independent' estimates were produced: an estimate by 'income received' and an estimate by 'source of production'. The government product in the former was determined by adding wages, salaries, interest, rent and pensions paid by government since it was 'clear that incomes paid to individuals by governments should count on the same basis as other incomes'. It was assumed that those who received incomes from government were contributing direct services of corresponding value which ought to be included in National Income. A few detractors argued that it was not appropriate to have a government product at all since government activity was primarily redistributive (Paton, 1922, p. 806). And, in 1923, the early study of national income and wealth carried out by the Federal Trade Commission also excluded government as a productive industry, though no theoretical discussion was provided since '(s)uch discussions would tend to show ... how difficult it is to draw the line between what is income and what is not income on the basis of any general principle.' (quoted in Carson, 1971, pp. 57–8) In reviewing the FTC study, Z. Clark Dickinson (1928) took issue with the exclusion of government services and advocated the practice adopted by the National Bureau, of deducting taxes which are added to selling prices and including those which are not added to selling prices, in calculating the value product of a taxed industry.

Measuring the final product in terms of tax payments was short-lived however. The standard procedure was instead to measure the net volume of services rendered in terms of the actual payments of government to the labour and capital employed by it. Income originating in government activity was thus equal to payments to employees plus interest on the government debt. In choosing this method the Department of Commerce (and Kuznets, who directed the first Commerce national income study) noted that there might be 'some doubt as to the propriety of classifying government ... as a branch of the country's economic system'. The following problems were noted: government activity is not characterized by a profit motive, there are no price payments for the services produced; government taxes based upon the ability to pay, not in terms of the value of services rendered to the taxpayer; and finally, the employment of capital and labour is not the same as in private industry (Department of Commerce, 1934, p. 125). Modern practice has substantially deviated from this early method; for example, interest on government debt is now excluded from the measure of gross national product.

The question of whether tax payments of business reflected the value of the intermediate product of government led to a debate concerning whether a direct method of estimating such an intermediate product could be developed. The issue of whether G should be in or out was left behind, and the debate solely concerned issues of valuation. According to the traditional definition of the national income, only final goods and services which satisfy the demands of final demands ought to be included. Consequently, in order to answer the question should government spending be included in the national income we have to ask: does government expenditure on goods and services constitute a final use? If the answer to the question is 'yes', then all government spending should be included in national income. If the answer is 'no', then again there is no valuation problem since all government spending would be excluded. However, the common view was that a part of government product was final and a portion was intermediate, so valuing the final product became a source of controversy. Differing views on the statistical feasibility of measuring the net product of government are generally claimed to be the source of the controversy. However, a more compelling explanation is that differing views on the role of government in the economy actually explain the divergence of opinions on how to value government final product.

In his major work on national income measurement, *National Income and Its Composition*, Kuznets was concerned with the proper valuation of government services and acknowledged substantial difficulties of statistical estimation. Yet he was not willing to treat the government as unproductive. He ruled out this option, noting that: 'governmental activities contribute too much to the satisfaction of need and are too closely interwoven with the entire network of market relations for their role as economic and productive pursuits to be ignored' (Kuznets, 1941, p. 31). When it came to determining which part of governmental services could properly be treated as final products, Kuznets claimed that differentiating final from intermediate services of government was so difficult that any division would necessarily have to be arbitrary. He acknowledged the problem with his own method that tax payments need not reflect benefits received, but nevertheless opted for adopting 'the most easily obtainable division' and made intermediate consumption of government services equal to the value of taxes and other payments of business enterprises to government.

The difficulties of drawing a line between the final and intermediate product of government noted by Kuznets had been recognized even earlier by the National Bureau investigators in the 1921 volume on national income. There is was noted that, in valuing the government product, the issues were even less clear when the estimators considered government expenditures item by item, asking whether each expenditure really represented services of corresponding value contributed in that year to National Income. This did not deter Gerhard Colm (1937) from making a division of government expenditures into cost services, political services, and consumption services of government. Kuznets took issue with Colm's proposed accounting (Which had the effect of raising Colm's ($44,592,000,000) estimate above Kuznets's ($39,365,000,000). Objecting to what he perceived as an arbitrary apportionment between services to individuals and services to enterprises, Kuznets argued that the nature of government's role was such that no classification of government activities and expenditures was proper (Kuznets, 1937, p. 235).

R.W. Nelson and Donald Jackson (1938) also objected to what they found to be an extreme position taken by Kuznets. For their purposes, (preparing an estimate of income in the form of final utilities received by farm residents from all government units and corresponding aids to productive activities of farmers) it was necessary to make the kind of distinction Kuznets was ruling out. They found it impossible, however, to make an integrated analysis of farm benefits and farm taxes and consequently proposed various allocations of expenditures to 'final use' or 'aid to production'. In some cases the apportionments were arbitrary (a 50–50 split was assumed), while in others there was an attempt to base the allocation on estimates of use by either consumers or business – use of highways based on gasoline consumption, for example. Nelson and Jackson (1938, p. 327) took the opportunity to bemoan the condition of the data as well as the 'subjective barriers' interfering with their ability to make imaginative estimates; namely, 'divergences of opinion concerning theories of the relationship between the government and the governed'.

It is clear from these few examples that one's opinion with regard to measurability of particular concepts depends upon the investigator's objectives as well as implicit theoretical assumptions. Measurability is not an objective standard but one which depends upon the subjective interpretation of the estimator. However, measurability issues cannot explain the decision to segregate government expenditures in type of product estimates.

On sectors and the spectre of war

It cannot be said that the government controversy was resolved, but a standardization of practice occurred nonetheless. This standardization cannot be attributed to a resolution of conceptual and statistical difficulties of distinguishing the intermediate from the final product of government on the basis of Keynesian theory or any other theory for that matter. The debate was effectively put to rest in 1947 when a major conceptual revision of the accounts was completed and the current practice of including total government expenditure in the national income was instituted. At that time Simon Kuznets was opposed to the change and made his opposition known in a lengthy review article in the *Review of Economics and Statistics* (1947). Members of the National Income Division of the Department of Commerce banded together to defend their practices (Gilbert, Jaszi, et al., 1947) and Kuznets' complaints held little sway. One even has to wonder whether Kuznets's decision to leave the field was prompted by dissatisfaction at his inability to dictate the course of national income accounting.

Kuznets did not like the accounting approach, which he felt could not help resolve important conceptual problems. Nor did he approve of the treatment of the government product. The 1947 exchange between Kuznets and the staff of the National Income Unit of the Commerce Department is an example of Kuznets's battle to limit the share of government spending in the accounts. With respect to valuing the government product, Kuznets was pushed into a defensive position, forced to backpedal (changing his views as to what constituted proper methods of accounting) in an attempt to influence the accounting to the extent possible while the Commerce Department estimators forged ahead, making the government contribution to national product even larger. In his 1941 conceptual discussion, Kuznets had argued that any division between the final and intermediate product of government would be arbitrary; in 1945 he retreated somewhat and argued that war expenditures could be treated as final product, but rejected the Commerce approach of making *all* expenditures of government final. His 'last ditch' effort came in 1951 when he proposed that national income estimators should, in fact, attempt an item by item breakdown of government expenditures into final and intermediate categories. Here, an accounting practice which he had rejected earlier on the grounds that it was not feasible was suddenly advocated as the most rational course of action.

Not only did Kuznets favour eliminating a large fraction of government spending from national income, but in his early work on commodity flows, Kuznets (1937) did not see fit to distinguish a separate category of government purchases. He argued that the volume of goods produced should be considered as being available for immediate consumption or for addition to the stock of capital ($Y = C + I$). Three types of products were said to constitute the final product:

(*a*) the value of finished products reaching their final destination;
(*b*) changes in stocks of all finished commodities not at their destination (in circulation) and of all other commodities;
(*c*) net change in claims against foreign countries, or net product flowing out of country's boundaries.

Had he carried this through, our textbooks might now carry the identity, $Y = C + I + (X - M)$, but Kuznets combined (*b*) and (*c*) and called this total net capital formation. Net national product or national income was thus separated into two categories: consumer's outlay (*a*) and net capital formation (*b*) + (*c*). While Kuznets acknowledged that public agencies contributed to gross capital formation – public highway construction, for example, was considered part of capital formation (Kuznets, 1937, Table 10, p. 40) – there was no rationale for considering government expenditures as a separate category, though Kuznets did provide a breakdown of the figures on gross domestic capital formation by type of user: business, consumers, and public agencies. When the Commerce Department began work on official estimates by type of product they were building on this early work by Kuznets. When Commerce took over the estimation, though, *G* now appeared as a separate category. In response to the Commerce Department's practice of equating the government product with total expenditures (a practice which coincided with the segregation of these expenditures in the accounts), Kuznets argued that the war had magnified the conceptual difficulties of estimating the national income and in particular the distinction between intermediate and final product: 'It shifts markedly the boundaries of free market institutions, of government controlled activities, of the family and of other institutions. And it accentuates the degree to which national interest is permitted to determine the scope of national product' (Kuznets, 1945, p. viii).

Kuznets consequently considered whether war production ought to be considered a final consumption good or a capital good. He hesitated to call defence expenditures consumption but admitted that winning a war was a valid social objective, so advocated incorporating defence expenditures – purchases of goods and services for defence purposes as well as war capital formation – into the measure of national product. Including the gross value of war output in the measure of final product had the effect of raising the measure of national product. Kuznets (1945, p. 19) argued that this was appropriate during wartime and contended that if a certain use for economic goods is accepted as a goal we must include their full value in national product; consequently, the more goals the more product categories included at their gross value, and the larger the resulting total. Kuznets's wartime concept of the national product thus included the flow of goods to consumers, nonwar capital formation (both private and public), and goods purchased by government for war purposes. ($Y = C + I +$ war expenditures)

While Kuznets restricted his measure to war expenditures, the Commerce Department estimate of 'gross national product at market prices' included **all** government purchases of goods and services as final consumption. Kuznets objected that the Commerce justification for their practice did not uniquely pertain to their measure of GNP at market prices but, he said, would be equally applicable to his wartime GNP. Thus, while Commerce maintained that achieving an accurate measure of civilian consumption as a residual after subtracting defence expenditures and other non-consumption expenditures required the inclusion of total government expenditures, Kuznets (1945, p. 29) argued that all government outlays would have to be included only on the implicit assumption that all are for final products or because government expenditure is thought to be an important independent variable determining the level of national product. It is this latter point which is most relevant. It seems as if the government bureaucrats were determined to emphasize the importance of government's role in the economy by enlarging the share of government expenditure in the national income. While this official change was motivated by the great increase in government expenditures caused by the war, the underlying explanation must relate to the Commerce estimators' philosophy of the proper role of government in the economy.

In the search for sources of the modern treatment of the government sector, Lauchlin Currie should also get credit for being among the first to assign a number to the government contribution to national income. While Assistant Director of Research and Statistics at the Federal Reserve in 1936, Currie was responsible for designing a series to measure the net contribution of the federal government to national buying power. While the series bears little resemblance to the modern government product component of the gross national product, Currie was ahead of the national income estimators in perceiving the need for a separate number for government. Once again, policy analysis, and not pure theory, set the context for the construction of a particular measure. The public debates of the New Deal era concerning the proper role of government in the economy could only be addressed if a separate number was assigned to government. A separate number could be pointed to and analysed as to whether it was too big or too small. Yet, to say that there ought to be an analysis of the 'net income increasing expenditures' of government is not sufficient to determine how the government contribution should be measured. The conclusion that should be drawn is that it is difficult to isolate a specific point at which the resolution of theoretical questions produced the correct solution to the problem of how to measure G.

Why does it matter how G got into the GNP?

In emphasizing the number of different treatments of the government sector and the fluidity of the definitions given the purpose at hand, I have sought to show how arbitrary the current designation of the components of GNP is. If Kuznets had had his way, there would be no separate government product in the expenditure totals and the textbook Keynesian model would look far different. Moreover, it cannot be claimed that the estimators simply experimented for a time before settling upon the correct accounting structure, nor can it be said that the stabilized version is best suited to the widest variety of uses. Instead, it is very particular construction which is an artifact of specific concerns.

The development of national accounts in the US was largely independent of Keynesian theory. The treatment of the government sector had a long history prior to the Keynesian Revolution and the resolution of the debate was not provided by Keynes. The fact that changing interests and objectives have affected the mode of accounting, moreover, is apparent in the confusion over whether the national accounting identity, $Y = C + I + G + X - M$, is meant to be a functional or institutional categorization. In their initial form, the estimates by type of expenditure were to reflect functional divisions. The estimators were concerned with types, and not sources, of spending. Kuznets for example, eventually, allowed for a separate category of war expenditures – *not* total government expenditures. Similarly, Richard Stone's treatment of sectoral accounts betrays an attempt to split the difference. He suggests that six accounts are necessary: consumption, investment, government, labour, and lending accounts. This is a very different accounting structure from what we are used to, though we might be more familiar with it had Stone (1951b, p. 12) not argued that the latter two accounts 'have very little independent existence and are always thought of as consolidated elsewhere'. If Irving Fisher had sole control of national income accounts, we might only have $Y = C$. If Warburton's method had won out, Y would equal $C + I$. The point is that there is no single correct accounting structure and understanding how we got from $Y = C + I$ to $Y = C + I + G + X - M$ must be understood as a social or historical process rather than as a neat relationship between theory and measurement.

Notes

1. The estimates in *National Income and Commodity Formation* (1937) were based on estimates Kuznets had published for the National Bureau in 1933.
2. For exceptions see Nordhaus and Tobin, (1972) and Higgs, (1992).

References

Boss, Helen (1990), *Theories of Surplus and Transfer; Parasites and Producers in Economic Thought*, Boston: Unwin Hyman.

Carson, Carol Stine (1971), *A History of the United States Income and Product Accounts: The Development of an Analytical Tool*, Ph.D. Dissertation, The George Washington University.

Clark, Colin (1932), *National Income, 1924–1932*, London: Macmillan.

Currie, Lauchlin and Krost, Martin (circa 1935), 'Federal Income-Increasing Expenditures, 1932–1935', reprinted in *History of Political Economy*, **10** (4), pp. 534–40.

Colm, Gerhard (1937), 'Public Revenue and Public Expenditure in National Income' Conference on Research in Income and Wealth, *Studies in Income and Wealth*, Vol. I. New York: National Bureau of Economic Research.

Department of Commerce (1934), *National Income 1929–32*, Senate Document 124, Washington D.C.: Government Printing Office.

Dickinson, Z. Clark (1928), 'The Federal Trade Commission's Report on the National Wealth and Income', *Quarterly Journal of Economics*, (42), pp. 117–30.

Gilbert, Milton, George Jaszi, Edward F. Denison, and Charles F. Schwartz (1948), 'Objective of National Income Measurement: A Reply to Professor Kuznets', *Review of Economics and Statistics*, (30), pp. 179–95.

Higgs, Robert (1992), 'Wartime Prosperity? A Reassessment of the U.S. Economy in the 1940s', *Journal of Economic History*, **52** (1), pp. 41–60.

Jones, Byrd L. (1978), 'Lauchlin Currie, pump priming and New Deal Fiscal Policy, 1934–1936', *History of Political Economy*, **10** (4), pp. 509–24.

Kendrick, John (1970), 'The Historical Development of National Income Accounts', *History of Political Economy*, **2** (1), pp. 284–315.

Keynes, John Maynard (1936), *The General Theory of Employment, Interest and Money*, New York: Harcourt, Brace & Company.

Keynes, John Maynard (1940), *How to Pay for the War*, New York: Harcourt, Brace & Company.

Kuznets, Simon (1937), *National Income and Capital Formation 1919–1935*, New York: National Bureau of Economic Research.

Kuznets, Simon (1941), *National Income and Its Composition*, New York: National Bureau of Economic Research.

Kuznets, Simon (1945), *National Product in Wartime*, New York: National Bureau of Economic Research.

Kuznets, Simon (1948), 'National Income: A New Version', *Review of Economics and Statistics*, (30), pp. 151–79.

Kuznets, Simon (1951), 'Government Product and National Income', *Income and Wealth*, Series I. International Association for Research in Income and Wealth, Cambridge: Bowes & Bowes.

National Bureau of Economic Research (1921), in Wesley C. Mitchell, Willford I. King, Frederick R. Macaulay, and Oswald W. Knauth, *Income in the United States: Its Amount and Distribution 1909–1919*, I and II, New York: Harcourt, Brace & Company.

Nordhaus, William and Tobin, James (1972), 'Is Growth Obsolete?' in *Economic Growth*, Fiftieth Anniversary Colloquium V, New York: National Bureau of Economic Research.

Nelson, R.W. and Donald Jackson (1938), 'Allocation of Benefits from Government Expenditures', *Studies in Income and Wealth*, Vol. 2, Conference of Research in Income and Wealth, New York: National Bureau of Economic Research.

Patinkin, Don (1976), 'Keynes and Econometrics: On the Interaction Between the Macroeconomic Revolutions of the Interwar Period', *Econometrica*, (44), pp. 1091–123.

Paton, W.A. (1922), 'Review of Income in the United States: Its Amount and Distribution, 1909-1919' Vol. II, *Journal of the American Statistical Association*, (18), pp. 804–9.

Perlman, Mark (1987), 'Political Purpose and the National Accounts', in Alonso, William and Paul Starr, (eds), *The Politics of Numbers*, New York City: Russell Sage Foundation for the National Committee for Research on the 1980 Census.

Porter, Theodore M. (1991), 'Interpreting the Triumph of Quantification in Economics: Metaphysical Hubris or Cultural Adaptation', mimeo.

Rosen, Sam (1963), *National Income: Its Measurement, Determination and Relation to Public Policy*, New York: Holt, Rinehart & Winston, Inc.

Samuelson, Paul A. (1975), 'The Balanced-Budget Multiplier: A Case Study in the Sociology and Psychology of a Scientific Discovery', *History of Political Economy*, 7 (1), pp. 43–55.

Spahr, Charles B. (1896), *An Essay on the Present Distribution of Wealth in the United States*, New York: Boston, T.Y. Crowell & Company.

Stone, Richard (1951a), 'The Use and Development of National Income and expenditure Estimates', in D.N. Chester (ed.), *Lessons of the British War Economy*, Cambridge: Cambridge University Press.

Stone, Richard (1951b), 'Functions and Criteria of a System of Social Accounting', *Income and Wealth*, Series 1, Cambridge: Bowes & Bowes.

Tew, Brian (1953), 'Keynesian Accountancy', *Yorkshire Bulletin of Economic and Social Research*, (August), pp. 147–53.

Tomlinson, Jim (1981), *Problems of British Economic Policy 1870–1945*, New York: Methuen.

Warburton, Clark (1934), 'How the National Income was Spent', *Journal of the American Statistical Association*, (30), pp. 175–82.

13 Farrell, data envelopment analysis and Leibenstein on efficiency measurement

Henry T. Burley[1]

Introduction

Farrell (1957, p. 232) grasped the essentials of the multi-factor production productivity problem at the empirical level and provided an elegant and fundamentally simple solution. His innovative technique not only specifically allowed for the realities of multiple factors of production and variable returns to scale, but also provided interpretive meaning to the deviations from his production frontier: perceiving them as technical efficiency evaluators rather than the hitherto unwanted and nebulous errors of least squares fit.

Clark (1957, p. 283), in the discussion on Farrell's paper, wrote 'I think we will agree, having heard this paper, that Mr Farrell has already reached some interesting and successful results and has come nearer than any previous investigator to a true measure of agricultural efficiency, which figures in their turn will send economists further down the road hunting for the social and other factors which lie behind them'. Farrell pioneered a systematic approach to measure productive efficiency in an environment of multiple inputs producing measured output. His efficiency method identified both productive, or technical, efficiency and price efficiency. The latter, which measures a firm's success in choosing the minimum cost set of inputs *on the production function*, is also known as allocative efficiency and, until then, had been of principal concern to economists.

Subsequent empirical studies such as Anndalingham and Kulatilaha (1987, p. 143) and many others, based on both time series and cross section data, have shown variations in productive efficiency to be far more predominant than variations in allocative efficiency. This result, indicating the relative unimportance of allocative efficiency, holds even when using or misusing the term in its widest sense to include as an apparent allocative inefficiency the short run non-adjustment to current prices for longer term goals. (See Forsund, Lovell and Schmidt, 1980, p. 5).

At the psychological and sociological interpretive level, Leibenstein (1966, p. 392) called attention to a source of economic inefficiency which he termed X-[in]efficiency, explaining output losses due to motivational deficiencies in the human actors in the production scene. This paper briefly explains first the

Farrell method, then Leibenstein's argument and goes on to show a possible interface between the two as a likely area for further inquiry. The research is in a world of both mathematical and institutional economics, which the author does not see as being in conflict with each other.

Farrell saw productive efficiency as a measure of a firm's success in producing as large an output as possible from a given set of inputs. Economists have traditionally emphasized capital and labour as inputs. Clearly there are other measurable and tangible inputs: such as energy, raw materials and other intermediate and primary inputs as considered in the input–output analysis. There are also the non-tangible factors, emphasized by Leibenstein, such as motivation.

Fundamentally the Farrell method evaluates a firm as 100 per cent efficient if it is on the frontier production function, the frontier being identified as that piece-wise linear surface convex to, and closest to, the origin in N dimensional (one for each production factor) space. Firms or processes not on the frontier are of less than 100 per cent efficiency in so far as they use more resources to produce unit output. Finally, as one who had the privilege of working with Farrell at Cambridge (England), I attempt to recall, as I see it, some of the motivational and historical background to his contribution.

The calculation of an optimum convex surface
Slater (1972 p. 14) supplies an algorithm and computer program to form a piece-wise linear surface convex to the origin which is the envelope of M points in N dimensional space. More recently, in the last decade, the integration of statistical and programming approaches has enabled economists to see the estimation of the production frontier for what it is – a convex data envelopment problem. Lovell and Schmidt (1988, p. 3) detail four approaches: (1) pure programming methods like the Farrell optimum surface, (2) a modified or parametric programming approach using programming approaches to curve fitting rather than statistical least squares, (3) a statistical frontier approach and (4) a stochastic frontier approach. There have been some landmarks in later developments in the estimation of the Farrell efficiency system which make significant and worthwhile methodological and algorithmic improvements. Early developments include the Slater (1972, p. 14) program for the calculation of an optimum convex surface and the linear programming formulations of Aigner and Chu (1968, p. 826). Then there is the Australian application by Burley (1980, p. 619) to economy-wide manufacturing efficiency changes and time.

If we do not allow for economies of scale then the Farrell method for two input factors can be seen in Figure 13.1. The input factors are x_1 and x_2, the dots represent the volume of the factors or inputs of the different firms to produce one unit of output. The efficient production frontier is the envelope

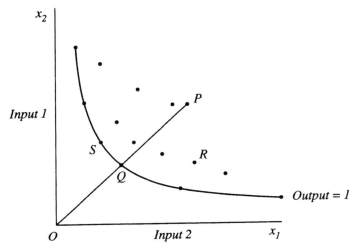

Figure 13.1   The Farrell method by pure linear programs

of the dots closest to 0. Firms using more x_1 and x_2 are clearly less efficient. Note no assumption is made about the shape of the production function. The envelope enforces convexity to the origin and negative slope e.g. positive factor substitution. Firm Q is efficient while P is not.

Now OQ/OP is defined as the technical efficiency of firm P, since it is producing unit output using fraction OP/OQ as much of the inputs as firm Q. In Figure 13.1 OP/OQ is exactly 2 so we conclude process P is half as efficient as Q, or that P requires exactly twice the inputs as Q. If x_1 and x_2 are the only factor inputs this analysis appears quite valid as OQP are on a straight line from the origin. In the case of a process R where there is no other observed process on the line OR we assume the envelope of adjacent efficient firms forms the efficient isoquant on the assumption that a linear combination of neighbouring efficient firms also represents an efficient firm, provided all weights are non-negative.

Generalization by linear programming in k constraints
Generalizing to k factors: the computation of the Farrell efficiency system where there are $k \geq 2$ factor inputs can be handled in an activity analysis approach. For n firms n linear programming problems, of k constraints each, need be solved. Consider n firms in an industry producing a homogeneous output. The output for each firm is q_j and the set of all outputs is represented by the vector q. Inputs of the k factors by the n firms are represented by matrix F of k rows and n columns. That is, the tth column of matrix F is a

Leontief production function of firm t. This vector, denoted $F_{,t}$ consists of k elements, one for each input factor.

The condition for a firm t to be technically efficient is that no linear combination of firms (with non-negative weighting) using in total less than the inputs of firm t, can produce greater output than firm t. In game theory language this condition implies that for an efficient firm no pure or mixed strategy of other firms could dominate the firm t strategy. If such a linear (non-negative) weighted sum of firms, using up to inputs $F_{,t}$, can produce greater output than firm t, say proportion z greater than firm t, then firm t has an efficiency of $1/(1 + z)$: since its inputs should theoretically be able to produce $1 + z$ times its output. So to compute the measure of productive efficiency of firm t one needs to solve a linear programming problem formulated thus:

$$
\begin{array}{ll}
\textit{Primal} & \textit{Dual} \\
\max q'x = Z_t^* & \min F'_{,t}y = Z_t^* \\
\text{s.t.} \quad Fx \le F_{,t} & \text{s.t.} \quad F'y \ge q \\
x \ge 0. & y \ge 0.
\end{array}
$$

x is the vector of weights of firms 1 up to n theoretically competing with firm t. The solution vector x is the optimum basis of the above linear programming problem and the value of the program Z_t is the output of the theoretically efficient firm using the same inputs as firm t. The functional Z_t^* is clearly a maximum amount of output with the known technologies that can be produced from inputs $F_{,t}$, as detailed in the constraints on factor use. The dual solution y, being the shadow prices of the primal, yields the minimum valuation of resources to produce output of at least q. The valuation of vector y is in terms of output as numeraire.

Here we have more explicitly the Primal Estimation Technique.

$$\max Z_t = q'x$$

subject to constraints:

$$
\overset{\textit{Firms}}{
\begin{bmatrix}
F_{11} & F_{12} & F_{13} & \cdots & F_{1n} \\
\vdots & & & & \vdots \\
F_{k1} & F_{k2} & F_{k3} & \cdots & F_{kn}
\end{bmatrix}}
\overset{\textit{Weights}}{
\begin{bmatrix}
x_1 \\
x_2 \\
x_3 \\
\vdots \\
x_n
\end{bmatrix}}
\le
\begin{bmatrix}
F_{1t} \\
\vdots \\
F_{kt}
\end{bmatrix}
\quad \text{Factor use by Firm } t
$$

$$x \ge 0$$

There are k constraint equations in the primal, one for each input factor, so the optimum basis may contain up to k firms, though it could contain only 1 (itself) if firm t was of 100 per cent efficiency.

Thus $Z_t^* = $ max $q'x$ which is $\geq q_t$ and E_t the efficiency of the firm t is q_t/Z_t allowing for the k factors and the set of n firms. A similar Z_t and E_t may be computed for each firm t by means of this procedure.

This input based efficiency measure based on production technology is generalized in the multiple output case of Lovell and Schmidt (1988, p. 3) to describe the production frontier as the maximum amount of output that can be produced, for given levels of production of the remaining outputs and given levels of input usage. The other outputs can be considered as the joint conventional products of the producer; or as indicators of the lack of 'constraint concern' introduced by Leibenstein and explained in the next section.

X-efficiency

The tenor of Leibenstein's argument is that allocative efficiency is trivial in practice and it is X-efficiency, which governs direct effort, that is important. This involves: (1) inter-plant motivational efficiency, (2) external motivational efficiency and (3) non-market input efficiency. He observes that neither individuals nor firms work as hard, nor do they seek for information as effectively as they could. The X-factor could loosely be described as 'spirit'. If an individual is the basic decision-making unit, then he or she will aim at striking a compromise between (a) what he or she likes to do, i.e. without constraints, and (b) what he or she must do, i.e. subject to constraints.

'Constraint concern' is a concept used by Leibenstein (1976, p. 77) to express the degree of compromise with constraints which is a characteristic of an individual's behaviour under constraining influences. He assumes that there is a vector of characteristics which is used by an individual to cope with his or her environment. 'Constraint concern' is one of the components of the vector; the other components are personality characteristics which determine the degree of engagement of capacities required to cope with the environment, the sense of obligation to commitments, the degree of satisfaction with established routines of performance, independence of judgement, etc. Each component of the vector takes on an 'intensity value' say from 0 to 1. Maximizing behaviour is obtained if the intensity value of every component equals unity. But most, if not all, of the values are likely to be less than 1. Each intensity value has a utility rating, the sum of which over all components renders a utility value for a given degree of 'constraint concern'. In Leibenstein's model 'pressure' is disutility that could be imposed by the outside world for disregarding constraints. Individuals can then be seen as trading off constraint concern against pressure. Other things being equal, people, as free agents, would prefer less pressure and less constraint.

There is a tangency solution between desires and standards which depicts the choice by an individual between pressure and constraint concern in a given environment, unless he or she is prevented from so choosing. Leibenstein's 'model of man' (1976, p. 77) shows a 'selectively rational' individual whose interests and those of the firm do not necessarily coincide. This is in direct contradiction with the traditional approach according to which there is a sharp division between (1) ends, (2) alternatives and (3) decision techniques and procedures in choosing among alternatives in the pursuit of ends. Elements (1) and (3) involve no choice whatsoever, that is, the traditional approach eliminates the person as an *interpretive* being.

By contrast to this, in Leibenstein's model a person participating in economic activities gives his or her own interpretation concerning membership in the firm and his or her job, and relationship with the groups within the firm and outside of it. It is this model of a person that produces the effort which forms the basis of X-efficiency, by balancing ones own desires against the interests of the enterprise and other collectives with which ones is involved. This immediately poses the question of how the effort itself is allocated.

According to Leibenstein, effort directed to maximization of utility or firm's output should not be seen as the only effort position. Another effort position is a choice of activity–pace–quality–time bundles, all of which are, in the last analysis, the result of job interpretation by the worker. One should note that each effort level is associated with a productivity value which need not necessarily be measurable, and with a utility value for effort which includes such things as the utility of income from the firm. The amount of effort therefore could be associated with the level of constraint concern that is consistent with the individual's psychological state. Leibenstein (1978, p. 33) speaks of 'inert areas' and 'frictional' costs as reasons for not moving to the production frontier from a position of X-[in]efficiency.

In Leinbestein's model 1 an individual is depicted as balancing his own desires against the interests of the firm and other collective interests. Given 'constraint concern' (which plays a central role in the way a person interprets a job) and 'inert area' (which indicates the bounds within which the cost of change of effort is greater than the utility gain) X-efficiency can only be improved when the job interpretation of an individual is enhanced. It is therefore largely an X factor deriving from the interpretations of individuals. Also a certain amount of X-efficiency will always be present because of the 'inert areas' in effort-utility relations which is equally applicable to workers and managers.

Relation of X-efficiency to productive efficiency measurement
Leibenstein's contributions suggests why there is a great deal of possible variation in output for similar amounts of production factors employed in

similar techniques. Stigler (1976, p. 213), commenting on the [e]xistence of X-efficiency, poses the question 'What is output?' and points out that in this case, and in every motivational case, no person ever seeks to maximize the output of any one thing. Strictly speaking Leibenstein focused on why the efficiency of a whole industry or economy is less than some absolute value by referring to external pressures and conventions beyond narrowly defined economic maximization acting alone. By contrast the Farrell method is a relative measure, as it references from the best observed firms or processes in the industry. In microeconomic terms Leibenstein thus sets us thinking about what are the dimensions of success of a firm.

To the owners of the firm the dimensions of success might be profits, share of the market and use of factors supplied by an associated firm. To the management it might be survival, growth, maximization of sales, retention of skilled employment, quality of product, expansion of enterprise, congeniality of employment, and avoidance of risk. To the employees success might be, real wage levels, fringe benefits, ease of working hours, full employment, overtime, bonuses, discount purchases, security of tenure, congeniality of employment, location, promotion possibilities, industry morale and prestige. To government the productive success of a firm might be the maximization of employment for a given investment in a given region. It might also relate to the use of a resource no longer so much in demand, the tax revenue implications, and the strategic, defence, or import substitution considerations. To consumers success would generally be the production of the physical output for a given price and level of pollution externalities.

Even assuming homogeneous physical outputs there are also practical difficulties associated with the measurement of outputs. These involve qualities, durability, after-sales service, credit, availability of specialized products, location of sales points and product continuity. However, given the measures of inputs and outputs and the set of firms under study, the Farrell method, with recent extensions, provides an unambiguous measure of efficiency for each firm. Without conceding all of Leibenstein's economic arguments about the theory of the firm we can acknowledge that he has pointed to many of the reasons why our measure of productive efficiency varies between firms. As with outputs, inputs need to be classified in homogeneous groups.

Conclusion

The contributions of Farrell and Leibenstein are quite important to the macroeconomist. To start with, the variation in efficiencies pointed to by both economists throws doubts on any theory which assumes that all firms are on the production function.

Secondly, on the empirical level, their contributions give us good reason to try to measure the relative production efficiencies of enterprises in an industry. The variation in this measure yields an indicator of the effectiveness of competitive pressures in the industry. Lack of competition may well be one of the factors explaining X-efficiency. In this quest the Farrell frontier efficiency method, taking into account all the input factors of interest and importance, can yield relative efficiency indicators which are far more reliable than concentration ratios or output over labour indicators.

More importantly, it would allow us to estimate the amount by which industry might raise output, by increasing efficiency of inefficient plants, without increasing the total amount of conventional factors used. This very question was posed by Stigler (1976, p. 213); and a little previously by Fisher (1976, p. 371) in his review of the work of Farrell in the *Review of Economic Studies*. Both saw the connection between the less efficient and most efficient plants as measured by Farrell and the X-efficiency concept used by Leibenstein. Fisher legitimately asks whether the elimination of such inefficiency is costless.

On the applied econometric level, Leibenstein's concept of pressure and constraint concern rate among those variables not very amenable to empirical measurement. The presence of these non-observable variables and the scarcity, until recently, of available data envelopment analysis software may be reasons why the Farrell measure has seldom been used to test the claim of Leibenstein. De Alessi (1983, p. 64), in a review of transactions costs, property rights and X-efficiency, also sees a central difficulty with X-efficiency in that it focuses on preference relations that are not observable and thus fail to yield testable hypotheses.

Before concluding we may take a quick look at the apparent coincidence of ideas of Farrell and Leibenstein given their very different disciplines. Were they in contact prior to 1966? I think not. Farrell's paper, which very completely spelt out his ideas was read to the Royal Statistical Society in 1957. He had then been employed since 1949 at the Department of Applied Economics at Cambridge under Richard Stone. His interests seem to have included activity analysis, linear programming and econometrics.

Harvey Leibenstein was born in Russia in 1922, became a US citizen, took his first degree at Northwestern, was a professor at Berkeley in the 1960s and from 1968 was located at the Department of Economics, Harvard. Leibenstein's formal introduction of X-efficiency appeared in 1966 and is couched in sociological and psychological terms. Fisher (1976, p. 371) reports that Farrell's insights into firm behaviour arose from the works of Philip Andrews at Oxford where Farrell took a first in PPE. He points out, however, that Farrell's mathematical tools of thought were very much his own, for example, the integration of linear programming into the theory of the firm. Fisher also reports that Farrell's emphasis was intended to be on practical measurement. Colin Clark, who was a commentator at Farrell's Royal Statistical Society presentation, recollected to me that it arose out of Farrell's sheer intellectual curiosity. Leibenstein (1971, p. 12) includes Farrell in a footnote and sees X-efficiency as broader in nature than technical efficiency though comes closer to using the Farrell input based measure in 1978, p. 13.

My own association with Farrell concerned his developments in the ingenious technique of performing step-wise multiple regression by linear programming techniques – Hald's process. That was in an age when one used punched paper tape as a computer input medium. I found it impressive that he should refine and exploit (for the National Coal Board) the essential common matrix pivoting aspect of both algorithms. To start with, in the canonical formulation of linear programming, the vectors X and Y are unknowns while A and b are known. In regression X and Y are known while a and B are unknowns. I believe he thus saw least squares as just one form of a (parametric) objective function. His frontier estimation method, and more modern variants of it, involve other specifications of the (error term) objective function.

In my experience properly specified mathematical economic models give rise to insights and side effects that are also properly specified. In Farrell's written reply to Maurice Kendall's heuristic approximation method of efficiency ranking, proposed at the Royal Statistical Society discussion, Farrell stresses that he has attempted to produce a measure with a clear economic interpretation and not just a method to show which firms ought to get medals and which need gingering up. In this and other aspects Farrell's analytical framework has elegantly endured the test of time.

Note
1. I am grateful to discussant Jinbang Kim (University of California, Riverside) for helpful comments on an early draft.

References
Aigner, D.J. and Chu, S.F. (1968), 'On Estimating the Industry Production Function', *American Economic Review*, 58, pp. 826–39.
Anandalingham, G. and Kulatilaka, N. (1987), 'Decomposing Production Efficiency into Technical, Allocative and Structural Components', *Journal of the Royal Statistical Society*, Series A, 150, pp. 143–51.
Burley, H.T. (1980), 'Productive Efficiency in U.S. Manufacturing: A Linear Programming Approach', *Review of Economics and Statistics*, **LXII**, (4), November, pp. 619–22.
Chambers, Robert G. (1988), 'Recent Development in Production Economics', *1988 Australian Economics Congress*, Canberra.
Clark, Colin, (1957), 'Discussion on Mr Farrell's Paper', *Journal of the Royal Statistical Society*, A, **120**, Part III, p. 282.
De Alessi, Louis (1983), 'Property Rights Transaction Costs, and X-Efficiency', *American Economic Review*, **73**, (1), pp. 64–81.
Fare, Rolf (1975), 'Efficiency and the Production Function', *Zeitschrift fur Nationalokonomie*, 35, pp. 317–24.
Farrell, M.J. (1957), 'The Measurement of Productive Efficiency', *Journal of the Royal Statistical Society*, A, Vol. 120, pp. 253–90.

Fisher, Malcolm, R. (1976), 'The Economic Contribution of Malcolm James Farrell', *Review of Economic Studies*, Vol. 43, pp. 371–82.

Forsund, F.R., Lovell, C.A.K. and Schmidt, P. (1980), 'A Survey of Frontier Production Functions and their Relationship to Efficiency Measurement', *Journal of Econometrics*, Vol. 13, pp. 5–25.

Leibenstein, H. (1966), 'Allocative Efficiency vs. X-Efficiency', *American Economic Review*, 56, pp. 392–415.

Leibenstein, H. (1971), 'Notes on X-Efficiency and Technical Progress', Discussion paper number 162, Harvard Institute of Economic Research.

Leibenstein, H. (1975), 'Aspects of the X-Efficiency Theory of the Firm', *Bell Journal*, Vol. 6.

Leibenstein, H. (1976), *Beyond Economic Man, A New Foundation for Microeconomics*, Cambridge MA: Harvard University Press.

Leibenstein, H. (1978) *General X-Efficiency Theory and Economic Development*, New York: Oxford University Press.

Lovell, C.A. Knox and Schmidt, Peter (1988), in Ali Dogramaci and Rolf Fare, *Applications of Modern Production Theory: Efficiency and Productivity*, Boston, Kluwer, pp. 3–32.

Slater, L.J. (1972), *More Fortran Programs for Economists*, DAE Occasional Paper: 34, Cambridge University Press, pp. 14–34.

Stigler, George G. (1976), 'The Existence of X-Efficiency', *The American Economic Review*, Vol. 66, pp. 213–16.

Name index

Adler, Max, 113
Aigner, D. J., 257
Åkerman, Gustav, 99–100
Amadeo, E. J., 158
Amariglio, Jack, 33, 45
Anandalingham, G., 256
Anderton, Charles, 87–8
Andrews, Philip, 263
Aristotle, 219
Arrow, K. J., 26, 130, 151
Asimakopulos, A., 158
Aumann, Robert, 10–11

Backhouse, Roger, 28n
Bartley, W. W., 25, 26
Bellamy, Ian, 84
Bergson, H., 123n, 222
Beveridge, William, 81
Blanchard, Oliver, 9–10
Blaug, Mark, 4, 21, 22–4, 93, 149, 184, 187
Böhm-Bawerk, Eugen von, 91, 92, 94, 96–7, 99, 100, 101, 102n, 114, 115, 122
Boland, L., 3
Boltzmann, Ludwig, 107, 109–10, 112, 113
Boss, Helen, 243
Boulding, Kenneth, 85, 86, 87
Boumans, M., 109
Boyd, R., 3
Brisman, Sven, 91, 97, 98, 100
Brito, D. L., 86
Burley, H. T., 257

Caldwell, Bruce J., 3, 4, 15, 23, 25, 28n, 29n, 143
Callari, Antonio, 45
Carabelli, A., 158, 209, 210, 223, 224, 234
Carson, Carol Stine, 244
Chick, Victoria, 158, 160
Chu, S. F., 257
Clark, Colin, 244, 256, 263

Clark, J. B., 115
Coase, R. H., 142
Coddington, Alan, 189
Cohen, I. B., 8
Colm, Gerhard, 249
Cournot, A.-A., 132
Crouch, Robert L., 185
Cruz, J. B., 86–7
Currie, Lauchlin, 242, 252

Dardi, M., 210, 215, 236n
Davis, John B., 157, 197
De Alessi, Louis, 263
DeLong, J. Bradford, 201
de Marchi, Neil, 28n
Dickinson, Z. Clark, 248
Dillard, Dudley, 33, 37
Duhem, Pierre, 3, 5, 19, 116
Dyer, Alan W., 33

Edgeworth, F. Y., 123n, 236n
Edison, Thomas, 81
Ellis, L., 132
Engels, Friedrich, 40

Farrell, M. J., 256–60, 262–4
Ferguson, Charles E., 93
Fischer, Stanley, 9–10
Fish, Stanley, 16n
Fisher, Irving, 129
Fisher, Malcolm R., 263
Forsund, R. R., 256
Foucault, Michel, 33
Friedman, Milton, 8–9

Gasper, P., 3
Gaynor, W. B., 38
Gelderen, J. van, 109, 123n
Gilbert, Milton, 244, 250
Goes, Frank van der, 108
Gordon, S., 127

Hacking, I., 132, 133, 152
Hahn, Frank H., 26

Subject index

accounting *see* national income accounting
aesthetic preference, 33
anthropological studies, 40
antimodernism, 20, 24
arms races, model of, 81–8
Austrian economics, 91, 122
average expectations, 162–71

banks, 137
below capacity working, 63, 66–70
business cycles, 38, 44, 51, 186, 190–202

Cambridge tradition of imperfect
    competition, 66–74
capital, 45
    durable theory of, 99–100, 101
    evolution of Wicksell's view of, 90–101
    Keynes on, 191–2, 194
    markets for, 150–51, 163–77, 195
    money as, 38, 43, 44, 51
    uncertainty and, 150–51
capitalist system, development of, 50–51
chaos theory, 85
classical probability theory, 132, 133, 135, 140, 149
comestibles, 98
commodity fetishism, 45
competition
    imperfect, 63, 65–74
    monopoly, 64, 66, 68, 70, 72
    perfect, 64–6, 68, 72, 128
complexity (Duhemian) problem, 3, 5, 19
confirmation theory, 6–7, 10, 11, 13
conflict, mathematical models of, 79–88
contraction, economic, 193–202
conventions, 160, 162–76
correct expectations, 145
cost(s)
    in competition theory, 64–5, 66–70, 71–2
    of uncertainty, 137–8

credit cycles, 38, 44
critical rationalism, 20, 21, 24–7
cycles, economic, 38, 44, 51, 186, 190–202

demand
    competition theory and, 64, 65, 66, 68–70, 71, 73
    effective, 73, 74, 161, 193
    money and, 35–6, 50, 52
disutility of labour, 115, 117
dogmatism, 32
Duhemian problem, 3, 5, 19
durable capital theory, 99–100, 101
dynamics, 111, 141, 142
    Keynes on, 181, 186, 234–5

econometrics, 32
economic cycles, 38, 44, 51, 186, 190–202
economic theories *see* theories
effective demand, theory of, 73, 74, 161, 193
efficiency measurement, 256–64
empiricism, 3, 4, 9–10, 34, 45
employment, 158–9
    full, 181–2, 183, 185, 190
    see also unemployment
entropy, 107, 110–11, 112
equilibrium, 141–2, 144, 145
    Keynes on, 159, 180–81, 183–4, 185, 186, 187, 189, 190–93
evolution, 112
evolutionary epistemology, 25–6
expansion, economic, 190–93
expectations, 159, 196–7
    average, 162–71
    correct, 145
    interdependent, 171–6
    perfect, 143–6
    rational, 151
exploitation, 45

falsificationism, 19, 20, 21, 24

271